From Eastern Partnership to the Association. A Legal and Political Analysis

From Eastern Partnership to the Association. A Legal and Political Analysis

Edited by

Naděžda Šišková

CAMBRIDGE
SCHOLARS

PUBLISHING

From Eastern Partnership to the Association.
A Legal and Political Analysis,
Edited by Naděžda Šišková
Reviewers: Rainer Arnold
Josef Blahož

This book first published 2014

Cambridge Scholars Publishing

12 Back Chapman Street, Newcastle upon Tyne, NE6 2XX, UK

British Library Cataloguing in Publication Data
A catalogue record for this book is available from the British Library

ISBN (10): 1-4438-5819-6, ISBN (13): 978-1-4438-5819-9

CONTENTS

Part II: General Overview of the Bilateral Agreements with Eastern Partnership Countries: A New Generation of Bilateral Agreements

Part III: From Eastern Partnership to the Association in the Light of Legal Approximation, Human Rights and the Rule of Law

CONTRIBUTORS

Editor – Assoc. Prof. et Assoc. Prof. JUDr. **Naděžda Šišková**, PhD, Head of the Department of European law, Jean Monnet Professor in EU law, Faculty of Law, Palacky University in Olomouc, President of the Czech Association for European studies, (Czech Republic)

JUDr. **Ondrej Blažo**, PhD, Institute of International Relations and Comparative Law, Faculty of Law, Comenius University in Bratislava, (Slovakia)

Archil Chochia, Consultant, Tallinn Law School, Tallinn University of Technology, (Estonia and Georgia)

Assoc. Prof. **Liudmyla Falalieieva**, Ph.D, Department of Human Rights, International and European Law, Academy of Advocacy of Kiev, (Ukraine)

Dali Gabelaia, chief specialist, Tallinn Law School, Tallinn University of Technology, (Estonia)

JUDr. **Ondrej Hamul'ak**, PhD, Department of European Law. Vice-Dean, Faculty of Law, Palacky University in Olomouc, (Czech Republic)

Assoc. Prof. **Tanel Kerikmäe** PhD, Jean Monnet Professor in EU Law, Tallinn Law School, Tallinn University of Technology, Estonia, President of Estonian Association for European studies, (Estonia)

Assoc. Prof**. Vlasta Kunová**, CSc., Jean Monnet Professor in EU Law, Faculty of Law, Comenius University in Bratislava, Slovakia, President of Slovak Association for European studies (Slovakia)

PhDr. **Petra Lustigová**, MA, Faculty of Social Sciences, Charles University in Prague, (Czech Republic)

JUDr**. Soňa Matochová**, Ph.D, Analyst of the Constitutional Court of the Czech Republic (Czech Republic)

Prof. Dr.iur.habil.Dr.h.c.mult.**Peter-Christian Müller-Graff**, Director of the Institute of Administrative and European law, Faculty of law, Jean Monnet professor in EU law, Universität Heidelberg, President of Germant Association for European studies (Germany)

Prof. **Katrin Nyman-Metcalf**, Tallinn Law School, Tallinn University of Technology, (Estonia)

JUDr. **David Petrlík,** Court of Justice of the European Union, Legal secretary, (Luxembourg)

JUDr. **Michal Petr**, Ph.D, Vice-chairman of the Office for Protection of Competition of the Czech Republic, (Czech Republic)

Assoc. Prof. **Roman Petrov**, Ph.D, National University of Kyiv-Mohyla Academy in Kyiv, Jean Monnet Professor in EU Law, President of Ukrainian Association for European Studies (Ukraine)

JUDr. **Emil Ruffer**, PhD, Director, EU Law Department, Ministry of Foreign Affairs of the Czech Republic and External Collaborator of the Department of EU Law, Faculty of Law, Charles University in Prague, (Czech Republic)

Assoc. Prof. JUDr. **Pavel Svoboda**, PhD, DEA, Department of European Law, Faculty of Law, Charles University in Prague, (Czech Republic)

ACKNOWLEDGEMENTS

This book creates the main output of the Jean Monnet project entitled "Eastern Partnership and its prospects with a view of legal approximation, rule of law and human rights".

The project was completed by the Jean Monnet Multilateral Research Group in the framework of the Consortium of four European Universities from four countries, namely: Palacky University in Olomouc, Czech Republic (Naděžda Šišková as coordinator), University in Heidelberg, Germany (Peter Christian Műller-Graff), National University of Kyiv-Mohyla Academy in Kyiv, Ukraine (Roman Petrov) and Comenius University in Bratislava, Slovakia (Vlasta Kunová), with the involvement of academics from other universities in Estonia, Ukraine and Georgia, as well as legal experts from practice (Court of Justice of the EU, Ministry of Foreign Affairs, Constitutional Court, Office for the Protection of Competition).

The authors would like to express their deep gratitude to the European Commission and Executive Agency for Education and Culture for their financial support, which enabled the research and preparation (including the publication) of this book.

PREFACE

ŠTEFAN FÜLE

COMMISSIONER FOR ENLARGEMENT AND EUROPEAN NEIGHBOURHOOD POLICY

The way to secure a prosperous European neighbourhood in the East

I welcome very much the publication of this book, which is focused on legal and political aspects and current issues of the Eastern Partnership.

The Eastern Partnership is an ambitious initiative aimed at closer political association and economic integration between the European Union and six Eastern European countries. Launched in Prague in 2009 and marking its fifth anniversary in May, this unique and comprehensive element of the European Neighbourhood Policy has achieved remarkable progress.

The Eastern Partnership contributes to sustainable democracy and market-oriented reforms in the region, along with enhanced mobility for citizens. The overarching goal of the initiative is a secure a prosperous European neighbourhood with a shared commitment to democracy, the rule of law and fundamental freedoms. The European Union also strives to create the necessary conditions for long-term growth and enterprise. This is in the interest not only of the citizens of Eastern Partnership countries, but also of those of the European Union.

To achieve the ambitious goals of the Eastern Partnership, the European Union employs two parallel approaches: a bilateral track aimed at strengthening relations with the partner countries, and a multilateral track to address challenges common to all partners. The EU has taken significant steps to increase mobility and person-to-person contacts. Concrete cooperation in a wide range of sectors has likewise intensified.

Through the Eastern Partnership the European Union supports jointly agreed sector reforms to boost partner country economies. It provides financial assistance and provides know-how to ensure that aid brings about lasting change in the partner countries. For instance, support for local SMEs/business initiatives or reforms in vocational education and training sectors brings about increased growth and jobs. Upgraded transport connections and common regulatory standards boost trade. Enhanced mobility means easier movement of people and goods through modernised border crossings. Greater energy efficiency and more renewable energy sources lead to a greener economy.

Eastern Partnership countries face significant challenges, and the European Union must shape its policy towards the region in a way that ensures continued momentum. It is important to be ambitious, creative and at the same time realistic about the future.

Differentiation, sustained political engagement and public diplomacy are key elements to take the process forward towards the next Eastern Partnership Summit which will be in Riga in 2015. We will have to tailor our approach with each Eastern Partner country, with options ranging from full political association and economic integration to unique relationships that take account of our partners' other regional integration commitments. At the same time, the European Union will continue to place respect for the common values of democracy, human rights and the rule of law at the heart of our relationship with each of our partners. Whatever the level of ambition our partners have in their relationship with the European Union, steps towards ensuring the independence and effectiveness of the judiciary, tackling corruption and improving the quality and accountability of public administration will be essential for the European Union and partners to get the most out of their relationships. Equally it is imperative that we maintain the inclusive nature of the partnership and build a sense of joint ownership. The increasing range of multilateral meetings under the Eastern Partnership, provide important opportunities in this respect.

But the Eastern Partnership is much more than government to government cooperation. Through the Eastern Partnership we are creating a dense network of contacts between the European Union and partners across society as a whole. From the Civil Society Forum with its National Platforms in each partner country, through the Euronest Parliamentary Assembly and the Conference of Local and Regional authorities (CORLEAP) to the Business and Youth Fora, we are building constituencies who can carry the transformation message to the citizens of our partner countries. We will continue to build these contacts in the years ahead which will be facilitated by the gradual process of visa liberalisation for our partner countries' citizens to be able to travel to the European Union.

The European Union respects the historical, cultural, economic and political links among all its neighbours. The market-oriented reforms will make Eastern European Partner countries more attractive for investment and trade, and will improve energy security and interconnections. Improved public administration in Eastern European partner countries and a more effective judiciary are elements of better governance that benefit business as well as society as a whole.

I am strongly convinced that closer political Association and economic integration with the European Union will be of substantial benefit to Eastern European countries but also to the European Union. The Association Agreements (AAs) and Deep and Comprehensive Free Trade Area (DCFTA) currently on the table are not just about legal and regulatory convergence with European Union standards. They have been shaped by the European Union's own integration experience–one in which common rules have not only fostered trade links and laid the groundwork for increased prosperity but also demonstrated the capacity of states to work together in meeting the challenges of today's increasingly globalised world. In this sense, the Eastern Partnership will contribute to a more peaceful and prosperous European continent.

December 2013

INTRODUCTION

NADĚŽDA ŠIŠKOVÁ

The book entitled "From Eastern Partnership to the Association. A legal and Political Analysis" is published at the key moment of preparation of the historically first transition of one of the Eastern Partnership countries-Ukraine-into the association relationship. The dramatic development in Ukraine in connection with the delay of the signature of the EU-Ukraine Association Agreement shows that this contract instrument is considered to be much more than merely an agreement, but also as a powerful symbol of the future orientation of the Partnership state.

This coincidence, reflected in the text of the publication, still more underlines the significance of the covered material and the up-to-dateness of the chosen topic.

The monograph is dedicated to the legal and political dimension of the European Union's policy towards the EU's Eastern neighbours (Ukraine, Belarus, Moldova, Azerbaijan, Georgia and Armenia).

The relevant material is examined from a broader perspective and attention is paid to the analysis of the Eastern Partnership Agreements from the viewpoint of their place in the External Relations law of the EU, including the legal mechanisms of their operation.

Taking into account the fact that the Association Agreements with some of the Eastern Partnership were already prepared (Ukraine, Moldova, and Georgia), an analysis is performed concerning general issues of the association and their specific manifestation in the case of the mentioned states.

In this respect a comparison with the previous Association Agreements with the states of Central Europe is also made. The core lies in the analysis of the issues of human rights, the rule of law and legal approximation as the key elements of the acceptance of the duties of the Partnership and Association countries.

Attention is paid also to some important issues which are relevant in order to grasp the problems of coping with the obligations concerning the law of competition.

The monograph is prepared by a multi-national team consisting of leading scholars and experts from the old and new Member States as well as from the Partnership States. Namely, they are academics from Germany, Czech Republic, Slovak Republic, Estonia, Ukraine and Georgia and also prominent legal experts on EU matters from different institutions (who deal with the mentioned issues in practice), particularly the Court of Justice of the EU, Ministry of Foreign Affairs, Constitutional Court, Office for the Protection of Competition. The structure of the team involving academics and experts from practice representing the old and new Member States as well as the Partnership state enabled the analysis to be performed from various points of view and to reflect a diversity of approaches, including the fresh experiences of the Czech Republic, Slovakia and Estonia with the implementation of the Europe Association Agreements.

The last mentioned fact also holds a symbolic meaning since the strategy of the Eastern Partnership originates from the Summit held in Prague in May 2009, i.e. right in one of these new Member States. Also, the continuous efforts of Štefan Füle, the Czech Commissioner for Enlargement and the Eastern Partnership, in the form of his involvement into the process of European integration of those countries, including the emphasis put on the European values and the adoption of relevant legislation as reflected, *inter alia*, resulted in the so-called Štefan Füle plan, which gives a clearer picture of this symbolism.

Therefore, we hope that the "lessons learned in Central Europe" in the process of implementing the Association Agreements, the adoption of *acquis communautaire* and the preparation to access the EU, as reflected in this monograph, will be an inspiration to the states of the Eastern Partnership and for the new Association states, respectively.

Despite the fact that the book is prepared in the form of a collection of essays, it offers a coherent text thanks to its contentual connection between the topics and general conclusions at the end of the book, which embrace and summarize the whole material of the monograph.

The monograph presents the main output of the Jean Monnet Multilateral Research Project funded by the European Commission bearing the title "Eastern Partnership and its prospects with a view to legal approximation, the rule of law and human rights", within which three conferences were held (in Slovakia, Ukraine and the Czech Republic). In particular, they were "EU Law and Human Rights in Education and the Civil Sector of the Partnership States", which was organized by Comenius University and held in Bratislava, "Preparation for the Acceptance of the Duties of the Association Country in the Field of Human Rights, the

Approximation of Laws and Judicial and Administrative Capacity", organized by Kiev-Mohyla University and held in Kiev, and "From the Eastern Partnership to the Association – the Great Debate" organized by Palacky University and the Czech Ministry of Foreign Affairs, which was held in Prague.

The monograph draws from the herein mentioned scientific forums and presents the content of the most important contributions and conclusions.

As the Partnership and Association Agreements create an important part of the External Relations law of the EU, the book is intended for pre-graduate and postgraduate students from the Faculties of Law, Political Sciences and International Relations, and it could be also recommended to academics, practical lawyers, diplomats, journalists and others who are interested in EU matters.

1 December 2013

PART I

EASTERN PARTNERSHIP AND ASSOCIATION AS A PART OF EUROPEAN EXTERNAL RELATIONS LAW

CHAPTER ONE

THE PLACE AND STATUS OF THE EASTERN PARTNERSHIP POLICY IN THE EUROPEAN EXTERNAL RELATIONS LAW

PETRA LUSTIGOVÁ

1.1 Introduction

This contribution will focus on the creation and development of the Eastern Partnership, which represents an important pivot in the European Union's relations with the countries in the post-soviet region and serves as a platform to foster good neighbourly relations, stability, security and economic cooperation in different areas of mutual interest. In the wider context of the European Neighbourhood Policy (hereinafter the "ENP"),[1] the Eastern Partnership is thus a sort of counterbalance to the well established southern dimension, which was initially called the 'Barcelona Process'[2] and which was then re-launched as the ambitious Union for the Mediterranean in 2008 (under the French Presidency of the Council).

---

[1] The ENP was established in the aftermath of the 'eastern' enlargement of the EU in 2004 and stems from two essential documents of the European Commission: *Wider Europe – Neighbourhood: A New Framework for Relations with our Eastern and Southern Neighbours* (COM [2003] 104 final of 11 March 2003) and *European Neighbourhood Policy – Strategy Paper* (COM [2004] 373 final of 12 May 2004). Another significant document, which outlined some of the security goals of the ENP, was the European Security Strategy approved by the European Council at its meeting in Brussels on 12 December 2003 (*A Secure Europe in a Better World – European Security Strategy*). The following countries are taking part in the ENP: Algeria, Armenia, Azerbaijan, Belarus, Egypt, Georgia, Israel, Jordan, Lebanon, Libya, Morocco, Moldova, Palestinian Authority, Syria, Tunisia and Ukraine.

[2] The 'Barcelona process' was a designation for the Union's partnership with the Mediterranean countries, which dates back to the adoption of the 'Barcelona

We shall look at the context of the establishment of the Eastern Partnership, the role and contribution of individual EU Member States, as well as the involvement of the institutions of the Union, especially the European Commission (hereinafter the "Commission"). Further, we shall evaluate the multilateral and bilateral dimensions of the project and describe the political and legal instruments available for the attainment of its objectives. Finally, we shall discuss the preparations, expectations and possible outcomes of the forthcoming Eastern Partnership summit in Vilnius, taking place in November 2013, where the much expected and much delayed signature of the Association Agreement with Ukraine[3] should take place, provided all the political conditionals are fulfilled.

1.2 A star is born? Establishment of the Eastern Partnership as part of the ENP

The Union has basically two strategies with regard to its neighbours: (i) the offer of a future membership, i.e. a dynamic Association process with candidate status; or (ii) attempts to stabilise the country (or its wider region) by offering cooperation, but without closer integration into the EU and without the membership prospect. The European Neighbourhood Policy essentially reflects the second approach, which, however, does not mean that some of the countries involved would not be interested in full membership. The very opposite is true and by way of illustration, one might recall the statement of Ukraine's leaders on the country's future membership in the EU, made in 2004, which took the Union's representatives slightly by surprise and was met with moderate reactions.[4]

The concept of the ENP is a fairly ambitious project, which attempts to provide a coherent general framework for such different countries as e.g. Ukraine, Georgia, Israel or Tunisia.[5] It faces multiple challenges, one of

---

Declaration' at the first Euro-Mediterranean conference of Ministers of Foreign Affairs on 27-28 November 1995 in Barcelona. The original partner countries were Algeria, Cyprus, Egypt, Israel, Jordan, Lebanon, Malta, Morocco, Palestinian Authority, Syria, Tunisia and Turkey. Libya received an observer status later in 1999.

[3] Association Agreement between the European Union and its Member States, of the one part, and Ukraine, of the other part (hereinafter as the "AA with Ukraine").

[4] M. Koopmann, Ch. Lequesne (Eds.): *Partner oder Beitrittskandidaten? Die Nachbarschaftspolitik der Europäischen Union auf dem Prüfstand* (1st ed.), Nomos Publishing, Baden-Baden, 2006, p. 12.

[5] The ENP was initially (prior to the Treaty of Lisbon) not founded on any particular legal basis and "*took shape through an ad hoc interplay between the*

them being the fact that for those countries not eligible for EU membership, it has to offer other tangible benefits than becoming a member of the Union. It must further set clear and attainable objectives and avoid creating false expectations that could lead to frustration in partner countries. Last but not least, the regional and multilateral elements should be strengthened and the bilateral cross-border projects should be integrated into the wider ENP framework. It is thus necessary to convince the partner countries that large scale structural reforms of their economic and political systems are necessary, even if the EU membership cannot be guaranteed, and that the harmonisation with *acquis communautaire* (especially in the internal market area), along with the removal of trade barriers and the increase in mutual trade, would bring concrete benefits for their economies and businesses. In this context, it might be useful to recall the ideas and theories of Karl Deutsch (1912-1992), who focused, in his research, on the relations between the integration of political elites and intensity of mutual communication. His theory of *transactionalism* was based on the assumption that the increase in the number of transactions (in the broad sense of the word) among the states leads to a deepening of the integration and elimination of the use of force in dealing with conflicts.[6] This theoretical approach appears to be relevant also for the concept of the ENP and its objectives, namely the stability and security in the regions closest to the EU borders.

The difficulties briefly outlined above, as well as the shift of the EU borders further to the East after the enlargement in 2004, were among the reasons for creating the Eastern Partnership as a specific and enhanced Eastern dimension of the ENP for achieving stability, better governance and economic development at the Union's Eastern borders. The idea to intensify the EU's relations with the countries of Eastern Europe and Southern Caucasus materialised at the European Council meeting of 19 and 20 June 2008, which invited the Commission to prepare a proposal for an Eastern Partnership (EaP) and emphasised the need for a differentiated approach respecting the character of the ENP as a single and coherent policy framework. The Extraordinary European Council of 1 September 2008 requested that this work be accelerated, in response to the need for a

---

Commission (particularly DG External Relations) and the Council (including the High Representative [HR] for CFSP), with the blessing of the European Council." Ch. Hillion: *The EU's Neighbourhood Policy towards Eastern Europe*, In: A. Dashwood, M. Maresceau: *Law and Practice of EU External Relations*, Cambridge University Press, 2008, p. 315.

[6] K. W. Deutsch: *The Analysis of International Relations*, Englewood Cliffs, N.Y.: Prentice-Hall, 1978, Chapters 14 and 17.

clearer signal of the Union's commitment following the conflict in Georgia and its broader repercussions.

The Commission duly complied with the requests of the European Council and prepared a Communication on the Eastern Partnership.[7] The main objectives of this new project were stated in the following terms:

> The EaP should bring a lasting political message of EU solidarity, alongside additional, tangible support for their democratic and market-oriented reforms and the consolidation of their statehood and territorial integrity. This serves the stability, security and prosperity of the EU, partners and indeed the entire continent. The Eastern Partnership will be pursued in parallel with the EU's strategic partnership with Russia.[8]

As to the essential elements of the Eastern Partnership, the Commission declared that "*The EaP will be based on mutual commitments to the rule of law, good governance, respect for human rights, respect for and protection of minorities, and the principles of the market economy and sustainable development.*"[9]

According to the Commission's outline, the goals of the Eastern Partnership should be achieved both on a bilateral and a multilateral track. The bilateral track should create a closer relationship between the EU and each of the partner countries to foster their stability and prosperity. This would include the upgrading of contractual relations towards Association Agreements (hereinafter as the "AAs"); the prospect of negotiations to put in place Deep and Comprehensive Free Trade Agreements (hereinafter as the "DCFTAs") with each country, leading to the establishment of a network of DCFTAs that can grow into a Neighbourhood Economic Community in the longer term; progressive visa liberalisation in a secure environment; deeper cooperation to enhance the energy security of the partners and the EU; and support for economic and social policies designed to reduce disparities within each partner country and across borders. Further, a new Comprehensive Institution-Building (CIB) programme would be needed to improve the institutional and administrative capacity of each partner to undertake the necessary reforms.

---

[7] Communication from the Commission to the European Parliament and the Council: Eastern Partnership (COM [2008] 823 final of 3 December 2008). The Eastern Partnership covers the following six ENP countries: Armenia, Azerbaijan, Belarus, Georgia, Moldova and Ukraine.

[8] *Ibid.*, p. 2.

[9] *Ibid.*, p. 3.

The multilateral track would provide a new framework for addressing the common challenges in the whole region, including democracy, rule of law and energy security. To this end, four policy platforms were proposed on the following themes: (i) democracy, good governance and stability; (ii) economic integration and convergence with EU policies; (iii) energy security; and (iv) contacts between people. The multilateral track was also supposed to advance through a number of Flagship Initiatives supporting the aims of the Eastern Partnership, to be funded through multi-donor support, international financial institutions (IFIs)[10] and the private sector.

The Commission's communication was accompanied by the Commission Staff Working Document,[11] which elaborated in more detail on (i) potential subjects for the work of the multilateral thematic platforms and panels; (ii) the indicative list of potential Flagship Initiatives (e.g. the Integrated Border Management Programme or the Southern energy corridor[12]); and (iii) the interface with other regional and international initiatives (e.g. the Black Sea Synergy).[13] Both documents taken together thus give a good illustration of the content and structure of the proposal for the Eastern Partnership and provided the European Council with a basis for future action.

The Eastern Partnership was officially launched at the Heads of State (or Governments Summit) held in Prague in May 2009,[14] in an effort by

---

[10] The World Bank and the International Monetary Fund (IMF) are the main IFIs; the European Investment Bank (EIB) and the European Bank for Reconstruction and Development (EBRD) represent the European Financial Institutions.

[11] Commission Staff Working Document accompanying the Communication from the Commission to the European Parliament and the Council: Eastern Partnership (SEC[2008] 2974/3).

[12] Since the EU and its ENP partners share an interest in enhancing energy security by diversifying energy transport routes and energy sources, the development of the strategic Southern energy corridor was one response to this issue and has been identified as one of the EU's most important energy security priorities.

[13] The Black Sea Synergy is a regional cooperation initiative covering five ENP countries (Armenia, Azerbaijan, Georgia, Moldova and Ukraine), as well as the Russian Federation and Turkey. For more details, see e.g. Communication from the Commission to the Council and the European Parliament: Report on the First Year of Implementation of the Black Sea Synergy (COM [2008] 391 final of 19 June 2008).

[14] The summit took place on 7 May 2009 during the Czech Presidency of the Council and was attended by the Heads of State or Government and representatives of the Republic of Armenia, the Republic of Azerbaijan, the Republic of Belarus, Georgia, the Republic of Moldova and Ukraine, the representatives of the European Union (President of the European Council, President of the European

the EU and its Eastern European partners to emphasise the importance of political and economic reforms and assist the countries of the region to move closer to the EU. The Czech Republic, as the then Presidency of the Council, was amongst the strong supporters of the Eastern Partnership and considered the Prague Summit as the actual crowning of its previous initiative, introduced in 2007.[15]

In the Joint Declaration of the Prague Eastern Partnership Summit[16] the participants confirmed that the Eastern Partnership "*will be based on commitments to the principles of international law and to fundamental values, including democracy, the rule of law and the respect for human rights and fundamental freedoms, as well as to market economy, sustainable development and good governance.*"[17] The main goal of the Eastern Partnership was "*to create the necessary conditions to accelerate political Association and further economic integration between the European Union and interested partner countries*" and it was considered to significantly strengthen the development of a specific Eastern dimension of the European Neighbourhood Policy.[18]

As to the bilateral dimension, the Joint Declaration stressed the new Association Agreements (including DCFTAs) with individual partner countries as an important legal instrument that "*will provide for the establishment or the objective of establishing deep and comprehensive free trade areas, where the positive effects of trade and investment liberalization will be strengthened by regulatory approximation leading to convergence with EU laws and standards.*"[19] Further, the participants recalled the need for administrative capacity building, declared their support for the mobility of citizens and visa liberalisation in a secure environment, mentioning explicitly visa facilitation and re-admission

---

Commission, Secretary-General of the Council of the European Union/High Representative for the Common Foreign and Security Policy) and the Heads of State or Government and representatives of EU Member States. Also present was the President of the European Parliament, the representatives of the Committee of the Regions and the Economic and Social Committee, the President of the European Investment Bank and the President of the European Bank for Reconstruction and Development.

[15] A Czech non-paper, drafted in collaboration with like-minded EU Member States, was entitled "*The European Neighbourhood Policy and the Eastern Neighbourhood: Time to Act*" and was followed by a joint Polish-Swedish Eastern Partnership initiative in 2008.

[16] See Council document 8435/09 (Presse 78) of 7 May 2009.

[17] *Ibid.*, p. 5, para. 1.

[18] *Ibid.*, p. 6, para. 2.

[19] *Ibid.*, p. 7, para. 5.

agreements. Last but not least, the Joint Declaration stressed the importance of energy security with regard to long-term stable and secure energy supply and transit and provided that "*provisions on energy interdependence could be included in the new Association Agreements or other bilateral arrangements between the EU and the partner countries*."[20]

The multilateral framework, which should complement the bilateral initiatives, would consist of the four thematic platforms, as originally proposed by the European Commission: (i) democracy, good governance and stability; (ii) economic integration and convergence with EU sectoral policies; (iii) energy security; and (iv) contacts between people. As to the institutional arrangements to oversee the "work in progress", it was declared that meetings would be held at least twice a year at the level of senior officials engaged in the reform work in the relevant policy areas. The thematic platforms were then supposed to report to the annual meetings of Ministers of Foreign Affairs. At the highest level, the Meetings of Heads of State or Government of the Eastern Partnership would be held in principle every two years.[21]

The Eastern star was then born in Prague, with high expectations and an ambitious set of objectives to be achieved, as well as a number of challenges to be accommodated due to the difficult political and economic situation in some of the partner countries. The main goal of the Eastern Partnership was set to create the conditions to accelerate political Association and deepen economic integration between the EU and the Eastern European partner countries. We shall now look at the instruments available for the Union and its Member States to attain the objectives of the Eastern Partnership.

1.3 What's in your toolbox? Union's legal and political instruments

The development of relations with third countries in general is one of the objectives of the Union's external actions, stipulated in Art. 21 of the Treaty on European Union (hereinafter as the "TEU").[22] However, there is a specific Art. 8 TEU concerning exclusively neighbouring countries,

[20] *Ibid.*, pp. 7-8, paras. 6-8.
[21] *Ibid.*, pp. 8-9, paras. 10-12.
[22] Art. 21 TEU provides that "*The Union shall seek to develop relations and build partnerships with third countries* (…)".

which was introduced in the TEU by the Treaty of Lisbon[23] and confirms the importance of the Union's Neighbourhood Policy:

> 1. The Union shall develop a special relationship with neighbouring countries, aiming to establish an area of prosperity and good neighbourliness, founded on the values of the Union and characterised by close and peaceful relations based on cooperation.
> 2. For the purposes of paragraph 1, the Union may conclude specific agreements with the countries concerned. These agreements may contain reciprocal rights and obligations as well as the possibility of undertaking activities jointly. Their implementation shall be the subject of periodic consultation.

This provision constitutes the general framework for the implementation of the ENP, as well as the Eastern Partnership. As for the concrete legal instruments to be used, Art. 8 (2) TEU explicitly mentions "*specific agreements*" that "*may contain reciprocal rights and obligations as well as the possibility of undertaking activities jointly.*" Therefore, the Association Agreements with partner countries, including provisions on DCFTA, should constitute one of the tools for fostering relations and cooperation. In addition, there are a number of political instruments such as Action Plans, Programmes and Flagship Initiatives, which complement the legal framework and are more flexible to address particular priorities and outline concrete steps to be gradually taken.

Association Agreements represent the main legal instrument to secure enhanced and deeper contractual relations between the EU and partner countries. They should also include Deep and Comprehensive Free Trade Areas (DCFTAs), where regulatory approximation can serve to strengthen the positive effects of trade and investment liberalisation, leading to convergence with EU laws and standards.[24] The standard legal basis for the AAs is Art. 217 TFEU, which stipulates as follows:

> The Union may conclude with one or more third countries or international organisations agreements establishing an Association involving reciprocal rights and obligations, common action and special procedure.

---

[23] Treaty of Lisbon amending the Treaty on European Union and the Treaty establishing the European Community, signed on 13 December 2007 (OJ C 306, 17.12.2007, p. 1).

[24] Joint Communication to the European Parliament, the Council, the European Economic and Social Committee and the Committee of the Regions - Eastern Partnership: A Roadmap to the autumn 2013 Summit (JOIN [2012] 13 final of 15 May 2012), p. 3.

This is the legal basis also used for all the "new generation" AAs with partner countries of the Eastern Partnership, which are currently being negotiated.[25] It is interesting to note in this context that the above mentioned (new) Art. 8 TEU is not used as a concrete legal basis, and the more general Art. 217 TFEU serves this purpose, despite the fact that Art. 8 (2) foresees the conclusion of "specific agreements". It can be well argued that Art. 8 TEU "*is essentially a framework provision and a declaration of intent*"[26] and thus not fit for this purpose. Indeed, it might be the case that Art. 8 TEU does not stretch to cover 'fully-fledged' AAs which could be perceived as a stepping stone to EU membership.[27] For these reasons, the partner countries might prefer the standard AAs with recourse to Art. 217 TFEU, which leaves the potential for future accessions at least open.[28] Given the fact that all AAs currently negotiated with Eastern partners refer to Art. 217 TFEU, it "*renders the original intention of art. 8 TEU virtually redundant.*"[29] However, it can still serve the purpose of the framework provision which enhances the political importance of good neighbourly relations for the EU.

As for the content of the AAs, they are usually designed as very comprehensive, covering all areas of mutual interest and also creating a

---

[25] Negotiations on the AA with Ukraine, including a DCFTA, have been finalised and the agreed text of the AA was already initialled on 30 March 2012 (DCFTA was initialled later on 19 July 2012). Negotiations of AAs have been launched with the Republic of Moldova, Georgia, Armenia and Azerbaijan, while the decision to launch negotiations on DCFTAs, as an integral part of the AAs with Georgia and Moldova, was taken in December 2011 and with Armenia in February 2012.

[26] P. Van Elsuwege, R. Petrov: *Article 8 TEU: Towards a New Generation of Agreements with the Neighbouring Countries of the European Union?* 36 E.L. Rev. (2011), pp. 688-703 (at p. 696).

[27] Since the objective of Art. 8 (1) TEU is to "*establish an area of prosperity and good neighbourliness, founded on the values of the Union and characterised by* ***close and peaceful relations based on cooperation***" (emphasis added), it seems that it does not encompass anything going beyond this objective, such as enlargement of the Union.

[28] Ch. Hillion gives two reasons why the standard AAs should be used: (i) the initial rationale of not offering to e.g. Moldova and Ukraine an AA in the 1990s, i.e. to distinguish them from other Central and Eastern Europe Countries bound for EU accession under the so called 'Europe Agreements', ceased to exist when these countries joined the EU in 2004; and (ii) since the current Euro-Mediterranean Agreements with the Southern ENP countries are AAs, for the sake of ENP coherence any downgrade of the legal instruments for Eastern Partnership countries below the level of AAs is hardly conceivable. Hillion, op. cit. in note 6 *supra*, p. 328.

[29] Van Elsuwege, Petrov, op. cit. in note 27 *supra*, p. 703.

specific institutional structure. They are based on shared values and principles, notably democracy and rule of law, respect for human rights and fundamental freedoms, good governance, market economy and sustainable development. The provisions on 'Political Dialogue' include enhanced cooperation in foreign and security policy, with the focus on regional issues, WMD (Weapons of Mass Destruction), non-proliferation and disarmament, conflict prevention and crisis management. The AAs also include a section on Justice, Freedom and Security, covering the rule of law, data protection, migration, movement of persons (including gradual steps in the visa policy based on the Visa Liberalisation Action Plans), the fight against money laundering and financing of terrorism, illicit drugs, the fight against organised crime and counter-terrorism.

The provisions of a DCFTA are then supposed to go much further than classic free trade areas, foreseeing not only the mutual opening of markets for most goods and services, but also binding provisions on gradual approximation with EU norms and standards in trade and trade-related areas (such as standards and conformity assessment rules, sanitary and phytosanitary rules, intellectual property rights, trade facilitation, public procurement, and competition). The DCFTA also covers energy policy (including nuclear issues if applicable), with particular focus on issues concerning security of supply, the gradual integration of energy markets, energy efficiency, renewable energy sources and nuclear safety. Further, the AAs contain provisions for enhanced cooperation in key sector policy areas, based on gradual approximation with EU *acquis* and, where relevant, also with international norms and standards. These areas include transport, the environment, cooperation on industrial and enterprise policy, public finance, macroeconomic stability, company law, banking, insurance and other financial services, the information society, information technology and telecommunications, tourism, agriculture and rural development, fisheries and maritime governance, mining, cooperation in science and technology, space cooperation, consumer protection, social cooperation, public health, education, training and youth, cooperation in the cultural and audio-visual field, civil society cooperation, cross-border and regional level cooperation.

To complement and implement the comprehensive and wide reaching scope of the legal framework, there are a number of non-binding, political measures and instruments, which nevertheless appear to be of great significance. To begin with, there are jointly agreed documents (by the EU and the partner country concerned) in the form of Association Agendas and ENP Action Plans. These political documents lay out strategic objectives for cooperation within a certain timeframe (three to five years, subject to periodic review by the Commission) and include a list of priority areas and specific actions to be taken.[30]

The achievement of objectives specified in Association Agendas and ENP Action Plans requires significant financial resources. They are provided within the framework of the European Neighbourhood and Partnership Instrument (ENPI),[31] and the EU financial instruments supporting the implementation of the Neighbourhood Policy. The additional Eastern Partnership resources aim to support two particular initiatives in the bilateral track: the Comprehensive Institution Building programme (CIB) and the Pilot Regional Development Programmes (PRDPs). To implement these programmes, specific Memoranda of Understandings (MoUs) are signed with individual partner countries.

On the multilateral track, there are five regional Flagship Initiatives financed from ENPI, namely (i) the Integrated Border Management Flagship Initiative; (ii) the Support to Small and Medium Enterprises (SMEs) Flagship Initiative; (iii) the Regional Electricity Markets, Energy Efficiency and Renewable Energy Sources Flagship Initiative; (iv) the Prevention, Preparedness and Response to natural and man-made Disasters Flagship Initiative (PPRD-East); and (v) the Environmental Governance Flagship Initiative.

As regards to the enhanced mobility of persons, for the partner countries which have already concluded and implemented the visa facilitation and re-admission agreements (Moldova and Ukraine), Visa Liberalisation Action Plans are in place for future gradual loosening of visa requirements. Georgia has also concluded and implemented the visa facilitation and re-admission agreement and will start negotiations on the Visa Liberalisation Action Plan. For the rest of the partner countries, the Mobility Partnerships were arranged, and the negotiations on visa

[30] Even though not legally binding, these instruments are capable of reformulating the objectives of the Eastern Partnership, widening its scope and even revisiting some of the provisions of the existing legal framework with a view to give guidance and enhance compliance of the partner countries. See Ch. Hillion, op. cit. in note 6 *supra*, p. 321.

[31] Regulation (EC) No 1638/2006 of the European Parliament and of the Council of 24 October 2006 laid down general provisions establishing a European Neighbourhood and Partnership Instrument (OJ L 310, 9.11.2006, p. 1). As of 1 January 2014, the ENPI Regulation will be replaced by a new Regulation of the European Parliament and of the Council establishing a European Neighbourhood Instrument (proposal COM [2011] 839 final of 7 December 2011), with an increased budget of EUR 18.2 billion for the period 2014-2020, which is 40 per cent up on the amount available under the ENPI from 2007-2013.

facilitation and re-admission agreements are in progress (Armenia and Azerbaijan).

As we have seen, there is a wide range of tools in the Eastern Partnership toolbox, both of a legal and political nature. Taken together, they constitute a complex framework for assistance and cooperation and confirm the importance of the Eastern Partnership in the Union's external action. In the final section, we shall look at possible future developments of this key external policy with a view to the forthcoming Summit in Vilnius.

1.4 The long and winding road to the Vilnius Summit

The second Eastern Partnership Summit was held in Warsaw (under the Polish Presidency of the Council) in September 2011 and it reaffirmed the agenda agreed at the Prague Summit in 2009. It also offered an opportunity to review the progress achieved so far in a number of areas. However, Summit participants also recognised that the reform efforts needed to be reinforced and declared that the pace of reforms would determine the intensity of cooperation and that partners most engaged in reforms would benefit most from their relationship with the EU (the so called 'more for more' principle). It was also stressed that it is essential to build sustainable democratic institutions, resolve protracted conflicts peacefully and to create a solid foundation for sustainable and inclusive economic growth and job creation. All these elements were considered to be crucial in terms of the development of future relations between the EU and its Eastern European partners.[32]

As the third Eastern Partnership Summit approaches, to be held under the Lithuanian Presidency of the Council in Vilnius on 28-29 November 2013, the expectations and tensions rise. There has been progress in a number of areas, including successful completion of negotiations of AAs/DCFTAs with some of the partner countries, namely Armenia, Georgia, Moldova and Ukraine. However, due to the difficult political situation in Ukraine and the criticism of the 'selective justice'[33] and other

[32] Joint Declaration of the Eastern Partnership Summit, Warsaw, 29-30 September 2011 (Council document 14983/11 PRESSE 341 of 30 September 2011). For a brief summary of the Warsaw Summit outcomes, see also: Eastern Partnership: A Roadmap to the autumn 2013 Summit (JOIN [2012] 13 final of 15 May 2012), p. 3.

[33] In particular, the issue concerns the former Prime Minister of Ukraine Yulia Tymoshenko, who is currently serving a seven-year sentence for abuse of office. The Ukrainian government allegedly has a draft law prepared which would release her on humanitarian grounds and allow her to travel abroad for medical treatment;

structural problems with regard to the democratic principles and rule of law (such as the electoral reform), it remains to be seen whether the AA with Ukraine (incl. DCFTA) will be signed. Moreover, another problem concerns the set of remaining AAs/DCFTAs with Georgia, Moldova and Armenia, which was prepared to be initialled at the summit. Despite this fact, Armenia declared in September 2013 its intention to join the Customs Union with Russia, Belarus and Kazakhstan, which is incompatible with the DCFTA and the initialling of the AA with Armenia seems to be postponed indefinitely.[34] The road to the summit is thus rather cumbersome and given the above mentioned difficulties, it is uncertain what the overall outcomes will be and whether they will be perceived as a positive message. It has been suggested that the Vilnius Summit represents a critical benchmark for the Eastern Partnership and there is a pressing need for tangible results.[35] The stakes are rather high: the EU is playing for its influence and strategic partnership with the region against Russia, which will not be an easy game.

1.5 Conclusions

The Eastern Partnership clearly occupies a privileged position in the Union's external relations and constitutes an important "Eastern axis" of the ENP, along with its Southern/Mediterranean dimension. The Treaty of Lisbon confirmed the importance of cooperation with neighbouring countries in Art. 8 TEU, which is a framework provision and a "declaration of intent" to foster relations with the Union's neighbours.

Since its establishment at the Prague Summit in 2009, the Eastern Partnership has flourished and a complex framework of legal and political

---

but it would not void her conviction. See I. Bond: *Ukraine: Edging towards the EU?*, Centre for European Reform, 24 October 2013.

[34] *EU loses Armenia to Russia's Customs Union*, EurActiv.com: http://www.euractiv.com/europes-east/eu-loses-armenia-russia-customs-news-530224, accessed on 30 October 2013. As I. Bond rightly remarks, "*Russia has so far paid more attention to geopolitics than economics in building its Customs Union*", op. cit in note 34 *supra*.

[35] See e.g. A. Duleba, A. Rácz, V. Řiháčková, R. Sadowski: *Visegrad 4 the Eastern Partnership: Towards the Vilnius Summit (Policy Paper)*, Research Center of the Slovak Foreign Policy Association, 2013, p. 5: "*If no tangible contractual deal has been achieved with partner countries by the 2013 Vilnius summit, for instance, the signing of an AA/DCFTA with Ukraine and/or finalization of talks and initialling of agreements with Armenia, Georgia and Moldova, it might undermine the future dynamics of the EaP.*"

instruments has been created, along with the necessary financial resources to implement the defined objectives. However, the overall success of this project will be put to the test at the Vilnius Summit at the end of November 2013, and some tangible results (the signing and initialling of AAs/DCFTAs) would be much needed and appreciated. The future dynamics and progress of the Eastern Partnership depend on it to a great extent, as much as the stability and security of the Union depends on the developments in its neighbourhood.

CHAPTER TWO

EVOLUTION OF ASSOCIATION AGREEMENTS IN EU EXTERNAL RELATIONS LAW

PAVEL SVOBODA

2.1 Introduction: Association as an EU law concept

Whoever tries to analyse the evolution of Association Agreements in EU external relations law, he/she needs first of all to define what the EU Association Agreements are. As it turns out, this is a task similar to shooting at a moving target for three reasons. Firstly, EU law[1] uses the notion of Association in different meanings (see para 0 below). Secondly, the Court of Justice of the European Union ("CJEU") generally follows the substantive (material) approach towards EU legal acts[2] and, therefore, it is not important what an Agreement is called, but whether it falls under the concept of Association as per its content (cp. part 0). Thirdly, Association Agreements have been part of the EU law from the very beginning; however, over time similar concepts have been added thus narrowing the content of the Association pursuant to today's Art. 217 TFEU. Consequently, legal relationships that fell under the Association in the early post-war integration years often do not fit into this legal concept today (cp. part 0).

The structure of this analysis follows from the foregoing: after the introductory part dedicated to diverging meanings of Association under the EU law, we shall concentrate on the most frequent types of Association under Article 217 TFEU, including a current and historical overview of Agreements falling under this concept (cp. part 0); finally, we

---

[1] EU law is understood as encompassing its predecessor–the Community law. The continued existence of EAEC has, for the purpose of terminological simplification, not been considered.

[2] Cp. CJEU case law - 22/60 Elz; 307/81 Alusuisse Italia; 322/88 Grimaldi; 303/90 France v. Commission.

shall compare Association with similar EU concepts (cp. part 0) and outline its perspectives *de lege ferenda* (cp. part **Error! Reference source not found.**).

2.1.A Types of EU Association

The notion of Association has been used in several different meanings in the EU law:

- Association of entities with international legal personality (countries and international organisations) with the EU objectives, be it:
  - all objectives (general Association pursuant to Art. 217 TFEU), or
  - some of the objectives and policies of the EU. An example being namely the Association of some EFTA countries to the Schengen acquis (Article 6[1] of the Protocol annexed to the TEU, integrating the Schengen acquis into the framework of the European Union [for Iceland and Norway]). The EEC Agreement associating most of the EFTA countries with the EU internal market policies and allowing for their participation in EU programmes and actions, i.e. not in all EU activities, could also fall under this type of Association.[3]
- Association of dependent territories of EU member states (Art. 198 to 204 TFEU) which are not international legal persons.

It follows from the above mentioned that the term "Association" has a broad meaning which varies, in the different cases, in terms of legal basis, content and entities to which may be applicable.

2.1.B Lack of common doctrinal definition

Therefore, it wouldn´t come as a surprise that there exists no single legal doctrine, nor court definition of "Association with the EU". Whilst

[3] Cp. also Agreement EU/EC-Swiss Confederation on the Swiss Confederation´s Association with the implementation, application and development of the Schengen acquis of October 29, 2004, Commission document 13054/04. This type of sectoral Association entices to interpret Association extensively, which should, however, be avoided. This Association with the Schengen acquis needs to be read in light of the fact that the associate countries in question are already associated within the EEA based on Art. 217 TFEU. Therefore this type of Association cannot be apprehended as a stand-alone type.

primary law lays down some defining elements regarding the specific types of Association, the doctrine keeps on attempting (and failing) to do so.

2.1.C Common content characteristics

It is, though, possible to find some *content characteristics* common to all three types of Association: (i) adherence to some of the EU objectives, (ii) lack of internal relationship with the EU (external Association), (iii) perennial nature of Association Agreements, (iv) asymmetry of rights and obligations.

2.2 "The Association": Article 217 TFEU

Bellow we shall examine the EU law concept of Association solely as regards international legal persons and their Association with the Union´s objectives, including the European Economic Area, before comparing this legal institution with other related concepts, i.e. Association Agreements based on Article 217 TFEU, albeit that their content might not fully correspond to this provision (e.g. the Cotonou Agreement), or Agreements based on another legal basis, provided that the content of the respective Agreement corresponds de facto to Article 217 TFEU. A comparison with neighbouring concepts shall follow at the end of this paper (cp. part 0).

Article 217 TFEU (and Art. 206 TEAEC) empower the EU to *"conclude with one or more third countries or international organisations agreements establishing an Association involving reciprocal rights and obligations, common action and special procedure".* The conditions are, however, formulated in such general terms that most EU External Agreements, not only those establishing an Association, fulfil them. These are structural, formal and procedural elements that tell us almost nothing about the content of such Association Agreements.

As one can read on the web of the European Union External Service,[4]

> Association agreements are international agreements that the European Community / European Union has concluded with third countries with the aim of setting up an all-embracing framework to conduct bilateral relations. These agreements normally provide for the progressive liberalisation of trade (to various degrees: Free Trade Area, Customs Union…).

---

[4] http://eeas.europa.eu/Association/index_en.htm.

In certain cases, they prepare for future membership of the European Union. Although Association Agreements differ in their exact content and finality depending on the partner country, nevertheless, they meet the following criteria:

- The legal basis for their conclusion is Article 217 TFEU (ex Article 310 TEC);
- Intention to establish close economic and political cooperation (more than simple cooperation);
- Creation of paritary bodies for the management of the cooperation, competent to take decisions that bind the contracting parties;
- Offering Most Favoured Nation treatment;
- Providing for a privileged relationship between the European Union and its partner;
- Since 1995 the clause on the respect of human rights and democratic principles is systematically included and constitutes an essential element of the agreement;

In a large number of cases, the Association agreement replaces a cooperation agreement thereby intensifying the relations between the partners."

From a practical point of view, these characteristics are more or less true; however the matter is slightly more complicated. Therefore, let us look in more detail into the material and personal scope of this provision.

2.2.A Material Scope of Article 217 TFEU

The above mentioned vague definition of the content of Association was complemented by the Court of Justice of the EU ("CJEU") which ruled that it was *"an agreement creating special, privileged links with a non-member country which must, at least to a certain extent, take part in the Community system ... Article [217] must necessarily empower the Community to guarantee commitments towards non-member countries in all the fields covered by the Treaty"* (C-12/86 Demirel, para 9).[5] Such a definition has to be interpreted as follows:

---

[5]A reference for preliminary ruling submitted by Germany regarding a Turkish national, Mrs Demirel, who came to Germany in 1984 on a tourist visa to rejoin her husband living in Germany. Mrs Demirel remained in Germany after the expiration of the visa and defended herself against expulsion by reference to the Association Agreement signed with Turkey which aims, inter alia, at further liberalisation of the access of Turkish workers to the EU territory within a privileged Association status, the purpose of which was to allow for a convergence between the Association agreement regime and the Community system. It led to an analogous application of the regime intended for community workers to EU

- "*Take part in the Community system*" does not mean taking part in the work of the EU internal bodies since Association pursuant to Article 217 TFEU is an external one (see above). It therefore refers to the involvement in the EU policies and freedoms, in particular trade facilitation between the parties.
- The vague wording "*at least to a certain extent*" is confusing. Conceptually, an Association cannot exist if the Associated entity does not, at least to a certain extent, take part in the life of the organisation with which it is Associated. Otherwise it would not be an Association. If the Associated entity takes part in the life of the organisation more than "*at least to a certain extent*", in other words, completely, we can no longer talk about Association, but about full membership.
- The requirement stipulated in Article 217 TFEU i.e. "*reciprocal rights and obligations*" is, in this kind of Association Agreement, typically modified by an asymmetry in favour of the Associated entity, involving:
  - obligations incurred by the EU and its member states with no similar obligations being imposed on the Associated country (e.g. financial aid), or
  - tighter or less favourable conditions regarding the fulfilment of such reciprocal obligations (a typical example is a more rapid removal of custom or quantity trade barriers by the EU and its member states),[6]
  - direct effect of the provisions of such Association Agreements which become EU legal acts and therefore an integral part of member states′ legislation[7] (i.e. application asymmetry). It means that while a national of the Associated country can invoke some of the rights granted by the Association Agreement before national courts in the EU, an EU citizen cannot claim the same rights in the

external relations. But, more importantly, the CJEU decided favourably on its own jurisdiction to rule on immigration matters, which are, content-wise, necessarily related to the regime of foreign nationals/workers but for which no intra-community competence existed at the time!

[6] The EU usually commits to apply zero or reduced import duties (except for the Association Agreement with Israel according to which custom duties are reciprocal) in exchange for a clause on the most favoured treatment and interdiction of tax discrimination in the Associated country.

[7] Cp. C-268/99 Jany regarding Association agreements (Czech and Polish, self-employed" prostitutes in the Netherlands before the EU accession).

Associated country, if the country´s domestic law is based on a dualist system.

This asymmetry is often offset by the:

- o adoption of voluntaristic anti-dumping duties on sensitive goods by the EU,
- o inverse legal asymmetry vis-à-vis the Associated country. Association Agreements contain many *standstill clauses* preventing the adoption of less favourable legal provisions than those in force prior to the signature of the Agreement. Associated countries, which often lack experience with all the artifices of the EU internal market, may have less rigorous, more liberal legislation compared to the EU and its Member States. Due to the standstill clauses they are not allowed to tighten up their legislation in order to reach the same level of restriction as applicable in the EU. They thus open up their liberal market to EU undertakings, while their own businesses will not be allowed to enter on the more regulated markets of older member states.[8]

- "*... commitments towards non-member countries in all the fields covered by the Treaty*" is therefore the most significant statement of this ruling. In fact, according to the CJEU, the material scope of the Association pursuant to Article 217 TFEU, i.e. delimitation of the EU objectives in which the associate country takes part, may cover all EU policies.[9]

As for the power to conclude an Association Agreement pursuant to Article 217 TFEU, it is quite obvious that such Agreements govern areas, which fall, within the EU, both under exclusive and shared competences. That´s one of the reasons why these Agreements are concluded as mixed Agreements (see para 3.3. hereafter).[10]

---

[8] This inverse asymmetry contained in Art. 45/2 of the European Agreement raised issues in the Czech Republic during discussions regarding the Act on Lotteries in 1998.

[9] Cp. also C 181/73 Haegeman.

[10] Cp. NEFRAMI E.: L'action extérieure de l'Union européenne, LGDJ, Paříž 2010, p. 100: „*La politique de voisinage regroupe ainsi les accords de coopération et de partenariat ou d'Association existants*". (Neighbourhood policy thus pools existing cooperation, partnership or Association agreements).

Since 1996, following the provision on political dialogues in the form of joint declarations,[11] Associated countries (and EFTA countries) have also been associated with *the common EU positions in the CFSP*.[12] From the legal standpoint, such declarations can't be considered international Agreements in a simplified form, but unilateral acts, because they can be modified independently of the joint declaration. Moreover, any country, even a non-member country, can make such declarations, even against the will of the EU.[13]

The extent of participation in the EU system depends also on whether the Association is *dynamic*, leading to subsequent EU membership, or *static* without such an outlook. Following the progressive narrowing of the content of an Association, namely by the introduction of Economic, Financial and Technical Cooperation with third countries (see para 0 hereinafter)–the European Neighbourhood Policy can be considered to be part of it–the use of Article 217 TFEU has shifted significantly towards dynamic Association.

2.2.B Personal Scope of Article 217 TFEU

Pursuant to Article 217 TFEU, an Association can be established not only with a country (as had been the case until the entry into force of the Treaty of Amsterdam) but also with an international organisation. Although in the past Association meant that an entity was brought closer to the EU, the provision can in theory be also used the other way round,

---

[11] Cp. press release N° 10752/97 on the Common Position 1997/625 on Bosnia and Herzegovina: *The Associated countries of Central and Eastern Europe, the associated country Cyprus and the EFTA countries members of the EEA declare that they share the objectives of the common position defined by the Council of the European Union on 15 September 1997 on the basis of Article J.2 of the Treaty on the European Union on restrictive measures to be taken against persons in Bosnia and Herzegovina acting against the peace agreements and that they will see to it that their national policies conform to that common position."* On behalf of the EU Presidency it declares: *"The European Union takes note of this commitment and welcomes it."*

[12] Regarding the list of Common Positions up to 2001 comp. KRONENBERG V.: Third Countries and EU Common Positions in: The European Union and the International Legal order: Discord or Harmony?, T.M.C. Aster Press Haag 2001, p. 370.

[13] Cp. VENTURINI G.: La portée et les effets juridiques des attitudes et des actes unilatéraux des Etas, RCADI 112/1964, s. 400; KRONENBERG V.: cit. Third Countries … p. 361.

i.e. as an Association of the EU with another international organisation or a third country.

It is worth noting that this provision has never been used vis-à-vis any international organisation.

2.2.C Conclusion and Amendment of Association Agreements

- Conclusion of an Association Agreement: an Association is conceivable only with the EU and the EAEC at the same time; therefore procedural conditions stipulated both in the TFEU and TEAEC have to be met. Although there is no explicit provision in this sense, so far it has not been possible to choose to establish an Association with only one of the two partners.
  The EU system is, from the procedural standpoint, based on Article 218 TFEU.
  Association Agreements are concluded as **mixed** external agreements, i.e. international agreements concluded, on the Union´s side, jointly by the EU (or the EAEC) and by all its member states. The facts that there are several signatories on the Union´s side (member states, EU, EAEC) mustn´t, however, obliterate the fact that this aggregate acts, especially in terms of liability, as one single party to the international Agreement. The reference to the parties to the Agreement makes it quite clear-all the signatories from the EU *"on the one hand..."*, whilst the other party to the Agreement is *"on the other hand"*. Implications of the mixed nature of such Agreements include (a) Member States´ right to veto the conclusion of such an External Agreement by means of an internal ratification process. This right can be exercised even when the country in question has voted for the conclusion of the Agreement in the EU bodies; (b) delay in the entry into force, and therefore in the full effectiveness[14] of mixed Agreements. For example, the EU-Algeria Cooperation Agreement signed on 26 April 1976 entered into force only on 1 November 1978.[15]

---

[14] The agreement can be applied on a provisional basis, although usually only parts which fall under the competences of the EU.

[15]At the time when the provisional application of external agreements had not yet been possible (today Art. 218/5 TFEU), the EU was obliged to sign stand-alone provisional agreements allowing for an immediate application of trade provisions of these cooperation agreements. This was possible only since trade provisions fall under the exclusive competence of the EU: *"... in so far as aid granted to a non-member country by an Agreement with that country is financed from the*

The system set out in Article 206 TEAEC is similar to the one in the TFEU, with one significant difference regarding the role of the different institutions. The most important role is conferred to the Commission who negotiates and concludes such agreements alone.

- External Association Agreements may be amended (besides using the same procedure applicable to their adoption) based on the so-called "flexibility". In this case we talk about double or two-tier flexibility. First, Article 217 TFEU provides that an External Agreement shall include *"common action and special procedure"*. The External Agreement then specifically vests, as a common action or special procedure, the power to amend the Agreement in the common bodies established pursuant to the Agreement. Only the actual use of this amending power constitutes an act of substantive law.

  For instance, according to Article 50(4) of the EC-Albania Stabilisation and Association Agreement[16], the Agreement is amended by the decision of the Stabilisation and Association Council[17] that *"shall establish the modalities to extend the above provisions to the establishment of nationals of both Parties to take up economic activities as self-employed persons"*.[18] We are faced here with a predictable modification of the original act, moreover in a predictable time frame. On the other hand, the power of the Stabilisation and Association Council to *"extend or modify the scope"* of financial services pursuant to Article 49(i) of the same Agreement is far less predictable, and it constitutes a real and fully-fledge modification of the rules of conduct.

Community budget, only the Community has the authority to conclude such an Agreement. This holds true whatever the source of the funds contributing to the Community budget (national contributions or own financial resources)". See Answer by the Council to the written question no 396/77 by M. Dodlinger. OJ 1997 C 277 p. 7-8.

[16] Full title "Stabilisation and Association Agreement between the European Communities and their Member States, on the one part, and the Republic of Albania, of the other part", OJ 2009 L 107/166.

[17] A paritary body whose main task is to administer the agreement in question and settle disputes arising from the agreement.

[18] Similarly also pursuant to Art. 50/5(b) of the same agreement: *"Seven years after the date of entry into force of this Agreement the Stabilisation and Association Council shall establish the modalities for extending rights under this paragraph to the excluded sectors"*.

2.2.D The definition of Association remained, in substance, unchanged

Although the Lisbon Treaty has had a significant impact on the legal setting of the so called external relations of the EU as a whole,[19] if we compare the original Article 238 TEEC,[20] the same provisions as revised by the Maastricht Treaty-Article 310 TEC[21] and today‘s Article 217TFEU[22], we find that in its essence the definition of Association has remained unchanged. Minor changes in wording (the Community-the Union, union of States–one or more third countries, procedures-procedure) have had, as we shall show below, no impact on practice, and therefore their analysis is not addressed in this paper. Likewise, the transfer of procedural provisions from the original Article 238 TEEC to the current Article 218 TFEU itself is not important. However, one change is significant: the adoption of an Association Agreement requires today not merely a consultation of the European Parliament, but - according to Article 218(6)(2)(i) TFEU–its consent.

---

[19] Abundant literature has been published on this subject; namely on the institutional changes it brought about and the new legal basis of the Common Foreign and Security Policy. Cp. namely literature referred to throughout the excellent work-EECKHOUT P.: EU External Relations Law, Oxford University Press 2011. Cp. Also VAN ELSUWEGE P., EU External Action after the Collapse of the Pillar Structure; in: In Search of a New Balance between Delimitation and consistency; CMLR 47/2010, p. 987.

[20] Treaty establishing the European Economic Community (1957). Article 238 TEEC: „*The Community may conclude with a third State, a union of States or an international organisation agreements establishing an Association involving reciprocal rights and obligations, commonaction and special procedures.*

These agreements shall be concluded by the Council, acting unanimously after consulting the Assembly.

Where such agreements call for amendments to this Treaty, these amendments shall first be adopted in accordance with the procedure laid down in Article 236."

[21] Treaty establishing the European Community (1992). Article 310 TEC: „*The Community may conclude with one or more States or international organisations Agreements establishing an Association involving reciprocal rights and obligations, common action and special procedure.*“

[22] Treaty on the Functioning of the European Union (2007). Article 217 TFEU: „*The Union may conclude with one or more third countries or international organisations Agreements establishing an Association involving reciprocal rights and obligations, commonaction and special procedure.*"

2.2.E Gradual indirect limitation of the EU Association concept

At the time when the European Communities, and later the European Union had not yet had any specific legal basis for development cooperation, for economic, technical and financial assistance, or for neighbourhood policy, Association represented an umbrella category covering all privileged relations with third countries who wanted to get closer to the EU/EC politically and economically, including, in particular, candidate countries for EU accession. It held true then that "*Association can be anything between full membership minus 1% and a trade and cooperation agreement plus 1%*".[23] This claim is not valid anymore. As we shall show hereinafter, the notion of Association can nowadays take on a number of different meanings that do not share a more specific common denominator than the "getting closer" to the EU.

Following the Treaty of Amsterdam (1997), laying down a specific legal basis for development cooperation (ex. Art. 177-181 TEC), the Treaty of Nice (2001), expressly providing for economic, financial and technical cooperation with third countries (ex. Art. 181a TEC), and the Lisbon Treaty, introducing, in Article 8 TFEU, the basis for the European Neighbourhood Policy (ENP), the term "Association Agreement" can apply only to those Agreements which explicitly fall under one of the expressly mentioned types of Association.

2.2.F Material approach to legal acts, legal basis and appellation of Association Agreements

It ensues from that mentioned above that there exists a *variability of denomination of Association Agreements*. The EU is empowered by Article 217 TFEU to conclude *"Agreements establishing an Association"*. Such wording allows for a great diversity in terms of the content of the Agreements, but also for a great variety of their titles. In its answer to a question raised by the European Parliament the Commission emphasised that *"the EEC Treaty does not state in precise terms what the various categories of Agreements which the Community can conclude under those powers should be called. The titles of Agreements concluded by the Community—like their content—are not decided solely by the Community but are often the result of negotiations with its partners"*.[24] It means that

---

[23] Cp. HALLSTEIN W, Österreich und die EWG, Das Salzburger Expertengespräch, p. 30.

[24] Answer by the Commission to the written question n° 731/77, OJ 1978 C 88/ 2.

Agreements that are similar in content can bear different titles, and vice versa Agreements with different contents can have the same name. In its answer to a similar question the Council maintained that *"the so called 'Cooperation Agreements' concluded by the Community with third countries may differ widely as regards their actual content and it depends on the content what legal basis is adopted*".[25]

This flexibility resulting from the material rather than a formal approach made it possible for Switzerland, for example, not to have its Agreements with the EC/EU called "Association Agreements". Similarly, the currently drafted Agreement with Russia shall refrain from being called an Association one.

2.3 Overview of EU Association agreements

Below we shall first attempt to provide an indicative list of the 217 TFEU Association Agreements in force; secondly, an overview of previous EU Association Agreements shall be proposed.

2.3.A EU Association agreements in force

Association Agreements currently[26] in force concluded pursuant to Article 217 TFEU include:

- *Association Agreement* with Turkey (1963), expressly providing for future membership;[27]
- *Porto Agreement* (1992), establishing the European Economic Area with most of the European Free Trade Association (EFTA[28]) member states–Norway, Iceland and Lichtenstein.[29] The aim of this

[25] Answer by the Council to the written question n° 732/77, OJ 1978 C 88/ 3.
[26] Cp. MARESCEAU M., Bilateral Agreements Concluded by the European Community, Hague Academy of International Law, 2004, 309 Recueil des cours, Part II; PEERS S., EC Framework in International Relations, in: DASHWOOD A., HILLION C. (eds), The General Law of EC External Relations, Sweet & Maxwell 2000, p. 160-176.
[27] *„Recognizing that the support given by the European Economic Community to the efforts of the Turkish people to improve their standard of living will facilitate the accession of Turkey to the Community at a later date"* (paragraph 4 of the Preamble of the Turkey-EC Association Agreement (1963), OJ 1964 L 217/ 3705.
[28] European Free Trade Association.
[29] At the time of the conclusion of the agreement also Austria, Finland, Sweden. In Switzerland it was rejected in a referendum. For more detail concerning this

external agreement is to *"provide for the fullest possible realisation of the free movement of goods, persons, services and capital within the whole EEA, so that the internal market established within the European Union is extended to the EFTA States"* (C-72/09 Rimbaud, para 20);[30]

- seven *agreements* with Switzerland (1999),[31] which rejected the EEA Agreement by way of referendum;
  ▫ *Stabilisation and Association Agreements*, which expressly provide for future membership, concluded with Macedonia (2001), Croatia (2001),[32] Albania (2006), Montenegro (2007), Bosnia and Herzegovina (2008) and Serbia (2008, not yet in force);
- *Euro-Mediterranean Association Agreements*, which today fall under the Neighbourhood Policy (see para 0 hereinafter): Tunisia (1995), Israel (1995), Morocco (1996), Palestinian Authority (1997 Interim), Jordan (1997), Egypt (2001), Algeria (2002), Libya (2002), Syria (currently under negotiation);
- *Association Agreement* with Chile (2002), establishing not only a free trade area, but also a political dialogue, and defining many areas of cooperation. Today, such an agreement would probably be concluded based on Article 212 TFEU as part of the economic, financial and technical cooperation with third countries (see para 0 hereafter);

---

agreement Compaq e.g. C-321/97 Andersson, paras 26 to 31; C-300/01 Salzmann, para 65; C-452/01 Ospelt, para 27.

[30] The EEA creates a common market (free movement of goods, persons, services and capital), but not a custom union; the trade between the EEA countries is free; however there are no common economic and custom borders. This common market, though, shows its specificities. Firstly, the EEA members are subject to the same discipline as EU member states, namely the principle of loyalty, including the obligation to adopt measure to implement the Treaties, interdiction to adopt measures jeopardising the application of the Treaties, or interdiction of discrimination on grounds of nationality. The Porto Agreement imposes on the EFTA countries to approximate their legislation with the legislation of the EU, in conformity with the interpretation of the CJEU based on the state-of-affairs existing prior to the conclusion of the Porto Agreement.

[31] The relationship with Switzerland has been governed by the original agreement on free trade concluded in 1972 (OJ 1972 L 300/198) amended by seven agreements in 1999 (OJ 2002 L 114/1) on free movement of persons, air and land transport, public procurement, scientific and technological cooperation, mutual recognition in relation to conformity assessment, and trade in agricultural products. This legislative framework has been regularly extended and updated.

[32] Croatia will become member of the EU as of July 1, 2013.

- *Agreement on trade, development and cooperation* with South Africa (1999) (amended in 2009, not yet in force);
- *ACP-EU Partnership Agreement* signed in Cotonou (2000, amended 2005), which is, by its content, a development cooperation Agreement with 78 countries from the African, Caribbean and Pacific regions, mostly former colonies of EU member states. The Agreement was concluded for a period of 20 years with a retroactive effect as of 1 March 2000 (Article 95[1] of the Agreement). It has for a legal basis former Article 310 TEC on Association (now Article 217 TFEU), as if, in substance, it did not aim at development cooperation which, at the time of conclusion, had its own legal basis (since the MT ex-ex Article 130u to 130y TEC).

2.3.B Historical chronological overview of other EU Association agreements

Having in mind the twofold evolution of the EU Association concept (see paras 0 and 0 above), we can put forward a non-exhaustive chronological overview of Agreements falling under today's Art. 217 TFEU at least by their content, if not by their legal basis. Agreements already mentioned in para 0 above are not repeated.

- Agreements Establishing an Association: Greece (1961), Malta (1970), Cyprus (1972);
- Agreements: Sweden, Norway, Island and Portugal (1972);[33]
- Cooperation Agreements: Yaoundé (ACP countries),[34] Lomé (1975);
- "Conventions on economic Association" envisaged by declarations attached to the Rome treaties with three Maghreb countries–Tunisia (1969), Algeria, Morocco (1976); previous agreements: Tunisia (1963), Morocco (1969), entitled—despite their content—Association Agreements; with three Mashriq countries-Egypt, Syria, Jordan–and Israel (1977);
- Europe Association Agreements with Poland, Hungary (1994), Romania, Bulgaria, Czech Republic, Slovakia (1995), Estonia, Lithuania, Latvia (1998), Slovenia (1999).[35]

---

[33] These Agreements go beyond mere commercial agreements by their economic competition clauses; see OJ 1972 L 300, 301.

[34] Cp. OJ 1963 L 26/296; OJ 1964 L 27/3685; OJ 1964 193/1430.

2.4 EU law concepts similar to Association pursuant to article 217 TFEU

We have said that the material scope of Association has been progressively restricted following the adoption of the specific legal basis for special external relations of the EU which had previously been covered by the concept of Association. It is therefore useful to appreciate the differences between these policies and institutions on the one hand, and the notion of Association pursuant of Article 217 TFEU on the other hand.

2.4.A Association of Overseas Countries and Territories

This kind of Association, based on Articles 198-204 TFEU[36] is designed for relationships with *"non-European countries and territories which have special relations with Denmark, France, the Netherlands and the United Kingdom",* listed in Annex II of the TFEU ("OCT").[37] Its purpose is "*to promote the economic and social development of the countries and territories and to establish close economic relations between them and the Union as a whole*" (Art. 198(2) TFEU). In today's practice, it covers economic and trade cooperation, including trade in services and other related areas, and thus also involves social development and human resources development, regional cooperation and integration, and cultural and social cooperation.

The nature of the Association of the OTCs is however arguable: constitutionally, the OTCs have a dependency status vis-à-vis a EU member state, but, at the same time, they are not part of the EU territory. The fact that the EU and the OTCs are distinct entities follows clearly e.g. from the wording of Article 198 TFEU. OTCs thus benefit from a narrow cooperation with the EU, which is provided for in the Treaties themselves, without however being party to these Treaties. Therefore, this relationship

---

[35] Cp. CJEU case law relating to these Agreements, in particular C-235/99 Kondova; C-257/99 Barkoci and Malik; C-63/99 Gloszczuk; C-268/99 Jany; C-162/00 Pokrzeptowicz-Meyer.

[36] Cf. implementing secondary acts-Decision 2001/822 on the Association of the overseas countries and territories with the EU (as amended by the Decision 2007/249); Regulation 2304/2002.

[37] Cp. C-100&101/89 Kaefer, C-260/90 Leplat, C-430/92 Netherlands v Commission, T-480&483/93 Antillean Rice Mills, C-310/95 Road Air BV, C-110/97 R Netherlands v Council, C-106/97 Dutch Antilles Dairy, C-301/97 Emesa Sugar; also generally see Declaration no. 25 of the Treaty of Maastricht on the representation of the interests of these territories (1992).

cannot be considered as a treaty-based sovereign-to-sovereign Association according to international law. In fact, Association pursuant to Article 198 TFEU is not a real Association but rather (i) a singular way of extending the geographic scope of the Treaties or (ii) a hidden internal Association. Content-wise, this Association is quite similar to the development cooperation with the ACP countries according to the Cotonou Agreement.

2.4.B Economic, Financial and Technical Cooperation with Third Countries

Economic, financial and technical cooperation (EFTC) with third countries was introduced by the Treaty of Nice (2001, ex Art. 181a TEC) as one of the EU competences in a new kind of external relationship. Its application is still being refined because, firstly, it has not been used very frequently, and, secondly, the Treaty of Lisbon has restricted its applicability by providing for a new legal basis, i.e. Article 8 TEU on the neighbourhood policy. The EFTC comprises *"economic, financial and technical cooperation measures, including assistance, in particular financial assistance"*, but *"[w]ithout prejudice to the other provisions of the Treaties, and in particular Articles 208 to 211"*, i.e. provisions on development cooperation. Moreover, the EFTC measures *"shall be consistent with the development policy of the Union"*. This distinction, and the relation of speciality between Articles 212-213 TFEU and Article 208 ff. TFEU were sanctioned by the CJEU in the case C-155/07 European Parliament v. Council, paras 39-48.

Since the EU is allowed to provide financial assistance within the EFTC, there exist an asymmetry of rights and obligations in favour of the non-EU party. This is a characteristic feature of a privileged relationship that is, in the case of the EFTC, combined with development cooperation, neighbourhood policy and Association.

Later on we will point out that in neighbourhood policy agreements the cooperation relationship between the parties is a sign of a lack of perspective for the non-EU party to eventually join the EU. However, within the EFTC we cannot overlook Article 218(8) TFEU which stipulates that the Council *"shall act unanimously...as well as for Association agreements and the agreements referred to in Article 212 with the States which are candidates for accession"*. The primary law thus also envisages a so-called dynamic form of EFTC agreements, similar to Association Agreements pursuant to Article 217 TFEU. There is, however, no real life example of such Agreement.

The EFTC addressees are different from those of development cooperation since the EFTC is carried out *"with other than developing countries"*. This constitutes a clear-cut distinction from the development cooperation that is carried out pursuant to Article 208 ff. TFEU. Implementing regulations (2112/2005 and 1905/2006; see hereinafter 4.2.6) indicate that the EFTC is intended for some non-developing countries on the OECD lists.

Unlike Association Agreements, the EFTC is not intended for international organisations (i.e. international organisations are not potential beneficiaries of these relationships). However, in contrast to the neighbourhood policy, cooperation with international organisations is envisaged within the EFTC, i.e. by way of external Agreements. In fact, the EU is empowered, within the EFTC, to conclude such Agreements with *"third parties"* which includes States, but also international organisations.

2.4.C European Neighbourhood Policy

Today, the European Neighbourhood Policy (ENP) is recognised as the key priority of EU external relations.[38] It was established in 2003,[39] however its origins date back to the Partnership and Cooperation Agreements the EC had concluded with the former Soviet Union countries after 1990.[40]

Article 8 TEU constitutes a new legal basis introduced by the Lisbon Treaty and intended for a "*special relationship*" "*based on cooperation*" with *"neighbouring countries"* respecting *"the values of the Union"*. To formalise them, the EU concludes *"specific agreements"* that may contain "*reciprocal rights and obligations*" allowing to "*undertake activities jointly*", and subject to "*periodic consultation.*"

The objective of the ENP is to bring neighbour countries closer to the EU in security, economic and political matters, to create *"special*

---

[38] See Communication to the Commission by the Commissioner Ferrero-Waldner "Implementing and Promoting the ENP", 22.11.2005, SEC (2005) 1521.

[39] See the Commission, Wider Europe–Neighbourhood: A New Framework for Relations with our Eastern and Southern Partners, COM (2003) 104 final.

[40] For a very detail legal analysis of the ENP see CREMONA M., The European Neighbourhood Policy–More than a Partnership?, in: CREMONA M. (ed.), Developments in EU External Relations Law, Oxford University Press 2008, p. 244. For a brief and clear political analysis of the ENP see KUROWSKA X., PAWLAK P., The EU's Eastern partnership–More for More or More of the Same? Yearbook of Polish European Studies, Vol. 14/2011, p. 109.

relationships" with EU neighbours and to *"establish an area of prosperity and good neighbourliness, founded on the values of the Union and characterised by close and peaceful relations based on cooperation"* (Art. 8 TEU). In practice, this means opening up some EU internal market sectors to the ENP partners and intensifying political dialogue with them in exchange for significant political, economic and legal reforms. This cooperation should, among other things, prevent the creation of new dividing lines in Europe and ensure its stability. It covers areas such as sustainable development, participation in a common market, legislative convergence, market opening by way of free trade areas, integration into EU transport, energy and telecommunication infrastructures, contractual protection of investments, legal migration (in connection with the dying out of the EU population), prevention of security threats, or promoting human rights.

Within the ENP we talk about special relationships, i.e. privileged relations with the EU based on shared values, peace and cooperation, and governed in each individual case by an external agreement. The EU (population of 0.5 billion, GDP amounting to €12,000 billion) enters into direct contact with its poorer neighbours with whom it wishes to create a *"ring of friends"*.

The inspiration by Article 217 TFEU on Association is quite manifest– we talk about *"special relationships"*. Therefore, part of the doctrine considers that Association, and namely "static Association" (with no perspective of subsequent accession), constitutes an element of the ENP, which consequently makes the ENP part of the EU Association policy.[41]

However, unlike the Association pursuant to Article 217 TFEU, relationships arising from Article 8 TEU consist in *"cooperation"*, which expressly rules out any perspective of future accession.[42]All the same, it surely must involve more than just cooperation, otherwise the ENP could not create a *"special relationship"*. It is, in fact, difficult to delimit the boundaries of cooperation within the ENP. We can agree with the former President of the Commission M. Prodi that the only thing that can be excluded is the participation of the neighbouring country in the EU decision making, i.e. sharing the EU bodies and institutions.[43]

---

[41] Cp. LAENERTS K., VAN NUFFET P. European Union Law, 3rd edition, Sweet & Maxwell, London 2011, p. 980.

[42] Cp. e.g. CRAIG P., DE BÚRCA G., EU Law, 5th edition, Oxford University Press 2011, p. 324.

[43]Cp. PRODI R., A Wider Europe–A Proximity Policy as the Key to Stability, cit. in: VAN ELSUWEGE P., PETROV R., op.cit, p. 696.

Article 8 TEU covers exclusively relationships between the EU and its *"neighbouring countries"*. This restriction of its personal scope has several implications.

Firstly, international organisations–unlike in Article 217 TFEU–cannot enter into this kind of relationship.

Secondly, the notion of neighbourliness has evolved. According to the *travaux préparatoires* of the Convention, during the drafting of the Constitutional Treaty a proposal to include a specific title and article "the Union and its immediate environment" was discussed.[44] However, since countries without a common border with the EU were to be covered, such as Georgia[45], Armenia or Azerbaijan, the notion of neighbourliness in Article 8 TEU cannot be read in its narrow geographical meaning.

Countries and their geographical position-the nearest EU neighbours-concerned by the ENP are listed, in the most perspicuous manner, in the Annex of Financial Regulation 1638/2006 laying down general provisions establishing a European Neighborhood and Partnership Instrument. It includes two categories of countries, each subject to a different approach to cooperation–the Eastern Partnership and the Union for the Mediterranean.

2.5 Conclusion

Over the last few years, the scope of the legal institution of "Association with the Union", and especially its material scope, has changed fundamentally. It was mainly due to the modifications of the EU primary law, namely the adoption of specific legal bases for external relations which, in the founding Treaties, had been covered by the notion of Association.

The current state of affairs-following the introduction of a separate legal basis for development cooperation by the Amsterdam Treaty (1992) (ex Art.177-181 TEC); the express regulation of the EFTC by the Treaty of Nice (2001) (ex Art. 181 TEC), and the ENP provisions in Article 8 TEU of the Lisbon Treaty–allows the EU to adopt two not entirely coherent approaches. The first option is to conclude a specific external agreement on as precise a legal basis as possible; the other–and in our view more likely–option is to use flexibly the vague definitions of Association, EFTC and ENP to account for the political will of the other party. Differences between these concepts of external relations, and even

---

[44] Cp. document CONV 649/03 z 2.4.2003.

[45] Since the accession of Romania and Bulgaria (2007), Georgia has a maritime border with the EU.

more so their overlapping, indeed give the EU quite a lot of leeway allowing them to reflect on the political wishes of the non-EU contractual parties and, at the same time, to respect the EU principle of delegated powers which requires any EU action to have a sufficient legal basis in the Treaties.

In this context, Article 8 TEU (ENP) constitutes an *alternative* to Article 217 TFEU (Association).[46] Some countries do not wish to be "associated" because of their political ego (Russia, in the past also Switzerland); other countries require Association status (because of the vision of future membership) even if the EU is not that enthusiastic about it.

This flexibility potential first needs to be tried out in practice. The scope of Article 212 TFEU on EFTC had not been given enough time to be used more extensively between the adoption of the Treaty of Nice (2001) and the introduction of the new Lisbon article 8 TEU on the ENP. Both institutions are based on the principle of cooperation and thus should rule out any possibility of subsequent membership for the non-EU partner, however, Article 218(8) TFEU foresees that even an EFTC Agreement may constitute an antechamber to accession: "*The Council shall act…unanimously…as well as for…agreements referred to in Article 212 with the States which are candidates for accession.*" Whilst article 212 TFEU on EFTC introduces a clear link to the development policy, article 8 TEU on ENP talks about privileged relations and bears thus more resemblance to the Association pursuant to Article 217 TFEU.

We could conclude from the above that, implicitly, there exists a hierarchy between these comparable legal bases of the EU external relations: development cooperation–EFTC–Association–ENP. This order is backed up also by the structure of the TFEU, (provisions on ENP being an exception): Articles 208-211, 212-213 and 217 TFEU (and Article 8 TEU), as well as by suggestions indicating a possible use of Article 8 TEU as a legal basis for the "advanced status" of the southern countries within the ENP, as opposed to the current Association pursuant to Article 217 TFEU. This hierarchy is, though, set into perspective by the aforementioned possibility to use EFTC agreements as an antechamber to accession expressly provided for in Article 218(8) TFEU. Therefore we

---

[46] Cp. NEFRAMI E., op.cit. p. 100; the opinion developed by the author suggests that the neighbourhood policy encompasses Association as well as economic, technical and financial cooperation. Before the entry into force of the Treaty of Nice these Agreements had been concluded exclusively based on ex Art. 133 TEC (trade policy) and on the flexibility clause in ex. Art. 308 TEC i.e. not on the "Association basis" ex. Art. 310 TEC.

need to wait and see whether the actual application of the EU external relations policy will respect and comfort this legal-theory hierarchy.

CHAPTER THREE

INTERPRETATION, IMPLEMENTATION AND ENFORCEMENT OF ASSOCIATION AGREEMENTS: INSTITUTIONAL STRUCTURES, DISPUTE SETTLEMENT MECHANISMS AND THE JURISDICTION OF THE COURT OF JUSTICE OF THE EU

EMIL RUFFER

3.1 Introduction

Association Agreements (hereinafter the "AA[s]")[1] concluded under Art. 217 of the Treaty on the Functioning of the European Union (hereinafter as the "TFEU") constitute an important element in the European Union's external relations and as such contain a complex legal framework between the EU and the associated country.[2] It is therefore essential that their provisions are applied in a uniform manner, that they

---

[1] The names of the AAs can differ: they can be called "Stabilisation and Association Agreement", "Partnership and Cooperation Agreement", "Euro-Mediterranean Agreement establishing an Association" or simply an "Association Agreement", which I chose to use as a general term. In the words of W. Shakespeare: "*What's in a name? that which we call a rose / By any other name would smell as sweet*" - *Romeo and Juliet*, Act II, Scene II, In: *The Illustrated Stratford Shakespeare*, Chancellor Press, London, 1982, p. 708.

[2] Art. 217 TFEU stipulates: "*The Union may conclude with one or more third countries or international organisations agreements establishing an Association involving reciprocal rights and obligations, common action and special procedure.*"

are properly implemented and that the rights and obligation can be effectively enforced.

To this end, the AAs usually establish an institutional structure which is designed for the implementation of the agreement (by means of acts of 'secondary Association law') and for dispute settlement among the Parties (by means of negotiations through diplomatic channels). Moreover, they provide access to courts for natural and legal persons, both in the EU Member States and the third country concerned, and their provisions may be subject to jurisdiction and interpretation by the Court of Justice of the European Union (hereinafter as the "CJEU" or the "Court"). We shall look at these elements in turn and assess their nature and function in legal terms, focusing on the issue of the Union's competences and the role of the CJEU.

3.2 Institutional framework

An institutional framework[3] is crucial for the application and implementation of AAs and is one of the advanced features of an Association which falls under the scope of "*common action and special procedures*" within the meaning of Art. 217 TFEU. The institutional framework usually consists of the following main structures: the Association Council (composed from representatives at ministerial level), the Association Committee (composed from representatives at senior official level) and the Parliamentary Association Committee (composed from members of the European Parliament and members of the national parliament of the Associated country).

---

[3] The institutional framework is a common feature of all AAs, but individual arrangements may of course differ. For the purposes of this article, I will use the elements and procedures contained in the most recent AAs available, such as the *Stabilisation and Association Agreement between the European Communities and their Member States, of the one part, and the Republic of Montenegro, of the other part* (OJ L 108, 29.4.2010, p. 3, hereinafter as "SAA EU-Montenegro") or the *Stabilisation and Association Agreement between the European Communities and their Member States, of the one part, and the Republic of Albania, of the other part* (OJ L 107, 28.4.2009, p. 166, hereinafter as "SAA EU-Albania"). Nevertheless, the description should be relevant and appropriate also with regard to other AAs currently negotiated within the Eastern Partnership, which have not been signed and officially published yet (including the *Association Agreement between the European Union and its Member States, of the one part, and Ukraine, of the other part*, which is supposed to be signed at the next Eastern Partnership Summit in Vilnius on 28-29 November 2013, if all goes well).

The Association Council has the duty to supervise the application and implementation of the AA and to examine any major issues arising within its framework or any other bilateral or international issues of mutual interest. It consists of the members of the Council of the EU and members of the European Commission, on the one hand,[4] and of members of the Government of the Associated country on the other, and it usually holds meetings at a ministerial level once a year. The Association Council is chaired in turn by a representative of the Union and a representative of the Associated country, in accordance with the provisions laid down in its Rules of Procedure.[5]

The Association Council also has the power to take decisions for the purpose of attaining the objectives of the AA and within its scope, which are binding on the Parties. These decisions constitute so called "secondary Association legislation", comparable to the Union acts of secondary legislation,[6] and the CJEU jurisprudence gave them the status of an integral part of Union law[7] (as the AAs themselves). The decisions of the

---

[4] The President of the Council is predominantly supposed to represent the Union, whereas other members of the Council represent the EU Member States, which are also Parties to the AA. Members of the Commission represent the Union. By way of example, the composition of the EU delegation at the fourth EU-Montenegro Stabilisation and Association Council meeting (Brussels, 26 June 2013) was as follows: Ms Lucinda Creighton, Minister for European Affairs of Ireland (representing the Irish Presidency of the Council), led the EU delegation (on behalf of the EU High Representative for Foreign Affairs and Security Policy, Catherine Ashton), and Mr Štefan Füle, Commissioner responsible for Enlargement and European Neighbourhood Policy, represented the European Commission. See Joint Press Release UE-ME 3605/13 PRESSE 296 of 26 June 2013, p. 1.

[5] The Rules of Procedure also govern, *inter alia*, the conditions under which the members of the Association Council may arrange to be represented (substituted) in its meeting. *Cf.* Art. 1 (Chairmanship) and Art. 3 (Representation) of the Decision No 1/2010of the EU-Montenegro Stabilisation and Association Council of 14 June 2010 adopting its rules of procedure (2010/390/EU), OJ L 179, 14.7.2010, p. 11.

[6] These are regulations, directives and decisions within the meaning of Art. 288 TFEU.

[7] See cases 87/75 *Bresciani* [1976] ECR 129, para. 29, case 30/88 *Greece v. Commission* [1989] ECR 3711, para. 13 and C-192/89 *Sevince* [1990] ECR I-3461, para. 12. It is interesting to note that in the *Bresciani* case the CJEU merely stated that the decisions of the Associated Council were adopted under powers conferred on it by the AA, and thus relied on the direct connection with the AA, which in itself constitutes an integral part of EU law. In the later *Sevince* case, however, the CJEU went further and treated the decisions of the Association Council as "acts of an EU institution" for the purpose of preliminary ruling procedure, whereby effectively giving them the status equivalent to Union secondary law (which is by

Association Council serve as an important instrument for implementing the AA and ensuring its proper functioning, and the Parties (the Union and/or its Member States and the Associated country) are required to take the measures necessary to implement the decisions of the Association Council. Apart from legally binding decisions, the Association Council is entitled also to make appropriate recommendations on different policy areas, which might be of political relevance. Both categories of its acts, decisions and recommendations, must be drawn up by agreement between the Parties (i.e. by consensus/unanimity).

The Association Council is assisted in the performance of its duties by an Association Committee, its composition reflecting that of the Association Council itself, but only at a senior official level (representatives of the Council of the EU and representatives of the Commission on the EU side and representatives of the Government of the Associated country on the other side). The duties of the Association Committee as an expert and preparatory body include the preparation of meetings of the Association Council, whose Rules of Procedure usually also contain provisions on the functioning of the Association Committee.[8] The Association Council may also delegate some of its executive powers on the Association Committee; in such situations, the Association Committee shall take the relevant decisions and/or recommendations by the same procedure and under the same conditions (i.e. consensus/unanimity) as the Association Council itself. Specialised sub-committees or other bodies within certain fields covered by the AA may be also created by the Association Committee (such as a sub-committee on migration issues).[9]

The parliamentary dimension of the Association is reflected in an Association Parliamentary Committee, which serves as a forum for members of the parliament of the Associated country and of the European Parliament to meet and exchange views on all aspects of relations between the Parties to the AA. The intervals for its meetings are determined by the

---

definition an act adopted by the Union's institution). The approach adopted in *Bresciani* case was initially criticised in academic circles, *cf.* Hilf, Meinhard: *Organisationsstruktur der Europäischen Gemeinschaften*, 1982, p. 182 ff, but has become firmly established since then.

[8] The relationship between the Association Council and the Association Committee can be thus described by way of analogy with the Council of the EU and its preparatory body, the COREPER (the Committee of Permanent Representatives). Of course, the meetings of the EU Council are much more frequent (several Council formations meet within one month) and the COREPER meetings are held on a weekly basis.

[9] See e.g. Art. 123 of the SAA EU-Montenegro.

Committee itself in the Rules of Procedure,[10] which also set the periods of chairmanship of the Committee. Whereas the Association Parliamentary Committee can serve as an important forum for contacts at the parliamentary level, it has no formal decision making powers[11] and its direct involvement in the application and implementation of the AAs should therefore not be overestimated.[12]

3.3 Dispute settlement mechanism between the Parties

Generally, the Parties to the AA are required to take any general or specific measures in order to fulfil their obligations and to ensure that the objectives set out in the AA are attained. The AA usually contains a clause that the Parties agree to consult promptly through appropriate (diplomatic) channels and to discuss any matter concerning the interpretation or implementation of the AA. The initial consultation and discussions may lead to the clarification of the issue or to the identification of a potential dispute.

Any disputes regarding the application and interpretation of the AA may be brought to the Association Council and then consulted between the Parties. The Parties are obliged to try to resolve the dispute by entering into good faith consultations within the Association Council and/or other bodies established for this purpose,[13] with the aim of reaching, as soon as possible, a mutually acceptable solution. As long as the dispute is unresolved, it should be discussed at every meeting of the Association Council and thus kept 'on the agenda'.

The Association Council may settle the dispute by a binding decision or it can declare, following the consultations having taken place, that there

---

[10] See e.g. the Rules of Procedure of the EU-Montenegro Stabilisation and Association Parliamentary Committee (SAPC), whose Rule 6 provides for meetings twice a year.

[11] The Association Parliamentary Committee is not empowered to adopt binding decision, but it may be entitled to adopt recommendations for the European Parliament, the parliament of the Associated country, the Council of the EU and the European Commission. *Cf.* Rule 3 of the Rules of Procedure of the EU-Montenegro SAPC.

[12] This assertion can be supported e.g. by the Declaration and Recommendations from the 6th EU-Montenegro SAPC, adopted on 30 April 2013, para. 14: *"[The SAPC] Called upon the Parliament and the Government [of Montenegro] to make additional efforts aimed at* ***more efficient monitoring of implementation of the SAPC recommendations and conclusions****"* (emphasis added).

[13] E.g. Association Committee or special sub-committee established in one of the fields covered by the AA.

is no dispute anymore. If the Association Council is unable to settle the dispute, an arbitration procedure may be initiated, subject to certain conditions and limitations (see below). It appears, from the practice of Association relations, that the dispute settlement by the binding decision of the Association Council is rather rare and unique. However, it raises interesting legal questions along the following lines:

1. Firstly, such a binding decision of the Association Council would seem to breach the interpretation monopoly of the CJEU, which is otherwise within the meaning of Art. 19 TEU of the competent Court to ensure that in the interpretation and application of the Treaties (and provisions of the Union legal order adopted to give them effect)[14] the law is observed. The jurisdiction of the CJEU could be respected if it had an opportunity to rule on the interpretation of the disputed provisions of the AA in the preliminary ruling procedure under Art. 267 TFEU, prior to the adoption of the binding decision by the Association Council. However, such arrangements are hardly conceivable, since the Court itself in Opinion 1/09 confirmed very strict limits on compatibility of courts (by analogy any dispute settlement bodies), established under international agreements, with the Union legal order.[15]
2. Another interesting aspect seems to be the fact that should the Association Council adopt a decision on interpretation of a certain provision of the AA, then such a decision would constitute an act of the 'secondary Association law' and according to the CJEU case-law, it could also be regarded as an integral part of the Union law.[16] Given this status, such a decision could then be the subject of a preliminary ruling procedure on validity or interpretation, initiated before the CJEU under Art. 267 TFEU by the competent court or

---

[14] AAs (as well as other agreements concluded by the Union) form an integral part of the Union law and as such should also be subject to interpretation by the one and the only CJEU.

[15] See *Opinion 1/09* [2011] ECR I-1137, paras. 74-78. The CJEU acknowledged in para. 74 that "*As regards an international agreement providing for the creation of a court responsible for the interpretation of its provisions, the Court has, it is true, held that such an agreement is not, in principle, incompatible with European Union law.*" However, the conditions applicable to courts would not be automatically met by executive bodies, such as the Association Council, empowered to settle disputes under an international agreement.

[16] See note 8 *supra*.

tribunal of a Member State in the context of national judicial proceedings.

3. Finally, a question arises to what extent (if any) should the CJEU be bound by a previous interpretation in the decision of the Association Council, if it is called to interpret a similar or identical provision of the AA (e.g. in the preliminary ruling procedure under Art. 267 TFEU). If we approach this situation from a different perspective, we confront the issue of the binding nature of such a decision of the Association Council for the Parties. If one of the Parties of an AA is always the EU, it would effectively mean that the decision is binding, as a matter of international law, for the Union and its institutions.[17] Would then a decision of the Association Council be binding for the CJEU as one of the Union's institutions?[18]

For the sake of completeness, it should be mentioned that if either Party considers that the other Party has failed to fulfil an obligation under the AA, it may take appropriate measures. However, before doing so, except in cases of special urgency,[19] the Party willing to take the measures is obliged to supply the Association Council with all relevant information required for a thorough examination of the situation, with a view to seeking a solution acceptable to the Parties. In the selection of measures, priority must be given to measures which least disturb the functioning of the AA. If they have been taken, the measures must be notified immediately to the Association Council and shall be the subject of consultations, if the other Party so requests. Again, an attempt at the peaceful settlement of disputes is preferred if the circumstances permit.

---

[17] See e.g. Art. 121 SAA EU-Montenegro, which stipulates: "*The decisions taken [by the Stabilisation and Association Council] shall be binding on the Parties, which shall take the measures necessary to implement the decisions taken.*"

[18] Moreover, should the Association Council be requested by one of the Parties to decide on the interpretation of certain provision(s) of the AA, it cannot take recourse to the preliminary ruling procedure before the CJEU, since it is certainly not "a court or tribunal of a Member State" within the meaning of Art. 267 TFEU.

[19] The cases of special urgency are situations when one of the 'essential elements' of the AA has been breached. The essential elements (or 'political clauses') provide for fundamental values shared by the Parties and usually contain the following: respect for democratic principles and human rights; the fight against proliferation of Weapons of Mass Destruction (WMD); the fight against terrorism; and promotion of international peace and justice by ratification and implementation of the Rome Statute of the International Criminal Court (ICC).

The AA may also contain detailed rules on arbitration proceedings applicable with respect to differences concerning the interpretation and application of certain provisions of the AA.[20] Such rules on arbitration are usually set out in a separate protocol and would cover the initiation of the arbitration by one of the Parties, the composition of the arbitration panel, the form and the structure of its ruling, compliance measures and their review procedure and compensation awarded for non-compliance. Due to relative flexibility of the arbitration procedure, the issue of interpretation principles applied by the arbitration tribunal becomes crucial with respect to the safeguarding of the unity and coherence of Union law. It is therefore not surprising that the provisions on arbitration proceedings usually contain an 'Interpretation principles' clause, such as that in Art. 13 of Protocol 7 to SAA EU-Montenegro:

> Arbitration panels shall apply and interpret the provisions of this Agreement in accordance with customary rules of interpretation of public international law, including the Vienna Convention on the Law of Treaties. **They shall not give an interpretation of the acquis communautaire.** The fact that a provision is identical in substance to a provision of the Treaty establishing the European Communities shall not be decisive in the interpretation of that provision.[21]

It is comprehensible why such limitations on the interpretation of the Union law is explicitly included, given the wide-ranging jurisdiction of the CJEU which might be otherwise jeopardised. On the other hand, it is not entirely clear what remedies can be taken if the arbitration tribunal trespasses its limits and gives an interpretation of the EU law. Indeed, as the AA as such constitutes "an integral part of Union law", all its provisions can be perceived as constituting "*acquis communautaire*" and it might get extremely difficult to settle a dispute arising under the AA without interpreting any of its provisions: however, this is clearly not what is meant by the "Interpretation clause" quoted above, which itself

---

[20] The arbitration procedure is thus applicable only to specific provisions of the AA, whereas in cases of disputes concerning the remaining parts thereof, the Parties must use the consultation procedure through the Association Council. By way of example, Art. 2 of Protocol 7 to SAA EU-Montenegro limits the arbitration procedure to the following most significant sections: (a) Title IV (Free movement of goods); (b) Title V (Movement of workers, establishment, supply of services, capital); and (c) Title VI (Approximation of laws, law enforcement and competition rules), and further sets out concrete Articles within these Titles to which the arbitration is applicable.

[21] Emphasis added.

explicitly anticipates that the arbitration tribunal will strive to interpret the provisions of the AA. What is less clear is where to draw the dividing line between the provisions of the AA open for interpretation, and the provisions which are forbidden due to its nature as "*acquis communautaire*". Perhaps in the context of interpretation by the arbitral tribunal, the provisions of the AA do not form an "integral part of the Union law" and the term "*acquis communautaire*" means solely provisions of the TEU / TFEU and the EU secondary law adopted to give them effect. This would seem to be the only logical approach, which would not render the interpretation exercise performed by the arbitration tribunal effectively impossible and devoid of any purpose.

3.4 Access to national courts and judicial protection

Another important element for enforcement of the AAs is the mutual obligation of the Parties to ensure that natural and legal persons of the other Party have access to the competent courts and administrative organs to defend their individual rights and their property rights. Such access to the courts in one Party by natural and legal persons from the other Party must be free of discrimination in relation to its own nationals.

The provision on access to the courts, however, does not mean that every single provision of the AA can be directly relied on before the courts. On the one hand, as a matter of Union law, the national courts of the EU Member States should apply the AAs in a uniform manner and give their provisions direct effect, if the respective conditions under EU law are fulfilled.[22] On the other hand, it depends on the relevant constitutional framework which governs the relationship between the international and domestic law in the Associated country (*monist* vs. *dualist* systems)[23] whether the provisions of the AA can have a direct effect before its national courts.

Monist legal systems[24] are then founded on the concept of unity of international and domestic law, which form one legal order with its own

---

[22] Provisions which confer rights on individuals and which are clear, precise and unconditional.

[23] For a more theoretical explanation of dualist and monist approaches see e.g. M. N. Shaw: *International Law*, Cambridge University Press, 1997, pp. 100-101.

[24] Among the EU Member States, the monist systems are to be found e.g. in France or the Netherlands, as well as in Bulgaria, Cyprus, the Czech Republic, Estonia, Latvia, Lithuania, Poland, Slovakia, Slovenia and Romania (from the Member States which acceded to the EU in 2004). For more details see F. Hoffmeister: *Integration of the Europe Agreements/Association Agreements into National Law*,

hierarchy, in which the international law is supreme to the domestic law. The constitutions of monist states usually contain a general reception norm (clause), which incorporates all international treaties binding for that state into the domestic legal order. International treaties to which such monist state is a Party are no more regarded as an autonomous source of international law, but become part of the domestic legal order which takes precedence in applications before all other sources of domestic law (the doctrine of supremacy).[25] The AAs in monist states, after their entry into force following their ratification and their publication in the Official Journal/Collection of Laws, then become an integral part of the domestic legal order.

In dualist legal systems, provisions of international law are perceived as an isolated system, separate from domestic law. The provisions of international law may me applied by national courts only in cases where they have been duly implemented in domestic law. AAs in dualist countries[26] then have the status of an international treaty that is not part of the domestic legal order, which has an impact on their applicability and potential direct effect. As a general rule in a dualist system, an international treaty may not be directly applied by domestic courts unless it has been transformed into the domestic law in the form of e.g. a statute or other legislative act. The effects of the international agreements are provided by the ratification act of the parliament (an act of giving consent to the conclusion of the treaty and empowering the government to execute its transposition by means of domestic legislation) or by adopting a special law promulgating the international treaty. The status and effects of an international treaty in the hierarchy of sources of domestic law is then dependent on the nature of the domestic transformation law.

Due to the facts described above, in certain situations, only the domestic legislation implementing the AA can be invoked by natural and

---

In: A. Ott, K. Inglis (eds.): *Handbook on European Enlargement*, T.M.C. Asser Press, Hague, 2002, pp. 209-214, where the relevant provisions of the constitutions of these Member States are quoted.

[25] See e.g. Art. 10 of the Constitution of the Czech Republic, which stipulates: "*Promulgated international agreements, the ratification of which has been approved by the Parliament and which are binding on the Czech Republic, shall constitute a part of the legal order; should an international agreement make provision contrary to a law, the international agreement shall be applied.*" However, precedence of international treaties is usually given only in relation to laws and other legal acts which do not have a constitutional status, although constitutionally based precedence before the constitution itself is not excluded.

[26] Dualism is applied e.g. in Austria, Hungary, Germany, Malta or the United Kingdom.

legal persons trying to enforce their rights and benefits. This makes their position in an Associated country rather difficult in situations where the implementing legislation has not been adopted on time or even at all and leads to asymmetric situations.

Legal asymmetry at the application level may arise among the EU Member States and the Associated country with a dualist system. In the Member States, due to the doctrine of the direct effect established by the CJEU, the provision of the AA can be directly invoked and relied on in court proceedings, and the natural and legal persons from the associated countries can thus enforce their rights contained in the AA. In contrast, the dualist associated countries require the adoption of a domestic implementing legal act, which can be then applied before the courts (not the provisions of the AA themselves). If the adoption of such an implementing act is delayed or even does not take place at all, EU nationals (both natural and legal persons) cannot invoke their corresponding (reciprocal) rights from the AA, and are thus in a less favourable position compared to nationals from the Associated country.

3.5 Role of the Court of Justice of the EU and its jurisdiction

As regards the CJEU, it plays a crucial role in interpreting and enforcing AAs. Since the AAs form an integral part of the Union law, as acts adopted (concluded) by Union institutions,[27] they can be subject to interpretation by the CJEU within the preliminary ruling procedure under Art. 267 TFEU. [28] As parts of the EU law the AAs are also capable of having direct effects and thus can be relied on directly before the courts in

---

[27] This notion has been established and confirmed in influential cases 181/83 *Haegeman*, 270/80 *Polydor* and 104/81 *Kupferberg* and is now considered as 'settled case-law'. However, such an approach, used by the Court for the first time in case 181/73 *Haegeman*, was also subject to criticism. According to T. C. Hartley, the Council Act on conclusion of an Agreement (which is an act of Union institution) should be strictly distinguished from the Agreement as such, which cannot be considered as an act of Union institution. The CJEU should thus only have jurisdiction to interpret the Council acts (i.e. act on conclusion of the Agreement), but not on the interpretation of the Agreement itself, attached to the Council Act on conclusion. See T. C. Hartley: *The Foundations of European Community Law*, 2003, pp. 273-274.

[28] The principles of the CJEU jurisdiction were established in the case 12/86 *Demirel*, and further developed and clarified in the case C-459/03 *Commission v. Ireland* and recent case C-240/09 *Lesoochranárske zoskupenie*.

the EU Member States, in the same way as any other EU legislation fulfilling the criteria for direct effect.[29] Therefore, the provisions of an AA concluded by the European Union and its Member States with a third country must be regarded as being directly applicable when, given their wording and with regard to the purpose and nature of the agreement, the provision contains a clear and precise obligation which is not subject, in its implementation or effects, to the adoption of any subsequent measure.[30]

In order to be able to rule on the direct effects of certain provisions of the AAs and thus ensure their uniform application in Member States, the Court had to first clarify the issue of its own jurisdiction. The limits of the CJEU jurisdiction should, as a matter of principle, mirror the limits of the Union's competence to conclude AAs.[31] Since the EU does not have the competence in relation to all fields covered by AAs, they must be concluded as 'mixed agreements' with the participation of Member States alongside the Union. Thus the provisions of the AAs in the competence of the Member States should not be subject to jurisdiction of the CJEU.

However, the dividing line might be difficult to find, due to the complexity of AAs and the interrelation of their various provisions. Generally speaking, the CJEU is usually willing to assert its jurisdiction even in situations where there is only a limited or disputable link to EU law and/or EU competence. The seminal judgement on this matter was delivered in the case 12/86 *Demirel*,[32] where the CJEU established its jurisdiction with regard to the so called 'mixed agreements'. The Court had to rule on the delimitation of competences between the (then) Community and the Member States, which in turn inescapably determined the scope of its own jurisdiction. The subject matter concerned interpretation of the so called 'Ankara Agreement' establishing the Association of Turkey[33] and its Additional Protocol. But the CJEU had to

---

[29] See note 23 *supra*.

[30] See, in particular, case C-265/03 *Simutenkov* [2005] ECR I-2579, para. 21 and case C-372/06 *Asda Stores* [2007] ECR I-11223, para. 82.

[31] However, we should bear in mind the warning by P. Eeckhout: *EU External Relations Law (Second Edition)*, Oxford University Press, 2012, p. 279: "*If competence is the criterion for jurisdiction, the latter will be the hostage of the complexity of the former.*"

[32] 12/86 Demirel [1987] ECR 3719.

[33] Agreement establishing an Association between the European Economic Community and Turkey, signed at Ankara on 12 September 1963 and concluded on behalf of the Community by a Decision of the Council of 23 December 1963 (OJ C 113, 1973, p. 2) and the Additional Protocol, signed at Brussels on 23 November 1970 and concluded on behalf of the Community by Council Regulation No 2760/72 of 19 December 1972 (OJ C 113, 1973, p. 18).

first deal with the objections of the German and United Kingdom governments, which both argued that it lacked jurisdiction to interpret provisions of the Ankara Agreement on free movement of workers (regarding conditions for entry and residence in the territory of Member States for the purpose of family reunification), since the commitments to implement these provisions were assumed by the Member States in the exercise of their powers.[34]

Despite their efforts to contest the jurisdiction, the Court dismissed the arguments of Germany and the United Kingdom and declared that the powers of the Member States were not infringed, with the following reasoning:

> In that connection it is sufficient to state that that is precisely not the case in this instance. Since the agreement in question **is an Association agreement creating special, privileged links with a non-member country which must, at least to a certain extent, take part in the Community system**, Article 238 [now 217 TFEU] must necessarily **empower the Community to guarantee commitments towards non-member countries in all the fields covered by the Treaty**. Since freedom of movement for workers is, by virtue of Article 48 [now 45 TFEU] et seq. of the EEC Treaty, one of the fields covered by that Treaty, it follows that commitments regarding freedom of movement fall within the powers conferred on the Community by Article 238 [now 217 TFEU]. Thus **the question whether the Court has jurisdiction** to rule on the interpretation of a provision in a mixed agreement containing a commitment which only the Member States could enter into in the sphere of their own powers **does not arise.**[35]

As if this reasoning seemed insufficient to the CJEU itself, it tried to deal with the fact that implementation of the provisions on free movement of workers was the responsibility of the Member States, and offered additional arguments in favour of its jurisdiction:

> Furthermore, the jurisdiction of the Court cannot be called in question by virtue of the fact that in the field of freedom of movement for workers, as Community law now stands, **it is for the Member States to lay down the rules which are necessary to give effect in their territory to the provisions of the Agreement** or the decisions to be adopted by the Association Council.
>
> As the Court held in its judgment of 26 October 1982 in Case 104/81 Hauptzollamt Mainz v Kupferberg [1982] ECR 3641, in ensuring respect

[34] 12/86 Demirel, para. 8.

[35] *Ibid.*, para. 9 (emphasis added).

for commitments arising from an agreement concluded by the Community institutions **the Member States fulfil, within the Community system, an obligation in relation to the Community, which has assumed responsibility for the due performance of the agreement**.[36]

Despite the clear and understandable aim of the CJEU to ensure proper and, above all, uniform interpretation and application of AAs, its reasoning is not entirely persuasive. First of all, the CJEU refers to the case 104/81 *Kupferberg*, which did not concern a 'mixed agreement' establishing an Association, but a free trade agreement falling under the exclusive competence of the (then) Community. Further, as precisely noted by *P. Eeckhout*,[37] the CJEU established an external competence in the area of Association which went far beyond the powers contained in the (then) Treaty or derived from them. Although the Court refers solely to free movement of workers, it actually resulted from the judgement that by means of an AA the (then) Community may assume obligations in the field of immigration and residence of third country nationals,[38] since the exact subject matter of the case were conditions for entry and residence in Germany.

In the *Demirel* case the CJEU thus confirmed its broad jurisdiction to interpret provisions of AAs and at the same time distinguished essentially two areas of its jurisdiction:

a) The CJEU is always entitled to interpret commitments falling under the material competence of the Community / Union; and
b) In case of commitments falling under the competence of Member States, the CJEU might have jurisdiction necessary for the uniform application of the respective provisions in the Member States, since the Community/Union assumed responsibility for the due performance of the (whole) AA.

The broad delimitation of its jurisdiction effectively enables the Court to interpret also those provisions of AAs which fall under the shared competence between the EU and Member States, but have not been exercised by the Union, and this approach was confirmed and elaborated

---

[36] *Ibid.*, paras. 10-11 (emphasis added).
[37] P. Eeckhout, *op. cit.* in note 32 *supra*, p. 126.
[38] The EU competence in the area of immigration was explicitly added to Title IV of the EC Treaty by the Amsterdam Treaty, which entered into force on 1 May 1999. However, at the time of the *Demirel* judgment, the Community clearly had no such competence whatsoever

upon in subsequent lines of its case-law. Another important milestone in this direction is the judgement in case C-459/03 *Commission v. Ireland*,[39] where in the case concerning the United Nations Convention on the Law of the Sea ("the Convention"),[40] the Court made some important observations concerning the division of competences with regard to the 'mixed agreements' and the corresponding extent of its jurisdiction.[41]

The CJEU firstly recalled that 'mixed agreements' have the same status in the (then) Community legal order as purely Community agreements, in so far as the provisions fall within the scope of Community competence. Then it referred to the fact that in ensuring respect for commitments arising from an agreement concluded by the Community institutions, the Member States fulfil an obligation in relation to the Community, which has assumed responsibility for the due performance of that agreement. This led the Court to the necessity to examine whether the provisions of the Convention come within the scope of Community competence, in order to declare its jurisdiction.[42] For the purposes of this examination, however, the CJEU declared that "*the question as to whether a provision of a mixed agreement comes within the competence of the Community is one which relates to the attribution and, thus, the very existence of that competence, and not to its exclusive or shared nature.*"[43] This in fact means that the jurisdiction of the Court is conditional merely upon the existence of EU external competence, but is not dependent on whether the EU has already exercised its competence by adopting a secondary legislation in the relevant policy field. Such an approach arguably constitutes another extension of the CJEU jurisdiction to areas of non-exercised shared competence, although the reasoning in case C-459/03 *Commission v. Ireland* should be limited to a specific area of environment, where the EU has explicit external competence conferred in Art. 191(1) and (4) TFEU.

---

[39] C-459/03 *Commission v. Ireland* [2006] ECR I-4635.

[40] The Convention, which was signed at Montego Bay (Jamaica) on 10 December 1982, came into force on 16 November 1994. The Convention was approved on behalf of the European Community by Council Decision 98/392/EC of 23 March 1998 (OJ L 179, 1998, p. 1). The Convention has also been ratified by all of the Member States of the EU and from the Union's point of view, it represents a 'mixed agreement'.

[41] For a detailed analysis of the case and its international law context see annotation by N. Schrijver in 47 CMLRev. (2010), pp. 863-878.

[42] C-459/03 *Commission v. Ireland*, paras. 84-86.

[43] *Ibid.*, para. 93.

In the recent case C-240/09 *Lesoochranárske zoskupenie*,[44] concerning the interpretation of Art. 9 (3) of the Aarhus Convention,[45] the Court referred to its previous case-law concerning "mixed agreements" and firmly asserted that:

> Since the Aarhus Convention was concluded by the Community and all the Member States on the basis of joint competence, it follows that where a case is brought before the Court in accordance with the provisions of the EC Treaty, in particular Article 234 EC thereof, **the Court has jurisdiction to define the obligations which the Community has assumed and those which remain the sole responsibility of the Member States in order to interpret the Aarhus Convention.**[46]

Then the Court had to carry out the assessment of whether Art. 9 (3) of the Aarhus Convention[47] indeed fell within the obligations that the Community had assumed. It used the test of 'an area largely covered' by EU legislation and pointed out that "*a specific issue which has not yet been subject to EU legislation may fall within the scope of EU law if it relates to a field covered in large measure by it*". Somewhat surprisingly, the CJEU ultimately reached a conclusion that it "*has jurisdiction to interpret the provisions of Article 9(3) of the Aarhus Convention and, in particular, to give a ruling on whether or not they have direct effect.*" The decision on jurisdiction by the CJEU in case C-240/09 *Lesoochranárske zoskupenie* has been rightly criticised,[48] since it used 'the area largely covered' test in a dubious and puzzling way, assuming jurisdiction over the provision of a 'mixed agreement' which was in the competence of Member States.

The above described cases confirm that the Court retains the jurisdiction over 'mixed agreements' (incl. AAs) and can give interpretation

---

[44] C-240/09 *Lesoochranárske zoskupenie* [2011] ECR I-1255.

[45] Convention on access to information, public participation in decision-making and access to justice in environmental matters, approved on behalf of the European Community by Council Decision 2005/370/EC of 17 February 2005 (OJ L 124, 2005, p. 1) ('the Aarhus Convention').

[46] C-240/09 *Lesoochranárske zoskupenie*, para. 31 (emphasis added).

[47] Art. 9(3) of the Aarhus Convention requires the Parties to ensure that *"(...) members of the public have access to administrative or judicial procedures to challenge acts and omissions by private persons and public authorities which contravene provision of its national law relating to the environment.*"

[48] See e.g. M. Klamert: *Dark Matter-Competence, Jurisdiction and "the Area Largely Covered by EU Law": Comment on Lesoochranarske*, 37 E.L. Rev. (2012), pp. 340-350.

of all provisions (i) falling under the competence shared between the EU and its Member States, if it decides that such shared competence has been exercised by the Union within the context of the particular agreement at stake; or (ii) if the provision falls within 'the area largely covered' by EU legislation. Thus the jurisdiction of the CJEU tends to be wider than one could expect, which might be perceived as either (i) as a benefit for uniform interpretation and enforcement of AAs; or (ii) an undesirable extension of the sphere of EU competence by means of judicial activity.

This extensive approach from the CJEU appears to be justified in cases of the so called 'Accession Associations', where the Associated country should accede to the Union and become fully integrated within its legal system. It is more doubtful to apply the same approach to other types of Association relations, without the EU membership perspective, since this results in increasing the competence of the Union to the detriment of the Member States and the CJEU undertakes a risk of being accused of excessive "judicial activism".

The Court, however, rejects the notion that its interpretation methods should be determined by the nature of relations with the third country (e.g. Association with accession perspective vs. "merely" partnership and cooperation). A good example of this position is the case C-265/03 *Simutenkov*, where the Court applied criteria for the direct effect previously used with regard to the AAs with the Central and Eastern European states (which later acceded to the EU on 1 May 2004) to provisions of the Partnership and Cooperation Agreement (hereinafter as the "PCA") with Russia.[49] The CJEU ruled that the non-discrimination clause enshrined in Art. 23(1) of the PCA has a direct effect, even though the PCA is limited to establishing only a partnership and does not provide for future accession:

> The fact that the Agreement is **thus limited to establishing a partnership between the parties, without providing for an Association or future accession** of the Russian Federation to the Communities**, is not such as to prevent certain of its provisions from having a direct effect**. It is clear from the Court's case-law that when an agreement establishes cooperation between the parties, some of the provisions of that agreement may, under the conditions set out in paragraph 21 of the present judgment [i.e. the provisions contain a clear and precise obligation which is not subject, in its

[49] Agreement on partnership and cooperation establishing a partnership between the European Communities and their Member States, of one part, and the Russian Federation, of the other part, signed in Corfu on 24 June 1994 and approved on behalf of the Communities by Decision 97/800/ECSC, EC, Euratom: Council and Commission Decision of 30 October 1997 (OJ L 327, 1997, p. 1).

implementation or effects, to the adoption of any subsequent measure], directly govern the legal position of individuals.[50]

3.6 Conclusions

As far as the application and enforcement of rights and obligations from AAs is concerned, certain asymmetry in enforcement within the EU and its Member States, on the one hand, and the Associated country, on the other hand, may arise. Such asymmetry is a consequence of the position of AAs as one of the sources of Union law forming its integral part, which must be applied by the courts in the Member States and is subject to the jurisdiction of the CJEU. While the provisions of AAs conferring rights or benefits on individuals can be relied on by natural and legal persons from the Associated country before the courts in the Member States, the same may not be true *vice versa* for the EU nationals. It depends on the constitutional rules governing the incorporation of international agreements into the domestic legal order whether such agreements (including the AAs) can be relied on directly before the courts of the Associated country.

Regarding the jurisdiction of the CJEU, its approach is anything but restrictive and the Court apparently aims at exercising the widest jurisdiction possible in order to attain the uniform and coherent interpretation and application of AAs in the Member States. Whether the aims always justify the means is another matter.

---

[50] C-265/03 *Simutenkov*, para. 28.

CHAPTER FOUR

LEGAL ASPECTS OF THE EUROPEAN NEIGHBOURHOOD POLICY IN THE EU'S NEW APPROACHES

LIUDMYLA FALALIEIEVA

4.1 Introduction

The European Neighbourhood Policy (ENP) is one of the EU's external policies directed at its Southern and Eastern neighbours, aimed at avoiding the emergence of new dividing lines in Europe, and creating an area of security, stability and prosperity, founded on shared values and durable partnerships. ENP is the result of the continued evolution of the EU's policies towards its Eastern and Southern neighbours. The Mediterranean region is a vivid example of such evolution as the EU's relationship with the region began with the establishment of the Global Mediterranean Policy in the early seventies of the 20th century. In contrast to Southern neighbours the EU's relations with the Eastern ones got sufficient consideration at the end of the 20th century and thus are relatively new in legal, institutional and procedural dimensions.

The origins of the ENP can be traced back to the conclusion of the Partnership and Cooperation Agreements with the New Independent States of Eastern Europe and to the establishment of the Euro-Mediterranean Partnership (EMP). These processes were closely connected with the fourth and fifth enlargement of the EU. The European Commission (Commission) repeatedly emphasized the need for the establishment of a mechanism for cooperation with the new neighbours of the enlarged EU in its analytical reports on the candidate countries[1]. The concept of a new

---

[1] See e.g. Towards the enlarged Union – Strategy Paper and Report of the European Commission on the progress towards accession by each of the candidate countries, 2002, SEC(2002) 1400-1412.

"proximity policy" directed at the neighbourhood took shape in various Commission papers issued during 2001-2002. The new "proximity policy" should have included cooperation in a wide range of issues of common interest. It was then that the final choice was made to integrate the relevant regional policies into a single framework instead of developing separated relations with each group of states.

In December 2002 Commission President Romano Prodi delivered a speech stating the Commission's vision of a new policy directed at the neighbouring countries. He stressed that the new proximity policy should be "based on mutual benefits and obligations" and "offer more than partnership and less than membership, without precluding the latter"[2]. In March 2003 the Commission introduced the concept of ENP in the communication "Wider Europe – Neighbourhood: A New Framework for Relations with our Eastern and Southern Neighbours" followed in May 2004 by a communication entitled "European Neighbourhood Policy. Strategy Paper", which was more detailed and directed towards the practical implementation of the new policy.

At present the EU's partners within the ENP framework consist of 16 countries including its immediate neighbours by land or sea and a number of "neighbours of the immediate neighbours"[3]. The ENP partner-countries are divided into two large geographical groups: the Southern Dimension including Algeria, Egypt, Israel, Jordan, Lebanon, Libya, Morocco, Palestinian Authority, Tunisia and Syria; the Eastern Dimension including Ukraine, Belarus, Moldova, Armenia, Georgia and Azerbaijan. The Russian Federation has refused to participate in the ENP and develops its strategic partnership with the EU through the creation of four common spaces in the framework of the Partnership and Cooperation Agreement of 1994: the Common Economic Space, the Common Space of Freedom, Security and Justice, the Common Space for External Security, and the Common Space for Research and Education.

The main goal of the ENP is the creation of an area of security, stability and prosperity in the neighbourhood. The inclusion of security into the ENP indicates that it "represents a regional implementation of the European Security strategy"[4] aimed, inter alia, at "promoting a ring of well

---

[2] Prodi R. A wider Europe: A Proximity Policy as the Key to Stability. Brussels, 5-6 December 2002, SPEECH/02/619.

[3] Hanf D. The ENP in the Light of the New "Neighbourhood Clause". Research Paper in Law, No. 2 / 2011, College of Europe, Bruges, p.3.

[4] Hillion C. The EU`s Neighbourhood Policy towards Eastern Europe. In: A. Dashwood and M. Maresceau (eds) Law and Practice of EU External Relations:

governed countries to the East of the European Union and on the borders of Mediterranean"[5]. Stability in the ENP context combines national, regional and global levels, besides which it has political and economic components. Prosperity relies on economic reforms, successful transition of the neighbours to the market economy and deeper economic integration. Thus within the ENP the economic integration between the EU and neighbouring countries is an instrument for the successful development of market economies in the neighbouring states. The ENPs overall goal, as defined by the Council, is to reduce poverty and create an area of shared prosperity and values, based on free trade, deeper economic integration, intensified political and cultural relations, enhanced cross-border cooperation and shared responsibility for conflict prevention and conflict resolution[6]. The EU offers concrete benefits and the establishment of preferential relations within a differentiated framework, which enables the EU to respond properly to progress made by the partner countries in defined areas, namely political and economic reform as well as in the field of justice and home affairs.

4.2 The ENP Methodology and Instruments

The initial ENP methodology includes conditionality, joint ownership, regional cooperation and deeper integration. Conditionality is inherent in the ENP and was taken directly from the pre-accession methodology. It includes political and economic aspects which are deeply interconnected. Scholars commonly distinguish two types of conditionality: positive (ex ante) and negative (ex post)[7]. Positive conditionality connects the progress achieved in the implementation of commonly set goals with the future development of relations, the conclusion of a new advanced agreement, granting of financial assistance etc. Negative conditionality involves the EU's decision to suspend financial assistance or the signing of a new

---

Salient Features of a Changing Landscapes. Cambridge University Press, 2008, p. 314.

[5] A Secure Europe in a Better World: European Security Strategy, Brussels, 2003, p. 8.

[6] See: Council Conclusions of 16 June 2003 on Wider Europe – New Neighbourhood, Doc. 10447/03., p. 2.

[7] Fierro E. (2003) The EU`s Approach to Human Rights Conditionality in Practice. Martinus Nijhoff Publishers, the Hague, pp. 98-99; Smith K.E. (2005) Enlargement and Conditionality: Incompatible or Mutually Reinforcing?. In: R. Youngs (ed.) New Terms of Engagement: Global Europe Report 02. Foreign Policy Centre, London, pp. 23-24.

agreement if a partner country fails to adhere to its obligations. Conditionality and joint ownership may be able to co-exist and to add value to the partnership where there is a clear defined common goal (such as accession) and the understanding among the partners that certain obligations should be fulfilled in order to achieve that goal[8]. Joint partnership can't be applied in full to economic cooperation and harmonization of legislation as in these spheres conditionality will secure its dominant position. However, joint ownership is extremely important for the cooperation in the sphere of justice and home affairs, Common Foreign and Security Policy (CFSP), Common Security and Defence Policy (CSDP), where the main aim of the EU is to involve the neighbours in the elaboration of common approaches towards common security threats and challenges. In the context of the ENP the EU supports regionalism by providing support for existing regional structures, financing the establishment of a new "regional identities", and regional sectoral cooperation[9]. Deeper integration within the ENP framework is an important instrument for creating an appropriate condition for ensuring security, stability and prosperity. It encourages the neighbours to conform to certain criteria, which from the EU's point of view would contribute to its own and regional security. The concept of "sharing everything, but institutions"[10] proposed by R. Prodi envisages the neighbours' improved access to the EU's single market, the establishment of common approaches to the common threats and challenges, including illegal migration, organized crime, international terrorism, and environmental protection, as well as regional conflict resolution. Thus, deeper integration is not limited to economic issues, but also includes the cooperation in the sphere of security and defence, justice and home affairs. The legal framework for deeper integration is provided by the bilateral Agreements on the Deep and Comprehensive Free Trade Area (DCFTA), offering a high "degree of flexibility in the level of integration offered in different sectors"[11].

The EU attempts to spread its own concept of governance in the sphere of economic, environmental protection, border control and the rule of law. This goal is achieved through concrete commitments in bilateral agreements, general provisions on legislative harmonization, export of the EU acquis in the relevant spheres through bilateral and multilateral

---

[8] Cremona M., The European Neighbourhood Policy–More than a Partnership?. In: Cremona M. (ed.), Developments in EU External Relations Law, Oxford University Press, 2008, p. 282.

[9] *Ibid*, p. 290.

[10] Prodi R., *op. cit.*, p. 5.

[11] Cremona M., *op. cit.*, p. 290

agreements, and soft law instruments (namely action plans). The other effective instruments include conditionality, technical assistance, official and informal dialogue, and export of law, which is the method previously successfully used at the pre-accession stage of the enlargement process. Though it should be admitted that while exporting law through the ENP, the EU faces a challenge of adapting its complex system of rules to the partner's needs, while being constrained by a lack of political consensus on the final goal of relations[12].

The majority of the ENPs instruments belong to soft law and can be found in the Commission papers, Council and European Council Conclusions, letters, speeches and action plans. Soft law, according to Senden A., can be defined as "rules of conduct that are laid down in instrument which have not been attributed a legally binding force as such, but nevertheless may have certain (indirect) legal effects, and that are aimed at and may produce practical effects"[13]. The EU's large recourse to the soft law instrument within the ENP stems from its relative simplicity which allows it to reallocate human and financial resources to the implementation of the policy instead of spending them on lengthy negotiations and legislative procedures[14]. Action plans are the primary instrument of the ENP and determine the main goals for each partner country aimed at their deeper integration with the EU. Action plans usually cover a three to five year timeframe, which can be extended by mutual agreement. Based on the common set of fundamental principles, action plans should reflect the peculiarities of each neighbour, the progress in reforms and the nature of a partner's relationship with the EU. Action plans cover all the areas of cooperation, while providing the neighbours with tangible stimulus to reforms and setting a limited number of key areas for specific action: political dialogue and reform; trade and measures preparing partners for gradually obtaining a stake in the EU's Internal Market; justice and home affairs; energy, transport, information society, environment, research and innovation; social policy and people-to-people contacts[15].

---

[12] Dragneva R., Wolczuk K. EU Law Export to the Eastern Neighbourhood. In: Paul James Cardwell (ed.) EU External Relations Law and Policy in the Post-Lisbon Era. T.M.C. ASSER Press, the Hague, 2012 p. 236.

[13] Senden L. Soft Law in European Community Law, Hart Publishing, Oxford, 2005, p. 112.

[14] Van Vooren B. EU External Relations Law and the Neighbourhood Policy: A Paradigm for Coherence. Routledge, London, 2011, p. 214.

[15] Communication from the European Commission. European Neighbourhood Policy. Startegy paper, COM(2004) 373 final, p. 3.

Action plans are non-binding instruments adopted in the form of recommendations and thus the relevant negotiating procedures are exempt from the operation of the procedure for adoption of international agreements laid down in Article 218 Treaty on the Functioning of the European Union (TFEU). However, the implementation of the action plans often requires the adoption of legally binding documents such as national and EU legislation, bilateral international agreements. Action plans should promote joint ownership, but in practice the level of the parties' involvement is slightly different. The initial draft of an action plan comes from the Commission and reflects the EU's vision of bilateral relations with a partner and the final text is adopted by the relevant Cooperation or Association Council.

Bilateral Cooperation and Partnership Agreements (Eastern Dimension) and Euro-Mediterranean Agreements (Southern Dimension) constitute the legal basis for the EU's relationships with the neighbouring countries. With a number of partners, namely Ukraine, Israel, Jordan, Morocco, Moldova, Palestinian Authority and Tunisia, such agreements were concluded even before the official establishment of the ENP. Partnership and Cooperation Agreements (PCA) are less comprehensive, as they don't include provisions on free trade areas. For the relevant New Independent States they replaced the Agreement between the European Economic Community and the European Atomic Energy Community and the Union of Soviet Socialist Republics on trade and commercial and economic cooperation of 1989. PCAs are mixed agreements, i.e. their parties include the third state, the EU and its Member States. The PCAs' main goal was initially very similar to that of the ENP: to create the framework for elimination of the political and economic gap between the EU's new members and their Eastern neighbours. Upon the start of the ENP PCAs were immediately included in its framework, thus Cooperation Councils became the fora for discussions on action plans and their implementation. Common values are the important part of PCAs as they are binding international agreements, unlike action plans. PCAs also include provision for the gradual harmonization of the partners' national legislation with the EU law in the key areas of cooperation.

4.3 The Southern Dimension of the ENP

Within the Global Mediterranean Policy, during the 1970s the EU concluded Partnership Agreements with Algeria, Egypt, Jordan, Lebanon, Morocco, Syria and Tunisia. However, the Global Mediterranean Policy stagnated during the next decade, as the EU concentrated on its enlargement and the elaboration of a new institutional and legal basis for European integration. In 1994 the EU expressed its desire to reinforce Euro-Mediterranean relations and in October the Commission issued a communication entitled "Strengthening the Mediterranean Policy of the European Union: Establishing a Euro-Mediterranean Partnership", which endorsed the Euro-Mediterranean Conference in 1995 to agree on political and economic guidelines for future relations leading to setting up an institutional framework[16]. In November 1995 the Ministers of Foreign Affairs of the then 15 EU Member States and 14 Mediterranean countries launched the Barcelona Process, as the framework for bilateral and regional multilateral relations. The Barcelona Declaration of 1995 reflects the political will to develop a comprehensive partnership among the participants through bilateral agreements, which should contribute to the establishment of a bilateral framework, covering all Mediterranean countries. From the outset, the EMP was composed of three "baskets": political and security partnerships, economic and financial partnerships, partnerships in social, and cultural and human affairs, including migration. It should be noted that the structure of the Barcelona Declaration was influenced by the Helsinki Final Act of the Conference for Security and Cooperation in Europe (currently the OSCE)[17]. The political and security partnership within EMP is aimed at the establishment of a common area of peace and stability based on the rule of law, democracy and respect for human rights. The previous bilateral agreements between the EU and the Mediterranean countries were replaced with Euro-Mediterranean Association Agreements (EMAA), which form the legal basis of bilateral relations within the ENP's Southern Dimension. EMAAs cover a wider range of areas than their predecessors; inter alia, human rights promotion, establishment of a free trade area in manufactured and industrial goods, trade liberalization in agriculture, services and capital. The ambitious aim of the Barcelona Process was the establishment of a free trade area between the EU and all the Mediterranean partners, though its achievement appeared to be very complicated.

---

[16] Communication from the European Commission. Strengthening the Mediterranean Policy of the European Union: Establishing a Euro-Mediterranean Partnership, COM (94) 472 Final, p. 3.

[17] Lannon E., van Elsuwege P. (2004) The EU`s Northern Dimension and the EMP-ENP: Institutional Frameworks and Decision Making Process Compared. In: P. Xuereb (ed.) The European Union and Mediterranean – The Mediterranean's European Challenge. European Documentation and Research Center, Malta, 2004, p. 35-36.

The Joint Declaration of the Paris Summit of 13 July 2008 transformed the EMP into the Union for Mediterranean (UfM), building on the Barcelona Declaration and its acquis and aimed at strengthening regional integration through multilateral partnerships. The Joint Declaration defines six priority projects of the UfM: de-pollution of the Mediterranean, the establishment of maritime and land highways, civil protection initiatives to combat natural and man-made disasters, a Mediterranean solar energy plan, the foundation of a Euro-Mediterranean University (with its seat in Slovenia), and the Mediterranean Business Development Initiative focusing on micro, small and medium-sized enterprises[18]. The members of the UfM are 28 EU Member States and 16 Mediterranean partners: Albania, Algeria, Bosnia and Herzegovina, Croatia, Egypt, Israel, Jordan, Lebanon, Mauritania, Monaco, Montenegro, Morocco, the Palestinian Authority, Syria, Tunisia and Turkey. Libya is an observer state and the UfM expressed a desire to grant it full membership. Since November 2008 the League of Arab States participates in all UfM meetings at all levels. One of the key innovations is the establishment of a rotating co-presidency, where an EU and a Mediterranean representative preside jointly. UfM has its own joint Secretariat situated in Barcelona, which has a separate legal personality with an autonomous status. Biennial UfM Summits of Heads of States and Governments should result in a political declaration and a short list of concrete regional projects to be set in motion[19]. The Anna Lindh Euro-Mediterranean Foundation for the Dialogue between Cultures with headquarters in Alexandria (Egypt) is in charge of the cultural dimension of the UfM. Within the European External Action Service (EEAS) issues of UfM the geographical department "North Africa, Middle East, Arabian Peninsula, Iran and Iraq" deals with development and functioning.

4.4 The Eastern Dimension of the ENP

The development of the EU's policies towards its neighbours is influenced by the concept of "East-South equilibrium", which suggests that the EU's initiatives for the Southern neighbours should be counterbalanced by relevant initiatives for the Eastern neighbours and vice versa[20]. Thus, for example, Poland's agreement over the establishment of

---

[18] Joint Declaration of the Paris Summit for the Mediterranean. Paris, 13 July 2008, pp. 19-20.

[19] Joint Declaration of the Paris Summit for the Mediterranean. Paris, 13 July 2008, p. 13.

[20] Lannon E., *op. cit.*, p.13.

the Union for Mediterranean was conditioned upon "a new and specifically European approach to Ukraine"[21]. In May 2008 Poland and Sweden introduced a joint initiative of Eastern Partnership (EaP) between the EU and its neighbours in Eastern Europe, based on the ENP and aimed at strengthening horizontal links between these neighbours and the EU[22]. The concept of the Eastern Partnership was formulated in the Commission Communication "Eastern Partnership" and was inaugurated by the EU in Prague on 7 May 2009. The EU's Eastern Partners include Armenia, Azerbaijan, Belarus, Georgia, the Republic of Moldova and Ukraine. The communication states that these countries will get strong support from the EU in their efforts to come closer to the EU and will get all necessary assistance with the reforms this entails, through a specific Eastern dimension within the ENP[23]. The EaP provides for the upgrade of the current bilateral agreements with Eastern neighbours towards Association Agreements (AAs), which will be concluded with the partners willing and able to enter into far-reaching commitments with the EU. A Comprehensive Institution-Building programme for improving the administrative capacity in all the areas of cooperation will be established with each Eastern partner in order to provide the assistance necessary to meet the conditions for concluding AAs and to fulfil the commitment stemming from them.

Pursuant to the Joint Declaration of the Prague Eastern Partnership Summit of 7 May 2009 the EaP is a common endeavour of the EU Member States and their Eastern neighbours, founded on mutual interests and commitments as well as on shared ownership and responsibility[24]. The establishment of the EaP is a perfect example of the flexibility and dynamism of the ENP, in particular of the EU's approach to its Eastern neighbours, insisting that the EU should treat them differently from its Southern Mediterranean neighbours[25]. The EaP combines bilateral and multilateral forms of cooperation, governed by the principles of joint ownership, differentiation and conditionality. Bilateral cooperation is the

---

[21] *Ibid*

[22] Ministry of Foreign Affairs of the Republic of Poland. Polish-Swedish Proposal: Eastern Partnership, available at: http://www.enpi-info.eu/library/content/polish-swedish-proposal-eastern-partnership

[23] Communication from the European Commission. Eastern Partnership, COM (2008) 823 final, 3.12.2008, p. 2.

[24] Joint Declaration of the Prague Eastern Partnership Summit, Prague, 7 May 2009. Brussels, 7 May 2009, 8435/09 (Presse 78).

[25] Hillion C., Mayhew A. The Eastern Partnership – something new or window-dressing, SEI Working Paper No. 109 (2009), p. 21.

dominant element of the EaP and includes political Association and economic integration between the EU and its partners, as well as visa liberalisation. Multilateral cooperation is the EaP's major novelty, as the EU hasn't concentrated on the development of regional cooperation in Eastern Europe before. Besides, the development of regional cooperation in Eastern Europe wasn't among the ENP's priorities either. Cooperation within the framework of the EaP is developed without prejudice to individual partners' aspirations for their future relationship with the EU. The main objective of the EaP is to provide a foundation for political Association and deep economic integration between the EU and its partners, as well as support for regional cooperation and development of good neighbourliness. The new AAs including DCFTA will be negotiated with all partners in order to foster the implementation of the EaP goals. Moreover the EU within the EaP framework will support the mobility of citizens, visa liberalisation and the development of sectorial cooperation.

Multilateral cooperation within the EaP is developed on the following four levels: biannual meetings of EaP Heads of States or Governments, annual meetings of Ministers of Foreign Affairs, four thematic platforms at the level of Senior Officials, and various panels supporting the work of the platforms. Besides, EaP's multilateral institutional framework also includes the EU-Neighbourhood East (EURO-NEAST) Parliamentary Assembly, Conference of Regional and Local Authorities of the Eastern Partnership (CORLEAP) and Civil Society Forum. The multilateral dimension of the EaP will also advance through the flagship initiatives supporting its aims and funded through multi-donor support, international financial institutions and the private sector. The flagship initiatives cover six areas, viz: the Integrated Border Management Programme; the Small and Medium-size Enterprise (SME) Flagship Initiative; Regional energy markets and energy efficiency; Diversification of energy supply; Prevention of, preparedness to and response to natural and man-made disasters. Biennial summits of EaP Heads of States or Governments together with annual meetings of Ministers of Foreign Affairs provide the political impetus for the development of the EaP's multilateral track. The first meeting of Ministers of Foreign Affairs in December 2009 officially launched the programmes for each of the thematic multilateral platforms, namely: Democracy, good governance and stability; Economic integration and convergence with the EU sectoral policies; Energy security; Contacts between people. The EURO-NEST Parliamentary Assembly launched on 3 May 2011 is "the parliamentary institution of the EaP between the EU and its Eastern European Partners, to which Article 49 TEU in principle could be applied"[26]; it should be the forum for parliamentary discussion, consultation, supervision and monitoring in all issues of the EaP. The EURO-NEST Parliamentary Assembly is comprised of 60 members of the European Parliament and 10 members from each of the participating parliaments of the partner countries. For the abovementioned purposes, the EURO-NEST Parliamentary Assembly adopts resolutions, recommendations and opinions addressed to the EaP institutions and conferences as well as to the EU and partner countries' institutions.

The European Commission and the High Representative issued joint a communication in May 2012 entitled "Eastern Partnership: A Roadmap to the autumn 2013 Summit", which was agreed at the Warsaw Eastern Partnership Summit in September 2011. The Roadmap covers issues of bilateral and multilateral cooperation and is based upon the principles of joint ownership, conditionality and differentiation. The Roadmap sets out the jointly agreed objectives, the reform and progress necessary to meet the objectives, various instruments and support that the EU will provide to its partners, and targets, outputs or timelines[27]. The Roadmap reiterates the EaP's overarching goals, namely the acceleration of political Association and deepening of economic integration, support for mobility of citizens, promotion of regional cooperation and good neighbourly relations.

The negotiations on the EU-Ukraine Association Agreement, including DCFTA, have been finalised and the agreed text was initialised on 30 March 2012. The EU launched negotiations on AAs with the Republic of Moldova, Georgia, Armenia and Azerbaijan. Besides, the EU decided to launch the negotiations on DCFTA with Georgia and Moldova in December 2011 and with Armenia in February 2012. The implementation of the relevant visa facilitation and readmission agreements with the EU allowed Moldova and Ukraine to advance towards the implementation of Visa Liberalisation Action Plans. The EU signed protocols with Moldova and Ukraine, providing the legal basis for their participation in the EU programmes that are open to the ENP partners.

Sectoral cooperation within the EaP framework covers the following areas: energy, transport, freedom, justice and home affairs, regional development, agriculture and rural development, environment and climate change. Ukraine and Moldova became members of the European Energy

[26] Constituent Act of the EURONEST Parliamentary Assembly. 2011/C 198/06, Ofiicial Journal of the European Union, Vol. 54, 6 July 2011, pp. 4-7.

[27] Joint Communication from the European Commission and the High Representative of the European Union for Foreign Affairs and Security Policy. Eastern Partnership: A Roadmap to the autumn 2013 Summit. Brussels, 15.05.2012, JOIN(2012) 13 final

Community, which is perceived as a powerful tool for integration in the energy sector. Ukraine became the first EaP partner country with which the EU concluded a separate Action Plan in the Area of Freedom, Justice and Security. The European Neighbourhood Programme for Agriculture and Rural Development (ENPARD) was launched by the Commission to strengthen the cooperation in the field of agriculture with the partner countries. Thus, for example, a programme of €40 million in the agriculture sector "Support to the agricultural sector–ENPARD Georgia" was finalised.

The EaPs multilateral dimension will be further implemented on the basis of biennial programmes of its four thematic platforms, which are the forum, attended by senior officials from the EU Member States and the partner countries. The expert panels on public administration reform and on migration and asylum were launched within the platform "Democracy, good governance and stability". This platform also elaborates the programme for cooperation in the area of CSDP. The Platform "Economic integration and convergence with the EU policies" set up the Panel on Trade and Trade Related Regulatory Cooperation linked to DCFTAs, the Panel on Environment and Climate Change, the Panel on Small and Medium-sized Enterprises and business to business contacts. The core objectives of the Panel "Energy security" are the following: enhancement of framework conditions and solidarity; support for infrastructure development, interconnections and diversification of supply; promotion of increased energy efficiency and the use of renewable resources; regulatory framework and approximation of energy policies. The main aim of the platform "Contacts between People" is to foster interaction between the EU and partner countries' citizens, focusing on students, academic staff, researchers, young people and cultural actors.

Within the EaP the EU pays considerable attention to direct engagement with the civil society in partner countries. It was decided to invite representatives of the Civil Society Forum, established in 2009, to the four EaP thematic platforms as permanent participants. The Neighbourhood Civil Society Facility was set up in September 2011 to increase grant support for civil society organisations in EU neighbouring states. Furthermore, the EU agreed the main principles for the establishment of the European Endowment for Democracy, which will provide additional support for those who are engaged in democratic causes in the region. The Council of Europe also contributes to the development of the EaP through the EU-financed Council of Europe Eastern Partnership Facility.

4.5 The Treaty of Lisbon and the ENP review

Prior to the Treaty of Lisbon (ToL) the EU primary law didn't include any provision for its relations with the neighbourhood. The ToL introduced a number of provisions which are relevant for the programming and implementation of its policies towards the neighbourhood. One of such provisons is the introduction of the legal personality of the EU in Article 47 TEU, which put an end to debates whether the EU, as distinct from EC, had such a personality[28]. Article 8 Treaty on European Union (TEU) contains the neighbourhood clause, which obliges the EU to develop a special relationship with neighbouring countries, aiming to establish an area of prosperity and good neighbourliness, founded on the EU's common values and close relations. In practice the neighbourhood clause can be applied not only to the EU's immediate neighbours, but also to the neighbours of its immediate neighbours, as the ENP's geographical scope has already been extended to Azerbaijan and Armenia[29]. Article 2 TEU sets out the EU's fundamental values: respect for human dignity, freedom, democracy, equality, the rule of law and respect for human rights and minority rights. Article 8 TEU empowers the EU to conclude special agreements (Association Agreements) with the neighbouring countries, which may contain reciprocal rights and obligations. The implementation of such agreements shall be the subject of periodic consultations. Joint interpretation of Articles 2 and 8 TEU leads to a conclusion that the EU could conclude such special agreements only with the countries which recognize the EU's values or at least demonstrate sufficient progress in terms of the rule of law, democracy and protection of human rights. The term "special relationship" provides for deep forms of cooperation and precludes the existence of a single model for such a relationship. Thus, the previously successful, within the ENP, principles of conditionality and differentiation were introduced into EU primary law. It should be noted that such a special relationship precludes internal Association, i.e. formal participation of partner countries in the EU's institutions and decision-making processes. For those neighbouring states to which Article 49 TEU could, in principle, be applied, special agreements concluded under Article

[28] Eeckhout P. EU External Relations Law. Oxford University Press, Oxford, 2011, p. 166.

[29] Hanf D., *op. cit.*, p. 3.

8 TEU, given the favourable political context, could embody a "pre-pre-accession stage"[30].

A number of provisions in ToL are also relevant for the formulation and implementation of the ENP, as they introduce important changes to the EU's institutional framework. CFSP and CSDP have secured their role in the ENP. EU institutions will further rely on soft law in order to avoid competence complications[31]. The European Council has preserved its leading role as the forum for the Member States' debates on the EU's activities in the neighbourhood. The disagreements between the Member States, which constantly occur during the relevant debates, have resulted in the de facto geographical split of the ENP into the EaP and the UfM. The establishment of a new permanent position of the President of the European Council should contribute to continuity of the EU's external action, including the ENP. The mandate of the High Representative for Foreign and Security Policy (High Representative) does not include the ENP, though they can influence this policy through the framework of CFSP and CSDP. Thus, the external representation of the EU, in particular in the neighbourhood, can be performed by the President of the European Council, the Commissioner for Enlargement and ENP, the President of the Commission and the High Representative. The neighbouring states could have been confused with choosing the proper contact person for the relevant area of cooperation. In practice the High Representative intervenes in the ENP during crisis situations, for example the Lebanon crisis of 2011, while the day-to-day functioning of the ENP remains under the authority of the Commissioner for Enlargement and ENP supported by administrative and advisory capacities of the EEAS. Consequently, the smooth functioning of the EEAS is also extremely important. Moreover, all the documents relating to changes in regulations and programming of the European Neighbourhood and Partnership Instrument (ENPI) are prepared jointly by the EEAS and the Commission under direct supervision of the Commissioner for Enlargement and ENP.

ToL and political changes in the neighbourhood arranged the conditions for the review of the ENP. The EU's new approach to the ENP was introduced in the Joint Communications of the Commission and the High Representative entitled "A New Response to a Changing

---

[30] Bechev D., Nicolaidis K. From Policy to Polity: Can the EU`s Special Relations with its Neighbourhood be Decentred? Journal of Common Market Studies, Vol. 43, No. 3: 475-500 (2010), p. 494.

[31] Ghazaryan N. Pre and Post-Lisbon Institutional Trends in the EU`s Neighbourhood. In: P.J. Cardwell (ed.) EU External Relations Law and Policy in the Post-Lisbon Era. T.M.C. Asser Press, the Hague, 2012, p. 207.

Neighbourhood" of 25 May 2011 and "Delivering on a New European Neighbourhood Policy" of 15 May 2012. The EU's new approach is based on mutual accountability, commitment to common values of the rule of law, democracy, respect for human rights, as well as on higher levels of differentiation, which would enable the partners to develop their relations with the EU in line with their own aspirations, needs and capabilities. The new ENP aims to: provide support to partners engaged in building deep democracy; support inclusive economic development; strengthen the two regional dimensions of the ENP by working out consistent regional initiatives in areas such as trade, energy, transport or migration and mobility; provide the mechanisms and instruments fit to deliver these objectives[32].

The communications determine the common elements of deep and sustainable democracy, which, at the same time, will be the main benchmarks against which the EU will assess progress and adapt the levels of support[33]. These elements include: free and fair elections; freedom of Association, expression and assembly and a free press and media; the rule of law administered by an independent judiciary and right to a fair trial; fighting against corruption; security and law enforcement sector reform, including the police, and the establishment of democratic control over armed and security forces.

The principle of "more for more" is the keystone of the new ENP: only those partners willing to implement political reforms and to commit to common values of democracy, human rights and the rule of law are offered the most rewarding aspect of the ENP, notably economic integration through the creation of Deep and Comprehensive Free Trade Areas (DCFTA), mobility partnerships and greater financial assistance[34].

4.6 ENP financial instruments

The ENPI is the main financial instrument of the EU for ENP partners and the Russian Federation for the period 2007-2013, which from the 1 January 2007 replaced TACIS and MEDA. The ENPI budget is managed by the Commission through the Service for Foreign Policy Instruments

---

[32] Joint Communication by the High Representative of The Union for Foreign Affairs and Security Policy and the European Commission, A New Response to a Changing Neighbourhood, COM(2011)303, p 2.

[33] *Ibid* p. 3-4.

[34] Joint Communication by the High Representative of The Union for Foreign Affairs and Security Policy and the European Commission, Delivering on a new European Neighbourhood Policy, JOIN(2012) 14 final, p. 3-4.

placed under the authority of the High Representative. Financial assistance provided through the ENPI shall promote enhanced cooperation and progressive economic integration between the EU and the neighbours, effective implementation of bilateral agreements, as well as good governance and equitable social and economic development[35]. ENPI assistance is implemented through country, multi-country and cross-border strategy papers and multi-annual indicative programmes, joint operational programmes for cross-border cooperation, annual action programmes and special measures.

The review of the ENP in 2011 necessitated the relevant reform of its financial framework. The EU improved the coordination between the ENP's new approach and the existing programmes for financial assistance. In the Southern Neighbourhood the EU re-allocated €600m of existing funding towards the objectives defined in the joint communication from the Commission and the High Representative "A Partnership for Democracy and Shared Prosperity" on 8 March 2011. The Joint Communication "A New Response to a Changing Neighbourhood" of 25 May 2011 stresses the urgent need for additional financial resources for a full-fledged implementation of the ENP's new approach. Additional funding was allocated to the implementation of two regional framework programmes for 2011-2013: "Eastern Partnership Integration and Cooperation Programme" (EaPIC) for EaP and "Support for Partnership, Reforms and inclusive Growth" (SPRING) for the Southern Neighbourhood. Both regional programmes are focused on promoting democratic transformation and an institution-building programme and supporting sustainable and inclusive growth.

The ENP's new approach and other assessments identified a number of issues to tackle in the future by adapting the European Neighbourhood Instrument (ENI)[36] enabling the EU to provide effective financial support for its neighbourhood policy. The Commission made public its proposal for a Regulation of the European Parliament and of the Council establishing the ENI for the period 2014-2020 in December 2011. The new ENI will reflect the "more for more" principle, especially for programming and allocating support to the partners. It will address the

---

[35] Article 2 of the Regulation (EC) No. 1638/2006 of the European Parliament and of the Councilof 24 October 2006 laying down general provisions establishing a European Neighbourhood and Partnership Instrument. Official Journal of the European Union. – L 310, 9.11.2006.

[36] European Commission. Proposal for a Regulation of the European Parliament and of the Council establishing a European Neighbourhood Instrument, COM(2011) 839 final, 7 December 2011, Brussels

complexity and length of the programming process inherent in current ENPI through modernisation, shortening and simplification of procedures. The new approach should include new procedures that will help to streamline the scope of the EU financial instruments and strengthen links with relevant internal and external policies. The EU support under ENI will be programmed through bilateral programmes covering support to one partner country, multi-country programmes and cross-border cooperation programmes. The ENI brings down the 29 thematic areas of the current ENPI to six clearly defined objectives and provides for the establishment of the Single Support Framework.

4.7 EU-Ukraine relations within the scope of ENP

The current legal basis of EU-Ukraine relations is the Partnership and Cooperation Agreement that entered into force in 1998. The EU-Ukraine Cooperation Council in Brussels endorsed a Joint EU-Ukraine Action Plan within the ENP framework on 21 February 2005. Ukraine's accession to the WTO in 2008 created the necessary prerequisites for the launch of EU-Ukraine negotiations on a new enhanced agreement, including DCFTA. At the Paris Summit in 2008 it was agreed that the EU-Ukraine Partnership and Cooperation Agreement will be succeeded by the AA. The new AA will foster the development of EU-Ukraine relations, upgrade the joint institutional framework and facilitate political Association and economic integration through mutual rights and obligations. Considering that the negotiations and ratification of the AA will take a few years before it can enter into force, the EU and Ukraine decided that the Association Agenda would replace the Action Plan as a new practical instrument. The EU-Ukraine Association Agenda should facilitate the entry into force of the AA and promote further political Association and economic integration between Ukraine and the EU by creating a comprehensive and practical framework through which these overriding objectives can be achieved. The EU-Ukraine Association Agenda belongs to a soft law instrument and sets the principles, areas and instruments of bilateral cooperation. The representatives of the EU and Ukraine initialled the text of the Association Agreement on 30 March 2012 and expressed their common commitment to undertake the further technical steps. The EU-Ukraine AA Preamble contains references to common EU values shared by Ukraine and its European aspirations, as well as to the development of political Association and the economic integration conditionality on the Ukraine's progress in the implementation of the AA, commitment to common values, and progress in convergence with the EU in political, economic and legal areas. The EU-Ukraine Association Agreement consists of seven Titles which concern General Principles; Political Cooperation and Foreign and Security Policy; Justice, Freedom and Security; Trade and Trade related matters (DCFTA); Economic and Sector Cooperation; Financial Cooperation with Anti-Fraud Provisions; Institutional, and General and Final Provisions. The tailor-made institutional framework of the AA will include the EU-Ukraine Summit, the Association Council, the Association Committee, the Parliamentary Association Committee and the Civil Society Platform. The EU-Ukraine Association Agreement could be signed in the Vilnius Eastern Partnership Summit in November 2013, though only if Ukraine demonstrates tangible progress in the determined areas, namely addressing the issue of selective justice and implementation of reforms defined in the joint Association Agenda.

4.8 Conclusions

The establishment of the ENP was inspired mainly by the EU's fifth enlargement which necessitated the elaboration of a new comprehensive framework for the EU's relations with its new neighbours, bringing together the previous EU policies towards its neighbours. However, from its very inception the ENP covered two distinctly different groups of states, which impeded the EU's efforts to create a cohesive approach fully applicable to all of the neighbouring countries. The lack of consensus among the EU Member States for the finality of the ENP and the unwillingness of certain neighbouring countries to become a "permanent neighbour" provoked the geographical split of the ENP, resulting in the establishment of the UfM and the EaP. The UfM is an international organisation with its own institutional framework, while the EaP is perceived as a specific form of cooperation between the EU and its Eastern neighbours, implemented within the ENP framework.

The ENP methodology inspired by the EU pre-accession instruments includes conditionality, joint ownership, regional cooperation, deeper integration, differentiation and the "more for more" principle, which is the keystone of the revised ENP. Article 8 TEU constitutionalised the EU's ambition to become the global normative power by means of export of its common values, principles and legal acquis in different areas. Though while exporting its law through the ENP the EU should pay attention to the peculiarities of the partner's national legal system and provide each partner with sufficient incentives encouraging it to conduct ambitious political and economic reforms.

ToL and current developments in the neighbouring countries urged the EU to review the ENP. The new ENP approach stresses the importance of shared responsibility and mutual commitments to common values, while offering a higher level of differentiation, which provides the neighbouring states with the opportunity to develop their relationship with the EU in line with their own aspirations and capabilities. The ENP's main financial instrument is ENPI, which from the 1 January 2014 should be replaced with the new ENI, reflecting the "more for more" principle. The EU support under ENI will be programmed through bilateral programmes covering support to one partner country, multi-country programmes and cross-border cooperation programmes.

Participations in the ENP and EaP doesn't create any obstacles for Ukraine's EU membership in future, in case it satisfies the relevant membership criteria. Besides, Ukraine should effectively engage into sectoral cooperation with the EU within the EaP framework. The new enhanced EU-Ukraine Association Agreement could become an instrument for deep political and economic transformations in Ukraine, aimed at creating real grounds for the realization of its European aspirations.

Part II

General Overview of the Bilateral Agreements with Eastern Partnership Countries: A New Generation of Bilateral Agreements

CHAPTER FIVE

RELATIONSHIP BETWEEN THE EU AND UKRAINE

ROMAN PETROV

5.1 Retrospective view of the EU-Ukraine relations

This chapter is a study of the historical evolution of the relationship between the EU and Ukraine since its independence in 1991. It analyses a phenomenon of ups and downs of the approximation of law processes in Ukraine as a “non-applicant” country, which associates itself with the future enlarged Europe, and has thereby renounced the legacy of socialistic legal systems. Therefore, transparency, legal certainty and consistency of approximation of legislation constitute the core of the current partnership and future Association with the EU.

The chapter is focused on the process of the “europeanization” of the Ukrainian legal system that started shortly after independence in 1991. As a priority, Ukraine set, as a political objective, the integration into international political and economic structures and, consequently, membership of the Council of Europe. Once the Council of Europe set the criteria for achieving that goal, the first attempts were made to ensure the conformity of legislation in the spheres of democracy and human rights. As a consequence, Ukrainian criminal, penal and social legislation underwent substantial changes, such as the abolition of the death penalty, and the adoption of new criminal, criminal procedural and civil procedural codes. These reforms marked the first steps towards the reception of "European legal standards" into the developing Ukrainian legal system.

EU policy towards Ukraine has not been coherent. It has changed several times over the last decade. Our study concerns four stages of EU-Ukraine relations. The first stage lasted from 1994 to 1998. It started with the signing of the Partnership and Cooperation Agreement (PCA) by the EU and Ukraine on 16th June 1994, and ended with its entry into force on

1st March 1998. The Ukrainian Parliament–the Verkhovna Rada–promptly ratified the PCA on 10th November 1994.[1] However, the EU was reluctant to speed up the PCAs entry into force. This could be explained by serious economic and political constraints within the EU towards the whole set of PCA agreements. The former relate to the over-protectionist economic policies employed by the Newly Independent States (NIS) countries, which led to severe trade disputes with the EU.[2] The latter concerns the enhancement of Commonwealth of Independent States (CIS) structures and the dominant role of the Russian Federation throughout the entire post-Soviet area. In our opinion, the EU used the policy of conditionality with regard to the PCAs' entering into force. This means that the EU used all political and economic means to encourage the NIS countries to pursue internal market reforms, and to counterbalance Russian dominance before the PCA formally entered into force. The Ukraine was the first country to respond to this strategy. The change of domestic political elites took place in 1996 in the Ukraine. This was caused by economic crisis, hyperinflation and disintegration within the entire post Soviet area. In 1996, the first Ukrainian President Leonid Kravchuk (one of the initiators of the USSRs abolishment in 1991) lost his campaign for re-election to Leonid Kuchma. Kravchuk's successor quickly realised that the recovery of Ukrainian political and economic strength could be accelerated by a change of foreign policy towards Europe. Consequently, President Kuchma gradually reduced the participation of Ukraine in the CIS structures, in order to enable a possible rapprochement with the EU, with the perspective of eventual membership. These changes accelerated the formal entry into force of the EU-Ukraine PCA on behalf of the EU on 1st March 1998.[3] In fact, this was the second agreement, after the Russian PCA, to enter into force.

The second stage of EU-Ukraine relations lasted from the date of the PCA ratification to the issue by the European Council of the Common Strategy on the Ukraine on 11th December 1999. From 1st of March 1998 to the present day, the PCA has remained the major legal document

---

[1] Law issued by the Verkhovna Rada of Ukraine "On ratification of the Partnership and Cooperation Agreement between the European Communities and their Member States and Ukraine", No 237/94-BP.

[2] For example, see the 'Daewoo' trade dispute between the EU and Ukraine, in C. Hillion, 'Trade dispute overshadows entry into force of EC agreement', 6 EU Focus (1998).

[3] Council and Commission Decision of 26th January 1998 on the conclusion of the PCA between the EC and their Member States and Ukraine (O.J. 1998 L49).

governing EU-Ukraine relations.[4] In general, the EU-Ukraine PCA objectives focus on the establishment of a political dialogue; the facilitation of economic relations between the EU and Ukraine; the promotion of democratic reforms in Ukraine; human rights protection and the establishment of a legal order that guarantees the rule of law. The Preamble of the Agreement intentionally omits any reference to 'the process of European integration' or 'the objective of membership in the EU', as these are provided in the EU Association agreements.[5] Therefore, the EU-Ukraine PCA does not pursue the far-reaching objectives of either close economic cooperation between the Parties, or full EU membership. Instead, it is aimed solely at the development of close political relations; the promotion of trade, investment and harmonious economic relations between the Parties; sustaining mutually advantageous cooperation and the support of Ukrainian efforts to complete its transition into a market economy.[6] Thus, the EU-Ukraine PCA, as well as other PCAs, could be seen as a quite successful formula in EU external policy. At the time of there signing the PCAs certainly served their purpose as a reliable legal instrument in sustaining long-term relations with NIS countries, while holding them at a safe distance from closer access to the EU Single Market.[7] However, today the PCAs seem outdated and do not reflect the modern state of the EU's relations with the countries of the Eastern Partnership. The scope of EU legislation put forward as a pattern of approximation for Ukraine mirrors the narrow objectives of the EU-Ukraine PCA. It comprises "priority areas" defined in Article 51 PCA.[8] The "approximation clause" in Article 51 of the PCA imposes a soft law obligation on Ukraine merely to 'endeavor to ensure' the compatibility of its legislation to EC laws.

---

[4] Similar PCAs were signed with Armenia, Azerbaijan, Belarus (has not come into force), Georgia, Kazakhstan, Kyrgyzstan, Russia, Uzbekistan, Turkmenistan (has not yet entered into force).

[5] For example, the Preamble of the Hungary EA.

[6] Article 1 of the EU-Ukraine PCA.

[7] For the comparative overview and scrutiny of the PCAs see R. Petrov, 'The Partnership and Cooperation Agreements with the Newly Independent States' in A. Ott & K. Inglis (eds.), *European Enlargement Handbook* (Asser Press, the Hague 2002) pp. 175-194.

[8] These are: customs law, company law, banking law, company accounts and taxes, intellectual property, protection of workers at the workplace, financial services, rules on competition, public procurement, protection of life and health of humans, animal and plants, the environment, consumer protection, indirect taxation, technical rules and standards, nuclear laws and regulations and transport.

With the entering into force of the PCA in 1998, the Ukrainian government decided to push for a deeper level of cooperation with the EU. It openly promulgated the eventual objective of EU-Ukraine cooperation–full EU membership. One may suspect that the Ukrainian government seriously considered the possibility of replicating the example of the Central and Eastern European (CEE) countries which had managed to acquire candidate country status in a very short time after signing the Association Agreements (EAs) with the EU. In other words, the Ukrainian government made an attempt to "catch the train" of accelerating European integration by fulfilling formal commitments in the PCA.

With the purpose of "knocking" on the "European door", the Ukrainian government soundly proclaimed its European aspirations. The general framework of the integration process was set up in the Strategy of Integration of Ukraine into the EU (Strategy of Integration).[9] The purpose of this document was to declare Ukrainian ambitions to join the EU as soon as possible. Besides, this document determined the major priorities of the executive power to fulfil the objective of ultimate EU membership. Intrinsically, the President of Ukraine stated that 'joining the European political, economic and legal area and, subsequently, acquiring associate membership of the EU constitutes the major priority of the Ukrainian foreign policy in the medium term'.[10] Soon after, the scope of competence of the executive agencies was defined, and the corresponding institutional framework was established with the purpose of accelerating the process of integration and of implementing the PCA.[11]

The approximation of Ukrainian legislation to EU law was formally launched in 1999 when the Cabinet of Ministers of the Ukraine issued the Concept of Adaptation of Ukrainian laws to the legislation of the EU (Concept of Adaptation), in which the official understanding of the adaptation process was set up.[12] The Concept of Adaptation formulated the notion "adaptation" as a gradual and coherent process, which encompasses

---

[9] Edict (Ukaz) of the President of Ukraine "On approval of the 'Strategy of integration of Ukraine to the European Union'", 11 June 1998, No 615/98.

[10] *Ibid*, para 7 of the preamble.

[11] Ruling (Rasporiadzhenia) of the President of Ukraine "About the list of the governmental authorities responsible for fulfillment of the tasks defined by the 'Strategy on Integration of Ukraine to the European Union'", 27 June 1999, No 151/99-rp (as amended by Edict of the President of Ukraine, 06 July 2000, No 240/2000).

[12] To date, about 100 legal acts concerning the integration of Ukraine into the EU have been adopted by the Verkhovna Rada and the Government of Ukraine.

three basic stages, each of them guaranteeing a certain level of conformity of laws in the specified priority spheres.[13]

The first stage of adaptation is targeted at developing the Ukrainian legal system in accordance with the Copenhagen criteria, approximating Ukrainian laws in the priority areas envisaged in the PCA and other international treaties relating to EU-Ukraine cooperation and within the priority fields in the Concept of Adaptation.[14]

The second stage of adaptation comprises the reconsideration of Ukrainian legislation in force in the spheres, specified in Article 51 of the PCA with the purpose of *approximate adequacy* [emphasis added] with EU legislation. Furthermore, this stage anticipates the provision of legal assistance on the establishment of a free trade area between the Ukraine and the EU, as well as the consequent preparation of the Ukraine for an Association Agreement with the EU. It is envisaged that this stage of adaptation is likely to commence in time for the transition membership period of the first wave of accession of the Central and Eastern European countries into the EU. Of course, this timetable has not been met by the Ukrainian side.

The third stage of adaptation is the least well-defined. It could be launched upon the EU's acknowledgment of sufficient progress by Ukraine in pursuing tasks set for the first and second stages of adaptation. Initially, the final stage of adaptation was aimed at preparing the Ukraine for the negotiation of an accession agreement with the EU, and the subsequent harmonisation of the entire Ukrainian legislation with the whole "Community acquis". However the amendment in 2003 corrected these objectives. Today's wording of the third stage of adaptation is conditional on the entering into force of the Association Agreement between the EU and Ukraine and pursues the objective of Ukraine's integration into the EU Internal Market.

Undoubtedly, the EU noticed the integration efforts in Ukraine and decided to encourage its further progress, while underlining that the perspective of the EU membership for Ukraine is still remote. For this purpose, the EU sent the very first positive signal to the Ukrainian government by issuing the EU Common Strategy on the Ukraine (CS) (not

---

[13] Decree (Postanova) of the Cabinet of Ministers of Ukraine "Concept of adaptation of the legislation of Ukraine to the legislation of the EU", 16 August 1999, No 1496. Recently, legal acts issued by the Government of Ukraine seem to apply simultaneously and, sometimes interchangeably, the terms of definitions "adaptation", "approximation", "harmonisation", without clarifying the difference of their content.

[14] *Ibid*, Article 2 para 4.

in force anymore). This document (adopted by the European Council on 11th of December 1999 in Helsinki) complemented the PCA, thereby marking the emerging skeleton of laws governing relations between Ukraine and the EU, wherein the PCA occupies the upper level.[15] The CS displayed clear political and economic guidelines to Ukraine for the purpose of enhancing the nature of its relations with the EU. In response to Ukraine's reiterated diplomatic calls for a new framework agreement, the CS merely acknowledges and welcomes Ukraine's European aspirations, and states its major objective of working with Ukraine to facilitate further rapprochement with the EU.[16] The CS towards Ukraine prioritised the support for the democratic and economic transition in Ukraine, including the progressive approximation of its national legislation,[17] and foresaw the possibility of studying the circumstances of the establishment of a free trade area between Ukraine and the EC.[18] The CS on Ukraine has further endorsed the importance of the approximation of Ukrainian legislation to the EU, and complemented the list of priority areas.[19] On the one hand, the CS towards Ukraine supported Ukraine's European aspirations, and encouraged Ukraine to pursue the voluntary harmonisation of its legislation to that of the EU. On the other hand, it confirmed its unwillingness to revise and enhance the modest objectives of the EU-Ukraine cooperation outlined in the PCA.

In general, very little progress was made during the second stage of the harmonisation/adaptation programme in the Ukraine. Neither of the stages envisaged in the Concept of Adaptation has been achieved. The Ukrainian government failed to move further than enunciating "pro-European slogans". It has become apparent that the success of the

---

[15] Presidency Conclusions, Helsinki European Council (O.J. 1999, L 331/1, at 56). The same is envisaged in the CS towards Russia. The European Council meeting in Cologne in June 1999 adopted the first CS towards Russia. Presidency Conclusions, Cologne European Council (O.J. 1999, L 157/1, at 78).

[16] Article 6 of the CS towards Ukraine.

[17] It is stressed in Article 20 of the CS towards Ukraine that approximation should take place in such areas as: competition policy, standards and certification, intellectual property rights, data protection, customs procedures and environment.

[18] Article 61 of the CS towards Ukraine.

[19] These are issues of fiscal policy, personal data protection and money laundering. Decisions of the Helsinki Summit with regard to the approximation were implemented into Ukrainian legislation by the decision of the 4th Interministerial Coordination Council on that adaptation of the Ukrainian legislation to EU legislation by Decree (Postanova) of the Cabinet of Ministers of Ukraine "Regulation on Interministerial Coordination Council on the adaptation of Ukrainian legislation to EU legislation", 12 June 1998, No 852.

harmonisation/adaptation programme is intrinsically linked to an efficiently-functioning institutional framework and comprehensive educational measures in the area of EU law. Unfortunately, the Concept of Adaptation did not ensure the achievement of these aims. EU technical assistance in the harmonisation/adaptation of Ukrainian legislation focused on the establishment of the Ukrainian-European Legal Advice Center (UEPLAC). The mission of this institution was to provide expertise to the Ukrainian government in EU law. However, the reach of this assistance did not attain the wider circles of Ukrainian society (higher education, NGOs, the general public). Besides, the functioning of the UEPLAC lacked strategy consistency. Successive teams of contractors specialised in various kinds of expertise, shifting from EU law to issues of macro and micro economics in Europe. As a result, the Ukrainian government failed to accumulate the considerable expertise in EU law necessary to pursue voluntary harmonisation on a more efficient level. In our opinion, this situation resulted from the lack of a general consensus within the EU on the scope and limits of the harmonisation/adaptation programme in Ukraine. A significant advance of the Ukrainian harmonisation/adaptation programme could encourage the EU to enhance the format of EU-Ukraine relations. We suspect that at that stage, the EU was not interested in the enhancement of bilateral relations with Ukraine, owing to its preoccupation with serious external (the approaching absorption of CEE countries into the EU), and internal (launch of EURO) challenges.

The third stage of EU-Ukraine relations lasted from 11th December 1999 (issue of the CS on the Ukraine) until 2004 (launch of the ENP). The impressive progress of the Central and Eastern European countries towards full EU membership encouraged the President of Ukraine, Leonid Kuchma, to reiterate calls for eventual EU membership. One of his first steps was the issue in 2000 of the comprehensive Programme of Integration to the EU (Programme of Integration),[20] which displayed a framework of short-term, medium-term and long-term objectives for the executive branch of power to integrate Ukraine into the EU. This is a legal document of a higher value than the Concept of Adaptation, since it was issued by the President of Ukraine. It therefore has priority over legal acts issued by the executive and municipalities. The Programme of Integration complements the Concept of Adaptation by establishing institutional and administrative mechanisms for the harmonisation/approximation process. In particular, the Programme of Integration binds the Cabinet of Ministers

[20] Programme of integration to the European Union, approved by the Edict of the President of Ukraine, 14 September 2000 No 1072/2000.

to ensure funding from the State Budget for the harmonisation/approximation process. Furthermore, the Cabinet of Ministers of Ukraine are requested to issue yearly Adaptation Action Plans,[21] which set up a precise list of organisational and legislative measures to be enforced and adopted in the course of the calendar year. The PCA common institutions (Cooperation Council and Cooperation Committee) are empowered to monitor the implementation of the yearly Adaptation Action Plans. The scope of these plans is not exclusive to the adoption of the acquis communautaire into Ukrainian legal order. In fact, the yearly Adaptation Action Plans could envisage the adoption of international rules which help to reach the general objectives of the EU-Ukraine partnership. For instance, the 2002 Yearly Action Plan paid particular attention to the cooperation with international institutions and the enforcement of international conventions (accession into the WTO is regarded as one of the major priorities for the time being). In response to the Cabinet of Ministers Action Plan, all ministries and government agencies involved in the process of Ukraine's integration into the EU were requested to issue their own yearly Adaptation Action Plans.[22]

Furthermore, Ukraine passed considerable institutional reforms following the launch of the Programme of Integration in 2000. Hitherto, the President of Ukraine has remained the main political figure enforcing European integration policy in the country. He guides and defines the strategy of integration, sets up the external policy priorities, and as part of his jurisdiction authorises agencies, organisations, institutions and civil servants to execute duties concerning integration.

The Cabinet of Ministries of Ukraine ensures the implementation of the Programme of Integration in practice. The major workload is divided between the Ministries, each of them responsible for a certain sphere, designated by the Cabinet of Ministers.[23] All legal acts to be issued by the Cabinet of Ministers must be taken through the monitoring and compliance procedure. Any draft that falls within the priority areas of adaptation must be screened by the Ministry of Justice for conformity with EU legislation. In case of a submitted draft's inconsistency with EU legislation, the Ministry of Justice issues its conclusion that could contain

---

[21] Action Plan for the fulfilment of priority provisions of the Programme of integration in 2002 adopted by the Ruling the Cabinet of Ministers of Ukraine on 28 January 2002, No 34-p.

[22] For example see the Action Plan 2002 of the Ministry of European Integration and Economy on 1 April 2002, No 90.

[23] Decree of the Cabinet of Ministers "On the approval of the Rules of Procedure of the Cabinet of Ministers", 18 July 2007, No 950.

the reasons for non-compliance. Nevertheless, it is up to the Cabinet of Ministers to have the final word in deciding whether it is necessary to pass the particular law, taking into account either the affirmative or negative conclusion of the Ministry of Justice. Such a juncture shows the wide scope of the discretion of the Cabinet of Ministers in shaping the speed and depth of the adaptation process in Ukraine. However, it could be argued that the work of the Cabinet of Ministers in the harmonisation/adaptation of Ukrainian legislation has not been sufficiently monitored by the judiciary and legislature or the general public. The Cabinet of Ministers is accountable to the President of Ukraine and the Verkhovna Rada. Nevertheless, the Cabinet of Ministers was not publicly criticised for the delay in the harmonisation/adaptation. Owing to the lack of transparency within the Cabinet of Ministers, the accountability for its work to the general public in Ukraine was also hampered. Yearly Adaptation Plans have not been adequately discussed in the media, and academics and students had very little chance to obtain prompt information about new initiatives within the harmonisation/adaptation process.

Until 2002, the adaptation process was exercised solely within the executive branch of power under the guidance of the President of Ukraine. Therefore, there was neither a comprehensive legal nor a coherent institutional mechanism for coordinating the adaptation process by all branches of power, including the legislature and the judiciary. As a result, many of the Ukrainian laws adopted by the executive were inconsistent with primary laws issued by the Verkhovna Rada. From 1999 to 2004, some attempts were made to bring all branches of power into the coherent institutional framework of the adaptation process.[24] The major breakthrough came after the parliamentary elections in 2002, when Ukraine's European aspirations were given a majority endorsement by the victorious political parties. The Verkhovna Rada has explicitly acknowledged the need to adopt laws aimed at the implementation of the PCA, the accession of Ukraine into the WTO, and the establishment of a free trade area with the EC. As a result, the Parliamentary Committee for issues of European Integration was established, chaired by the pro-Western ex-Minister of Foreign Affairs Boris Tarasyk. The Verkhovna Rada Rules of Procedure were amended so as to avoid the adoption of

---

[24] The Strategy on integration empowered the highest, central and local executive authorities of Ukraine to establish close cooperation with the legislative–the Verhovna Rada–and the relevant local council authorities to pursue integration into the EU at all levels of Ukrainian society.

laws which contradict EU legal standards,[25] and a framework law "On the All State Programme on the adaptation of Ukrainian legislation to EU laws" (Programme on adaptation) was issued in 2004.[26] In our opinion, the issue of the Programme on Adaptation was a desperate attempt to accelerate the integration of Ukraine into the EU. This law envisages the export of the whole "accession acquis" into the legal system of Ukraine, since the objective of this law is the 'alignment of the Ukrainian legislation with the acquis communautaire taking into consideration criteria specified by the EU towards countries willing to join the EU'. In other words, Ukraine readily agreed to implement the "accession acquis" on a voluntary basis, without any perspective of full EU membership. It should be noted that the EU never indicated that voluntary harmonisation would lead to the immediate recognition of Ukrainian perspectives to join the EU. Nevertheless, the Ukrainian government decided that the harmonisation/adaptation programme would be the most expedient way to step into one of the waves of European enlargement in the region of Eastern Europe. Despite such ambitious "approximation offers" on behalf of Ukraine, EU–Ukraine mutual relations have reached a deadlock. Until now the EU has remained reluctant to acknowledge any perspective of either full EU membership, or Association between the EU and Ukraine.

In order to rectify such a perplexing situation, the Commission initiated the "Wider Europe Neighbourhood" policy towards third countries sharing an immediate post-enlargement border with the EU.[27] The fourth stage of EU-Ukraine relations lasts from 2004 (launch of the ENP) until the present. The ultimate objective of the fourth stage of the EU-Ukraine relations is to enforce the EU-Ukraine Association Agreement. As a result of launching the ENP in 2004 the Commission acknowledged Ukraine as its "privileged partner" along with Russia, Belarus, and Moldova. In the case of Ukraine, the eventual objectives of the ENP are: 1) the establishment of a free trade area between the EC and Ukraine; 2) access to selected segments of the EC internal market and the EC "financial packages". In return, it encourages Ukraine to continue the

---

[25] Decree of the Verkhovna Rada of Ukraine "Recommendations after parliamentary hearings in issues of realisation of the governmental policy on integration of Ukraine to the EU", 17 January 2002, No 2999-III.

[26] Law "About the All State Programme of adaptation of Ukrainian legislation to that of the EU", 18th of March 2004, No 1629-IV.

[27] Communication from the Commission to the Council and the European Parliament "Wider Europe – Neighbourhood: A New Framework for Relations with our Eastern and Southern Neighbours". (COM [2003] 104 final).

voluntary adoption of the acquis communautaire, without participating in the EU decision-making and legislative procedures.

The adoption of the bilateral Action Plan in February 2005 by the Commission and the Ukrainian government marks the beginning of the fourth stage in EU-Ukrainian relations. Action Plans identified the format of bilateral relations between the EU and neighbouring countries for the next three-year term. Therefore, Action Plans are not identical. On the contrary, they are tailored to satisfy the individual needs of the neighbouring countries in the course of rapprochement with the EU. At the same time, Action Plans contain some common elements which respond to the overall objectives of the ENP. They are: adherence to common democratic values, the establishment of a functioning market economy, and the approximation of neighbouring countries' laws to that of the EU. The ENP encourages neighbouring states to embark upon the voluntary adoption of the acquis communautaire, without participating in the EU decision-making and legislative procedures. Bilateral Action Plans have been agreed to clarify the precise scope of the acquis communautaire to be adopted by a neighbouring state. Hitherto, bilateral Action Plans have been concluded with Ukraine, Israel, Jordan, Morocco, Moldova, the Palestinian Authority, and Tunisia.

Since 2009 the ENP has been complemented by the Eastern Partnership (EaP) which is the EU's policy towards the countries of Eastern Europe and Southern Caucasus. Launched in May 2009 at the Prague Summit, the EaP fosters the necessary conditions to accelerate political Association and further economic integration between the EU and Armenia, Azerbaijan, Belarus, Georgia, Moldova and Ukraine.[28] The EaP envisages stronger political engagement with the EU through: the prospect of a new generation of Association Agreements; integration into the EU economy with deep free trade agreements; easier travel to the EU through gradual visa liberalisation, accompanied by measures to fight illegal immigration; enhanced energy security; increased financial assistance; deeper cooperation on environment and climate issues; increased people-to-people contacts and greater involvement of civil society.

The EaP has gone a long way in shaping the agenda of cooperation between the EU and its Eastern neighbours and providing a solid framework for sharing expertise and best practices. The initiative has given rise to new platforms for dialogue at government and expert levels (thematic platforms), as well as in the fields of parliamentary and

---

[28] Communication from the Commission to the Council and the European Parliament "Eastern Partnership". (COM [2008] 823 final).

participatory democracy (Euronest; Civil Society Forum and the Conference of the Regional and Local Authorities).

The EaP enhances the scope of the acquis communautaire to be adopted by the neighbouring countries. First, similar to the ENP the EaP elaborates on the concept of "shared values". It "promotes the commitment to shared values" on behalf of neighbouring states. The level of the EU's ambition in developing links with each partner through the EaP will depend on the extent to which shared values are effectively shared. One of the major objectives of the EaP is to encourage voluntary legislative and regulatory approximation of the post-Soviet neighbouring countries to EU law in return for closer economic and political rapprochement of these countries with the EU. The Action Plans and Association Agenda towards the NIS countries contain specific priorities intended to strengthen the commitment to shared values and to the adoption of the EU dynamic acquis. The pace of the NIS countries reforms aimed at adoption of the EU acquis is being regularly monitored by the Commission which vigilantly scrutinizes the NIS countries' successes and failures and proposes specific measures for improvements.

As a consequence of the launch of the EaP the EU-Ukraine Action Plan was substituted by the Association Agenda by the EU-Ukraine Cooperation Council on 23 November 2009. The EU-Ukraine Association Agenda was built on the Action Plan and defines key priorities for reforms, which Ukraine should address in order to fully benefit from the new Association Agreement. Major emphasis of the EU-Ukraine Association Agenda is on intensified cooperation and improved market-access of Ukrainian nationals and companies to the EU Internal Market. The EU-Ukraine Association Agenda is unique and hitherto has not been applied towards other countries of the EaP.

In our opinion, the EU-Ukraine Action Plan/Association Agenda did not move further than the EU-Ukraine CS in terms of clarifying the possibility of Ukrainian accession to the EU. They merely acknowledge 'Ukraine's European aspirations and…. Ukraine's European choice'. Furthermore, they recognise the PCA as a 'valid basis for EU-Ukraine cooperation'. However, the Action Plan envisaged the further economic integration of the Parties 'through joint efforts' towards an EU-Ukraine free trade area, following Ukraine's accession to the WTO. Furthermore, 'consideration will be given to the possibility of a new enhanced agreement, whose scope will be defined in light of the fulfillment of the objectives of this Action Plan and of the overall evolution of EU–Ukraine relations'.

One of the major objectives of the EU-Ukraine Action Plan/Association Agenda is to outline the priority areas for the internal reforms to be implemented by Ukraine. The emphasis on voluntary harmonisation is the strongest among all the Action Plans. For example, the EU-Ukraine Action Plan/Association Agenda encourages Ukraine to enhance its legislative and institutional foundations, in order to absorb not all, but a wide range of the acquis communautaire. The priority areas of approximation exceed what is envisaged in the PCA and the CS. It covers the wide range of legal reforms to be undertaken by the Ukrainian government: the adoption and enforcement of EU common values (democracy, rule of law, human rights and fundamental freedoms); adherence to fundamental democratic principles (respect for free media, respect of rights of national minorities, protection of rights of children); the signing and enforcement of international conventions (Charter of the International Criminal Court, UNSC Resolutions); participation in international democratic and security initiatives (non-proliferation of weapons of mass destruction, combating terrorism); cooperation in EU foreign and security policy.

We believe that the EU-Ukraine Action Plan/Association Agenda must be considered separately from the "approximation clause" in the PCA. From a legal point of view, the EU-Ukraine Action Plan/Association Agenda did not alter Ukraine's approximation of law commitments within the PCA. However, the EU-Ukraine Action Plan/Association Agenda offers a new non-contractual means for Ukraine to enhance bilateral relations with the EU. There are several factors which indicated the specific role of the EU-Ukraine Action Plan/Association Agenda among other tools of EU external policy. Firstly, the EU-Ukraine Action Plan/Association Agenda significantly broadened the scope of the acquis communautaire to be exported into the Ukrainian legal system. The EU-Ukraine PCA/Association Agenda contains a non-binding approximation clause that circumscribes the priority areas of the harmonisation/approximation process. However, in contrast to approximation clauses in other EU external agreements (EAA, SAAs) the PCAs neither contain annexes with a relevant acquis, nor provide any information on the priorities of the harmonisation/approximation process. In our opinion, the EU-Ukraine Action Plan/Association Agenda mirrored the Commission's White Paper on the Preparation of the Associated Countries of Central and Eastern Europe to Integration into the Internal Market of the Union,[29] and serves as a comprehensive guide for the Ukrainian government in the course of the approximation of national legislation to that of the EU. Being repeatedly blamed for a lack of interest in

[29] COM (1995) 163.

the Ukrainian harmonisation/approximation programme, the EU outlined its vision of Ukrainian legal and political reforms in the Action Plan/Association Agenda. At the same time, the EU skillfully applied the conditionality policy to ensure that Ukraine takes her harmonisation/approximation commitments in the EU-Ukraine Action Plan/Association Agenda even more seriously than in the PCA. For instance, after having been negotiated for almost a year (2004), the EU-Ukraine Action Plan was formally adopted only after the "revolutionary" Presidential elections of 2004 that led to the establishment of a pro-European government in Ukraine. The perspective of access to limited segments of the EU Internal Market and common EU policies, as well as the conclusion of a new "enhanced agreement", forced the Ukrainian government *de facto* to enhance its harmonisation/approximation commitments. This strategy has proved successful. It is interesting to note that the political elite in Ukraine hardly mentioned the PCA as a relevant functioning legal foundation of EU-Ukraine relations. Instead, politicians have started to refer to the EU-Ukraine Action Plan as a "treaty" and a new enhanced form of EU-Ukraine cooperation. This either conscious or unconscious misperception allowed the Ukrainian public to perceive the EU-Ukraine Action Plan as a legal document of higher value than the PCA, and as a considerable step forward in EU-Ukraine relations. This example illustrates that, despite its non-binding character, the EU-Ukraine Action Plan paved the way for a "political re-orientation" of the general format of relations between the EU and Ukraine. Of course, the adoption of the EU-Ukraine Action Plan cannot be compared to the drastic "political re-orientation" of the EAs objectives towards full EU membership after the Copenhagen Summit. However, the objectives the EU-Ukraine Action Plan "informally" went beyond what is envisaged in the PCA (free trade area). In other words, on the one hand, the EU-Ukraine Action Plan/Association Agenda serves as a bridge between the PCA and the Association Agreement to be concluded upon the successful implementation of the Action Plan/Association Agenda. On the other hand, the EU-Ukraine Action Plan/Association Agenda could be perceived as a comprehensive guideline for neighbouring countries for their political, economic and legal reforms in the course of rapprochement with the EU.

Secondly, the EU-Ukraine Action Plan/Association Agenda served as a catalyst for the revision of the national constitutional order towards the better perception of international norms and values. For instance, the Constitutional Court of Ukraine has confirmed that recognition of the International Criminal Court jurisdiction does not comply with the Constitution of Ukraine, because it encroaches upon the sovereignty of national judiciary.[30] However, the EU-Ukraine Action Plan/Association Agenda encouraged Ukraine to prepare draft laws necessary for the ratification of the International Criminal Court Statute. Consequently, the fulfillment of this commitment would require Ukraine to implement necessary constitutional reforms in order to obtain a positive decision from the Constitutional Court. The same consequences could apply with regard to Ukraine's adoption of European common values and principles specified in the EU-Ukraine Action Plan/Association Agenda.

Thirdly, one may argue that the EU-Ukraine Action Plan/Association Agenda represents an excellent "playground" for European bureaucrats to apply experience already gathered in the course of the enlargement of CEE countries. Besides, the EU used tools such as country reports, similar to those that have been applied towards candidate CEE countries. In other words, the methods for monitoring are almost identical for former candidate countries and neighbouring countries. However, the final objectives of these processes are different. Candidate countries hope to join the EU, while neighbouring countries may be engaged in negotiations for new and yet unspecified "enhanced agreements" with the EU.

To conclude, we set out a number of considerations which concern the evolution of EU-Ukraine relations. The first consideration is that one-sided attempts by Ukraine to secure the possibility of joining the EU through the promulgation of the voluntary harmonisation of legislation has not brought about any positive results, irrespective of the actual progress made by the Ukrainian government. It must be admitted that the Ukrainian government has achieved quite modest results in the course of approximating national legislation to that of the EU. Most national legal acts in approximating laws have had a declarative character. The Ukrainian government has continued to maintain trade barriers in order to protect national producers. Anti-competitive behaviour and state aid to national enterprises has been sustained. However, the basic institutional framework has been established. All branches of power have started to cooperate to ensure the success of the voluntary harmonisation programme. The example of Ukraine shows that EU institutions should be interested in supporting and acknowledging the process of voluntary harmonisation within a third country through technical assistance and additional initiatives, such as the ENP. However, the EU has hardly changed the format of bilateral relations without serious political or economic justifications. That is why Ukrainian efforts to launch the "accession acquis" in 1999 and in 2004 did not have

[30] Judgement of the Consitutional Court of Ukraine on constitutionality of the International Criminal Court Statute, No 3-в/2001, 11 July 2001 (case No1-35/2001).

an effect on the general state of EU-Ukraine relations. In both cases, the EU welcomed Ukrainian approximation efforts, but did not push through Ukrainian chances to join the EU.

The second consideration is that the scope of the EU "acquis" to be implemented by Ukraine mirrors the changes in bilateral relations between the EU and Ukraine. The first significant change took place in 1999, when the CS towards Ukraine was adopted at the Helsinki Summit. This document endorsed the approximation as one of the major objectives of EU-Ukraine cooperation, and added new priority areas of the approximation process in Ukraine to what has been already specified in the PCA. The second significant change took place in 2005 after the adoption of the EU-Ukraine Action Plan and the EU-Ukraine Association Agenda in 2009. These EU "soft law" documents considerably revised the scope of the EU "acquis" to be adopted by Ukraine. In addition to the priority areas of approximation in the PCA, the Action Plan/Association Agenda put forward common values, and EU principles, as well as various political and economic criteria to be effectively implemented by the Ukrainian government. Furthermore, the EU-Ukraine Action Plan/Association Agenda contain detailed actions and elements of the EU "acquis" which must be implemented by Ukraine. To ensure that the Ukrainian government takes these commitments seriously, the EU applied strong a conditionality on Ukraine promising to sign a new enhanced Association Agreement upon the successful fulfilment of the Action Plan/Association Agenda. These changes influenced the Ukrainian government and encouraged further political, economic and legal reforms without altering the primacy of the PCA within EU-Ukraine relations.

In conclusion, we argue that the EU-Ukraine Action Plan/Association Agenda must be perceived as something different or parallel to the PCA. The EU-Ukraine Action Plan/Association Agenda serves as a practical tool to reach the far reaching objectives of the ENP and the EaP. One may argue that the EU-Ukraine Action Plan/Association Agenda brings Ukraine closer to the EU through other various non-contractual means than formal cooperation within the PCA. As stated above, this conclusion is based on three factors. Firstly, the launch of the EU-Ukraine Action Plan/Association Agenda stipulated the de facto enhancement of the political, economic and legal commitments envisaged in the PCA by the Ukrainian political elite and the general public. Of course, these commitments are of a non-binding nature and, therefore, cannot override commitments within the PCA. Nevertheless, the EU-Ukraine Action Plan/Association Agenda contributed to the re-orientation of the Ukrainian political elite towards Europe, and accelerated the voluntary harmonisation of Ukrainian legislation to that of the EU. Secondly, the EU-Ukraine Action Plan/Association Agenda persuades Ukraine to reconsider the application of international law sources within its national legal system, in order to enable the implementation of European common values and principles. Thirdly, the EU closely monitors the success of the Association Agenda implementation through means already developed and tested within the "pre-accession" of the CEE countries. In our opinion, the ENP and the EaP offer better means (action plans, country reports) to ensure the effective implementation of the EU "acquis" by Ukraine than under the PCA. One may predict that special attention will be paid by the EU to the effectiveness of the harmonisation/approximation process in Ukraine in the course of implementing the Association Agenda. Therefore, Action Plans/Association Agendas represent a successful model for how initiatives taken outside the PCAs may affect the approximation process, without imposing binding commitments on a third country.

5.2 Association Agreements in the domain of EU External Relations

Association Agreements between the EU and third countries have become one of the most recognisable brands of the EU external policy. In particular, this relates to the countries of the EU's Eastern neighbourhood (Ukraine, Moldova, Belarus and the Caucasus countries) that have either already started negotiations on Association Agreements with the EU, or are about to do so in the near future. These countries are participating in the EaP initiative launched by the EU in 2009. One of the EaP's objectives is to pave the way for the upgrading of these countries' existing bilateral contractual relations with the EU. As of now, almost identical, but outdated partnership and Association Agreements that were concluded in 1994-1998 are still governing the bilateral relations between the EU and the countries of the EaP. Therefore, it is important to clarify two questions. First, what actually is the meaning of an Association and a partnership under EU law? Second, what advantages may the Association Agreements bring to the countries of the EaP?

Ironically, it appears that neither EU legal sources nor academics can provide clear answers on the meaning of an Association or a partnership in EU external relations. The only way to comprehend the scope and content of an Association or partnership under EU law is to study the EU's founding treaties, the case law of the European Court of Justice (ECJ) and the bilateral Association and partnership agreements concluded by the EU with other countries. In short, one may say that an Association and a partnership differ in their specific legal bases in the EU's founding treaties and special procedures.

The legal base for concluding Association Agreements under EU law is Article 217 of the Treaty on the Functioning of the European Union (TFEU). It states that:

> The Union may conclude with one or more third countries or international organisations agreements establishing an Association involving reciprocal rights and obligations, common action and special procedure.

One of the few explicit guidelines on the scope of an Association in EU external relations comes from the ECJ in its Demirel judgment, wherein it is stated that an Association Agreement implies "creating special privileged links with a non-member country which must, at least to a certain extent, take part in the [Union] system".[31] Therefore, we may distinguish several elements which are inherent to Association Agreements under EU law: 1) reciprocal rights and obligations; 2) common action and special procedures; 3) privileged links between the EU and a third country; 4) the participation of a third country in the EU system. Some features of Association Agreements make this form of bilateral contractual relations particularly beneficial for a third country. These are: reciprocal rights and obligations, and the prospect of full EU membership. If the former feature constitutes a core of an Association between the EU and a third country, the latter feature means that the act of signing an Association Agreement does not automatically imply the eventual membership of that third country in the EU. EU law considers entering into Association relations with the EU and obtaining full EU Member State status as two different processes, although it is true that most of the EU Member States entered into Association with the EU prior to acquiring full EU membership.

In the past two decades, the EU has concluded several Association Agreements with far-reaching integration objectives, which either led or might lead to eventual EU membership (the European Economic Area Agreement between the EU and Norway, Iceland and Liechtenstein, the former Europe Agreements between the EU and Central & East European countries, the Stabilisation and Association Agreements between the EU and Western Balkan countries). These Agreements contain specific reciprocal obligations. For example, there are EU commitments to ensure access of the third country's nationals to its internal market, and to provide financial assistance for certain political and legal reforms. In return, the third countries accept specific obligations such as the voluntary

[31] Case 12/86, *Demirel v Stadt Schwäbisch Güdn* [1987] ECR 3719.

harmonisation of their national legislation with that of the EU, and the implementation of specified international conventions. However, most of the EU Association Agreements do not pursue the objective of EU membership. Instead, the Association Agreements are either narrow Agreements focused on sectorial cooperation (like the bilateral sectorial cooperation agreements between the EU and Switzerland) or Association Agreements on close political and economic cooperation leading to the establishment of free-trade areas between the parties (like the Association Agreements with Mediterranean countries [Morocco, Tunisia, Israel and others]). These Association Agreements aim at establishing a zone of peace, prosperity and stability in the region without formal EU membership, as well as at establishing, over a transitional period, free trade in industrial goods and the progressive liberalisation of trade in the agricultural sector; trade in services; cooperation in political, economic, social and cultural matters, and justice and home affairs. After the Treaty of Lisbon came into force, Association Agreements remained one of the major pillars of the EU's external policy. The Treaty of Lisbon distinguishes Association Agreements by a separate legal basis (Article 217 TFEU) and a specific procedure (Article 218 TFEU). In the latter case, Association Agreements differ from other EU external agreements by the fact that the decision to conclude an Association Agreement with a third country comes only after a unanimous vote by the Council and the consent of the European Parliament. This implies that any EU Member State or majority in the European Parliament may block the conclusion of an Association Agreement with a third country. Furthermore, the Treaty of Lisbon (Article 21[1] Treaty on European Union [TEU]) states that the EU's external policy should be "guided by the principles….of democracy, rule of law, the universality and indivisibility of human rights and fundamental freedoms, respect for human dignity, the principles of equality and solidarity, and respect for the principles of the United Nations Charter and international law", and third countries should share these principles in their pursuit of bilateral relations with the EU. Subsequently, it implies that future generations of EU external agreements will impose an obligation on third countries to share EU's democratic values. Such an obligation is likely to be subject to regular monitoring on behalf of the EU institutions.

The meaning of "partnership" under EU law is not completely clear either. Meanwhile, partnership agreements are being concluded on the basis of Article 212 TFEU, which states that such agreements pursue the objectives of economic, financial and technical co-operation measures, including assistance, in particular financial assistance, with third countries other than developing countries. Such measures shall be consistent with the developing policy of the Union and shall be carried out within the framework of the principles and objectives of its external action.

In contrast to Association Agreements, the procedure to conclude partnership agreements is less complicated. For instance, the Council may issue a decision to conclude a partnership agreement after a qualified majority vote and, in some cases, even without the consent of the European Parliament. It also follows that a partnership does not imply any prospect of full EU membership and, as a rule, does not designate common institutions to be set up under the agreement and issue binding decisions.

However, in our opinion, this does not mean that a partnership agreement should not contain at least some special privileged links and reciprocal rights, as in an Association Agreement. In fact, partnership agreements have been concluded by the EU with third countries that are characterised by elements that are reminiscent of Association Agreements. For instance, in the Simutenkov case, the ECJ drew a parallel between the EU-Russia PCA and the EU-Slovakia Association Agreement with regard to recognising the PCA provisions as having a direct effect within the EC legal order. It argued that a partnership agreement or an agreement other than an Association Agreement *may lead* [emphasis added] to the achievement of the objectives expected from an Association Agreement.[32]

One may argue that any future generations of Association Agreements between the EU and the countries of the EaP will pursue specific objectives inherent to the nature of the EaP initiative. On the one hand, Association Agreements with the countries of the EaP could be distinguished by greatly enhanced objectives that are typical of most EU Association Agreements (close political and economic co-operation, the establishment of a free trade area, far-reaching approximation of national legislation to that of the EU). On the other hand, Association Agreements with the countries of the EaP will be marked by some specific objectives aimed at ensuring the functioning of a democratic society, establishing a deep and comprehensive free trade area, the possibility of establishing a visa-free regime, cross-border and regional cooperation, and other objectives. The establishment of a deep and comprehensive free trade area would imply approximation of national laws and standards in line with the EU acquis.

Therefore, gradually moving to the second question, we may argue that signing an Association Agreement with the EU should trigger serious

[32] Case C-265/03 *Simutenkov v Ministerio de Educación y Cultura, Real Federación Española de Fútbol* [2005] ECR I-2579.

internal reforms in the Eastern Partnership countries. First of all, future Association Agreements will serve as a template for further political and economic reforms in these countries. The obligation to share the EU's common democratic values will imply regular monitoring by the EU institutions. Thereby this should prevent the EaP countries from undemocratic practices. Establishing a deep and comprehensive free-trade area will open new markets for the neighbourhood countries' products on the EU's internal market, and will enhance internal competition within the EU neighbourhood. The new joint institutions set up under the framework of Association Agreements will help to pursue the programme of approximating the laws with the help of its binding decisions. However, it is important that the EaP countries take full advantage of the reciprocity under the Association Agreements with the EU, and ensure their nationals' access to the freedoms of the EU internal market, and the visa-free regime with the EU. Eventually the principle of reciprocity should lead to the neighbouring countries' informal participation in the EU's decision-making processes.

The process of effectively implementing the Association Agreements will constitute the greatest challenge for the countries of the EaP. These countries have to prove their adherence to the EU's common democratic and economic values, and ensure the proper functioning of their deep and comprehensive free trade areas. The latter objective may be achieved only under the condition of establishing truly competitive market economies and the adoption of international and EU legal standards. What are the possible sanctions that could be imposed on the countries of the EaP in case of non-implementation and/or the violation of binding and soft obligations under the future Association agreements? Several factors could be relevant. First, the joint institutions to be set up under the framework of the Association Agreements could be given the role of dispute settlement bodies with the right to issue binding decisions. In this case, the parties to an Association Agreement will be bound by a decision of the dispute settlement body under international law. Second, following the widely used practice in the EU's external agreements, any future Association Agreements with the countries of the EaP may contain so-called 'evolutionary' and 'conditionality' clauses. These are provisions in the EU's external agreements with specific objectives (for instance, granting a visa-free regime, the status of a candidate country to join the EU), the attainment of which is conditional either on certain actions on behalf of a party to an agreement (such as the elimination of trade barriers and uncompetitive practices) or the effective functioning of democratic and market-economy standards (such as free and fair elections and fighting corruption). However, it should be acknowledged that these 'evolutionary' and 'conditionality' clauses are only effective if the general objectives of an Association Agreement are attractive. In the meantime, we can only hope that the overall objectives of the Association Agreement between the EU and the countries of the EaP will give enough encouragement for countries like Ukraine and Moldova to ensure its effective implementation.

5.3 Objectives and scope of the EU-Ukraine Association Agreement

Hitherto, there is no official text of the EU-Ukraine Association Agreement available. Relevant EU external documents have shed very little light on the EU-Ukraine AA's objectives and scope. However we argue that these objectives can be deduced from the general objectives of the ENP and the EaP, which offers to neighbouring countries the chance to participate in various EU activities through close political, security, economic and cultural co-operation. We deem that the AA's objectives will not be identical, but will differ to reflect the existing status of relations between the EU and each neighbouring country, its needs and capacities, as well as common interests. The AA's will be preceded by a jointly-agreed tailor-made Association Agenda, which covers a number of key areas specific to each neighbouring country as provided by the ENP: 1) political dialogue; 2) economic and social development policy; 3) participation in a number of EU programmes (education and training, research and innovation); 4) sectorial cooperation; 5) market opening in accordance with the principles of the WTO and convergence with EU standards; 6) Justice and Home Affairs cooperation. We speculate that the AA's will reproduce both general and individually tailor-made objectives of the Association Agenda. Thus, for instance, the general objectives of the EU-Ukraine AA will focus on close political, security, economic and cultural cooperation with the eventual access of Ukraine to the EU Internal Market. Individual objectives of the AAs will reflect various strategic priorities of the EU towards specific neighbouring countries. For instance, we expect that the new AA's with Mediterranean countries will emphasise enhanced regional cooperation with the purpose of ensuring cross-border cooperation, setting up energy networks and infrastructure, and the prevention of local conflicts. On the other hand, the AA's with the EaP countries will prioritise the promotion of EU democratic values, justice and home affairs cooperation, and anti-corruption and regional security issues, all over a purely economic partnership. This is because the EU would prefer to have the EaP countries as neighbours with properly functioning democratic institutions, and with effective mechanisms for fighting illegal immigration into Europe. The stability and security within neighbouring countries is also important for the EU.

Below we attempt to forecast the objectives and scope of the EU–Ukraine AA. Objectives of the EU–Ukraine AA will replicate both the general and individual objectives of the EU-Ukraine Action Plan/Association Agenda: 1) political dialogue, promotion of European and international democratic values, rule of law, human rights and fundamental freedoms, ensuring regional and global stability, as well as close cooperation in JHA; 2) social and economic development, encouragement of structural reforms towards a functioning and competitive market economy, limitation of state involvement in the economy and privatisation, liberalisation of services including financial sector, social and human development policies, fiscal management, monetary and exchange policy; 3) the participation in a number of EU programmes (education and training, research and innovation); 4) sectorial cooperation in the fields of energy, transport, environment and information society; 5) market opening in accordance with the principles of the WTO and convergence with EU standards; 6) Justice and Home Affairs cooperation in issues of border management, migration, the fight against terrorism, trafficking in human beings, drugs and arms, organised crime, money laundering and financial and economic crimes.

After clarifying the potential objectives of the EU–Ukraine AA, we seek to associate them with specific elements of the EU acquis. The objective of political dialogue between the EU and Ukraine will target the establishment of democratic freedoms, the protection of human rights, free press and media in Ukraine. For this purpose, the Preamble of the Ukraine AA will encourage Ukraine to follow EU values and principles as stated in the EU Constitution. Specific provisions of the Ukraine AA will call on Ukraine to adhere to recognised international principles and standards (UN Charter, the principles of the Helsinki Final Act and the Charter of Paris, the Council of European and the OSCE documents). It is most likely that Ukrainian commitment to adopt the EU and international human rights and democracy acquis will be underpinned by a conditionality clause warning that the AA could be terminated if Ukraine or the EU violated these values and principles.

The objective of social and economic cooperation will be the opening of access to Ukraine of the EU internal market. This could potentially envisage the establishment of a free trade area and a mutual recognition regime between the EU and Ukraine. In both cases, these objectives will be supported by conditionality and approximation clauses. The conditionality clause will foresee the access of Ukraine to EU internal market freedoms and the establishment of a free trade area on the progress of legislative and regulatory approximation and on the adherence to EU democratic values and principles. An approximation clause will impose binding commitments on Ukraine similar to those in the latest Association Agreements (similar to the stabilisation and Association Agreements). Besides, they will envisage specific stages and priorities of the approximation process. For example, the EU–Ukraine AA will list priority areas of the EU acquis to be adopted by Ukraine within specific deadlines. One may argue that these priority areas will concern the adoption of the EU competition and state aid acquis, the establishment of the principle of non-discrimination, and the liberalisation of the Ukrainian services market. Upon the successful adoption of the priority EU acquis, Ukraine could be urged to adhere to the dynamic EU acquis within the spheres of future mutual recognition agreements. Since the Ukrainian AA is unlikely to offer any prospect of EU membership, one may not expect binding commitments to adopt the whole "accession acquis". Instead, it is most likely that Ukraine will be encouraged to continue the process of voluntary harmonisation within areas of mutual interest.

We expect that Ukraine's participation in EU-funded programmes will concern areas of education, culture, and science cooperation. This means that Ukraine will be offered access to selected EU-funded programmes (Erasmus Mundus, Socrates), conditional on the observance of EU values and principles. Besides, the Neighbourhood Instrument will envisage the provision of informational, technical, and financial assistance to enable the success of the approximation of law programmes in Ukraine, as well as closer cooperation in other areas, such as JHA and cross-border trade. This assistance will focus on the provision of information on the EU acquis, EU institutions, the organisation of training events for Ukrainian officials, and legal advice on the approximation process. Of course, the EU in the case of Ukraine's potential breach of the Union's values and principles could terminate all these types of assistance.

Sectorial cooperation will focus on areas of mutual interest to the EU and Ukraine. Taking into consideration the Ukrainian geographic position and the advanced level of industrial development, this will concern cooperation within JHA, control on illegal immigration, transport, energy, information society, environment, innovation, and space. The Provision in the EU–Ukraine AA on sectorial cooperation will encourage Ukraine to embark upon the voluntary harmonisation of its legislation with the EU sectorial acquis. Within areas of particular importance, such as environmental protection, competition, state aid, and the control of illegal immigration, the EU–Ukraine AA will contain the relevant EU acquis in the annexes (if the EU–Ukraine AA targets the creation of a customs union and/or advanced access of Ukrainian undertakings to the EU Internal Market freedoms).

The institutional framework within the EU–Ukraine AA will also be determined by the objectives of the agreement. The objectives of advanced political dialogue between the EU and Ukraine will justify the existence of the three-pillar institutional framework: Council, Committee, and Parliamentary Committee. It is not likely that the EU–Ukraine AA will provide for any degree of informal involvement of Ukraine into the EU decision-making procedure. Instead, it is likely to offer an enhanced exchange of information on the pending EU acquis. In return, Ukraine could commit itself to informing the EU on new laws and regulations that influence the neighbourhood partnership with the EU. We argue that objectives of the EU–Ukraine AA will determine whether the EU/Ukraine joint institutions possess the competence to issue binding legal decisions. On the one hand, if the EU–Ukraine AA targets mere political and economic partnership aims without precise mutual commitments to enhance the level of cooperation, it is likely that the EU/Ukraine joint institutions will have competence to issue non-binding decisions. On the other hand, if the EU–Ukraine AA is to contain a perspective of the upgrade of mutual partnership (a free trade area, mutual recognition regime), the EU/Ukraine joint institutions could be given the power to issue binding decisions that are directly enforceable in Ukraine. This would give a decisive competence to the EU/Ukraine common institutions to undertake the export of the sectorial acquis into the Ukrainian legal system, by analogy with the EU-Turkey Association Council decisions.

5.4 Concluding remarks

To conclude, we believe that our attempt to forecast the objectives and scope of the future EU–Ukraine AA is not a merely theoretical exercise. Subsequently, we argue that the future EU–Ukraine AA should be regarded as a sophisticated tool of EU external policy. Recognising the established role of the EU as a "rule generator", we acknowledge that the objectives and scope of the EU–Ukraine AA serve as an appropriate "wrapping" for the export of EU-generated rules (EU acquis) abroad. Similar to a missionary, the EU–Ukraine AA pursues an objective of the gradual establishment of a friendly legal environment beyond EU borders through the export of its values, principles, and legal heritage abroad underpinned by the existence of binding harmonisation/approximation commitments.

CHAPTER SIX

THE EU – UKRAINE ASSOCIATION AGREEMENT AS AN INSTRUMENT OF A NEW GENERATION OF SO CALLED "TAILORED" ASSOCIATION AGREEMENTS: THE COMPARATIVE VIEW

NADĚŽDA ŠIŠKOVÁ

6.1 Introduction

At the moment of preparation of this Chapter, the EU–Ukraine Association Agreement[1] has not yet been signed, nevertheless the key information about its content and its scope has already been published on the website of the European Extrenal Action Service; therefore it is available to the general public.[2] This information enables us to make a number of conclusions concerning the character of the Agreement and its specifics in comparison with the previous Association Agreements. This part of the monograph will be focused on the comparison of some of the elements of the mentioned new contract instrument with one of the previous Association Agreements, known as the Europe Agreements, especially the one which was concluded with the Czech Republic.

---

[1] The full title reads: Association Agreement between the European Union and the European Atomic Energy Community and their Member States, of the one part, and Ukraine, of the other part.

[2] available at:
http://glavcom.ua/pub/2012_11_19_EU_Ukraine_Association:Agreement_English.pdf [31.3.2013]. EU- Ukraine Association Agreement. "Guide to the Association Agreement." http://eeas.europa.eu/images/top-stories/140912-C;
http://www.sonsilium.europa.eu/uedocs/ems_Dat

Obviously, at this moment we can provide only a general and brief overview with the emphasis on legal approximation; a deeper analysis may come into consideration only when the anticipated signatures will be made and the EU-Ukraine Agreement comes into effect, or after commencement of the implementation thereof and gaining experience from its realisation.

6.2 General outlook and characteristics of the EU–Ukraine Association Agreement

The first distinction is apparent at a fleeting glance even without a closer examination, since it lays in the extremely large scope and unique concept of the new Association Agreement with Ukraine, as compared with the previous so-called Europe Agreements. In this respect we would like to mention briefly that under the term Europe Agreements it is meant the kind of Association Agreements that had almost identical content and structure, and which were concluded with a number of states of Central and Eastern Europe, namely: Poland, Hungary (1991), the Czech Republic, Slovakia, Bulgaria, Romania (1993), Latvia, Lithuania, Estonia (1995) and Slovenia (1996).[3]

The term "European Agreement" was first used in the Communication of the European Commission on 27 August 1990, in relation to the group of the first three Association Agreements concluded in 1991 with Hungary, Poland and Czechoslovakia and later spread to the other mentioned countries. The attribute "Europe" was used by the Commission not only to underline the geographic location and cultural relationships of these states, but also to reflect the fact that they represent a qualitatively new grade of integration, and are characterised by the introduction of new elements into the Association relations, including, among others, the obligation for the Associating state to ensure that the compatibility of the norms of its legal order with EU law is reached.

Jurisprudence divides the Europe Association Agreements into two generations[4] that differ from each other not only by the time of their conclusion (in two waves), but also by the fact that the second generation of the Europe Agreements contains a clause concerning the respect for democratic principles and fundamental rights from the side of the

---

[3] For details see Cremona, M.: Citizens of Third Countries: Movement and Employment of Migrant workers within the European Union in: Legal Issues of European Integration, ELR 1995, vol. 2, p. 94.

[4] Šišková,N.: Základní otázky sbližování českého práva s právem ES. Codex Bohemia, Prague, 1998, p. 36.

Association countries as a *conditio sine qua non* for the legal life of the Agreement. Especially the Association Agreement between the Czech Republic and the European Communities (which was concluded after the division of Czechoslovakia) was a Europe Agreement of the second generation comprising the obligation to respect these principles as the essential element of the Association (article 6 of the Czech- ES Association Agreement).

As mentioned before, the Europe Association Agreements concluded in the 1990´s were in principle characterised by almost the same concept and wordings. It means that they had similar texts, a common pattern and even almost the same number of provisions and identical formulations. This approach is obvious from the fact that these Association Agreements "were concluded on the basis of the model agreement and differed only in the details, which were included in the protocols and the annexes, reflecting the compromises reached during the negotiations."[5] That is why representatives of legal science unambiguously consider all the Europe Agreements to be "almost identical from the point of view of structure and contents"[6] with only one "minor difference between the various Europe Agreements of the first round and others[7]", which consists in the introduction of human rights clauses into the European Association Agreements of the second generation (as we mentioned before with respect to the Agreement with the Czech Republic, for instance).

Contrary to this, the concept of the newly envisaged Association Agreements with the countries of the Eastern Partnership States is rather different. Under the Commission's proposal, "the new relations with the Eastern Partnership countries would be constructed on the basis of country-tailored new Association Agreements, which would provide a better response to partners' aspirations for a closer relationship."[8] In other words, each country will negotiate its own version of the Agreement with the EU, which will be quite unique, reflecting the progress reached and the specifics of each country and tailored for it personally. In this respect, we may state that this means a further strengthening of the approach of the so-

---

[5] Pitrová, L, Pomahač, R.: Průvodce judikaturou Evropského soudního dvora, Linde, Prague, 2001, p.265.

[6] Maresceau, M.: On Association, Partnership, Pre-accession and Accession, in Marescean, M (ed.): Enlarging the European Union, Relation between the EU and Central and Eastern Europe, Longman, London and New York, 1997, p. 7.

[7] ibid.

[8] http://eeas.europe.eu/top_stories/140912_ukraine_en.htm

called "variable geometry"[9] in relation to the mentioned states and stronger application of the principle of differentiation, already launched within the Eastern Partnership Agreements[10], reflecting the fact that concerned are states "which have divergent legal and political relations with the European Union under one policy umbrella"[11]. It is therefore no surprise that the principle of differentiation is a cornerstone of the EU's revised ENP[12], whereas a deepening of the tendency towards a greater differentiation may, in particular, be found in the new Agreement with Ukraine.

According to the European External Action Service, "the EU-Ukraine Association is the first of a new generation of Association Agreements with Eastern Partnership countries, a pioneering document, the first agreement based on political association between the EU and any of the Eastern countries, which is comprehensive, ambitious and innovative."[13]

Unlike the concept of the previous Europe Association Agreements, that in general were relatively brief instruments (in the case of the Czech Agreement, its length was only 124 articles consisting of about 130 pages, including Annexes and Protocols), the EU-Ukraine Association Agreement includes 486 articles of the Agreement and the very large annexes, which cover over 1,200 pages. So, it is several times more extensive and larger in scope than the Agreement with the Czech Republic. According to the European External Action Service "it is unprecedented in its breadth (concerning the number of areas covered) and the depth (detail of commitments and timelines)."[14]

In the following pages, we will try to get to the point and to find out the substance of this newly chosen concept and explain why the above-

---

[9] For content of this term see: Elsuwege, P. V.: Variable Geometry in the European Neighbourhood Policy. The principle of Differentiation and its Consequences, in: Lannon, E. (ed.): The European Neighbourhood Policy's Challenges, P. I. E. Peter Lang, Brussels 2012, p. 59

[10] For distinction between „Association" and „Eastern Partnership" see Maresceau, M.: On Association partnership, pre- accession and accession, in: Maresceau, (ed.): Enlarging the European Union, Longman, London- New York, 1997, p. 3-12.

[11] Elsuwege, P. V.: Variable Geometry in the European Neighbourhood Policy. The principle of Differentiation and its Consequences, in: Lannon, E. (ed.): The European Neighbourhood Policy's Challenges, P. I. E. Peter Lang, Brussels 2012, p. 59

[12] Ibid

[13] Information on EU-Ukraine Association Agreement, see: http://eeas.europa.eu/top_stories/2012/140912_ukraine_en.htm, references from 21.9.2012

[14] ibid

mentioned Association instrument is so unique as concerns its scope and content in comparison with the previous European Agreements. In this respect, the *ratione materiae* of the Agreement will be a relevant issue.

Right at the beginning, upon characterising this new contract instrument, we would like to mention that despite its unusual and non-ordinary concept, the EU-Ukraine Agreement belongs to the category of so-called 'mixed type' agreements, as concerns the External relations law of the EU. In addition to all issues involved, this also means participation in this Agreement on the part of the Union of the Member States who here act on their own behalf in the fields not covered by acquis communautaire.[15] Especially, it is used when the subject matter falls partly within the competence of the Union and partly within that of Member States. [16] Another important feature of the 'mixed type' agreements is their so- called "three-dimensional character",[17] therefore their effects within European, International and national law of the involved states.

Further, we may state that like the Europe Agreements, the EU-Ukraine Agreement is a complex instrument, regulating both the political association and cooperation in various fields as well as it bringing an institutional structure of bodies that implement the Agreement including the settlement mechanism. In fact, it is an instrument that is "used for establishing privileged links, across a broad spectrum of EU policies."[18] The complex conception of the EU-Ukraine Agreement is apparent already from its structure which covers many fields of Association, ranging from political association to the questions of the mutual opening of markets for goods and services, through to the issues of approximation of laws and of the area of justice, freedom and security.

It is obvious from this that the Association Agreement effectively covers almost all the fields contained in the Establishing Treaties and even reflects in some places its structure. First of all, economic provisions are concerned, as in the FEU Treaty, the subject of regulation in the EU-Ukraine Agreement are the four fundamental freedoms: movement of goods, persons, services, capital, as well as competition and other economic provisions, etc. In particular, provisions of Article 30 of the EU-

---

[15] For details see Eeckhout, P.: The External Relations Law of the European Union, Oxford University Press, Oxford - New York, 2004, p. 190-191

[16] Hartley, T. C.: The foundations of the European Union, 7th edition Oxford University Press, Oxford and New York, 2010, p. 196 – 197

[17] Svoboda, P.: K právní povaze tzv. asociačních dohod a sekundárního asociačního práva, Právník, 1996, vol.3, p. 201-206

[18] Eeckhout, P.: EU External Relations Law, 2. Edition, Oxford University Press, Oxford – New York, 2012, p. 127.

Ukraine Association Agreement and Article 30 of the Treaty on the Functioning of the European Union may serve as an example. However, despite the above-mentioned provisions regulating the same field–prohibition of imposing new customs duties (the so-called "stand-still clause")–the formulation in wordings thereof is different. That is why we may say that just like in the cases of the previous agreements with the states of Central and Eastern Europe, even though the subject of regulation is the same as concerns the four fundamental freedoms, the articles are not identical, since the contents thereof are different in the Treaty on the Functioning of the European Union and in the Association Agreement. In this respect we speak about a different operating regime that is "in particular embedded there where different integration intentions are clearly demonstrated."[19]

Such "borrowed" provisions from the texts of the Establishing Treaties were named in the jurisprudence as "mirror legislation".[20] In our opinion, the above-mentioned norms prove a gradual penetration of the content of the EU law into the Association Agreement and then consequently into the national law of the Associated State.[21] This conclusion is in full compliance with the definition of the term 'Association' given by the Court of Justice in the Demirel case, declaring that an "Association agreement creating special, privileged links with a non-member country which must, at least to a certain extent, take part in the Community system".[22]

Due to the limited space of this chapter, we cannot explain and analyse all relevant fields covered by the Agreement. We will therefore restrict ourselves to a short statement that the unprecedented scope of the Association Agreement with Ukraine reflects an enormous growth in the number of fields of the material scope of the Union in the intention of the Lisbon Treaty,[23] which is several times larger than that in the case of the

---

[19] Pauknerová, M.: Asociační dohoda – některé teoretické a praktické otázky, Právník, 1995, vol. 9, p. 841

[20] ibid

[21] Šišková, N.: Základní otázky sbližování českého práva s právem ES, Codex, Praha, 1998, p.69

[22] ECJ judgement C- 12/86 Demirel, point 9

[23] Under the words of Štefan Füle „after the adoption of the Treaty of Lisbon, the European Union is a different type of animal", in Füle, Š.: Ukraine and the World: Addressing Tomorrow´s Challenges Together, 9th Yalta Annual Meeting, Ukraine, 13 September 2012, Press Releases, available at http://europa.eu/pressReleasesAction.do?reference=SPEECH/12/603aformat=H, 21.9.2012, p. 3.

European Agreements which were concluded just before the Amsterdam Treaty.

In other words, upon the making of the Association Agreement with Ukraine, the extended acquis communautaire[24] inevitably caused a more extended embedding of contractual obligations in the respective fields. For comparison, in the case of the Association Agreement between the EC and the Czech Republic concluded in 1993, the relevant acquis communautaire that was to be taken over consisted of about 2,000 legal acts only.[25] The above-mentioned reason may be a key one, though not the only one to explain the extreme extent of the text of the Association Agreement with the Ukraine.

Another reason is the fact that as concerns the Czech Republic and the states of Central and Eastern Europe, the other instruments were adopted also, containing guidelines for the taking over of the Community and Union legislation which has not been directly incorporated into the text of the Agreements (for example the White Paper-see details herein below).

6.3 Future prospects of the Association Agreement and its connection with the political criteria

Concerning the future prospects of the compared instruments it should be mentioned in particular paragraph 17 of the Preamble to the Czech Association Agreements which declared: "*Recognizing the fact that the Czech Republic's ultimate objective is to accede to the Community, and that this Association, in the view of the Parties, will help the Czech Republic to achieve this objective*". In legal science, such a type of Association is classified as a "dynamic association" or "Association with the perspective of the accession" or a so-called "anteroom (antechamber)" of the future membership.[26]

The EU-Ukraine Association Agreement has no such provisions, so formally it looks like an association without any perspective of accession, or like the so-called "static association". Nevertheless, the eventuality of future membership of Ukraine in the EU is not in fact excluded, as under the wording of Art. 1 of the envisaged Treaty "*this Agreement shall not*

[24] For definitions of the acquis communautaire in modern legal science see Petrov, R.A.: Transpozicia "acquis" Europejskogo Sojuza v pravovyje sistemy tretjich stran, Publishing Istina, Kiev, 2011, p. 19-36.

[25] Palivec, J.: Aktuální problémy aproximace práve ČR s právem ES. Přehled předpisů Evropských společenství, 1997, vol. 1, p. 4.

[26] Svoboda, P.: Přidružení v teorii a praxi Evropská unie, Právník, 1994, vol. 2, p. 164

prejudice and leaves open future developments in EU–Ukraine relations." This idea was further specified by Štefan Füle, the Commissioner for Enlargement and Eastern Partnership, who stated "the Ukraine Association Agreement will constitute a new stage, aiming at a political association and economic integration and leaving open the way for further progressive developments, including a perspective for a country to accede".[27]

It is necessary to bear in mind that even in the case of the Czech Republic and other new Member States that concluded the same type of agreements, that the mentioned declaration of paragraph 17 of the Preamble concerning the aims and perspectives of the association was not assessed as a binding promise of future membership and an obligation on the side of the Union to enable the accession. Therefore, as concerns the Czech Republic, the issue of accession remained open until the accomplishment of the process of evaluation and "screening".

In fact, the accession to the EU is connected with the fulfilment of the conditions of the membership, formulated at the Copenhagen Summit in June 1993 as follows:

a) Political: stability of institutions which guarantee democracy, rule of law, human rights and the respect for and protection of minorities;
b) Economical: existence of a functioning market economy as well as the capacity to cope with the competitive pressure and market forces within the Union;
c) Other: the ability to take on the obligations of membership including adherence to the aims of the political, economic and monetary union[28]

The European Commission in its document Agenda 2000 specified these criteria and declared that "the acceptation of the acquis communautaire, which is introduced in the Treaty, other legislation and politics of the Union"[29] belong among the third group of criteria (so-called "other" criteria) and is an essential pre-condition for the membership. In other words, the approximation of laws and the acceptation of the legal rules of the Union create the key criteria for the accession to the Union. The obligation for the association country to ensure the approximation of norms of its legal system with the EU law and taking over of the acquis

[27] Füle, Š., ibid
[28] Conclusions of the European Council, Kopenhagen 21-22.6.1993,7/A/iii, JN 180/93, p.13.
[29] Bulletin EU 6 1993

communautaire was incorporated into the text of the Europe Association Agreements for the first time in the history of the association relationships.

The fact that all these preconditions are decisive and create *conditio sine qua non* for the future accession of the Associate State to the Union is confirmed in particular by the experience of Slovakia. At the Luxembourg Summit in December 1997, Slovakia was excluded from the list of candidate states for its failure to meet the political criteria, as in the Commission's opinion the government lead by Vladimír Mečiar did not guarantee democracy, the rule of law and human rights. Positive changes at the Slovak political scene after the parliamentary elections in 1998 were reflected in the conclusions of the Helsinki Summit in 1999, when Slovakia regained the status of a candidate country (for details see Chapter 11 of the monograph).

An almost identical formulation of those political criteria was incorporated directly into the Ukraine Association Agreement and occurs in the text several times:

- In the Preamble: "*A reference to common values on which the EU is built – namely democracy, respect to human rights and fundamental freedoms and rule of law – and which are shared by Ukraine*"
- In title 1 – Principles "*respect for democratic principles, human rights and the rule of law…*"
- In title 2 – Political dialogue and the reform: "*to strengthen the respect for democratic principles, the rule of law and good governance, human rights and fundamental freedoms*"

The analysis of these provisions and the fact of their incorporation thereof directly into the text of the Agreement even several times enables us to conclude that the mentioned pre-conditions played a really key and decisive role in reaching the aims of this instrument and the filling of the prospects of future relations between the EU and Ukraine. This fact is also confirmed by the Commission's message from the Yalta meeting on 13 September 2012 expressed in an unambiguous declaration-"no compromise on values".[30]

---

[30] Štefan Füle.: Ukraine and the World: Addressing Tomorrow´s challenges Together, 9th Yalta Annual Meeting, Ukraine, 13 September 2012, Press Releases, available at http://europa.eu/pressReleasesAction.do?reference=SPEECH/12/603aformat=H, 21.9.2012, p. 3.

It should be highlighted that the Copenhagen Summit mentions one other pre-condition that is not precisely named by some authors as the "fourth Copenhagen criterion".[31] By this particularly is meant the formulation of point 13, declaring *"Union capacity to absorb new Members, while maintaining the momentum of European integration, is also an important consideration in the general interest of both the Union and candidate countries*".[32]

In this respect we would like to stress that although the fact that this is undoubtedly an essential pre-condition for the enlargement of the Union, in our opinion it cannot be aligned to the previous Copenhagen criteria since they represent the requirements towards aspiring states only and are decisive for preparedness of those countries to "to assume the obligations of membership by satisfying the economic and political conditions".[33] Therefore, we are convinced that this pre-condition, that is related to the Union as such and that cannot be met by states aspiring to membership, creates its own specific category, referred to as "absorption capacity of the EU"[34]. Its incorporation thereof among the previous requirements is very unusual in science, and could even cause some confusions.

6.4. Approximation of laws – the new approach. "Regulatory approximation" and its comparison with the previous concept

As mentioned before, Europe Agreements launched a practice of including into the texts of Association Agreements the provision for imposing obligations on the Associated States to do the approximation of its legal orders with the acquis communautaire.

In this respect, we would like to mention that for a long period the approximation and harmonisation process was an exclusive domain of the Member States only, i.e. an internal affair of the Community. Non-member European states did not pay any attention to this issue, even in the cases where Association Agreements were concluded.

---

[31] Inglis, K.: EU Enlargement: Membership Conditions Applied to Future and Potential Member States, in Blockmans, S., Łazowski, A., ed.: The European Union and its Neighbours, A Legal Appraisal of the EU´s Policies of Stabilisation, Partnership and Integration. T. M. C. Asser Press, The Hague, 2006, p. 63 - 67.

[32] Bulletin EU 6-1993, point 13.

[33] Ibid.

[34] Svoboda, P.:Právo vnějších vztahů EU, C. H. Beck third edition, Praha, 2010, p. 209.

More substantial changes in this field took place in the early 1990s and the obligations to approximate the laws were included into the texts of the Europe Association Agreements. "The European harmonisation process on the basis of EC law thus crossed the borders of the European Communities."[35]

The process of approximation of laws within the European Union should not substitute the approximation of laws in the context of the Association. Approximation of laws of an Associated State is undoubtedly a wider term, of a general character, and must be assessed from the viewpoint of objectives on the basis of which the approximation should be reached. That is why the primary question, which must be solved from the very beginning, is the issue of terminology, or determination of the content of relevant terms and their differentiation.

It is of special importance, in particular due to the fact that European law has not yet defined the relevant terms, and in texts of the previous Europe Agreements, as well as in other instruments addressed for the States of Central and Eastern Europe (the White paper, for instance), the terms "approximation" and "harmonisation" were used essentially in a synonymic meaning, i.e. *promiscue.*

In this respect a vivid discussion on those issues took place namely in Czech jurisprudence, and among others it explored the semantic meaning of the expressions, highlighting that *harmonisation* means "bringing into accordance, into conformity", while *approximation* means "the process of approaching and reaching a similarity, in other words one-direction adaptation of the laws of an Associated State with the European law, performed only from the side of the Czech law towards the EU law."[36]

Even though the term *harmonisation* unambiguously predominated in jurisprudence in the beginning[37], nevertheless in late 1990s the opinion prevailed in Czech legal science (in reference to the mentioned subtle nuances in the particular meanings), that the term *harmonisation* should be reserved for the process of adaptation of legal norms of the Member States only, [38] i.e. exclusively within the EU. [39]

---

[35] Libánský, V.: Harmonizace čs. práva s právem ES, Právo a zákonnost, 1992, vol. 4, p. 197.

[36] Šišková, ibid, p. 20.

[37] See for instance, Honcová, R.: Procesy sbližování práva – některé aspekty, Právník 1998/8, p. 686.

[38] Cesta do Evropské unie. No. 9, Ministerstvo pro místní rozvoj ČR, Prague, 1997, p. 12.

Neither harmonisation nor approximation shall mean an establishment of legal rules that would be uniform to the EU and Associate State and which would substitute national law, it is not the elaboration of texts of legal norms precisely corresponding with the wording of the Union´s legal provisions and the creation of completely identical legal rules is not anticipated (though it cannot be excluded in advance). This is how approximation and harmonisation differs from that of the *unification* of law.

In this respect we absolutely share the opinion that "harmonisation may be contrasted with unification"[40], as "process unification would result in the complete replacement of particular aspects of the legal orders of the Member States with a new order adopted at the European level.[41] "In contrast, although harmonisation may result in the creation of a common set of rules which have the same substantive scope, the implementation of these rules utilises the legal principles and concepts familiar to each Member State."[42]

The legal approximation under the EC–Czech Agreement did not mean a verbatim adoption of the community legal acts and the incorporation thereof into the national legal order in the way as it was performed on the basis of the Agreement on the European Economic Area (for details see below). The Europe Association Agreement with the Czech Republic included only the obligation to approximate the law, not to ensure the immediate incorporation of a large amount of the Community legal acts into Czech legislation. Therefore, it is not a one-off and radical interference into the Czech law, but, in particular, a process of gradual ensuring of compatibility and removal of discrepancies between legal norms of the CR and EC law"[43], the requirement of "a maximum adaptation or readiness to integrate with the Community legal order so that

[39] For details concerning the nature of harmonisation through the Union see Stainer, J., Woods, L.: EU law, 10th edition, Oxford University Press, Oxford – New York, 2009, p. 360-384.

[40] Stainer, J., Woods, L.: EU law, 10th edition, Oxford University Press, Oxford – New York, 2009, p. 362.

[41] Stainer, J., Woods, L.: EU law, 10th edition, Oxford University Press, Oxford – New York, 2009, p. 363.

[42] Ibid, p. 363

[43] Šišková, N.: Obecné otázky sbližování českého práva s právem ES, Právník 1998/8, p. 704

the Czech economy could merger with the integral economy of the Communities."[44]

Therefore, we may definitely evaluate as positive the fact that the EU-Ukraine Association Agreement abandons the above mentioned disunity and consistently uses the term *approximation* of law.

Analysis of the experience from the implementation of the previous Association Agreements enables us to make the conclusion that *approximation of laws is a process of adaptation and transformation of legal systems of Associated States, in order to reach the full compatibility thereof with the European law in the fields which correspond to the material scope of the norms of EU law.*[45]

From a practical point of view, the content of approximation consists in the fulfilment of the following elements on the side of the associated state:

a) newly adopted legal provisions should be compatible with EU law;
b) previously existing legal provisions must be gradually brought into accordance with EU law;
c) new Union legislation must be constantly monitored and assessed as concerns the requirements for national law in relation to the approximation with the respective norms;
d) EU intentions must be taken into account, therefore, the drafts of the Union legislation published in the EU Official Journal must be assessed;
e) finally, important legislation of Member States must be taken in account as well.[46]

The subject of approximation includes not only the norms of material law, but the procedural rules as well (which regulate the judicial procedures when applying EU law).

Approximation does not mean only a contextual compatibility of laws of the Associated State with EU law, but also requires uniformity in the interpretation of the approximated legal provisions so that the objective of the approximation could be achieved. This can be reached only when taking into account the interpretation of the Court of Justice of the EU and its constant case-law that fills in the gaps in the European law and thus

[44] Kalenský, P.: Právo Evropských společenství a čs. právní řád se zřetelem k přístupu Československa. Právník, 1991/6, p. 542
[45] Šišková, N.: Základní otázky sbližování českého práva s právem ES, Codex Bohemia, Prague, 1998, p. 18
[46] Šišková, ibid, p. 26

influences the EU legal order in a substantial manner.[47] Even in the opinion of some representations of legal science[48] the "Court prefers to interpret texts on the basis of what it thinks they should be trying to achieve; it moulds the law according to what it regards as the needs of the Union. This is sometimes called the 'teleological method of interpretation', but it really goes beyond interpretation properly so called: it is decision-making on the basis of judicial policy."

The objectives of the approximation of law, considering the prospective membership of the Czech Republic to the Union, were defined in the Czech jurisprudence as "a *preparation of legal preconditions for the accession to the European Union and taking over of obligations arising from the membership after the accession. In this sense, the approximation was performed on two levels,*[49]" i.e. before and after the accession of the Associated State to the supranational entities. As concerns the EU-Ukraine Agreement, where dynamic association is not taken into account for the time being, the objective of the approximation of law could be defined in our opinion as the *achievement of the legal, political and institutional objectives under the Association Agreement and its complete implementation that will potentially enable further integration of Ukraine into the Union.*

Europe Association Agreements already contained not only one, but a number of provisions focused on ensuring the approximation of laws. Within these norms, it is possible to distinguish both general approximation provisions and special ones which regulate the process of ensuring of compatibility in particular fields covered by the Agreement (for instance movement of capital, economic competition, etc.).

Provisions for ensuring the compatibility of technical norms creates its own special approximation category (so-called technical approximation, see hereinafter).

---

[47] For details see Adams, M., ed.: Judging Europe´s Judges, The Legitimacy of the Case Law of the European Court of Justice, Hart Publishing, Oxford and Portland, Oregon 2013.;
Panke, D.: The effectiveness of the European Court of Justice. Why reluctant states comply. Manchester: Manchester University Press, 2010, p. 329.;
Corrias, L.: Tha passivity of Law. Competence and Constitution in the European Court of Justice. Dordrecht: Springer, 2011, p. 171.

[48] Hartley T.C.: The Foundations of European Union law, 7th Edition, Oxford University Press, Oxford- New York, 2010, p. 72.

[49] Pauknerová, M.: Asociační dohoda – některé teoretické a praktické otázky, Právník, 1995/2, p. 849.

As concerns the general approximation provision, its formulation was contained in particular in article 69 of the EC–Czech Republic Agreement that reads as follows: *"The Contracting Parties recognize that the major precondition for the Czech Republic's economic integration into the Community is the approximation of the Czech Republic's existing and future legislation to that of the Community. The Czech Republic shall endeavour to ensure that its legislation will be gradually made compatible with that of the Community."*

This was a usual "lump formulation"[50] that was contained in all Europe Agreements. In the case of the Agreement with Ukraine the analogical formulation could be found even in several places and thus creates several provisions of the same wording (for example art. 124, art. 133). These provisions declare that: "*The parties recognize the importance of the approximation of Ukraine's existing legislation to that of the European Union. Ukraine shall ensure that its existing laws and future legislation will be gradually made compatible with the EU acquis.*" (Art. 124 para 1, art. 133 para 1).

The analysis of the mentioned general approximation provisions contained in the previous Europe Agreements (with the Czech Republic for instance) and its comparison with the EU-Ukraine Agreement show substantial similarity as well as certain differences.

The above-mentioned formulations show the following:

- As concerns the Czech-EC Agreement, "*the parties recognise that approximation is an important precondition for economic integration of the Czech Republic into the Community*".
- In the case of the Agreement with Ukraine, "*the parties recognize the importance of the approximation of Ukraine's existing legislation to that of the European Union.*"

In both cases, considering the experience of the Czech Republic and other states of Central and Eastern Europe when assessing their level of preparedness to access the Union, we may state that this is really an essential requirement, *conditio sine qua non* for the implementation of the Association Agreement and the eventuality of future possible integration of the Associated State to the EU.

The formulations of other parts (EC-Czech Agreement, Art. 69 and EU-Ukraine Agreement, Art. 124[1] and Art. 133[1]) of said provisions in the two different agreements are almost identical.

---

[50] Pauknerová, ibid, p. 41

In particular, it follows from these provisions that:

- approximation involves "*existing laws and future legislation.* " It meant that not only valid EU law (the norms in force) must be respected, but also the Union law which will be adopted after the Association Agreement comes into force, entirely without any interference or influence from the side of the legislator of the Associated State.
- the objective of the approximation is to "*ensure that is legislation will be gradually made compatible with the EU acquis*". However, neither the limits, nor criteria for compatibility are contained in the provisions.

The ways, manners and procedures of the approximation, i.e. by which means the compatibility should be achieved, are formulated in rather a vague form-"*shall endeavour*" (in the case of the Czech Republic) "*shall ensure*" (in the case of Ukraine).

The analysis of these norms shows that it is a general obligation of the international law character and of the programme nature that determinates in a very rough form and only outlines the issues relating to the approximation of the national law with EU law. Nonetheless, the factual authority of these provisions is immense (as proved by the experience of the states of Central and Eastern Europe) and its importance to the future integration is decisive.

When determining specific fields of approximation of law, we notice considerable differences in the two compared instruments.

As concerns the Agreement with the Czech Republic (and with other country-signatories of the Europe Agreements) relevant fields were determined in another general provision of the Association Agreement separately (article 70 of the CR-EC Agreement), wherein the listing was a demonstrative one, not exhaustive or limitative as concerns article 69 EA. In other words, the approximation obligation was not limited only to the fields declared in article 70, but it embraced a number of others, mentioned in special provisions of the Agreement[51].

In the Association Agreement with Ukraine, relevant fields of approximation are included directly in Annex XVII to the Agreement, distinguished by a considerable scope as compared with the mentioned article of the Agreement with the CR, so they created an internal part of the contractual framework (on the contrary to the CR-EC Agreement).

[51] For more details see Šišková, ibid, p. 43.

The above-mentioned Annex XVII, titled "Regulatory Approximation", provides a list of specific fields of approximation of laws, presents enumeration of special approximation provisions and establishes "general principles and obligations on regulatory approximation", including the determination of horizontal adaptation and procedural rules. In other words, the Annex contains a very detailed guideline and a manual for the taking over of the Union legislation and for its incorporation into the legal order of Ukraine.

Even though the term "regulatory approximation" is not closely specified either in the Agreement or in any Annex to it, but by an analysis of namely article 2[52] of Annex XVII and Appendix XVII-2 we may come to the conclusion that it refers *to laid down in advance specific*

---

[52] Article 2 section 2 of Annex XVII reads as follows:
General principles and obligations on regulatory approximation
1. The applicable provisions of the acts referred to in Appendices XVII-2 to XVII-5 (to this Agreement) shall be binding upon the Parties in accordance with the horizontal adaptations and procedural rules laid down in Appendix XVII-I (to this Agreement) and with the specific arrangements provided in Appendices XVII-2 to XVII-5 (to this Agreement). The parties shall ensure full and complete implementations of those provisions.
2. The applicable provisions of the acts referred to in paragraph 1 (of this Article) shall be made part of Ukraine's internal legal order as follows:
(a) an act corresponding to a EU Regulation or Decision shall as such be made part of the internal legal order of Ukraine
(b) an act corresponding to a EU Directive shall leave to the authorities of Ukraine the choice of form and method of implementation
3. The Parties shall cooperate to ensure compliance with this Annex by Ukraine via: periodic consultations, within the framework of the Trade Committee on the interpretation of the applicable provisions for the sectors concerned by regulatory approximation and other related areas covered by the Agreement; periodic discussions on institutional, capacity and resourcing issues relevant to the process of regulatory approximation; consultations and exchange of information on existing and new legislation according to Title VII (Institutional, General and Final Provisions) of this Agreement.
4. The Parties shall inform each other of their respective authorities responsible for the sectors concerned by regulatory approximation.
5. Pursuant to the principle of sincere cooperation, the Parties shall, in full mutual respect, assist each other in carrying out the tasks which flow from this Annex and its Appendices. The Parties shall take every appropriate measure to ensure fulfilment of the obligations arising out of this Annex and its Appendices or resulting from the acts of the institutions of the Union. The Parties shall facilitate the achievement of regulatory approximation and refrain from any measure which could jeopardise or delay the attainment of the objectives of this Agreement.

procedures, including a time-line, for the taking over of acquis communautaire and its incorporation into the legal system of Ukraine in order to ensure compatibility of Ukrainian legal norms with the EU law in the fields of material scope covered by the Agreement.

Concerning the regulatory approximation, which is mentioned in Art. 2 (2) of Annex XVII, it must be underlined that the relevant provision is absent in the text of the Europe Agreements. However, an identical norm has already been used in practice, in the case of another agreement, namely the EEA Agreement.[53] In particular, article 7 EEA is in complete conformity with the cited provision.

The mentioned conformity in the methods used may be further illustrated and also confirmed by other similar provisions appearing both in the EEA Agreement and in the Association Agreement with Ukraine (Article 6 of Annex XVII to the Agreement with Ukraine and Article 6 of EEA Agreement) that set the obligation for the parties to interpret relevant acts in accordance with the relevant ruling of the Court of Justice.[54]

Especially, due to these specifics, the EEA Agreement is considered to be and often referred to as "the highest level of association relations".

While analysing the approximation provisions in the Agreement with Ukraine and comparing them with the European Agreements, we would like to stress *expressis verbis* the temporal aspect. We mean the fact that the approximation provisions of the European Agreements did not contain any concrete time limits for ensuring compatibility concerning the particular norms. We may therefore state that their *ratione temporis* basically followed from and was governed by the time schedule of the

[53] Agreement on the European Economic Area, OJ No L1, 3.1.1994, p. 3

[54] Article 6 of the EEA Agreement: Without prejudice to future developments of case law, the provisions of this Agreement, in so far as they are identical in substance to corresponding rules of the Treaty establishing the European Economic Community and the Treaty establishing the European Cole and Steel Community and to acts adopted in application of these two Treaties, shall, in their implementation and application, be interpreted in conformity with the relevant rulings of the Court of Justice of the European Communities given prior to the date of signature of this Agreement.

Article 6 of Annex XVII to the EU- Ukraine Agreements reads as follows:

Article 6 Interpretation: Insofar as the provisions of this Annex and the provisions of the applicable provisions specified in the Appendixes (to this Agreement) are identical in substance to corresponding rules of the Treaty on the Functioning of the European Union and to acts adopted pursuant thereto, those provisions shall, in their implementation and application, be interpreted in conformity with the relevant rulings of the Court of Justice of the European Union.

association relation itself (as concerns the Czech Republic, the period created was 10 years divided into two consequent five-year stages).[55]

On the contrary, as concerns the Association Agreement with Ukraine, Annex XVII brings an unambiguously drawn "road-map" that strictly determines a precise time framework that begins when the Agreement enters into force. In the Czech Republic's case the issue remained for the consideration and discretion of the state itself, when the sequence of taking over of the Union legislation was determined on the basis of a timeline scheduled in accordance with a Governmental decree (see below).

6.5 Technical approximation

While assessing the Association Agreement provisions on approximation of law, we would like to highlight in particular the technical approximation, as the Czech experience proves that the concerned field creates a very extended and substantial part of the approximation of law of the Associated State with EU law.

Its importance is given by the fact that technical obstacles in trade need to be removed in order to ensure the free movement of goods. These obstacles might prevent the realisation of the mentioned fundamental freedom not less effectively than customs and quantitative restrictions of exports and imports.

The classification of technical approximation as a separate category within the norms on the approximation of law is done in particular with respect to the special character on technical provisions.

As it is known, a legal regulation is connected with an officially recognised formal source of law and the execution of legislative powers, it contains legal norms and it is formally published in an appropriate form.[56] On the contrary to this, the act of technical regulation has a mixed character and accumulates within itself the elements of the pure technical nature as well as binding rules for human behaviour which are the subject of legal regulation. The content of a technical provision in particular consists of technical rules as an application of the laws of nature on technological procedures. In practice, it is the determination of characteristics of products, of testing, production and screening methods,

---

[55] Except for several provisions that were implemented before the Agreement came into force on the basis of the Interim Agreement.

[56] For more details see Havránek, J. et al.: Právní teorie. "Juridica Brunencia", Brno 1995, p. 138, 139

technical terminology, marking or labelling of products, and procedures for assessment of conformity of products with the certification basis.[57]

In other words, they are the acts that in particular contain technical requirements. The duty to meet these requirements (or only certain provisions) may be set consequently by normative or individual legal acts.

If normative legal acts refer in this way to the designed "technical specifications, then they specify the disposition of a legal norm, and the technical specifications thus become the construction element of the legal norm."[58]

Therefore, the technical approximation comprises only those technical norms that are contained in legal acts (in the form of a reference or quotation), thus having a legally binding effect.[59]

Technical harmonisation was regulated in the EC-CR Association Agreement in Article 75, which was formulated relatively vaguely[60]. The new EU-Ukraine Agreement brings a much more detailed and specified regulation, contained in several provisions (e.g. Art. 56-Approximation of technical regulations, standards and conformity assessment, and Art. 55-Technical cooperation, Art. 57–Agreement on Conformity Assessment and Acceptance of Industrial Products, Art. 64–Regulatory approximation [concerning sanitary and phytosanitary and animal welfare legislation]).

In particular, the subject of technical approximation in the new Agreement is determined in a substantially broader way, as opposed to the Agreement with the CR, which laconically mentions only "*Community technical regulations, European standardization, and conformity assessment procedures*".[61]

---

[57] Technická harmonizace. Cesta do Evropské unie, vol. No. 4. Ministerstvo hospodářství ČR, Praha 1996, p. 32

[58] Ibid.

[59] Šišková, N.: Základní otázky sbližování českého práva s právem ES, Codex Bohemia, Prague, 1998, p. 48

[60] Šišková, ibid

[61] The art. 75 of the ES-Czech Association Agreement states:
Industrial Standards and Conformity Assessment
1. The Parties shall co-operate with the aim to achieve the Czech Republicś full conformity with Community technical regulations and European standardization and conformity assessment procedures.
2. To this end, co-operation shall seek:
- to promote the use of Community technical regulations and European standards and conformity assessment procedures;
- where appropriate, to achieve the conclusion of agreements on mutual recognition in these fields;

As concerns the Agreement with Ukraine the subject of technical approximation comprises among others: "*technical regulations and EU standardization, metrology, accreditation, conformity assessment procedures and the market surveillance system, including the principles and practices laid down in relevant EU Decisions and Regulations.*"

While the objectives of the approximation are defined similarly: "*to achieve full conformity*" (in Agreement with the Czech Republic), "*to gradually achieve conformity*" (in the Agreement with Ukraine), substantial differences can be found in the determination of the means and procedures of the approximation. In the case of the EU-Ukraine agreement, the requirements (under art. 56(2)) are:

- incorporate the relevant EU *acquis* into the legislation of Ukraine;
- make the administrative and institutional reforms, that are necessary to implement this Agreement and the Agreement on Conformity Assessment and Acceptance of Industrial Products (hereinafter referred to as the "ACAA") mentioned in Article 57 of the Agreement;
- provide an effective and transparent administrative system required for the implementation of this Chapter.

In relation to the above mentioned provisions of the Association Agreement with Ukraine concerning technical harmonisation, we would like to stress particularly the absolute novelty in the regulation of association relations in the form of the mentioned realisation of relevant administrative and institutional reforms and assurance of an efficient and transparent system of administration.

Further, as concerns differences from the Europe Agreements, it is necessary to highlight the time schedule set in advance (contained in Annex III) of the EU–Ukraine Agreement and measures leading to the monitoring of the fulfilment of those provisions in the form of an obligation for Ukraine to submit annually a report to the EU (paragraph 4 article 56: "*Ukraine shall provide the EU party with reports on the measures taken in accordance with this Article once a year*").

- to encourage the Czech Republic´s participation in the work of specialized organizations (CEN, CENELEC, ETSI, EOTC).

3. The Community will provide the Czech Republic with technical assistance where appropriate.

6.6 Mutual obligation on the side of the Union

With the mentioned obligation of the Associated State to realise the approximation of its laws with EU law, corresponds the mutual obligation on the side of the Union to provide the relevant technical assistance. The aims of the approximation *de facto* will not be reachable without effective assistance from the side of the EU. This obligation was incorporated into Art. 71 of the EC-Czech Association Agreement, which brought the demonstrative list of such measures included *inter alia:*

- the exchange of experts;
- the provision of early information especially on relevant legislation;
- organization of seminars;
- training activities;
- aid for the translation of Community legislation in the relevant sectors.

In the case of the Association Agreements with Ukraine, the palette of these measures is much wider and impressive, including among others:

a) reinforcing regulatory cooperation through the exchange of information experiences and data, and scientific and technical cooperation, with a view to improving the quality of their technical regulations, standards, testing, market surveillance, certification, and accreditation, and making efficient use of regulatory resources;

b) promotion and encouraging cooperation between the respective organizations, public or private, responsible for metrology, standardization, testing, market surveillance, certification and accreditation;
c) fostering the development of the quality infrastructure for standardization, metrology, accreditation, conformity assessment and the market surveillance system in Ukraine;
d) promoting Ukrainian participation in the work of related European organisations;
e) seeking solutions to trade barriers that may arise;
f) coordinating their positions in international trade and regulatory organisations such as the WTO and the United Nations Economic Commission for Europe.

Art. 55 of the EU-Ukraine Agreement, which brings this non-exhaustive list of the forms of mutual cooperation in the field of technical assistance, also envisages the eventuality of the establishment of the regulatory dialogues at both horizontal and vertical levels as the precondition for the technical approximation.

6.7 "Dynamic approximation"

The envisaged EU-Ukraine Association Agreement brings also one more unknown concept of so-called "dynamic approximation"[62]. This entirely new term, not used in any other Association Agreement before, reflects the fact that "EU law is not static, but under constant evolution".[63] The mentioned general feature of European law nevertheless obtains the specific dimension right now, when the EU is in the period of preparation of Treaty reforms and in process of the acceleration of its legal changes. In other words, the approximation process in the Association State due to this fact has to be dynamic, must take into consideration the future development of the EU and should keep pace with the envisaged EU reforms, including the eventuality of the declared federalisation of the European Union in the near future.

6.8 The White paper and its role in the implementation of the European Agreements: other instruments of the approximation at the Czech national level

For a clearer understanding of the concept of the previous Europe Agreements and their difference from the new the EU-Ukraine Association Agreement, it is imperative to analyse the instrument known as the White paper.

This document of a non- binding character, which is known under the title: White paper for preparation of the Association States of the Central and Eastern Europe for integration into the Internal market of the EU, was adopted by the European Commission in May 1995.[64]

The mentioned instrument contained a very detailed description of the Union's legislation and included the recommendations concerning the

---

[62] EU-Ukraine Association Agreement – Guide to the Association Agreement, p. 5, available at: http://eeas.europa.eu/top_stories/2012/140912_ukraine_en.htm

[63] ibid

[64] The preparation of the Association states of the Central and Eastern Europe to integration into the Internal Market of the Union (White paper), 1995

optional ways and procedures on how to carry out the approximation by the Association countries in the related areas. To the specifics of the White paper belongs also the fact that this analytical document of the European Commission was not addressed to the Czech Republic personally, but was designated to the all Association States of Central and Eastern Europe and thus had a general character.

The second specific is that it was a document of a non-binding character. The European Commission itself named it as a "vademecum", non-binding instruction or the guidebook. It set out a number of gradual steps thought it were better to realize the approximation of the relevant norms of law in the Association States and to make them compatible with the acquis communautaire.

The third pecularity consisted of the specific material scope and direction of the White paper, which was focusing on the areas of the internal market only, contrary to the Association Agreements which were more complex instruments, also regulating the political dialogue, institutional structure, human rights and other fields.

The final characteristic of the White paper consisted of its very detailed description and specification in the related areas, as the internal markets "acquis" contained information concerning approx. 1,300 legal acts and the precise procedures and concrete steps on how to introduce them.

On the basis of the recommendations given in the White paper each Association State had elaborated its own National programme, containing its own timetables, priorities and procedures for the achievement of the approximation of laws in the mentioned areas[65].

Although the fact that the White paper had no binding character, nevertheless the fulfilment of its recommendations played a key role in the process of the accession, because it created a part of the assessment and the evaluation done by the Commission concerning the preparedness of the Association States and the screening during the negotiations about the accession.[66]

On the contrary to this concept, which was applied to the States - signatories of the Europe Agreements, in the case of the EU-Ukraine

---

[65] For instance in the case of the Czech Republic was adopted „Priorities of the fulfilment of the principles of the White paper in the Czech Republic." This analytic document, which was approved by the Czech Government on 13.12.1995, contained the programme of measures (including the time-schedule), which had to be realised as priorities till 2000.

[66] For details see Šišková, N.: Bílá kniha jako nástroj sbližování práva přidruženého státu s acquis communautaire vnitřního trhu, Právní rozhledy, 1999/ No5, p. 288

Association, the detailed and specified procedures concerning compatibility being reached and its timetables are incorporated directly into the text of the Agreement itself or its Annexes and thus create an integral part of the obligations under the Treaty.

6.9 Some other experience, which may be shared[67]

In the case of the Czech Republic other instruments for approximation of law became the relevant Government decrees. These acts had provided, on the practical level, the solution of issues of ensuring compatibility of Czech legal regulation with acquis communautaire,[68] established an institutional structure of bodies to administer the approximation of law[69], and also fixed timetables for particular steps of the gradual approximation of law.[70]

Particularly positive experiences and well-proven procedures shall be seen in the elaboration of the Government Decrees for ensuring compatibility of the Czech legal order with the EC law,[71] including definitions of the criteria for compatibility.[72]

Especially from the viewpoint of approximation of legal regulation of the Czech Republic with EU law, such grades of compatibility could be reached: full compatibility[73], prevailing compatibility[74], prevailing

---

[67] This expression was used by Jan Zemánek, who analysed some other aspects of the transformation of the Czech legal order, for details see: Zemánek, J.: The Czech pre-European Union accession experience from legal approximation and its relevance for the Eastern partnership, in: The Eastern Partnership and the Europe 2020 strategy: Visions of leading policy makers and academics, Directorate-General for Education and culture, Publications Office of the European Union, Luxembourg, 2012, p.89

[68] Governmental decree No 396 from 9.10.1991, No 432 from 16.7.1997, No 382 from 25.6.1997, No 709 from 12.11.1997 etc.

[69] Governmental decree N 631 from 9.11.1994

[70] Goverental decree No 151 from 15.3.1995

[71] CR Government Decree of 9.10.1991 No. 296 and CR Government Decree of 16.7.1997, No. 432

[72] Credits for the elaboration of these criteria belong to the outstanding Czech lawyer JUDr. Alexej Kohout, who not only theoretically prepared the drafts for the assessment of compatibility of national regulations with acquis communautaire, but also very actively aided the implementation and pursuing of these rules into bodies of the state administration. The mentioned procedures also became an inspiration to Slovakia.

[73] -where the Czech legal regulation is not in collision with any EC legal regulation and

compatibility with reservations[75], partial compatibility[76], partial compatibility with reservations[77], incompatibility[78], incompatibility with reservations[79].

-where all provisions of an EC regulation are materially covered by a Czech legal provisions and
-where the Czech regulation does not contain stricter provisions in comparison with EC regulations or an extra provisions that might disrupt the single market, unless such exceptions have been accepted by the Community law or by the European Agreement (must be specifically reasoned),

[74] -where most provisions of the EC regulation are materially covered by a regulation of the Czech Republic, and
-where the Czech regulation in not incompatible with any of the substantial provision(s) of a EC directive, and
-where the Czech regulation does not contain stricter provisions in comparison with EC regulations or an extra provision that might disrupt the single market, unless such exceptions have been accepted by the Community law or by the European Agreement (must be specifically reasoned),

[75] -where prevailing compatibility has been reached and full compatibility is achievable only under the conditions of the Czech Republic's membership in the EU, in particular
- as concerns provisions which are applicable only between Member States, due to their nature and content, or
-in the case of membership, a divergent regulation could be recognised as equivalent under relevant provisions of primary community law (Article 100a para 4 of the EC Establishing Treaty),
-where it follows from the special regulation of the European Agreement (including an Association Council Decision under article 106 or Association Commission Decision under article 108(2) of the European Treaty),

[76] where only some (or even one) substantial provisions of EC Directive are covered by Czech regulation(s),

[77] -where partial compatibility has been reached and full compatibility is achievable only under the conditions of the Czech Republic's membership in the EU, in particular
-as concerns provisions which are applicable only between Member States, due to their nature and content, or
-in the case of membership, the divergent regulation could be recognised as equivalent under relevant provisions of primary community law (Article 100a para 4 of the EC Establishing Treaty),
-where it follows from the special regulation of the European Agreement (including an Association Council Decision under article 106 or Association Commission Decision under article 108(2) of the European Treaty)

[78] -where a Czech legal regulation is in material collision with a substantial EC legal provision and
-where no substantial provision of a EC Directive is covered by a Czech regulation,

The efficiency of these criteria was examined and proved in practise in the case of the Czech Republic and Slovakia, where every draft of a legal act is accompanied by the elaboration of a compatibility clause including the mentioned pre-conditions of the compatibility. That is why we considered this experience to be an inspiration and eligible know-how that can be used by other Association States in the process of legal approximation.

6.10 Conclusions

The analytical view on the previous Association Agreements with the States of Central and Eastern Europe and their comparison with the new EU-Ukraine Agreement proves that as concerns the European Agreements, the issues of approximation of law have been left open to the broader discretion and consideration of the Candidate States themselves, including the provision of legally non-binding instruments (for example the White Paper).

Unlike the Europe Agreements, the EU-Ukraine Association Agreement brings specified procedures, methods and detailed instructions in the form of legal obligations as concerns the taking over of the Union's legislations, including the institutional questions, determination of the time sequence for ensuring compatibility on particular norms and monitoring the fulfilment of these obligations (in the framework of so-called regulatory approximation).

Even though the above outlined new concept may seem at first sight to be a little bit "paternalistic" in comparison with the previous Association Agreements, nevertheless it must be taken into consideration that to the more extensive obligations in approximation of law corresponds the substantially extended pattern of "assistance counter-obligations" on the Union side.

---

[79] -where the regulation in incompatible and full compatibility is achievable only under the conditions of the Czech Republic's membership in the EU, in particular
-as concerns provisions which are applicable only between Member States, due to their nature and content,or
-in the case of membership, the divergent regulation could be recognised as equivalent under relevant provisions of primary Community law (Article 100a para 4 of the EC Establishing Treaty),
-where it follows from the special regulation of the European Agreement (including an Association Council Decision under article 106 or Association Commission Decision under article 108(2) of the European Treaty)

In other words, it can be concluded that the generally declared principle "more for more"[80] will be fully applicable in the field of the legal approximation as well. Besides the precise specification of the *ratione materiae* and *ratione temporis* given in an Agreement enables the effective monitoring of the contractual obligations, including the fulfilment of the political and legal criteria.

The Association Agreement with Ukraine confirmed also the greater accentuation of the importance of the guarantees in the field of human rights and democratic principles (futher deepening of the general trend which was started by the conclusion of the Europe Agreements of the second generation).

The future association relationship between the EU-Ukraine is influenced also by a new term of dynamic approximation, which supposes the prompt reaction on the side of the national legislator of the Associate State to take over the envisaged modifications of EU law that are expected in the future. This concept enables a flexible approach without the necessity of changing contractual obligations.

From the point of view of the theory of External Relations law, the EU-Ukraine Association Agreement indicates also the future orientation and prospects for Eastern Partnership countries, which will be a transition to more privileged links with the Union in the form of a future association relationship. In this sense the Eastern Partnership could be evaluated as a certain intermediate level (grade) to the association.

This conclusion is also proved by the fact that the drafts of new Association Agreements with some other States of the Eastern Partnership (Moldava and Georgia) were already prepared on the basis of this "model" Association Treaty of the new generation.

Current political unrests and demonstrations in Ukraine in connection with the delay of the signature of the EU-Ukraine Association Agreement showed also that the mentioned contract instrument is considered to be a key indicator in geopolitical terms, as a concrete expression and powerful symbol of the future orientation and inclination of this former Soviet Republic either towards the European Union, or to Russia. In this respect the envisaged signature and the implementation of the EU-Ukraine Association Agreement and the realisation of this "pilot project" will

[80] Under European Commissioner for Enlargement and Neighbourhood Policy this principle means „the more you commit to reforms the more support you get". For details see Fűle, Š. „Ambitions of EU and East Partners for the Vilnius summit, 28.5.2013 available at http"//europa.eu/rapid/press-release_SPEECH-13-477_en.htm, p. 2.

influence to a great extent not only the destiny of Ukraine itself, but some countries of the former Soviet empire as well.

CHAPTER SEVEN

THE EUROPEAN NEIGHBOURHOOD POLICY FOCUSED ON SOUTH CAUCASUS

ONDŘEJ HAMULÁK AND ARCHIL CHOCHIA

7.1 Introduction

The subject of this research article is the relationship between the European Union and the countries of South Caucasus, Armenia, Azerbaijan and Georgia, precisely the European Neighbourhood Policy in the South Caucasus, due to its importance to the EU from one side and to these countries on the other. The EU is very much interested in keeping and improving the stability in the region and its direct cooperation with the countries from this region supports this idea. Therefore, the main question of this paper is why the EU is interested in cooperation with the countries of the South Caucasus and what are the factors for this policy?

The hypothesis is that the EU became more concerned about the region and interested in closer cooperation with the countries due to the fact that the Union considers it as an important part of the process aimed at solving cross-border problems, such as drug trafficking, illegal immigration, human trafficking, terrorism etc.

The aim of this research paper is to prove that the prevention of the problems the EU fears in the region or due to the situation in South Caucasus is the main motivation for the Union to be engaged locally as an active political actor and is the starting reason for its policy.

In order to understand the issue fully, studying the policy of the EU is essential: what is the policy in detail and why has the Union initiated the policy with its neighbours. This article will try to explain the matter using the theory of Neofunctionalism.

7.2 The beginning of the cooperation with the South Caucasus

After the collapse of the Soviet Union and the re-gained independence, the countries of the South Caucasus, Azerbaijan, Armenia and Georgia, actively engaged in the bilateral and multilateral programmes of the EU, including the national programmes supporting institutional reforms, the Comprehensive Institutional Building Programme (CIB), the INOGATE programme supporting energy policy cooperation between the EU and partner countries, the TRACECA programme promoting the development of regional transport dialogue and Euro-Asian transport connections, macro-micro financial support, the Partnership and Cooperation Agreement (PCA) starting in 1999. The EU has also established a regional representation in Tbilisi, Georgia, dealing with the regional issues and last but not least, in 2009 the Eastern Partnership Programme started working[1].

Describing the EU's cooperation with each country, in the case of Georgia, this cooperation has been stably developing since the 1990s. The EU regional representation opened in Tbilisi, the capital of Georgia, in 1995 and it has obviously been a huge factor in developing and improving cooperation with the country, between its government and the institutions of the EU. The representation holds negotiations with the Georgia government over the cooperation programmes, as well as, in general, it coordinates those programmes. The Partnership and Cooperation Agreement (PCA) that came into power on July 1, 1999, being a legal and political basis for the cooperation, regulates the cooperation between the EU and Georgia[2]. One more document within the European Neighbourhood Policy regulating the cooperation between the EU and the country is the European Neighbourhood Policy Action Plan, being a document that defines strategic goals of the bilateral cooperation for five years, with short-term and long-term priorities[3]. On the basis of the Action Plan, the EU and Georgia make a commitment to deepen economic integration and develop political cooperation in fields such as foreign policy, justice, energy, transport, fighting poverty, freedom and safety, and especially in the fields of boarder control and migration, and environment protection. The main priorities of the cooperation between the EU and Georgia are described in two documents: the Country Strategy Paper 2007-2013 and the National

---

[1] European Union External Action. European Neighbourhood Policy–Overview. Available at: http://eeas.europa.eu/enp/index_en.htm.

[2] Ibid.

[3] ibid.

Indicative Programme 2007-2010; each document includes priority fields for cooperation[4]. Furthermore, from the 1990s, the EU is helping Georgia to solve internal conflicts with its breakaway regions, Abkhazia and South Ossetia, providing various programmes for economic and humanitarian rehabilitation, as well as a trust and peace building process. Such programmes include projects on improving living conditions of Internally Displaced Persons (IDPs) and supporting them starting up their own small businesses[5].

For Armenia, the EU has prioritized three fields: strengthening of the democratic structure of the government, regular reforms and the building of administrational basis, and fighting poverty. The EU also has an Action Plan with Armenia that defines the cooperation and the priorities of this cooperation with the country, managing various programmes supporting the development in the above-mentioned priority fields[6].

The EU's cooperation with Azerbaijan has defined three priority directions as being investments in the country's infrastructure, economic integration and a partnership in exporting oil from the Caspian Sea. Similar to Armenia and Georgia, Azerbaijan also has an Action Plan with the EU, which defines the aspects of the cooperation between the country and the EU[7].

It is important to mention that the Neighbourhood Policy is dedicated to integrating the partner countries with the EU, but not with the intention of admitting them to the Union. The policy first of all is devoted to help the partner countries to develop and strengthen their democratic institutions; it also provides these countries with a privileged relationship with the EU and somehow, at least in the short term, as an alternative to membership. The cooperation promoted and regulated by this policy should be based on taking obligations on common values such as the rule of law, minority rights, good relations with neighbours, market economy and sustainable development. Thus, practically the main aim and objective

---

[4] ibid.

[5] Europa – summaries of EU legislation. European Neighbourhood Policy: recommendations for Armenia, Azerbaijan and Georgia and for Egypt and Lebanon. Available at:
http://europa.eu/legislation_summaries/external_relations/relations_with_third_countries/eastern_europe_and_central_asia/r14103_en.htm.

[6] ibid.

[7] ibid.

of the policy is to functionally integrate partner countries with the European Union[8].

The then President of the European Commission, Romano Prodi, stated, concerning the Neighbourhood Policy, that: in times of globalization, the existence of a transnational social society, foreign relations of the EU cannot exist without taking into account the direct neighbours of the Union. That, instead of so-called "dividing borders", there should be a path of deeper integration between the EU and its neighbours, which itself will accelerate the political, economic and cultural process of bringing these countries closer to the Union[9].

The European Neighbourhood Policy undoubtedly brings huge prospects to the countries of South Caucasus. By political dialogue between the countries of the region and the EU, the spectrum of political cooperation between them will naturally be broadened, the conditions of deeper cooperation in the fields of foreign policy and safety will improve, economic and trade relations will progress, cooperation in environmental protection and in economic sectors will expand (which itself will play an important role in the diversification of energy resources in the EU). Furthermore, the interest of the EU is also due to the conflicts in the region, which keep the region an unstable area very close to the borders of the EU.

7.3 European Neighbourhood Policy

At the beginning, one may suggest that there was little interest in South Caucasus from the EU, or less than in some other regions, but the interest slowly grew and from 2003 the EU has a special representative in the region[10]. When talking about the issues that might have contributed to an increase in interest a few could be mentioned, such as the so-called Rose Revolution in Georgia, which increased the possibilities in the country for democratic transformation and more cooperation with the west including the EU, the problem that arose between the Russian Federation and the Ukraine might have played a big role as well, due to the shortages of energy resources this resulted in for several European countries and once

---

[8] European Commission. European Neighborhood Policy. Available at: http://ec.europa.eu/world/enp/index_en.htm.

[9] Prodi, R. (2002) "A Wider Europe - A Proximity Policy as the Key to Stability", Sixth ECSA-World Conference, "Peace, Security and Stability International Dialogue and the Role of the EU".

[10] Europa–EU Delegations. Delegation of the EU to Georgia. Available at: http://eeas.europa.eu/delegations/georgia/eu_georgia/political_relations/index_en.htm.

more highlighted the need for the diversification of energy resources and in this concern South Caucasus is an important alternative. The same energy resources related matters have also contributed to the EU's more active involvement in conflict resolution processes in the region, of course together with the concerns of safety issues in general[11].

Therefore, the start-up of the Neighbourhood Policy was a very important step, which more clearly defined and more importantly planned the policy towards the partner neighbouring countries. In the cases of Armenia, Azerbaijan and Georgia, they all received individual recommendations even before the policy started operating and later a report of the commission was based on the individual reports concerning those recommendations. The commission studied in detail the economic and political situation in each of these three countries, and afterwards provided some recommendations for reform, which differed for each country, however some key elements were common, such as the recommendation to reform the business environment in the country, public sector modernization, resolution of local conflicts only in a peaceful way and through negotiations, improving the situation with human rights. The main differences concerned the advice on how to fight corruption, due to the fact that the level of corruption varied in each country, the situation in Georgia being better, while Azerbaijan was the worst of the three countries. Additionally, Azerbaijan was advised to take more active steps on its way to join the World Trade Organization, as the rest, Armenia and Georgia had already joined the organization by that time, Armenia joining in 2003 and Georgia in 2000[12]. Similarly, Armenia got a specific recommendation regarding the modernization of the nuclear power plant Metsamor[13], which was built back in the Soviet period, in 1970, and carried some concerns regarding its safety.

The big enlargement of 2004, when ten new members joined the EU, introduced some new members with a Soviet past, as well as bringing the EU geographically closer to a few other former Soviet states. And in that same year, it was decided that the European Neighbourhood Policy would

---

[11] European Parliament. The South Caucasus (Armenia, Azerbaijan, Georgia) Available at:
http://circa.europa.eu/irc/opoce/fact_sheets/info/data/relations/relations/article_7242_en.htm.

[12] World Trade Organization. Members and Observers. Available at:
http://www.wto.org/english/thewto_e/whatis_e/tif_e/org6_e.htm.

[13] Poviliunas, A. (2006) South Caucasus in The Context of European Neighbourhood Policy, Lithuanian foreign policy review. Available at:
http://www.lfpr.lt/uploads/File/2006/Poviliunas.pdf.

cover the countries of South Caucasus. The situation in the area for that period was quite problematic, due to the lack of democracy and the weakness of the democratic institutions in particular, unsolved local conflicts (Abkhazia, Nagorno-Karabakh, South Ossetia), generally the high level of corruption, the unstable political situation and similar difficulties. Therefore the decision to engage more actively in the region in order to improve the situation was a necessary and useful decision, which allowed the EU to have a better understanding of the developments made in the countries and the possibility to promote needed reforms to overcome the problems. Such a commitment would have a direct effect on bringing peace and stability to Europe's boarders and thus avoiding the problems caused by the instability in the region.

The three countries of South Caucasus became even closer to the EU geographically after two other new States, Bulgaria and Romania joined the Union. As a result, the problems such as drug trafficking, human trafficking, illegal immigration, terrorism, etc. became more worrying to the EU and in order to prevent such issues the Union turned to direct cooperation with these three countries. Moreover, the geopolitical importance of the region was an additional motivation to the EU, as it opened a direct route to Central Asia, including its energy resources, which gives Europe the possibility to lower its dependence on the Russian Federation by opening a new energy corridor, the trans-Caspian and the trans-Black Sea corridors. As, when it comes to energy, South Caucasus plays a very important role in the issue, being a part of the Black Sea region, which has been an important area when it comes to Europe's energy supply; "The Black Sea is a leading theatre in which the new dynamics of energy security are being played out, a theatre in which transit countries as much as producing countries are leading stakeholders"[14].

The European Neighbourhood Policy gives the countries involved the possibility to take part in various programmes for deeper cooperation with the EU in the fields of politics, economics, safety, culture, etc. Such activities, which are based on democratic values, protection of human rights, principles of market economy and sustainable development, bring these countries closer to the Union, while the ultimate goal is not necessarily membership[15].

---

[14] Lesser, I. (2007) "Global Trends, Regional Consequences: Wider Strategic Influences on the Black Sea", Xenophon Paper, No 4. International Centre for Black Sea Studies publications, p 13.

[15] Civil Georgia. European Neighbourhood Policy for the region. Available at: http://www.civil.ge/geo/article.php?id=15653.

Within the Neighbourhood Policy, the EU has an individual Action Plan with each State involved in the policy. In those Action Plans, the priorities of the cooperation are defined; priorities that are important specifically for that particular country, therefore the plans differ from each other. The Action Plans are composed with the involvement of both sides; the EU from one side and the country from another and these plans include issues such as political dialogue, economic cooperation, reforms in the social field, the creation of a market economy, the country's access to the European market, cooperation in the field of justice[16]. One part of the European Neighbourhood Policy is the Eastern Partnership, which is devoted to strengthening the European dimension of the policy; it sets additional goals to the countries for European integration, covering fields of democracy, stability, economic and political integration, energy safety, etc.[17].

The August war of 2008, between Georgia and the Russian Federation, also contributed to more active cooperation within the Eastern Partnership programme, admitted the President of the European Commission Jose Manuel Barroso. At same time underlining that it does not intend to draw new division lines, saying that stability in the 21st century will be brought about by economy, dialogue and partnership[18].

For Armenia, Azerbaijan and Georgia, involvement in the Eastern Partnership is an important step forward in their cooperation and relations with the EU, being an essential contribution in the countries' development. It provides countries with a real possibility to carry out needed reforms and start cooperating with the EU on a higher level.

The majority of scholars working on the issues of the European Neighbourhood Policy admit that it is, in a way, Europe's answer and a reaction to the newly arisen challenges and problems coming from the region of South Caucasus. Promoting democracy via the implementation of such a policy towards these countries and stabilizing the situation on the EU's borders could be the best prevention measure that the EU could take.

The implementation of the European Neighbourhood Policy in this region was a result of the existing safety problems in this area, according to Lilli Di Puppo, suggesting that the EU decided to promote European

---

[16] ibid.

[17] Europa – Eastern Partnership Summit to strengthen EU links with Eastern Europe and South Caucasus. Available at: http://europa.eu/rapid/pressReleasesAction.do?reference=IP/09/700&format=HTML&aged=0language=DE&guiLanguage=en.

[18] Civil Georgia. EU Offers Close Partnership to its Six Neighbours. Available at: http://www.civil.ge/eng/article.php?id=20070.

democratic values in the region in order to challenge the unstable situation there. She believes that when, in 2006, the President of Azerbaijan, Ilham Aliyev, was warmly received in Brussels despite the on-going struggle with the situation of human rights in this former Soviet republic, it was due to the fact that the country is a strategic partner of the EU because of its geopolitical status, being a direct neighbour of Iran, which, with its nuclear policy, remains as seen as a threat to the EU's safety[19].

Sabine Fisher, researcher at the Paris-based Institute for Security Studies thinks that the EU has several interests in South Caucasus and only one of them is the energy resource of Azerbaijan. It is also in Europe's interests to bring economic progress, democracy and stability into this region, as it has a direct effect on the EU itself[20].

The EU has a fundamental interest in the region, first of all due to the importance of the safety and stability in the region, and to the safety and stability of Europe itself, supposes Elkhan Nuriyev. The matters for concern are extremism, separatism, terrorism, conflicts over territorial disputes, drug and human trafficking, as well as the rise of organized transnational crime[21]. The instability of South Caucasus, especially due to the local conflicts in Abkhazia, South Ossetia and Nagorno-Karabakh, might cause serious problems to the EU, by the rise of illegal immigration, drug and arms trafficking, and the increase of organized crime[22].

7.4 The Dynamics of the Action Plans' implementation

It is interesting to follow the implementation process of the Action Plan and the dynamics of that implementation. And as the Action Plan differs in the case of each country, the implementation process should also be reviewed in each country separately.

The Progress Report of 2009 by the European Commission says that the Georgia government has reached some important priorities within the Action Plan, particularly mentioning key reforms carried out in the fields

---

[19] Puppo, L. (2007) The South Caucasus countries and the ENP: Three different paths to Europe? Available at: http://www.un-az.org/undp/bulnews45/caucasus.php.

[20] News. Az Energy not EU's only interest in South Caucasus. Available at: http://www.news.az/articles/politics/3268.

[21] Nuriev, E. (2007) The EU policy in south Caucasus: The Case of post-soviet Azerbaijan New opportunities and future prospects. Available at: http://swp-berlin.org/fileadmin/contents/products/arbeitspapiere/SWP_RP_Nuriyev_ks.pdf.

[22] Tangiashvili, N., Kobaladze, M. (2006) EU- Georgian Neighbourhood Relations. Central European University p 13.

of the penitential system, fighting corruption, and improving the business environment in the country. But the report also says that the situation with fighting poverty, unemployment and social policy remains quite difficult and challenging.

Concerning democracy, the Commission found the following steps taken by the government important: first of all the modernization of the election code and the establishment of a special working group where the members of the opposition parties were included; secondly working on a new constitution within the so-called "second wave of democracy" proclaimed by the President Mikheil Saakashvili. Furthermore, important progress was achieved in fighting corruption and taking into account the recommendations from the GRECO programme (Group of States against Corruption–Council of Europe).

In the field of protecting human rights, the principal advancement was achieved by the signing of the United Nation's Convention on the Rights of Persons with Disabilities in July 2009. However, an extremely difficult situation remained with the rights of the detained and prisoners, due to the fact that detention facilities continued to be overloaded. With regard to minorities, the government adopted a new national strategy, however it did not fully corresponded with the Council of Europe's Convention for the Protection of National Minorities, also Georgia had not signed the European Charter for Regional or Minority Languages.

In other important fields, a problematic matter for Georgia remained the Competition Policy, where little has been done in order to improve the situation. Progress was achieved in border control, where cooperation with other South Caucasus States has advanced; the same has been done with regards to the visa facilitation process, migration issues, fighting drug trafficking and human trafficking. Improvements were made in the transport system, including the safety of goods coming from the Caspian Basin through Georgia and to Europe[23].

Similar to Georgia, the Progress Report for Armenia has been released concerning the country's success in the implementation of the Action Plan. The report underlined Armenia's achievements in the field of human rights, via political dialogue with the EU. Success has been made regarding overcoming internal crises as well, which was due to problematic presidential elections in the country in 2008. Needed reforms were also carried out in the financial and competition policies sector.

---

[23] European Commission (2009) Progress Report Georgia. Available at: http://ec.europa.eu/world/enp/pdf/progress2009/sec09_513_en.pdf.

However, problems remain in such sectors as economy, where inflation has stayed high and there was a lack of direct foreign investment, especially after the global financial crisis. A significant achievement in the field of regional cooperation was the conducting of negotiations with Turkey to normalize the relations between the two countries, including the signing of an official protocol, but later the protocol was not ratified by the Armenian side despite the position of the EU, which supported the signing of such a document.

Armenia received principle recommendations for more implementations of the Action Plan, including a proposal to compile a working group that would investigate the political crisis after the presidential election in 2008. Furthermore, recommendations concerned the need to improve the electoral environment in the country, the freedom of the press, the judicial system, cooperation between the ruling political party and the opposition political groups, which is essential for a country's democratic development.

Concerning the country's fight against corruption, even though its legal system provides quite a good environment for improvements, not much has been done and the progress remains minor. Regarding the protection of human rights, even though success has been achieved, the report suggests that more actions should be made, particularly in the penitential system, as well as reports that journalists were beaten and tortured on various occasions.

As for the situation with the conflict in Nagorno-Karabakh, in 2009 there were six meetings held within the so-called Minsk group, but no significant progress has been made and the situation remains unstable, with, from time to time, escalation and gun-fire on the frontline[24].

When it comes to the third country of the region, Azerbaijan, it has achieved important progress in terms of reaching the goals set by the Action Plan, particularly in economic and social fields. It managed to keep its inflation rate low during the years following the global economic crisis of 2008 as well. Considerable improvements have been reached in energy cooperation, where Azerbaijan has made efforts in developing a new energy corridor, Nabucco–the EU initiated pipeline, which could link Europe not only with Azerbaijan, but could also allow European consumers to get direct access to gas and oil from other former Soviet republics, Kazakhstan and Turkmenistan, which itself would mean a huge step for Europe in the diversification of its energy resources.

---

[24] European Commission (2009) Progress Report Armenia. Available at: http://ec.europa.eu/world/enp/pdf/progress2009/sec09_511_en.pdf.

Meanwhile problematic issues remain the country's slow progress in joining the World Trade Organization, as Azerbaijan's steps in this direction have been rather dim. As for the protection of human rights in the country, the situation remains very difficult, including the rights of the detained, as well as the freedom of the press, as various occasions of beating and torturing civilians and journalists were reported and the situation was called critical[25].

The situation described in these reports of the Commission, showed a different picture in all three countries concerning the implementation of the Action Plans, some being more successful in certain fields than others. Georgia had better results in achieving progress in the strengthening of democracy in the country compared to other States in the region, where the country managed to carry out some necessary reforms, firstly the improvement of the election environment in the country by reforming its election code. Armenia and Azerbaijan had quite good election legislation, however the progress in improving the environment has been rather disappointing, especially highlighted by the events after the presidential elections in Armenia in 2008, therefore the situation requires urgent measures to be taken.

When it comes to the protection of human rights, countries' achievements have also been slightly different. Progress has been reported in each country, but still the situation needs to be significantly improved, in the main problems differ from country to country, for example several kidnappings have been reported in Armenia that still need to be investigated, as well as the issues of torturing civilians and journalists in Azerbaijan and the situation in the detention facilities in Georgia. Some differences were discovered in countries' achievements when fighting corruption also.

The above-described differences could be the result of the diverse political situation in each country, especially concerning the position towards the EU in general. In this regards, the Georgia government had a very clear pro-European policy, aiming for better and faster integration with the EU institutions. Armenia, while being involved in the Neighbourhood Policy and the Eastern Partnership, still remains an ally of Russia and does not have very clear pro-Western and pro-European policies.

---

[25] European Commission (2009) Progress Report Azerbaijan. Available at: http://ec.europa.eu/world/enp/pdf/progress2009/sec09_512_en.pdf.

7.5 Theoretical explanation

The theory of Neofunctionalism could well help to explain the matter and answer the question of this research. The theory describes well the issue of integration, when having common interests gives more possibility for integration. This theory pays more attention to regional matters rather than to global integration. Neofunctionalists argue that integration in one sector will promote integration in another via the spillover effect; in their opinion, supranational institutions and organizations will play a main role in the integration process[26], the EU is definitely one of such supranational organizations. Neofunctionalism suggests that as a result of integration, the role of national institutions will be lowered, as the power will be transferred to the above-mentioned new supranational organizations. The theory argues that integration starts from "low politics" such as economics and will go to "upper politics" such as defense and foreign policies[27].

If we apply the theory of Neofunctionalism to the cooperation between the EU and the states of South Caucasus, we may suggest that such closer cooperation and integration will benefit all parties involved and interest groups on both sides. As mentioned above, the EU does not want to draw a new division line, its programmes implemented in the region support such integration and deepening. As for the involvement of different interest groups from these countries, an important step could be the integration of local youth in different European programmes, where young people from Armenia, Azerbaijan and Georgia have the possibility to better understand European values, culture, ideas. At the same time cooperation in some sectors of the economy will have a spill-over effect and should result in a deeper cooperation and integration in the economy in general, thus bringing the economies of these three states closer to the EU economy and European standards.

7.6 Conclusion

The aim for this research was to analyse the European Neighbourhood Policy towards the South Caucasus states, namely Armenia, Azerbaijan and Georgia, and try to find out what might be the reasons for the EU engaging in such close cooperation with these countries and to have such a policy towards them. This work describes the history of the cooperation

---

[26] Dinana, D. (2000) Encyclopedia of the European Union. Macmillan press. pp. 278-283.
[27] ibid.

between the EU and three former Soviet republics, its development, the geopolitical importance of the region in general and for the EU in particular, how did the chances of these countries increase for more integration with the EU after their involvement in the policy actions and what are the main obstacles in the way.

The research shows that the prevention of possible problems coming from the region, or caused by instability there, definitely is a motivating factor for the EU to have a special, closer relationship with the region, having a special policy towards it and putting in effort to reform and modernize the countries. These possible problems, such as drug trafficking, illegal immigration, human trafficking, terrorism, might have a direct effect on the EU itself and therefore becomes a threat to its safety. That is why the EU is very much interested in being more active in this region, being able to monitor the situation very closely, having the possibility to influence the countries more on their way to modernization and democratization, carrying out necessary reforms, in order to build more successful States, with strong democratic institutions, a stable market economy, with the values that are common to Europe and in general, a safe and stable, developing country. Stability in the region would mean stability and safety on the EU borders in general.

The theory of Neofunctionalism was used to prove such a position, which pays attention to the integration and its importance for cooperating parties, and its effects on their future. As the theory suggests, integration in one sector has a spillover effect and causes integration in another, upper sector, thus causing more integration in general and bringing parties closer. In the case of the EU and the countries of South Caucasus, integration in some sectors gives good grounds for the integration in other sectors, thus making it possible to have the countries more similar to the EU and its way of development.

CHAPTER EIGHT

COOPERATION OF POST SOVIETS WITH THE AIM OF NOT BEING "POST" AND "SOVIETS"

TANEL KERIKMAE, KATRIN NYMAN-METCALF, DALI GABELAIA AND ARCHIL CHOCHIA

8.1 Introduction

Two decades have passed since Georgia gained independence. During its democracy building, the country has had to overcome serious obstacles: apart from difficulties caused by the transition from a communist regime to a democracy through reforms, Georgia had to cope with the destabilization caused in 1991-1993 by civil wars, wars in South Ossetia and Abkhazia and later in 2008 by war with Russia. Additional difficulties hindered the development process, but strong adherence to the main goal–becoming a European country-has not changed. In this regard, experience and help provided by European countries was and remains helpful. The experience of countries that have recently joined the European family is even more valuable than that of countries with a long democratic history as such experience can more easily be applied to Georgia. The similar background–being a post-Soviet country-is often named as a best explanation for the value of the example of certain states. This can be true, to some extent, but it should by no means be regarded as sufficient for the success of cooperation between certain states.

This chapter concentrates on a particular representative of the 2004 enlargement of the European Union: Estonia and the role it plays in the development of Georgia. The aim is not to analyse the development of Georgia and the reforms undertaken there so far, but rather to understand what role Estonia plays in helping Georgia to achieve its main foreign policy goals and what the preconditions are for this. The inclusion of

Georgia in the European Neighbourhood policy in 2004 and more specifically, the launching of the Eastern Partnership five years later emphasize the EU's intention not only to gradually strengthen relations between the EU and Georgia, but also to start the integration with possible enlargement in the near future (European Union, delegation to Georgia). Nevertheless, the internal instability and continuous fear of conflicts as well as fragile relations with Russia reduce Georgia's appeal to the EU. Naturally, Estonia, together with some other former Soviet states now belonging to the EU, have experienced the same; yet it still managed not only to join the EU but to be regarded as a Member State with an exceptionally booming economy (Estonia 2012). Therefore, Estonia is particularly competent to offer aid to Georgia, demonstrating that on-going endeavours together with external support can help to stabilize the economy and strengthen Georgia's status as a potential member of the EU.

8.2 Georgian independence and the goals of the country

Georgia proclaimed independence by adopting the Independence Restoration Act on 9 of April 1991;[1] however, it was not until December of 1991 that Georgia was recognized as an independent country. The country had to deal with a number of political, social and economic problems after the dissolution of the Soviet Union. The difficult political situation and incompetence of the ruling elite of the time resulted in a false start to democracy and state building in Georgia (Nodia 2007). Instead of uniting around the liberalization idea, the national movement was split, ethnic conflict in South Ossetia, civil war and overthrowing the government, devastating war in Abkhazia and losing control over approximately one fifth of its territory made the country almost a failed state. Georgia did not manage to follow the path of the Baltic States, whose national liberation movements were gradually developing into a success story. Rather, Georgia's resources spent on establishing the most basic order and democratic reforms, so necessary for the country, were forgotten for more than a decade (Nodia 2006: 138). With the new government, from 1994 the country slowly started to implement needed reforms and managed to achieve some results worth mentioning.

[1] On 31 March of 1991 a referendum was held in Georgia: the question to answer was whether people wanted to restore Georgia's independence on the basis of the Independence Act issued on 26 May of 1918. 90.3 per cent of the population took part in the referendum and 98.9 per cent of participants answered positively to the question.

During the transition period, the EU assisted Georgia in its endeavours in many ways: in 1995, the European Commission opened its Delegation to Georgia in Tbilisi; a year later a Partnership and Cooperation Agreement (PCA) was concluded between Georgia and the EU (European Union, delegation to Georgia). Therefore, it was in that period that Georgia's orientation towards the West emerged, though this was still not very obvious. The interests of the West in the region were strengthened at this time due to the project known as Baku-Tbilisi-Ceyhan. This project aimed to build a pipeline through the Caucasian countries, which would transfer oil from the Caspian Sea to the Mediterranean and from there, ship it to Europe (Cornell, Tsereteli, Socor 2005: 19). Thus, many expectations were based on the actual completion of the pipeline, which finally happened in 2005. In addition, Georgia's will to join the North Atlantic Treaty Organisation (NATO) was announced in that period (formal institutional cooperation started in 1994 when Georgia became a participant in the Partnership for Peace programme). The above mentioned PCA triggered Georgia to move towards the West from the very beginning; by laying out its objectives in Article 1 of the Agreement (European Union, EUR-Lex), the EU had a thriving effect on Georgia, which became a member of the Council of Europe[2] and the World Trade Organisation (WTO) in 1999 and 2000 respectively. However, it was only after the Rose Revolution in 2003, that joining NATO and the EU were declared as the main goals for the country and necessary consistent reforms were undertaken.

8.3 The main factors of inspiration for Georgia

As for several other ex-Soviet countries the main aim for Georgia became joining Western institutions. Being well aware of the scarcity of domestic resources (finances, knowledge), the Georgia government both needed Western support and received it. In this regard, the experience of Western European countries was helpful; however, due to the great difference between Georgia and such countries, the experience of "new Europeans" became even more valuable. This was despite the fact that the "old Europeans" (Western European countries) remain the main deciders when it comes to the most important issues defining Georgia's future (Nodia 2006: 144). There are several reasons for this situation, the main explanation for which examples are the most valuable to follow is the

[2] Georgia applied for membership of the Council of Europe in July of 1996 during the presidency of Estonia.

great gap that exists between Georgia and Western European countries, while the countries of Central and Eastern Europe have more in common with Georgia and can serve as better examples. Georgia may realistically follow a similar route of development and accession as t one of those countries.

However, the common history argument is not that strong. Indeed, at first glance, it may seem that all former Soviet countries have a very similar background, as they all were governed in more or less a similar fashion by Central Committees of the Communist Party with Moscow as the main decision-maker in all important issues (local government was simply following an indicated course). At a closer look, things are different and countries appear to have a lot less in common than it is believed (Racius 2006: 123-125). Nevertheless, cooperation between the countries exists and seems to have been getting more fruitful during the past years.

Discussing the relationship between all post-Soviet countries would take us beyond the scope of this article, so it will concentrate on Estonia and more specifically the relationship between Estonia and Georgia and the impact this relationship has on the development of the latter. An additional factor explaining the willingness for cooperation (rather than its success) which partly derives from the previous reason–a common background-is "greater sympathy towards the travails of a country struggling to secure its statehood in Russia's shadow" (Nodia 2006: 144), in other words, we are referring to the Russian factor. Post-Soviet countries, including Estonia, can be presumed to have an interest in weakening Russia's influence in its neighbouring countries.

In general, in the early 1990s, it looked like all post-Soviet states appeared to be in a more or less similar situation, however, each found (some are still looking for) their own way of democratization. Estonia in this regard was one of the most successful examples of a speedy democratization among post-Soviet states; it managed to carry out reforms serving a consistent general policy in such a way that by 1996 it was put on the short-list for EU membership (a year prior to Latvia and Lithuania) (Galbreath, Lamoreaux 2006: 106) and in 2004 Estonia achieved two key foreign policy goals by joining NATO and the EU (Dobrovoljec, Nyman-Metcalf 2001). This gives Estonia a unique opportunity to support the democratization processes in other post-Soviet countries.

Preparing for EU membership is not only a process of undertaking various economic and other reforms, but strengthening or building up systems of trust between states is an essential feature of the process for EU membership. The success of Estonia as a EU member indicates that it fitted well into the value family. For Georgia or any other potential new members the extension, potential or actual, of this value family is a criterion for how far the EU may expand but also for what other kind of relations the EU may create with certain states. There is also a question of the extent to which values can be shaped by external influences such as EU assistance and pressure for reform and to what extent they are given by cultural circumstances (Nyman-Metcalf 2006: 110-111).

In the framework of the previously mentioned Eastern Partnership, the aim is to involve those countries, including Georgia, in stronger socio-political relations with the EU (European Union, delegation to Georgia). Moreover, the negotiations for a EU–Georgia Association Agreement, the aim of which is the far-reaching economical integration of Eastern Partnership countries, as well as certain “deep free trade agreements” (European Union, delegation to Georgia) were already launched by Catherine Ashton in 2010. In September 2012 a “Joint statement by the High Representative/Vice-President Catherine Ashton and Commissioner Štefan Füle, on EU-Georgia relations and the upcoming elections” (European Union 2012) was published. This statement reaffirms the importance of Georgia as a partner of the EU, stresses the importance of the completion of negotiations of the Association Agreement and refers to a relatively new idea called the Visa Liberalization Action Plan. However, taking into account the values of the EU, the intensity of the future relations between the EU and Georgia crucially rely on the latter’s “consolidation of democracy,” especially as regards to Georgia’s upcoming (October 2012) parliamentary elections (ibid).

Before talking about Estonia’s intentional support or the impact of its expertise (one country learns from another how to do things better that it wants to do anyway), the impact of the encouragement Estonia provided (one country in some way encourages the other to do things that it might not otherwise dare to) should be referred to [Nodia 2006: 134]. The first example of Estonia’s influence is traced back to the times of the Soviet Union. The liberation movement, which started in Estonia showed to others that there was indeed an opportunity to change the existing regime, which influenced democratic encouragement, was unfortunately not completely followed by Georgians. Apart from several achievements mentioned above, the semi-authoritarian regime existing in Georgia in the aftermath of the civil war there did not provide any further opportunities for the country, although aid from the West always existed at least at some level. During this period, between the end of the 1980s until the early 2000s, there was no active cooperation between Estonia and Georgia.

8.4 Georgia after the Rose Revolution: The Western orientation

The situation changed in 2003 after the Rose Revolution in Georgia. It can be said that after the revolution Georgia returned to the same point of departure and started a new path on the same road that Estonia had already successfully travelled since 1991 (Lucas 2008: 173). Prior to the revolution, as the World Bank report puts it: "By 2003, reform momentum sputtered to a halt, and Georgia was a near failed state. Political power was increasingly fragmented, corruption and crime were rampant, there were massive arrears in pension payments and teachers' salaries, and the infrastructure was in a state of near collapse" (World Bank 2009: 1). After the revolution, with the new Georgian government, which had strongly defined Western preferences, a new wave of reforms (this time more fruitful) began. Western orientation was chosen not only by the political elite of the country, but had strong support among the population as well. According to surveys that were held in 2009 and 2011, a vast majority of the population would vote for joining the EU if asked about this in a referendum. This attitude towards integration has remained unchanged for years (79% of respondents supported the idea in 2009 and 80% in 2011) (Caucasus Research Resource Centre 2011).

The pro-Western orientation, which strives towards achieving membership of Euro-Atlantic organizations, requires from Georgia that she accepts Western values, indeed becomes Western herself. Historically, however, Georgia's contact with the West has always been minimal. During the Medieval Ages, Georgia had close ties with Byzantium, which later changed to relations with the Ottoman Empire and Persia. Georgia started socializing with Western countries in the early nineteenth century, but after becoming part of the Russian Empire, Georgia could share only the Russian version of modernity and gained direct access to the 'real thing' only after becoming independent in 1991 (Coppieters, Legvold 2005: 69). That explains why there is no definite European country model which can be used as an example in the case of Georgia. In this regard Estonia, which achieved visible results in its development, can serve as an orienteer. Unlike previous periods when Georgia did not have a well-defined Western orientation and seemed to be unmotivated to receive Western help-although it was essential for the country and was also provided-the post-revolution government is well aware of the scarce resources of the country (not only financial ones but also competent human resources, absolutely necessary to ensure the building of democratic institutions) and values cooperation with European countries, especially post-Soviet countries (Nodia 2006: 143).

Discussing general issues concerning the relationship between Georgia and the Euro-Atlantic community would again lead us beyond the specific topic of this article, but nevertheless this topic has to be mentioned briefly in order to understand what role Estonia can play in this relationship. In this regard, it must be noted that the potential role of Estonia is not determined only by its own will, but also by the policy the EU plans to carry out regarding Georgia. Relations with the EU started long before the Rose Revolution. An Agreement on Partnership and Cooperation was signed in 1996 and came into force in 1999.[3] Closer cooperation began after Georgia became involved in the European Neighbourhood Policy (ENP); the latter provides a "privileged relationship, building upon a mutual commitment to common values (democracy and human rights, rule of law, good governance, market economy principles and sustainable development),"[4] but not more and by no means can be regarded as a guarantee for accessing the EU. By offering ENP, the EU did not deprive Georgia of the hope of eventual accession, but showed that it was unwilling to extend its borders further to the East, at least in the near future. Consequently EU membership can be seen as a very distant perspective for Georgia. From the EU's viewpoint, the accession of Georgia is undesirable because of the unstable situation, which still exists in the country (Coppieters, Legvold 2005: 52). Added to this is a general enlargement fatigue in the EU, quite apart from the question of how far to the East any future enlargement may reach.

Even if assuming that the Georgia government successfully carries out reforms and builds a democratic country in order to achieve "stability of institutions guaranteeing democracy, the rule of law, human rights and respect for and protection of minorities" (Copenhagen criteria) (European Council 1993), the EU enlargement to the East is still questionable. Some members are sceptical about the general idea of enlargement due to the problems it may bring to the EU. According to their logic, the EU needs to stop accepting new members and focus on the development of existing ones. Those who are in favour of enlargement only slightly outweigh those

---

[3] Partnership and Cooperation Agreement between the European Communities and their Member States, of the one part, and Georgia, of the other part - Protocol on mutual assistance between authorities in customs matters - Final Act - Joint Declarations - Exchange of Letters in relation to the establishment of companies - Declaration of the French Government. Document was signed on 22 April 1996 and entered into force on 01 July 1999.

[4] Council Regulation 1638/2006, OJ 2006 L 310/1.

who are against. Opposition is stronger in old member states Germany, France and the United Kingdom (Mayhew, 2007: 10). However, despite this view, the enlargement process still continues. Croatia signed an accession agreement in December of 2011 and is expected to become the 28th member of the EU in 2013 and there is still talk about further enlargement. Enlargement of the EU to the East will inevitably cause strains in the relationship with Russia (which Brussels tries to avoid). With regard to Georgia the problem is even worse than for some other potential further enlargements, as due to its geopolitical position its extraction from what is perceived by Russia as its near abroader, is likely to cause an even more severe reaction than that experienced regarding, for example, the Baltic states (Galbreath, Lamoreaux 2006: 99-102).

Despite all the negative connotations with the Eastern Countries, the European External Action Service (EEAS) regards the Eastern Partnership as a particularly important aspect of European Foreign Policy. The EEAS claims that events in countries such as Georgia affect the EU, especially due to their wish to come closer to the EU (European Union, delegation to Georgia). Therefore, in order to enhance the cooperation and actualize possible further integration, domestic reforms need to be made to effectuate local democracy since without internal harmonization and unanimous aspirations by all layers of the society to jointly follow the objectives of the EU the fragmented society may prevent quality integration.

8.5 The aftermath of the Russian-Georgian war of 2008

It is inevitable that what can be called the Russian factor plays a significant role in determining Georgia's development process, by influencing the decision making process not only of Georgian politicians but most importantly of European ones. Russian powers have always tried, if not to strengthen, at least not to lose their influence in the post-Soviet countries that gained independence after the collapse of the Soviet Union (which was always dominated by Russia) (Lucas 2008). Thus, the Western orientation of Georgia has been an annoying factor for Russia. The escalation of tension between the countries grew into the Georgian-Russian war in August of 2008 (Kerikmäe, Nyman-Metcalf, Põder 2010) over a tiny separatist republic of South Ossetia that had declared its independence from Georgia in 1991. After the war the diplomatic relationship between the countries was broken off. Since the Russian government refuses to talk directly to Saakashvili's government under any circumstances (United Press International 2012), there are at the moment no chances of changing the situation; logically there is no other way for Georgia but to concentrate all forces on approaching the West. Any chances–even the most illusory ones–of improving the tense relationship with Russia vanished after the war.

Two sets of problems, which emerged in the after-war period, hindered the development process of the country once again. On the one hand, there were inner problems. Georgia's economy was seriously threatened; control over territories was lost (as after the war, the Georgian government controls less territories of Georgia than it did before August 2008); thousands of Georgians were forced to leave their homes; protests organized by opposition leaders lasted for months in Tbilisi and created an additional basis for destabilization.

On the other hand, there was the reaction of the West to the war. Although its assistance was sufficient to play a key role at the end of the war, the assistance could still be characterized as weak and inconsistent. Such a reaction was caused by the absence of a common opinion on what the response to Russia's actions should be. Russia's actions could be regarded as aggression against NATO and the West. In this case severe measures were required. However, applying strict measures against Russia would mean returning to a hostile relationship with that country–something the West tried to avoid, in order not to destroy the existing international consensus (Nodia 2008). As a result no dramatic sanctions were used against Russia. From Georgia's perspective, this gave rise to doubts that Georgia was left alone vis-à-vis its powerful northern neighbour. Indeed, the EU–Georgian relations cooled significantly on the publication of the Tagliavini Report (Meister 2010). Although dividing blame for the conflict between both sides (Russia was blamed for provoking Georgians for years, also for a number of violations of international law) (Civil Georgia 2010), in its report the Independent International Fact-Finding Mission on the Conflict in Georgia (IIFFMCG)[5] came up with the conclusion that it was Georgia that triggered off the war (Civil Georgia 2010) by attacking Russian peacekeepers deployed in Georgia. This action, according to the commission, equalled an attack on Russian territory and created a lawful basis for the latter to take actions of

---

[5] The Independent International Fact-Finding Mission on the Conflict in Georgia was mandated by the Council of the European Union with Heidi Tagliavini as the head of the mission. The aim of the initiative was to investigate the origins and the course of the conflict in Georgia, including regard to international law, humanitarian law and human rights, and the accusations made in that context. See http://www.ceiig.ch/Index.html

self-defence (Independent International Fact-Finding Mission on the Conflict in Georgia 2009: 265).

However, some steps taken by the EU in the after-war period, such as financial support, sending a monitoring mission to Georgia (the EUMM[6]), active involvement on behalf of the EU in order to de-escalate the conflict between the opposition and the government of Georgia, proved that Georgia was not 'abandoned'. The EUMM has proved to be effective; for instance, after the war, certain EU-mediated agreements were made between Moscow and Tbilisi, and since they are now monitored by the EUMM, there have not been any critical signs of arising conflicts. In addition to surveillance, the EUMM's mandate is also the "stabilisation, normalisation and confidence building" in Georgia, so as to "contribute to the future EU engagement in the region". In addition, the EU demonstrated its support despite the fragile relations with Russia, by continuing its diplomatic mission-Delegation of the European Union to Georgia (European Union, delegation to Georgia). In the framework of the latter, financial support has been granted to Georgia several times, for instance in order to mitigate the effects of war, as well as to "support democratic development, rule of law, good governance; trade and investment, regulatory alignment and reform; regional development, sustainable economic and social development, poverty reduction as well as peaceful settlement of conflicts" (EU Monitoring Mission in Georgia). What is more, the launch of the previously discussed Eastern Partnership in 2009 also indicates the will of the EU to upgrade relations with Georgia, but as has become obvious over the previous years, the EU still has no common strategy regarding Georgia.

8.6 Estonian –Georgian relations

While the EU could not reach a consensus regarding its position in the Georgian-Russian conflict, Estonia openly expressed its solidarity with Georgia. The joint declaration by Estonia, Latvia, Lithuania and Poland issued on 9 August 2008 is one of such expressions of support in which the presidents of the abovementioned countries urged that "The EU and NATO must take the initiative and stand-up against the spread of imperialist and revisionist policy in the East of Europe" (Estonia 2008). An active role of the EU in conflict solving was stressed by the Estonian president Toomas Hendrik Ilves in a telephone conversation with Javier Solana: "War has broken out in Europe, a European nation has fallen

[6] See http://www.eumm.eu/en/

victim to the aggression of its neighbour, and the European Union, as the bearer of European values, cannot remain a helpless bystander" (Estonia 2008). On 12 August 2008, President Ilves visited Tbilisi together with other leaders of former Eastern Bloc states (Ukraine, Poland, Lithuania, and Latvia) to show their support and become acquainted with the situation on the ground. Apart from showing solidarity, Estonia additionally provided humanitarian aid during the period after the war as well as sending specialists to Georgia to give advice regarding cyber-attacks. Today, Georgia continues to receive support in relieving the problems of war. Within the framework of different projects, Estonia is building child friendly spaces; organizing vacations for refugee children in summer camps in Estonia and providing first aid and psychological assistance in the city of Gali, in Abkhazia (Estonia 2011).

Officially, a relation between Georgia and Estonia were established in 1992 and though at some level aid was provided for Georgia from the beginning of the 2000s (in 2000 to relieve famine as a result of a drought in Georgia and later to support civil society projects), active cooperation did not start until after the Rose Revolution in 2003. This was caused on the one hand by the fact that only with the coming of a new government, had Georgia once and for all announced its adherence to the Western orientation in foreign policy and had started actively seeking cooperation with countries, which were able to share their experiences and provide support for reforms. On the other hand, by that time Estonia had been rather successful in rebuilding a democratic state and society and was very close to EU membership, which enabled it to share its experience and knowledge with others. In other words, by that time from aid receiver Estonia had turned into an aid provider. According to the Estonian Development Cooperation Strategy for 2006-2010, Georgia was one of the four priority partner countries for Estonia and Georgia is once more listed among priority partner countries in the "Strategy of Estonian Development Cooperation and Humanitarian Aid 2011-2015" (Estonia 2011).

Since 2003 an active and consistent cooperation developed between the countries and there are no signs so far of that relationship changing. Although Estonia provides assistance to Georgia in various fields (for instance: economic development, environmental sustainability), the main fields of cooperation are education, good governance and democracy building (Estonia 2011).

As a concrete example of the kind of assistance Estonia offers to Georgia, first the area of educational support will be mentioned. Estonia played an important role and is still very active in helping the Georgian government to successfully carry out reforms in the education system. The first steps in order to change the education system which was rooted in the Soviet legacy (aimed to be used in a different era with a different ideology) were made in 1995, but due to their irregular character, they were not effective. In 1999, by bringing to life the "Education System Realignment and Strengthening Program Project for Georgia" (World Bank 1999) financed by the World Bank, some useful changes were made. However, reforms continued with greater commitment after 2003.

According to the studies held during the first years of reforms, more than 80% of students hired private tutors (as passing entrance exams relying only on the knowledge provided by schools was very difficult) during the final phase of study. The research made it obvious that knowledge provided by schools was not of a sufficient quality and thus the situation created serious social inequality (The International Institute for Education Policy, Planning and Management 2007).[7] The main aim of the reforms was to create a high quality educational system, which could provide pupils/students with the knowledge and skills necessary in the modern world and to ensure the availability of education for all. To ensure this, a number of reforms were made, but since the sphere of our interest is limited to Estonia-Georgia relations, the part of the reforms where Estonia played a significant role will be touched upon–the project known as the "Deer Leap".

The Deer Leap is a school computerization programme elaborated on the basis of a similar project in Estonia known as the Tiger Leap.[8] An idea to equip all Estonian schools with computers was officially announced by Estonian President Lennart Meri in 1996. The programme was launched in 1997 after the necessary funds were raised and accomplished its aims in 2000. After the successful accomplishment moving to the next stage of the program–providing IT competency to all teachers and students–became possible. Slowly the aims broadened and the programme focused on e-learning and the development of various e-learning related content services. As the project launched by Georgian ministers was created relying on the Estonian model and in cooperation with Estonian

---

[7] The scale of private tutoring does not depend only on the poor quality of general school education. According to the studies provided by the International Institute for Education Policy, Planning and Management such factors as strict and high demands for entrance exams in to universities, low teachers' salaries, low confidence in school education in general also are of crucial importance.

[8] Symbolizing the designed radical changes and technological leap the programme was named Tiger Leap as an allusion to the "East Asian Tigers", the countries whose economy boomed, in part as a result of information technology use. See also http://www.tiigrihype.ee/?op=body&id=45

specialists, it was possible to establish its goals clearly and consistently. Starting in 2005 the programme is being carried out in several stages. The aim of the programme is to promote the modernization of Georgia's education system. Launched initially for four years, the programme was supposed to end in 2009 and aimed to ensure availability of computers and internet access for every school, create educational computer programmes and related services, as well as to provide teachers and students with sufficient knowledge in the ICT field. As the programme was assessed as successful by experts, the second stage was launched introducing additional goals such as access to computers and the internet to every pupil; ICT skills for all pupils, teachers and principals; collaboration between schools; digitally enriched learning environments with the integration of ICT into the curriculum. The Georgian Prime Minister once again stressed the role Estonia plays in improving education standards during a 2012 meeting with the President of the Estonian Parliament (Riigikogu) by expressing the hope that close cooperation in this field would continue (Georgia 2012).

Apart from that project, the Estonian government also provides MA scholarships for students from Georgia at Estonian universities, as well as offering places to young Georgian diplomats and civil servants at the Estonian School of Diplomacy. The latter also arranges training and seminars on EU and NATO matters, to support Georgia's integration processes. At the beginning of 2011, Estonia took the task of development cooperation to the next level, by establishing the Estonian Centre of Eastern Partnership (ECEAP). It was launched in cooperation with the Ministry of Foreign Affairs and the Estonian School of Diplomacy. What is more, the work is not conducted simply in theoretical ways; for instance in June 2012 a seminar on effective management of the EU assistance to Eastern Partnership countries was held in Tbilisi (Estonian Center of Eastern Partnership 2012). Estonia regards the educational work of the organisation especially important, since it considers Georgia as a priority economic partner to have an even closer cooperation with within the near future and education is an area of specific attention.

As this brief example may highlight, a concrete element of the success of Estonia such as the introduction of modern information and communication technologies in education and other measures to reform and modernise the education system at all levels and getting rid of the Soviet legacy, is the kind of practical assistance that a country like Estonia is well placed to offer Georgia and Georgia has been able to assume quite successfully. Estonia possesses not just the experience of how to leave the Soviet legacy behind, but more importantly, has an educational system that in an international comparison and not just among post-Soviet states is very good and well regarded.

Estonia has also assisted in many spheres outside that of education. For example, the previous Estonian Prime Minister Mr. Mart Laar worked via the United Nations Development Programme (UNDP) as an adviser to the Georgian president in economic matters, especially on issues of taxation. It is telling of the above-mentioned perception of spheres of interest that Russia objected to this nomination (Lucas 2008: 179).

Estonia has proclaimed that it supports Georgia's integration with the EU and possible NATO membership. The Estonian Minister of Foreign Affairs has confirmed plans to change the cooperation between Estonia and Georgia into a more organized structure, to determine priorities in different spheres and to lay down long-term objectives (Estonia 2012). The Ministry has moreover emphasized that the desire for collaboration indeed is twofold, since if on the one side, Georgia seeks Estonia's expertise and experiences in free trade and agricultural spheres; then on the other side, Estonia is interested in marketing and selling Estonian goods in the Georgian market, developing transit-related cooperation as well as providing services and know-how. Estonian entrepreneurs are interested in investments in the Georgian market, such as buying real estate or marketing Georgian wine in Estonia (Estonia 2012). Therefore, in order for the business relations and collaboration to be effective and prosperous, Estonia is interested in Georgia's integration with the EU, to ensure democracy building and a steady economy as a basis of strong trade relations.

8.7 Conclusion

Estonia and Georgia provide examples of two quite different roads taken by post-Soviet states, but roads that in some ways have converged on similar goals. Still, the timing of steps taken to reform the countries and the consistency of such reforms have meant that now Estonia is in a position to assist its partner and such assistance has in many ways proven to be more consistent and effective than that of European and Euro-Atlantic organisations in general.

Estonia has been considered as not only a partner and a close friend, but also a strong supporter of reforms undertaken in Georgia (Georgia 2007). The country has become very important for Estonian foreign policy and the increasing number of activities with the cooperation between the countries proves this. Furthermore, the fact that cooperation with Georgia has been so far much closer than those with the other two countries in

South Caucasus, namely Armenia and Azerbaijan, shows that Estonia chooses a reformer over just poor countries. Despite an unfavourable context, Georgia stays adherent to Westernization. At this point it means basing foreign policy on long-term objectives and planning and focusing on cooperation issues rather than aiming at membership of specific bodies. Estonia, which is interested in closing the gap between the West and other post-Soviet states (Galbreath, Lamoreaux 2006: 98), and thus acquiring more allies in the enlarged Europe, continues its cooperation with Georgia. Although membership of Georgia in Euro-Atlantic institutions seems to lie in a very distant future, by sharing its experience in fields in which it succeeded and by reminding the EU and NATO about the importance of Eastern partners, Estonia may turn into a bridge to Europe for Georgia. Support from Estonia can also play a role in keeping Georgia on the path to Westernization, not least through its influence on public opinion and efforts in the sphere of education. It is not possible to reliably predict how such influences would survive a changed political situation in Georgia, but they do have an effect on the expectations of people in making political choices and what they expect from the governing structures.

Today, the concept of post-Soviet countries does not make sense anymore. Some successful examples, such as Estonia, have proven that being a post-Soviet country does not prevent blooming of the economy; Estonia has fulfilled the EU criteria of becoming a member, is a member of the Eurozone, belongs to NATO and is perfectly capable of taking care of its own economic affairs. Nevertheless, international opinion including at the highest level among the states of "Old Europe" and other groups of countries together based this only on a shared history. Due to this, the post-Soviets are striving for closer cooperation with each other in order to lose the negative connotations of being Eastern European countries that are too fragile in the economic sense to be in collaboration with. Two decades have passed since the collapse of the Soviet Union: it should now be high time to accept that those countries that have gained independence and proven to have thriving economies are worthy of being regarded as full members of the European family and indeed instrumental in assisting those yet not quite as far on the road to "Westernization".

PART III

FROM EASTERN PARTNERSHIP TO THE ASSOCIATION IN THE LIGHT OF LEGAL APPROXIMATION, HUMAN RIGHTS AND THE RULE OF LAW

CHAPTER NINE

THE IDEA AND RULE OF LAW AS THE FOUNDATION OF THE EU ACQUIS

PETER-CHRISTIAN MŰLLER -GRAFF

The rule of law is the essential cornerstone of the legal acquis of the European Union. It includes three general dimensions (A) and it implies three specific dimensions in the domestic order of the Member States of the Union (B).

9.1 The Three General Dimensions of the Idea and Rule of Law in the European Union.

The idea and rule of law which brought to existence the former three European Communities as the historical forerunners of the European Union and which is supposed to guarantee and govern the functioning of the European Union extends into three general dimensions: the trans-national dimension between the Member States (I), the internal dimension of the European Union (II) and the domestic dimension of every Member State (III).

9.1 A The Trans-national Dimension of the Rule of Law

The trans-national dimension of the idea and rule of law is the formally binding foundation and lifeline of the acquis of European Union law and the Union itself. This is due to the fact that the Union is based on voluntarily concluded treaties between 28 sovereign states in 24 authentic legal languages, from which Dutch, French, German and Italian are the original languages of the former European Economic Community. The Union is a historically unique project. It can be assumed that the Union can function only as long and in so far as the Member States voluntarily respect and fulfil the obligations that they mutually incurred in the treaties.

It is true that due to their trans-national character these obligations cannot be enforced in the same way as national law in a state. However, other mechanisms are in place which generate an astoundingly high degree of compliance and enforcement.

Already the first President of the European Economic Community, Walter Hallstein, a former German professor of private law and economic law, called the European Economic Community a "community of law" ("Rechtsgemeinschaft"). This well observed character of the supranational organisation implies on the other side an obvious risk. If Member States do not comply with their obligations, the "Rechtsgemeinschaft" is endangered–and with it the European Union altogether. In the regular and normal course of the Union approved legal mechanisms cope fairly with violations of Union law and the non-fulfilment of obligations. However, if the non-compliance of a Member State concerns a main obligation such as the obligation to avoid excessive government deficits very serious problems and challenges can arise concerning the integrity of the Union as shown by the experiences with the budget failures of some members of the Monetary Union since 2010. Hence the loyalty to the obligations incurred with the ratification of the treaties is a matter of essential necessity which is nevertheless explicitly spelled out in the Treaties with the words that "the Member States shall take any appropriate measure, general or particular, to ensure the fulfilment of the obligations arising out of the Treaties or resulting from the acts of the institutions of the Union."

9.1.B The Internal Dimension of the Idea and Rule of Law

The internal dimension of the rule of law within the European Union concerns its inner structure and functioning. In this respect the acquis of primary law is composed of three legal core elements: the principle of conferral, the existence and the general task of the Court of Justice of the European Union and the rule of law as a constitutional value of the European Union.

a) The Principle of Conferral.

First: Since the European Union is based on Treaties all its measures have to comply with the principle of conferral as defined by the Treaty on European Union with the words: "Under the principle of conferral, the Union shall act only within the limits of the competences conferred upon it by the Member States in the Treaties to attain the objectives set out therein." This principle implies not only the legal framing and confining of the subject matters in which the Union can act (in particular: the internal market; the monetary union; the area of freedom, security and justice; the common external action). The principle also obliges the institutions of the Union to use only the procedures and instruments provided by the Treaties (e.g. the ordinary legislative procedure; the instruments of regulations, directives or decisions).

b) The Existence and the General Task of the Court of Justice of the European Union.

A second legal anchor of the primary law acquis of the idea and rule of law is based on the existence and the general task of the Court of Justice of the European Union (CJEU). It was a brilliant innovation of the six founding states of the former ECSC to set up a mandatory dispute resolution mechanism by establishing the jurisdiction of this independent trans-national institution.

Today the relevant basic provision in the Treaties provides that the CJEU "shall ensure that in the interpretation and application of the Treaties the law is observed." This raises the question of how the law has to be defined in this specific context of an international treaty and its implementation by secondary measures. Since the Treaties do not establish a complete codified legal order the law as mentioned in the basic task of the CJEU must not be understood as only referring to the explicit provisions of primary and secondary law, but also as implying the general principles of law as conceived, identified, formulated and articulated by the CJEU itself in accordance with the legal principles which are common to the Member States such as–in the past-the protection of fundamental rights, the principle of proportionality or the protection of legitimate expectations in administrative law. The formulation of the task of the CJEU also implies that the observation of the law is a task of all institutions of the Union ("on the interpretation and application"). This obligation is accompanied by several practical devices in the Treaties in order to make it effective. If a measure taken by an institution of the Union contradicts primary law or the general principles of law the CJEU can declare the act concerned (regulation, directive, decision) to be void. This is not only a hypothetical possibility, but is practiced by the CJEU. In this respect a spectacular case concerned the first tobacco advertisement directive that was adopted by the European Parliament and the Council although the Community held no competence for harmonising the laws of the Member States in the area of health policy.

c) The Rule of Law as a Constitutive Value of the European Union

The third anchor of the rule of law in the inner legal structure of the European Union is placed right at the beginning of the Treaty on European Union in two of its head provisions. The first one says "the Union´s aim is to promote peace, its values and the well-being of its people." The other one answers the question of how the values are substantially composed. It reads "the Union is founded on the values of respect of human dignity, freedom, democracy, equality, the rule of law and respect for human rights." Here we encounter the explicit expression "rule of law" (in German "Rechtsstaatlichkeit" which corresponds to the fundamental principle embodied in Articles 20 and 23 of the Basic Law–"Grundgesetz" of Germany). As a consequence of the external relations of the Union the provision on the Union's neighbourhood policy includes this requirement when prescribing that "the Union shall develop a special relationship with neighbouring countries, aiming to establish an area of prosperity and good neighbourliness, founded on the values of the Union."

9.1.C The Domestic Dimension of the Rule of Law in Every Member State

In the general dimensions of the idea and rule of law in the legal acquis of the European Union we find as a third feature of it the primary law requirement that the domestic structure of every Member State respects the rule of law. This is unfolded in three directions: in the direction of a mandatory obligation, in the direction of a requirement for applying for membership and in the direction of a special enforcement procedure.

a) The Rule of Law as a Binding Value Common to the Member States

The requirement of every Member State's respect for the "rule of law" also anchors in the relevant Article of the TEU on values. While its first sentence lists the quoted six basic values of the Union (among them the "rule of law") the second sentence transforms the values into requirements for every Member State by saying that "these values are common to the Member States …" It might be possible to argue that this wording is a pure description without any normative character and hence without any obligation for the Member States. However, such an understanding would take a rather idealistic view, since the attainment of these values is never guaranteed by itself. Therefore Article 2 TEU is properly understood as to establish the permanent obligation of Member States to realise the rule of law in their domestic order.

b) Respect for the Rule of Law as a Requirement of the Application for Membership

The understanding of Article 2 TEU as an obligation of the Member States is supported by the Treaty's provision of accession. Article 49 TEU provides that any European State "which respects the values referred to in Article 2 and is committed to promoting them may apply to become a member of the Union". It is noteworthy that the text provides that this requirement has already to be fulfilled at the time at which the application for membership is lodged. It certainly would be paradoxical if this requirement for a State would vanish in the moment in which this State becomes a member of the Union.

c) Enforcement Procedures

The perception of Article 2 TEU as an obligation of the Member States is confirmed by the specific device that Member States can be supervised in this respect and, in case, a Member State can even be sanctioned by the Union if it does not respect these values. To these ends specific procedures exist: a pre-warning system and a repressive system. A pre-warning can be given by the Council (acting by a majority of four fifths of its members) determining "that there is a clear risk of a serious breach by a Member State of the values" (Article 7 par. 1 TEU). If this warning fails its objective, the European Council "may determine the existence of a serious and persistent breach by a Member State of the values referred to in Article 2" and, as a consequence, the Council "may decide to suspend certain of the rights" deriving from Union law to the Member State in question."

9.2 The Three Specific Dimensions of the Rule of Law in the Domestic Order of the Member States of the European Union.

The fixation of the rule of law as a condition for applying for membership and accession to the Union and as an obligation of full membership is only a general point of orientation. The primary law of the Union does not specify its content in detail. Rainer Arnold has shown in a comparative study that the Western European doctrine has not elaborated a uniform understanding of the rule of law in the different national social, economic and political orders. It is true that, e.g. in the German legal doctrine a substantive understanding prevails over a formal one, while this relation is differently balanced in other legal orders. But it is also true that a common core of several single elements can be identified, although systematisations and the main accent vary. In some national orders the separation of powers is emphasized, in others the legality of public and, in particular, administrative conduct is accentuated. Such results which derive from comparison contain clues for the content of the term and concept in Union law as laid down in Article 2 TEU, but do not determine them, since Union law has to be interpreted autonomously in order to give it the authority of neutrality. However, in Union law we encounter the relative uncertainty of a "frame concept" (Rahmenbegriff) that has to be interpreted and understood in relation to the specific objectives and characteristics of the Union as a trans-national polity. Here I propose to distinguish three specific dimensions: the horizontal dimension (A), the vertical dimension (B) and the structural dimension (C).

9.2.A The Horizontal Dimension of the Rule of Law

The horizontal dimension of the rule of law is the very basis of any legal order. It is the legal structuralisation of the free exchange and interchange of individuals among themselves. Using the collective public authority of the State can enforce their agreements. Within the framework of mandatory laws their relations can be governed by rules of commutative reasonableness provided by the legislator as far as the parties do not agree otherwise. Mirrored in terms of law the horizontal dimension is synonymous to private agreements and private law. These can be understood as the basis of any living rule of law, since in reasonable and generally accepted rules for solving interest conflicts between individuals the value of law is experienced, understood and appreciated in daily life, e.g. in issues where an offeror is bound by his offer or which general terms of an agreement which have been unilaterally drafted by one party are binding on the other in a contract or by which damage of a person has to be compensated by an other. One can presume that the consented authority of private law rules in a society is the fertile soil for understanding the positive function of legally enforceable norms (in the sense of rules enforced by the legitimate collective public authorities of a democratic state). In other words: if rules of private law do not enjoy social authority in daily conduct it can hardly be expected that any legal provision will enjoy authority, perhaps except the very essential rules of criminal law.

9.2.B The Vertical Dimension of the Rule of Law

The most widely quoted aspect is the vertical dimension of the concept of the rule of law. It concerns the relationship between the collective public power with its legitimate enforcement potential on the one side and its addressees on the other side (in particular: individuals, undertakings, private Associations, but also single public bodies). Here we encounter the classical substantive legal principles for controlling, reviewing and limiting the far reaching potential of public means and instruments in order to prevent or sanction their arbitrary, disproportionate or otherwise illegitimate use. In this respect a comparative view over the legal orders of the member states produces common ground in principles, although not in detail and terminology. This is in particular true for (1.) the principle of the legality of the actions of public administration (headwords: legally conferred competence; compliance with procedural rules; compatibility of the content of administrative measures with statutes and other binding law); (2.) the classical principles of administrative law in order to protect individual freedom against infringements (headwords: principle of legal certainty and the protection of legitimate expectations–Vertrauensschutz); and (3.) the pivotal requirement that any public measure is compatible with the standards of human rights (in particular: respect for human dignity and all relevant fundamental rights; proportionality between the objective and the effect of a concrete measure which restricts the leeway of individuals).

9.2.C The Structural Dimension of the Rule of Law

The structural dimension of the rule of law serves the horizontal and vertical dimensions by making them effective in reality. Here the classical concept of the division of public power is located, which, in the tripartite definition of Montesquieu, distinguishes between the powers of legislature, administration/execution and jurisdiction. This idea of division of powers is an essential condition for the existence of a free polity. It stands contrary to any ambition to concentrate all or most public power functions in an omnipotent authority. One basic element of the structural dimension of the rule of law is the guarantee of the effective legal protection of individuals, undertakings, private Associations and single public bodies by independent courts. Independent courts also require independent judges. Effective legal protection by courts contains in particular three elements: the institutional and individual independence and impartiality of professional judges, the "access to justice" and the authority and effective enforcement of judgements.

a) Institutional and Individual Independence and Impartiality of Professional Judges

The very first and pivotal element of effective legal protection by courts and, by that, for a living rule of law in a State is to be seen in the institutional and individual independence of professional judges who are sufficiently qualified for this intellectually, professionally and morally most demanding task and who realise the ethics of impartiality. Still, even shortly before the accession of new States to the Union in 2004 and 2007 the European Commission reported difficulties in this respect in some of the (then) candidate and "transformation" States under the heading of "judicial capacity". While this situation seems to have widely improved since then, in 2013 the Commission took an initiative towards achieving more positive equivalence of the judiciary systems in the Member States.

b) "Access to Justice"

A second element of effective legal protection is the "access to justice" in the sense of guaranteed access to courts that is not barred by factual hindrances. This objective requires of the horizontal and vertical dimension alike sufficient capacities of the courts to deal with actions, requests and complaints in a reasonable time on the one side and the abolition of financial and technical barriers to initiatives to pursue a judicial procedure on the other side. Moreover, for the vertical dimension the existence of a functioning independent jurisdiction with the competence of controlling and, in case, nullifying administrative measures is indispensable. In addition the establishment of an adequate mechanism of judicial review of the constitutionality of legislative acts within a pending judicial procedure ("konkrete Normenkontrolle") is a good standard of the rule of law in an advanced social system.

c) Authority and Effective Enforcement of Judgements

The rule of law also encloses the requirement of authority and effective enforcement of judicial decisions. Such a situation is functionally closely linked to a general social acceptance and appreciation of judicial decisions. In the tradition of Immanuel Kant the latter can be considered to mirror an essential element of an enlightened society and polity. The experience in Central and Eastern European States after 1989 shows that this social foundation of the rule of law is a specific great challenge in polities which transform from dictatorships into free societies. However, a living rule of law evidently needs the consciousness and conviction of the members of the respective society for the civilising and pacifying potential of the role of legal rules. The bottom line is the concept that: The rule of law is us. Hence, the authority of law lives in the respect of law. This has a pre-condition of not only a general understanding and acceptance of the basic abstract distinction between "right" and "wrong" and not only an instinctive perception of the mutual conditionality of individual freedom and social community. It also demands a basic respect for legal rules, courts and, by that, for judges as autonomous authorities in a polity within the law. Here we arrive at the very foundation of the rule of law in the legal acquis of the European Union. The connection between every national court and the Court of Justice of the European Union in issues of Union law by way of the preliminary reference procedure becomes the more effective reality the more this basic respect is a reality. The functioning and success of the European Union as a trans-national community of law essentially depends upon this appreciation, which, on the other side, burdens all professional protagonists of normative conceptions, legislative creations and administrative and judicial applications of Union law with the great responsibility for permanent reasonableness. Hence scholars, legislators, administrators and judges are foremost responsible for creating and supporting this respect–in the common interest of the desired high standards of societal civilisation in Europe.

CHAPTER TEN

NEW CONCEPTION OF PROTECTION OF FUNDAMENTAL RIGHTS IN EUROPEAN UNION

DAVID PETRLÍK

As the original founding Treaties did not contain any provision guaranteeing the protection of fundamental rights in the then European Communities, the European Court of justice[1] protected these rights, for almost 40 years, according to a self-created conception. The main characteristic of the latter was that it was based on a unique unwritten formal source of fundamental rights, i.e. general principles of law. The Court of Justice began protecting fundamental rights under those general principles of law in the 1970s[2] and its conception of protection was validated in the Treaty of Maastricht, and more specifically in the former Article 6(2) TEU, under which the Union was obliged to respect fundamental rights, as guaranteed by the European Convention for the Protection of Human Rights and Fundamental Freedoms ("ECHR") and as they resulted from the constitutional traditions common to the Member States, "as general principles of Community law".

The Treaty of Lisbon changed this conception as it created a regime of triple protection of fundamental rights in the Union. Firstly, Article 6(1) TEU proclaims that the Union recognises the rights, freedoms and principles set out in the Charter of Fundamental Rights of the European Union ("Charter") which has the same legal value as the Treaties.[3]

[1] "Court of Justice" or "ECJ".

[2] See Cases 11/70 *Internationale Handelsgesellschaft* [1970] ECR 1125 and 4/73 *Nold v Commission* [1974] ECR 491.

[3] The Charter was already adopted on 7 December 2000 but, until the Treaty of Lisbon, it was a non-binding document which served only as a material source of fundamental rights, and not as a formal one. However, despite its non-binding

Secondly, under Article 6(2) TEU, the Union is bound to accede to the ECHR and this Convention will therefore become an integral part of the Union legal order. Thirdly, Article 6(3) TEU reaffirms that fundamental rights, as guaranteed by the ECHR and as they result from the constitutional traditions common to the Member States, continue to exist in the Union legal order as unwritten general principles of Union law.

This new conception of protection of fundamental rights, based on the co-existence of several formal sources of law, has given rise to three main consequences. First of all, the Charter has become a central instrument of protection of fundamental rights in the Union legal order (I). At the same time, the Court of Justice has lost a part of its discretionary power in this field (II). Finally, the level of protection of fundamental rights has been increased (III).

10.1 Centrality of the Charter

From a formal point of view, all three sources of fundamental rights mentioned in Article 6 TEU (Charter, ECHR and general principles of law) are independent, parallel and they have a similar binding force. However, having regard to the structure of this provision, the explicitly recognised legal value of the Charter and its detailed catalogue of rights, the authors of the Treaties have made clear that the Charter shall become the main and preferred source of fundamental rights in the Union legal order. The Court of Justice has respected this will and it has been, in particular, gradually ceasing to refer to general principles of law. Thus, when possible, the Court of justice started replacing the analysis based on general principles of law by the one based on the Charter and the latter is thus replacing, step-by-step, the general principles in its case-law. Furthermore, the Court of Justice prefers to refer to the Charter instead of the ECHR, even in cases in which referring courts or applicants base their arguments on provisions of the ECHR. In some cases, the Court of Justice preferred however to complete the provisions of the Charter by references to the provisions of the ECHR.[4]

---

nature, the Court of Justice applied the Charter before the Treaty of Lisbon (see Case C-540/03 *Parliament v Council* [2006] ECR I-5769), although with a certain caution. The Charter was adapted in Strasbourg on 12 December 2007.

[4] See Cases C-163/10 *Patriciello* [2011] ECR I-7565, paragraph 31; C-391/09 *Runevič-Vardyn and Wardyn* [2011] ECR I-3787, paragraph 66; C-208/09 *Sayn-Wittgenstein* [2010] ECR I-13693, paragraph 52 and C-145/09 *Tsakouridis* [2010] ECR I- 11979, paragraph 52.

The Court of Justice clearly demonstrated this attitude in Volker und Markus Schecke in which the national court referred essentially to the ECHR when it demanded a review of the validity of certain provisions of EU Regulations. Instead of analysing the validity in light of the ECHR, the ECJ stressed that the Charter shall have the same legal value as the Treaties and it deduced from it that the validity of these provisions had be assessed in light of provisions of the Charter.[5] Similarly, in Chalkor and in Otis, the Court of Justice held concerning arguments based both on Charter and the ECHR, that Article 47 of the Charter secures in EU law the protection afforded by Article 6(1) of the ECHR and that "it is necessary, therefore, to refer only to Article 47".[6]

By these statements, the ECJ has introduced a sort of hierarchy between the Charter, on the one hand, and the ECHR and the general principles of law on the other hand. This hierarchy is not a "value" hierarchy in the sense that the Charter would have, in general, a higher legal value that the latter. In this respect, it would be difficult to argue that the Charter has a higher legal value than the ECHR given Article 52(3) of the Charter, according to which "in so far as [the latter] contains rights which correspond to rights guaranteed by the [ECHR], the meaning and scope of those rights shall be the same as those laid down by the said Convention", unless the Charter recognises a more extensive protection. Hierarchy introduced by the Court of Justice is rather a "scope" hierarchy. It means that the Charter is, from now on, the principal source of reference for fundamental rights in the Union legal order. It constitutes, therefore, a cornerstone and a starting point for every legal analysis in this domain, the ECHR and the general principles of law serving solely to clarify the meaning of its provisions and to fill its gaps. As a result, the ECJ will continue to reformulate pleas of applicants in direct actions and references for a preliminary ruling, which refer to the ECHR and the general principles of law.[7]

---

[5] Joined Cases C-92/09 and C-93/09 *Volker und Markus Schecke and Eifert* [2010] ECR I-11063, paragraphs 44 to 46.

[6] Case C-386/10 P *Chalkor v Commission* [2011] ECR I-0000, paragraph 51 and Case C-199/11 *Otis and Others* [2012] ECR I-0000, paragraph 47. Italics added.

[7] See recently Case C-396/11 *Radu* [2013] ECR I-0000, paragraph 32.

10.2 Reduction of margin of disretion of the Court of Justice

The Court of Justice has traditionally enjoyed an important margin of discretion concerning the scope and content of fundamental rights in the Union legal order. The new conception of protection of these rights has reduced this margin of discretion as it changed the philosophy of judicial review and it strengthened the position of the ECHR legal system and, in particular, of the European Court of Human Rights ("ECtHR").

10.2.A Positivist approach

Before the Treaty of Lisbon, the judicial review in the domain of fundamental rights was based on a conception of natural law. Following this conception, the Union courts "discovered" fundamental rights in an unwritten source of law and they had therefore some margin of appreciation in finding and interpreting these rights. This liberty was only partially framed by the ECHR and constitutional traditions common to the Member States that had to be taken into account in the interpretation of these rights.

After the Treaty of Lisbon, the conception of fundamental rights is rather positivist in nature given that they are set out, above all, in two written sources of law, the Charter and the ECHR, which contain detailed catalogues of rights and liberties. Such a nature of fundamental rights limits the freedom of action of the ECJ as it would now be difficult for the Court of Justice to proclaim a fundamental right as a general principle of law if this right is not mentioned in the Charter. The absence of intent on the part of the authors of the Treaties to provide for such a right–despite the comprehensive catalogue of rights in the Charter–is in fact a serious argument for the non-existence of any such right in the Union legal order. Conversely, if the Charter protects a right that is an important indication for the Court of Justice that this right exists also as a general principle of law.[8]

---

[8] Concerning the right to take collective action, including the right to strike, see Case C-438/05 *International Transport Workers' Federation and Finnish Seamen's Union, 'Viking Line'* [2007] ECR I-10779, paragraphs 43 and 44, and Case C-341/05 *Laval un Partneri* [2007] ECR I-11767, paragraphs 90 and 91; regarding the principle of non-discrimination on grounds of age, see Case C-555/07 *Kücükdeveci* [2010] ECR I-365, paragraphs 21 and 22.

This does not mean that the EU system of protection of fundamental rights has become completely rigid and that it does not preserve dynamic features any more. As difficult as it may be, the co-existence of the general principles of law guarantees the Court of Justice the possibility, at least a theoretical one, to recognise additional rights which are not listed in the Charter.[9] In practice, the ECJ will however prefer, when possible, to recognise them as derivative rights of written rights set out in the Charter, rather than to proclaim them as completely autonomous rights in the form of general principles of law.

The positive nature of fundamental rights reduces, moreover, the margin of discretion of the Court of Justice in interpreting the scope and content of fundamental rights, as it is formally obliged to respect the wording of the Charter, the ECHR, the Explanations relating to the Charter,[10] the case-law of the ECtHR[11] and national constitutional rules.[12] It is true that the ECJ used these sources even before the Treaty of Lisbon (except for the Explanations). However, it used them only as a source of inspiration in the process of determining the scope and content of fundamental rights. It was not bound by them and it enjoyed, therefore, a broader margin of discretion.

In this context, it is worth noting that the Court of Justice has not only started applying the Charter as the main formal source of the fundamental right but, at the same time, it applied it in light of the other above-

---

[9] For a discussion on this point, see S. Iglesias Sánchez, The Court and the Charter: The impact of the entry into force of the Lisbon Treaty on the ECJ's approach to fundamental rights, Common market law review, 49, 2012, p. 1597 and L. F. M. Besselink, The Protection of Fundamental Rights post-Lisbon. The Interaction between the EU Charter of Fundamental Rights, the European Convention on Human Rights and national Constitutions, FIDE Congress 2012, available at www. fide2012.eu, p. 13.

[10] Explanations drawn up under the authority of the Praesidium of the Convention, which drafted the Charter, and updated under the responsibility of the Praesidium of the European Convention (OJ 2007 C 303, p. 17) ("Explanations"). Pursuant to Article 52(7) of the Charter, these explanations shall be given due regard by the courts of the Union.

[11] Union courts are de facto bound by the case-law of the ECtHR by virtue of Article 52(3) of the Charter (see *infra*).

[12] The Treaty of Lisbon has confirmed the binding force of these constitutional traditions because the rights of the Charter must be interpreted "in harmony with those traditions" when the Charter recognises the same fundamental rights as these traditions (Article 52[4] of the Charter). Before the Treaty of Lisbon, the Treaties did not contain such an explicit obligation, Article 6(2) TEU being in particular more vague in this respect.

mentioned sources. Besides the case-law of the ECtHR (see *infra*),[13] the Court of Justice applied in particular the Explanations as they contained clarifications on the scope and content of fundamental rights.[14]

10.2.B Strengthened position of the ECHR legal system

As before the Treaty of Lisbon, the ECHR remains a material source of fundamental rights as expressed in the form of general principles of law, because Article 6(3) TEU states that "[f]undamental rights, as guaranteed by the [ECHR], shall constitute general principles of the Union's law". However, this treaty has also increased the binding force of the ECHR and strengthened the position of the whole ECHR legal system in the Union legal order.

Firstly, EU courts have become formally bound both by the provisions of the ECHR and by the case-law of the ECtHR by virtue of Article 52(3) of the Charter which requires that the meaning and scope of fundamental rights set out in it shall be the same as those laid down by the ECHR, unless the Court of Justice recognises a more extensive protection.

In this regard, it must be recalled that, already previously to the Treaty of Lisbon, the Court of Justice respected the case-law of the ECtHR. Since 1989, it stressed repeatedly that the ECHR, as interpreted in this case-law, had special significance for the interpretation of fundamental rights whose protection the ECJ ensured.[15] However, this respect was "voluntary" because no provision of the Treaties obliged the Court of Justice to comply with the requirements following from this case-law.[16] Conversely, that Article 52(3) of the Charter imposes such an obligation as its wording is in reality an euphemism for an obligation to interpret the Charter in conformity with the case-law of the ECtHR given that the latter is an

---

[13] See, for example, Case C-400/10 PPU McB. [2010] ECR I-8965, paragraphs 54 to 58 and Joined Cases C-411/10 and C-493/10 N.S. and Others [2011] ECR I-0000, paragraphs 88 to 90.

[14] See, for instance, Case C-279/09 *DEB* [2010] ECR I-13849, paragraphs 32 and 39, Case C-426/11 *Mark Alemo-Herron and Others* [2013] ECR I-0000, paragraph 32, Case C-233/12 *Gardella* [2013] ECR I-0000, paragraph 39. See also the case-law of the Civil Servants Tribunal: Case F-103/06 REV *Saintraint v Commission*, paragraph 53.

[15] Joined Cases 46/87 and 227/88 *Hoechst v Commission* [1989] ECR 2859, paragraph 13 and Case C-260/89 *ERT* [1991] ECR I-2925, paragraph 41.

[16] In this respect, the only relevant provision was former Article 6(2) TEU which was, however, too vague concerning the binding force of the case-law of the ECtHR.

authority competent for determining the "meaning and scope of fundamental rights guaranteed by the [ECHR]" in the sense of this provision.

Secondly and more significantly, the Union is obliged to accede to the ECHR according to Article 6(2) TEU. Negotiations on the Agreement on Accession began in June 2010 between the Member States of the Council of Europe and the EU. In April 2013, negotiators finalised the agreement. In July 2013, the Commission made a request to the Court of Justice for an Opinion pursuant to Article 218(11) TFEU, in which the Court of Justice will hold whether the said Agreement is compatible with provisions of the Treaties (Opinion 2/13). If it is compatible, Member States of the Council of Europe and the EU will ratify, accept or approve the Accession Agreement. Afterwards, the latter will enter into force that could occur around 2016.

From this moment on, judgments of the Court of Justice will be subject–for the first time in the history of European integration– o a judicial review by a different judicial body, i.e. the ECtHR. Put differently, not only will the Court of Justice be formally bound by the case-law of the latter but, moreover, enforcement of this obligation will be ensured by a system of judicial review of its judgments by the ECtHR.
This will limit the Court of Justice's role as a guardian of the sovereign and autonomous nature of the Union legal order, as this Court will no longer have the last word on the interpretation of the scope and content of fundamental rights in the EU. It will be for the ECtHR to determine to which extent the specificity of the Union legal order may justify a particular approach for the EU in this domain.

It is true that the Protocol on the Accession of the Union to the ECHR states that the Accession shall respect the specificity of the Union legal order.[17] However, the draft Accession Treaty takes into consideration the specific characteristics of the Union only with regard to procedural aspects. From the substantive point of view, it does not provide for any safeguards in respect of any specific features of the EU,[18] which is a logical consequence of the fact that the latter accedes to the ECHR, as a

---

[17] Protocol No 8 relating to Article 6(2) TEU on the accession of the Union to the ECHR, annexed to the Treaty of Lisbon.

[18] See Draft Revised Agreement on the Accession of the European Union to the Convention for the Protection of Human Rights and Fundamental Freedoms set out in Annexe I to the document of the Council of Europe 47+1(2013) 008. Available at http://www.europarl.europa.eu/meetdocs/2009_2014/documents/libe/dv/5thmeeting_finalrep_/5thmeeting_finalrep_en.pdf

matter of principle, on an equal footing with other Council of Europe Members, that is, with the same rights and obligations.[19]
In Bosphorus, the ECtHR has admittedly adopted an approach towards the EU that has taken into account specific characteristics of the Union, in particular its supranational character and the fact that it protects fundamental rights at a supranational level.[20] The question remains, however, whether this approach will be maintained after the accession to the ECHR, because the Bosphorus case-law is based on a premise that the EU is not a Contracting Party of the ECHR and it is not formally bound by this convention.[21] After its accession, this situation will change and the ECtHR may treat the EU in the same way as other Contracting Parties.

10.3 Increased level of protection of fundamental rights

10.3.A Increase of importance of fundamental rights in the case-law

The effect of incorporation of the Charter into the EU binding legal framework goes beyond the mere consolidation and clarification of fundamental rights. The Charter contributed to reinforcing the centrality of these rights in legal reasoning[22] and gave them more importance. Such incorporation was a signal to all EU institutions and formal recognition of the importance of fundamental rights in the EU legal order.

As already mentioned, the Court of Justice respected, in particular, this importance and began to regularly apply the Charter. Whereas it referred

---

[19] See also Draft Explanatory report to the Agreement on the Accession of the European Union to the Convention for the Protection of Human Rights and Fundamental Freedoms set out in Annexe V to the document of the Council of Europe cited in previous note, paragraph 7.
[20] See judgment of 30 June 2005 *Bosphorus Hava Yollari Turizmve Ticaret Anonim Şirketi v Ireland* (ECHR 2005-VI) in which the ECtHR decided in that the protection of fundamental rights by EU law can be considered to be, and to have been at the relevant time, "equivalent" to that of the ECHR system. Consequently, a presumption arises that an EU Member State does not depart from the requirements of the ECHR when it implemented legal obligations flowing from its membership of the EU. Such a presumption could be rebutted if, in a particular case, it is considered that the protection of ECHR rights is manifestly deficient (see *Bosphorus*, paragraphs 155 to 165).
[21] See *Bosphorus*, cited in previous note, paragraph 152.
[22] S. Iglesias Sánchez, The Court and the Charter: The impact of the entry into force of the Lisbon Treaty on the ECJ's approach to fundamental rights, cited above, note 12, p. 1582.

to the latter not even in 10 rulings in 2009 (although the Charter was already part of EU legal order since 2000, albeit a non-binding one[23]), the number of rulings quoting the Charter increased significantly afterwards. It reached 43 rulings in 2011 and this number doubled to 87 in 2012. Such a twofold increase of cases cannot be explained by the mere fact that more cases are in the scope of application *ratione temporis* of the legally binding Charter. It illustrates rather a general increase of the importance of fundamental rights in the ECJ's case-law and it announces also their growing importance for the future.

The same is true for applications of EU fundamental rights on a national level as national courts increased, in particular, the number of references for a preliminary ruling related to the Charter. It indicates that they tend more and more to control the compatibility of national law with the Charter and, more generally, with EU fundamental rights. Whilst there were almost no such references in 2009, this number rose to 27 in 2011 and has since reached 41, which is an increase of 65% in a year.[24] Although a notable number of these references were inadmissible, many of them were serious, the Charter playing a predominant role above all in the field of immigration and asylum.[25]

Perhaps even more significant is the fact that more and more national constitutional courts, possibly under the influence of the increased importance of fundamental rights, have begun to address references for a preliminary ruling to the Court of Justice. Four more constitutional courts did so since the adoption of the Treaty of Lisbon: the Spanish Constitutional Court in Melloni, the French Constitutional Council in Jeremy F., [26] the Italian Constitutional Court in Presidente del Consiglio dei Ministri[27] and the Lithuanian Constitutional Court in Sabatauskas.[28]

---

[23] See supra note 3.

[24] See 2012 Report on the Application of the EU Charter of Fundamental Rights, p. 22. Available at http://ec.europa.eu/justice/fundamental-rights/files/charter_report_2012_en.pdf.

[25] See General report of the Association of Councils of States and of Supreme Administrative Courts, seminar of the Hague of 24 November 2011, p. 5. Available at http://www.aca-europe.eu/en/colloquiums/colloq_en_23.html.

[26] Case C-168/13, pending.

[27] Case C-169/08 *Presidente del Consiglio dei Ministri* [2009] ECR I-10821. This case does not concern fundamental rights but it shows the readiness of the Constitutional Court to address a reference for a preliminary ruling even in this field in future.

[28] Case C-239/07 *Sabatauskas and Others* [2008] ECR I-7523. Similarly to the case cited in the previous note, this case does not concern fundamental rights, but it illustrates the general tendency of this court.

Other national constitutional courts continued to address such references, in line with their previous practice.[29]

10.3.B Bold application of a high standard of fundamental rights

Since the 2000s, the Court of Justice has had a courageous stance in the field of fundamental rights. In this regard, it is sufficient to mention the case of Kadi I, in which the Court of Justice contested the very approach of the international community concerning the treatment of persons suspected of terrorist activities. Contrary to the Court of First Instance of the EU (now the General Court), it did not accept the restrictive, albeit inexistent, regime of protection of procedural rights of these persons and it forced the Security Council of the United Nations to introduce certain procedural guarantees.[30]

Positivist methods and the above-mentioned limitations of the Court of Justice have not changed this trend and it could not have changed it. In fact, the purpose of the incorporation of a clear and written source of fundamental rights to the EU legal binding framework was to increase legitimacy of the control of respect of fundamental rights by Union institutions and by Member States. Consequently, the authors of the Treaty of Lisbon wanted the ECJ to enhance the level of protection of these rights. Similarly, the said limitations restricted the margin of appreciation of the Court of Justice in the interest of the highest possible standard of fundamental rights and they aimed therefore at increasing the level of protection of these rights. Accordingly, whereas the EU must respect the minimum standard of protection of fundamental rights as guaranteed by ECHR, Article 52(3) of the Charter stressed that it can provide a more extensive protection. Article 53 of the Charter has the same purpose when it provides that "[n]othing in this Charter shall be interpreted as restricting or adversely affecting human rights and fundamental freedoms as recognised, in their respective fields of application, by Union law and international law and by international agreements to which the Union or all the Member States are party, including the [ECHR], and by the Member States' constitutions."

---

[29] For Belgian constitutional court, see Case C-73/08 *Bressol and Others and Chaverot and Others* [2010] ECR I-2735). For Austrian constitutional court, see Case C-594/12 *Seitlinger*, pending.

[30] Joined Cases C-402/05 P and C-415/05 P *Kadi and Al Barakaat International Foundation v Council and Commission* [2008] ECR I-6351.

It can be stated that the level of protection of fundamental rights has indeed been increased. This is not necessarily a direct consequence of adoption of the Charter, but rather its indirect result. It has created a climate of an enhanced protection which influences the judges of the Court of Justice and leads applicants and national courts to rely more on fundamental rights and on the Charter. Consequently, the ECJ has set the standard of protection of fundamental rights very high and it has been ready to deliver bold judgements. This boldness results in particular from the fact that the Court of Justice did not fear to deliver unpopular judgements, i.e. judgments which were favourable for the persons whose rights are endangered, but which were unpopular not only with Union institutions or Member States, but also with the general public.

This was the case of a recent judgement Test-Achats,[31] in which the Court of Justice declared invalid Article 5(2) of Directive 2004/113 on equal treatment between men and women in the access to and supply of goods and services which provided for a derogation from the general rule of unisex premiums and benefits in the insurance services sector.[32] The ECJ ruled that, for the purposes of applying the principle of equal treatment for men and women, enshrined in Articles 21 and 23 of the Charter, the respective situations of men and women with regard to insurance premiums and benefits contracted by them were comparable. This principle of unconditional equal treatment is courageous because it applies, in particular, to the life assurance sector and requires therefore the same premiums and benefits for men and women even if it is undisputed that women have a longer life expectancy and their life assurance premiums should be accordingly less expensive. The judgment resulted in a significant increase of prices of premiums of life insurance for women and, in consequence, it was obviously very unpopular among them.

Another bold and unpopular ruling is Volker und Markus Schecke, in which the Court of Justice condemned Union Regulations that imposed an obligation to publish personal data relating to each natural person who was a beneficiary of agricultural aid. In light of the general opinion according to which these persons receive disproportionate aid from Union budget, this judgement was not very popular either.

The Court of Justice has applied the same strict and bold approach towards national measures. In this regard, the most important recent

---

[31] Case C-236/09 *Association belge des Consommateurs Test-Achats and Others* [2011] ECR I-773.

[32] Council Directive 2004/113/EC of 13 December 2004 implementing the principle of equal treatment between men and women in the access to and supply of goods and services (OJ 2004 L 373, p. 37).

judgement is N.S. The ECJ ruled in this judgment that the Member States, including the national courts, may not transfer an asylum seeker to the Member State indicated as responsible for examination of his or her application for asylum where they cannot be unaware that systemic deficiencies in the asylum procedure and in the reception conditions of asylum seekers amount to substantial grounds for believing that the asylum seeker would face a real risk of being subjected to inhuman or degrading treatment. The boldness of this judgment is however relativized by the fact that the Court of Justice has relied on the judgement M.S.S. of ECtHR and it applied it as regards the solution.[33]

A better example is the ruling of 4 June 2013 ZZ.[34] The Court of Justice admitted in the latter that when a State refuses a Union citizen from another Member State an admission to its territory on public security, above all related to his or her presumed link to terrorist activities, the right to effective judicial protection does not require precise and full disclosure of the grounds on which a decision refusing entry is based if it turns out that State security stands in the way of disclosure of these grounds. However, national authorities must ensure, to the greatest possible extent, that the adversarial principle is complied with, in order to enable the person concerned to contest the grounds on which the decision in question is based and to make submissions on the evidence relating to the decision and, therefore, to put forward an effective defence. In particular, the person concerned must be informed of the essence of the grounds on which a decision refusing entry is based, as the necessary protection of State security cannot have the effect of denying him his right to be heard and, therefore, of rendering his right of redress ineffective.

By this statement, the Court of Justice follows its case-law Kadi I and it continues to go against the flow. In fact, general public requires, in principle, more public security in the context of the fight against terrorism and it may be ready to sacrifice, in this field, even the substance of procedural guarantees of the concerned persons.[35] Conversely, the ECJ

---

[33] Judgment of 21 January 2011, *M.S.S. v Belgium and Greece*, application No 30696/09.

[34] Case C-300/11 *ZZ* [2013] not yet reported.

[35] A 2010 YouGov/Sun poll in the United Kingdom showed, for example, that the general public agrees with robust anti-terrorist powers and lacks concern for civil liberties in relation to terrorist issues. On the overarching question of whether people suspected of terrorist offenses should benefit from the full protection of human rights or not, 31% of people thought that they should, but 60% thought that some human rights should be suspended for people suspected of terrorist offenses.

attempts to strike an appropriate balance between the requirements flowing from State security and those of the fundamental rights, ensuring that even this fight guarantees some essential fundamental rights. Such an approach is bold as the judges are fully aware of the fact that it is very popular neither among the general public nor between Member States.

10.4 Conclusion

The new conception of protection of fundamental rights, which is based on several formal sources of these rights and on a central role of the Charter, has not provoked a revolution in the approach of the Court of Justice. Rather, it has resulted in an important evolution as it has strengthened features that were already present in its previous case-law. In particular, as before the Treaty of Lisbon, the Court of Justice is limited, to a certain extent, concerning the scope and content of fundamental rights because it is bound to take into account the ECHR, the case-law of the ECtHR and the constitutional traditions common to Member States. After the Treaty of Lisbon, the ECJ is however limited to a greater extent and it can be stated that it respects the limitations imposed.

Furthermore, it follows from its recent rulings that the level of protection of fundamental rights has been increased even though, before the Treaty of Lisbon, its case-law was already very human rights friendly. In light of the case-law of the ECtHR, the case N.S. may have had the same outcome. However, it is more to say if the judgements such as Volker und Markus Schecke, Test-Achats or ZZ would have had the same wording.

45% of respondents thought terrorist suspects should be able to be held for 42 days or longer without charge (http://today.yougov.co.uk/sites/today.yougov.co.uk/files/YG-Archives-Pol-ST-results-051110_0.pdf).

CHAPTER ELEVEN

QUESTIONS OF DEMOCRACY AND RULE OF LAW PROCESS AND THEIR IMPORTANCE FOR THE ASSOCIATION AND MEMBERSHIP IN THE LIGHT OF THE EXPERIENCE OF THE SLOVAK REPUBLIC

ONDŘEJ BLAŽO

11.1 Introduction

Respect of human rights, principles of democratic regime and rule of law are substantial elements in agreements within the Eastern Partnership. These elements are not mere political declarations but also legal obligations and commitments as a part of the international agreement. The example of Slovakia clearly shows the importance of such criteria as a condition sine qua non for further and deeper integration of an Eastern-Partnership country into the EU.

Despite its neighbours Slovakia was not called to open bilateral negotiations on accession to the European Union at the European Council meeting held in Luxembourg on 12 and 13 December 1997 because it did not fulfil the political and legal criteria of democracy and rule of law. This situation can be considered similar to the situation of Ukraine since the Association Agreement signature was frozen because of objections to the level of democracy and rule of law in Ukraine. The story of Slovakia can be inspiring for Ukraine since thanks to quick reforms after the parliamentary elections in 1998 it was able to successfully commence and finish negotiations on accession. This paper maps objections of the EU's institutions and bodies regarding the situation in Slovakia in the 1990s compared to those regarding Ukraine, describes their solution and analyses basic reforms that enabled Slovakia to begin accession negotiations. The bitter legal heritage of Mečiar's government in the form of controversial amnesties cannot be omitted in this context as an example of interference of executive power into the investigation and prosecution of politically sensitive infringements.

11.2 Democracy as a Legal Obligation in the European Accession Process

Although the requirement of fulfilling the criteria of a democratic regime is a political question, the Treaty on the European Union introduced this requirement as a legal prerequisite. The Treaty on the European Union (1992) stated in Article F(1) that "The Union shall respect national identities of its Member States, whose systems of governments are founded on the principles of democracy."

In the first place this provision enacted the legal obligation of the Union to respect national identities of its member states. In the second place it also referred to the system of governments of the members states founded on the principles of democracy. However, we can read the second part of the provision in two ways: (1) the Union is not obliged to respect the national identity of the member state whose system of government is not founded on the principles of democracy, or (2) a government founded on the principles of democracy is a condition of membership in the Union.

Another legal problem of this provision was that it provided neither legal definition of democracy, substantial features, nor reference to other documents.[1] Karen Henderson suggests that the rationale of this provision was due to a fear of unexpected turns from democracy to undemocratic regimes (example of Greece) or the threat of returning back to authoritarian regimes (Spain, Turkey) and the the notion of democracy was based on the Western-European understanding of it[2]. The development of the countries of Central and Eastern Europe was different. After the fall of the communist regime they started to try to establish democratic governments. It was an unprecedented movement since these countries were establishing democratic regimes after more than forty years of dictatorship and the total de-installation of democratic institutions and traditions. A definition of the consolidation of democracy given by Juan Linz and Alfred Stepan could

---

[1] E.g. Article F (2) that dealt with respect to fundamental rights referred to the European Convention for the protection of Human Rights and Fundamental Freedoms as well as to constitutional traditions of Member States,

[2] HENDERSON, K.: Slovakia and the democratic criteria of EU accession. In HENDERSON, K. (ed.): Back to Europe: Central and Eastern Europe and the European Union. London: UCL Press, 1999, p. 211.

be very useful for the explanation of this process. Juan Linz and Alfred Stepan defined three dimensions of the political development towards democracy: behavioural, attitudinal, and constitutional: *"Behaviorally*, a democratic regime in a territory is consolidated when no significant national, social, economic, political, or institutional actors spend significant resources attempting to achieve their objective by creating a non-democratic regime or turning to violence or foreign intervention to secede from the states. *Attitudinally*, a democratic regime is consolidated when a strong majority of public opinion holds the belief that democratic procedures and institutions are the most appropriate way to govern collectively life in a society such as where and when the support for anti-system alternatives is quite small or more or less isolated from the pro-democratic forces. *Constitutionally*, a democratic regime is consolidated when governmental and non-governmental forces alike, throughout the territory of the state, become subjected to, and habituated to, the resolution of conflict within the specific laws, procedures, and institutions sanctioned by the new democratic process."[3] In the further analysis it will be shown that democracy in EU member States as well as in candidate countries shall be consolidated behaviourally, attitudinally and constitutionally.

The conclusions of the Presidency of the European Council held on 21-22 June 1993 in Copenhagen explained the condition of democracy in the EU enlargement context. Implicitly it confirmed that a democratic regime is an obligation of member states when it defined democratic regime as a *conditio sine qua non* for accession to the European Union: a country shall be "able to assume the obligations of membership by satisfying the economic and political conditions required." The Copenhagen conclusions further explained that membership[4] (i.e. conditions for incumbent members and accessing members) requires (1) stability of institutions guaranteeing (a) democracy, (b) the rule of law, (c) human rights and (d) respect for and protection of minorities, (2) the existence of a functioning market economy as well as the capacity to cope with competitive pressures

---

[3] LINZ, J. J. - STEPHAN, A.: Problems of Democratic Transition and Consolidation: Southern Europe, South America, and Post-Communist Europe. JHU Press, 2011, p. 5-6.

[4] Membership requires that the candidate country has achieved stability of institutions guaranteeing democracy, the rule of law, human rights and respect for and protection of minorities, the existence of a functioning market economy as well as the capacity to cope with competitive pressure and market forces within the Union. Membership pre-supposes the candidate's ability to take on the obligations of membership including adherence to the aims of political, economic and monetary union.

and market forces within the Union. The candidate country shall be also (3) ready to follow the aims of the political, economic, and monetary union and adopt the *acquis communautaire,* the rights and obligations derived from EU treaties, laws, and regulations over the years. These three sets of criteria (political, economic and the adoption of *acquis*) became known as the Copenhagen criteria and their fulfilment was diligently checked during accession processes[5].

The requirement of a democratic regime and market economy in the case of Slovakia also became a legal obligation under Article 6 of the Europe Agreement establishing an Association between the European Communities and their Member States, on the one part, and the Slovak Republic signed on 4 October 1994 in Luxembourg (hereinafter as "Europe Agreement" or "Association Agreement"). This article refers to the democratic principles as one of the essential elements of the Association: "Respect for the democratic principles and human rights established by the Helsinki Final Act and the Charter of Paris for a new Europe, as well as the principles of market economy, inspiring the domestic and external policies of the Parties and constitute essential elements of the present Association."

Since fulfilling the democratic criteria became a legal obligation for both Member States and Associate members of the EU, putting the political regime of such a country under scrutiny cannot be deemed an illegal interference into internal affairs as prohibited by Article VI of the Helsinki Final Act of 1975. Furthermore, since the adoption of the Amsterdam Treaty the right to interfere into the political regime of a Member State has been strengthened by the right of the Council to suspend certain rights of such Member States derived from the Treaty on the European Union in case of the existence of a serious and persistent breach of principles of the Union, i.e. principles of liberty, democracy, respect of human rights and fundamental freedoms, and the rule of law; principles which are common to the Member States (later extended by the Lisbon Treaty).

---

[5] Political criteria were incorporated into the Treaty on European Union (Article F, later Article 6): The Union is founded on the principles of liberty, democracy, respect for human rights and fundamental freedoms, and the rule of law, principles which are common to the Member States.

11.3 Slovak Government 1994-1999 and Failure to Fulfil the Political Criteria

11.3.A Major cases perceived contrary to democratic principles

After the premature general election held in autumn 1994 the course of the Slovak political regime followed a course that disqualified the Slovak Republic from negotiations to accession to the EU.

The whole political situation was influenced by the strong position of Vladimír Mečiar[6] and his political party "the Movement for Democratic Slovakia" (HZDS) and particularly the following acts and situations were perceived to be contrary to democratic principles:

- Disputing the legality of parliament mandates of the Democratic Union (DU);
- The attitude to the political opposition and the position of the political opposition after the "night of long knives";
- The tension and deteriorating relationship between Prime Minister Mečiar and President Kováč;
- The case of Mr. Gaulieder; attitude to Hungarian minority; Referendum in May 1997.

The DU was a political party formed mainly by the former members of the HZDS and its political ally the Slovak National Party (SNS) and their members contributed to the fall of Mečiar's second government. In the 1994 elections the DU obtained 15 seats in the parliament. However, the HZDS and its leader Mečiar disputed the legality of the DU's seats in the parliament by disputing the validity of signatures which the DU as a non-parliamentary party had to collect in order to be eligible for parliamentary election. Although the Constitutional Court dismissed the charges raised by the HZDS, Mečiar went on to accuse the DU for election fraud.

The second move against the parliamentary opposition was made during the establishing session of the parliament on 3 and 4 November 1994. Although the new government had not been named yet, the new coalition led by Mečiar and his HZDS tested its power against the opposition. The new coalition did not respect the results of the election or the proportional representation of political parties in committees of the parliament (the National Council of the Slovak Republic). Only members

---

[6] Vladimír Mečiar became Prime Minister in three governments: I. June 1990-April 1991, II. June 1992 – March 1994, III. December 1994-October 1998.

of the new coalition were elected as the Chairman and Deputy Chairmen of the parliament as well as the chairmen of all the parliament committees. Leaders of the parliament opposition were "transferred" to the environmental committee as "sweet revenge" as one of HZDS deputies noted[7]. During the night from 3 to 4 November the parliament declared censure of three ministers and dismissed the Council of Slovak Radio, the Council of Slovak Television[8], the Chairman and Deputy-Chairmen of the Supreme Audit Office of the Slovak Republic, the Prosecutor General and all members of the Board of the National Property Fund of the Slovak Republic and appointed new officials to these positions, as well as new members of the parliament's surveillance body for the secret service, all members of the new coalition. After this night session of the parliament (later labelled as the "night of long knives") the political opposition lost the possibility to participate effectively in surveillance of the government and to effectively participate in parliamentary work.

The tension between the Prime Minister and President Kováč, former HZDS member, and the deteriorating relationship between them may have started very soon after the election of President Kováč. Attacks from the governing party were in a political as well as personal sphere. For example, in October 1995 civil servants were invited to sign a petition from the Minister of Culture seeking the dismissal of the President and those who did not wish to sign were threatened with sanctions. In November 1995 the parliament passed a resolution asking the President to resign. The abduction of the President's son in August 1995 was generally believed as a personal attack on the President because the major suspect in this case was the Slovak Secret Service and its Director. However, the criminal investigation of this case was not possible because after the expiry of President Kováč's term Prime Minister Mečiar as the Acting President amnestied this crime and it was insinuated by the government that the President's son had kidnapped himself.

The case of Mr. Gaulieder showed how the HZDS understands and enforces the loyalty of its members and was also an example of when the parliament ignored constitutional checks performed by the Constitutional Court. Mr. Gaulieder was a HZDS Deputy who in November 1996 left the party and its parliamentary faction in order to sit in the parliament as an independent deputy. Although there is no legal obligation for deputies to resign after leaving a parliamentary faction, in December 1996 the parliament removed Mr. Gaulieder's mandate on the basis of a resignation

---

[7] LEŠKO, M: Mečiar a mečiarizmus. p. 126.

[8] The new councillors, during the same night, dismissed respective general directors of public broadcasting organisations.

letter allegedly sent by Mr. Gaulieder. During the proceedings of the Constitutional Court[9] it was found that the HZDS asked its members for "bianco resignation letters" and the Constitutional Court considered this practice of achieving loyalty illegal and unconstitutional[10]. The Constitutional Court declared that the constitutional rights of Mr. Gaulieder had been broken by the parliament[11] and that the body responsible for the unconstitutional state was obliged to provide a remedy. However, the parliament did neither annul its removal of Mr. Gaulieder's mandate nor adopt any decision to returning Mr. Gaulieder's mandate. Therefore Gaulieder's case showed not only the unconstitutional political practice of the ruling party aimed at maintaining the loyalty of its deputies, but also a refusal to respect the findings of the Constitutional Court by the parliament.

Although during Mečiar's third government the Treaty of friendship and co-operation with Hungary was signed and the Hungarian minority had a strong position, permanent hostility and legislative proposals aimed against minorities (e.g. a law on the use of the state language) were a matter of concern for European institutions. This was also one of the reasons for the disqualification of Slovakia in the integration process on political grounds.

The referendum held in May 1997 resulted in real constitutional, legal and political turmoil since the parliament proposed to call a referendum on NATO membership (three questions) and the opposition, via collecting enough citizens' signatures, proposed to call a referendum in the direct

---

[9] Finding of the Constitutional Court of the Slovak Republic File Ref. No. I. ÚS 8/97 of 23 July 1997.

[10] „The pledge which has the form of a special understanding (commitment) entered into between a political party and a candidate nominated by this party for the elections violates the Constitution because the political party concerned may use such pledge to permanently and effectively demand its former candidate (and/or deputy after the elections) with whom it concluded the "pledge agreement" to exercise his mandate exclusively according to party instructions, and may use the previous written statement of the candidate whereby he agrees to give up his parliamentary seat in the future pursuant to Article 81 paragraph 1 of the Constitution of the Slovak Republic." (Finding of the Constitutional Court of the Slovak Republic File Ref. No. I. ÚS 8/97 of 23 July 1997).

[11] „Not even the Plenary Session of the National Council of the Slovak Republic may strip its deputy of his mandate arbitrarily, i.e. without a personally made and legally relevant declaration of his will. This procedure is in conflict with the very foundations of law and of the State governed by the rule of law." (Finding of the Constitutional Court of the Slovak Republic File Ref. No. I. ÚS 8/97 of 23 July 1997).

election of the president. President Kováč fixed that both referenda should be held on the same day. The government disputed the legality of the opposition's question and the decision of the Constitutional Court in this matter was understood differently by the government and by the Central Referendum Committee. Notwithstanding the decision of the president, the Minister of Interior ordered the print and distribution of another set of ballot papers without the opposition's question. This resulted in the situation where in some regions ballot papers were distributed with three questions while in other regions there were four questions. The Central Referendum Committee declared the referendum obstructed by not distributing ballot papers with four questions and the Constitutional Court confirmed that there was a breach of the right of citizens to participate in the administration of public affairs directly.[12] The Constitutional Court also ruled that the Minister of Interior had obstructed the referendum[13], but the Prime Minister as an Acting President amnestied the obstruction of this referendum.

11.3.B Reaction of European institutions on state of democracy in Slovakia

As a reaction to the political development in Slovakia the EU via its representatives handed two demarches to Slovak representatives. The first of them was handed to the President, the Prime Minister and the Chairman of the Parliament on 23 November 1994 as a reaction to the "night of long knives". Concern about the incipient concentration of power in the hands of the incoming government was expressed in this demarche but the representatives of the new coalition interpreted it as positive in general

[12] Finding of the Constitutional Court of the Slovak Republic File Ref. I. ÚS 76/97 of 6 February 1998.

[13] „It is not possible to accept any reason put forward by the Ministry of Interior to support any other action than that provided for in the Act of the Slovak National Council No. 564/1992 Coll. on the Procedures for Holding a Referendum for this central administrative body. The Ministry of Interior did not have the competence to change the content (i.e., including the questions) of the referendum announced by the President of the Republic in the Collection of Laws under No. 76/97 Coll. The actions designed to lead to the exercise of the right to participate in the referendum announced by the President of the Republic under No. 76/97 Coll. were obstructed by (unlawful) actions of the Ministry of Interior carried out in contravention of Section 15 paragraph 3 and Section 30 paragraph 1 of Act of the Slovak National Council No. 564/1992 Coll. on the Procedures for Holding a Referendum."

terms. The second demarche was handed over on 25 October 1995 and the European Union expressed its concern about the political and institutional tension prevailing in Slovakia and in particular about measures taken against the President of the Republic which could infringe the Constitution and run counter to normal democratic practice in the Union. It reaffirmed obligations stemming from the Association Agreement and from Copenhagen criteria and emphasized the importance of a democratization process. The demarche also pointed to a continuing concentration of power in the hands of the government and called for the return of representatives of the opposition to government bodies.[14]

European Parliament also passed several resolutions regarding the political situation in Slovakia as a reaction on certain situations and also assessing the fulfilment of the democratic criteria as a whole.

The European Parliament reacted to the attitude of the Prime Minister towards DU members of the parliament, "the night of long knives" and the abduction of the President's son by a resolution of 16 November 1995[15] and asked:

- The Slovak government to abandon its attempts to deprive democratically elected members of the Slovak parliaments of their seats;
- To allow the Slovak police to complete its inquiry into the abduction of the President's son without political interference;
- The Prime Minister to guarantee all citizens, regardless of political affiliation, the right to freedom of expression in the media and in the public life.

Furthermore, the resolution warned the Slovak government that in case the Slovak government continued to follow policies which "show insufficient respect for democracy, human and minority rights and the rule of law", the European Union could reconsider its programmes of assistance and cooperation under the Europe Agreement and might suspend them. This threat declared in the European Parliament's resolution is similar to the power to suspend rights of the incumbent under the Treaty on European Union in case of the existence of a serious and persistent breach of principles of the Union.

---

[14] VACHUDOVA, M. A.: Europe Undivided: Democracy, Leverage, and Integration After Communism. Oxford University Press, 2005.

[15] OJ C 323, 4.12.1995, p. 116.

The resolution of 12 December 1996 on the case of Frantisek Gaulieder, Member of the Slovak Parliament[16] stressed in its preamble that the Europe Agreement between the European Union and Slovakia requires respect for human rights and the rights of minorities, democracy and the rule of law. In the operative part the European Parliament inter alia emphasized that a member of parliament exercises his mandate freely and reminded the Slovak Government that respect for fundamental democratic principles, including the free exercise of parliamentary mandates, is a condition for entering into and developing cooperation with the EU. Regarding Mr. Gaulieder the European Parliament urged the Slovak Parliament to reconsider its position on this matter and called on the Slovak authorities to undertake a proper investigation into the bomb explosion near Mr Gaulieder's house.

Meantime on 15 July 1997 the European Commission submitted a document called "Agenda 2000 - Commission Opinion on Slovakia's Application for Membership of the European Union". The Commission stated regarding political criteria that:

1. The Parliament in Slovakia does not carry out its duties in conditions which comply with the normal rules for the operation of democracy;
2. The rights of the Opposition are not fully respected, particularly with regard to its membership of Parliamentary committees;
3. Respect for the mandates of members of parliament and the procedures governing the work of Parliament is not always guaranteed;
4. The present government does not fully respect the role and responsibilities of the other institutions and frequently adopts an attitude which goes beyond the confrontations traditionally accepted in a democracy;
5. There is inadequate control of the work of the secret services in Slovakia by the civil authorities, particularly Parliament;
6. The judicial process in Slovakia is marked by excessive delays, and judges would benefit from stronger guarantees of their independence;
7. While the minorities live harmoniously alongside the rest of the population of Slovakia, there are nevertheless some tensions between the government and the Hungarian minority.

---

[16] OJ C 020, 20.1.1997, p. 145.

On the abovementioned grounds the European Commission concluded that, while the institutional framework defined by the Slovak Constitution corresponds to that of a parliamentary democracy, the situation with regard to the stability of the institutions and their integration into political life was unsatisfactory. In light of these considerations, the European Commission concluded that Slovakia did not fulfil the political conditions set out by the European Council in Copenhagen in a satisfying manner, because of the instability of Slovakia's institutions, their lack of rootedness in political life and the shortcomings in the functioning of its democracy. Satisfying the economic criteria and a firm commitment to take on the acquis could not validate this. In this document the European Commission considered that negotiations for accession to the European Union should not be opened with Slovakia.

Following the resolution of the European Parliament adopted on 23 October 1997[17] it used rather sharp wording, too. It recalled the previous resolutions, particularly the one on Mr. Gaulieder's case and the abovementioned position of the European Commission. The European Parliament in its resolution inter alia urged the Slovak parliament and government to reinstate Mr Gaulieder as a Member of Parliament and to take all the necessary steps to fully respect human rights and the rights of minorities, democracy and the rule of law, in order to fulfil the necessary conditions for the continuation of the process of Slovakia's integration in the structures of the European Union. These democratization steps should be performed particularly through the implementation of the recommendations adopted at the meeting of the EU/Slovakia Joint Parliamentary Committee in June 1997. This meeting recommended the re-creation of parliamentary committees on a proportional basis, increasing the chances of the opposition to control the intelligence services and a consensual preparation and adoption of a law on minority languages[18]. The European Parliament also explicitly warned Slovakia that, if political conditions were not fulfilled, serious obstacles would be put in the way of the process of the country's European integration.

These positions of the European Parliament and the European Commission were de facto endorsed by the European Council during its Luxembourg session on 12 and 13 December 1997 when it decided to

---

[17] OJ C 339, 10.11.1997, p. 158.

[18] MALOVÁ, D. - RYBÁŘ, M.: European Union's Policies towards Slovakia. Carrots and Sticks of Political Conditionality. In RUPNIK, J. ZIELONKA, J (eds.): The Road to the European Union. Volume 1. Manchester University Press, 2003, p. 105.

begin negotiations on the conditions for their entry into the Union merely with Cyprus, Hungary, Poland, Estonia, the Czech Republic and Slovenia.

Since the expiration of President Kováč on 2 March 1998 his powers passed on to the government and its Prime Minister, and the European Parliament in its resolution of 12 March 1998 repeated its concern "about the concentration of power in the hands of a Prime Minister who continues to display increasingly totalitarian attitudes".[19]

11.4 The Comparison of EU reactions to Slovakia's development and resolutions addressed to the Ukraine in 2012

The attitude to political opposition and political rivals became one of the key concerns of the EU in the accession process of Slovakia as well as the Association process of Ukraine. Via its resolution of 24 May 2012 on Ukraine the European Parliament stated conditions for signing and ratification of the Association Agreement with Ukraine and its effective implementation[20] since it expressed "dismay at the state of the democratic

---

[19] OJ C 104, 6.4.1998, p. 232.

[20] The European Parliament called and urged:

1. an improvement in the human rights situation, including decriminalisation of political decisions under a reformed penal code, in the rule of law and in deep democracy, with an end to the stifling of the political opposition and with free, fair and transparent elections;

2. to carry out and implement the necessary reforms, in particular of the legal and judicial system, with the aim of full adherence to the principles of democracy and respect for human rights and fundamental freedoms, minority rights and the rule of law;

3. the unconditional immediate release of all prisoners sentenced on politically motivated grounds, including leaders of the opposition;

4. to distinguish between political and criminal responsibility and to change the existing criminal penal code accordingly;

5. the democratic must not be destroyed by personally or politically motivated acts of criminal prosecution and manipulated judgments in the criminal courts;

6. to clarify the situation of prisoners sentenced on politically motivated grounds before the start of the election campaign;

7. to guarantee the impartiality and transparency of the cassation process in Ms Tymoshenko's case,

8. end to the use of selective justice targeting political and other opponents;

9. to respect fully the legal and human rights of defendants and detainees, including the right to medical care, in line with international standards;

freedoms, as well as at the practice of instrumentalising state institutions for partisan purposes and political revenge". The major common feature of Mečiar's regime in Slovakia and Yanukovich's regime in Ukraine seems to be the attitude to political opposition and the efforts to eliminate its leaders or to limit their possible influence. However, we can see several differences between the cases of Slovakia and Ukraine. First, in the case of Slovakia the major objections regarding democracy were aimed at the performance of the political system, but in the case of Ukraine the EU is asking also for structural improvements. Second, the state of democracy in Slovakia was also determined by a permanent conflict between supreme state institutions that were designed to form a system of "checks and balances". In the case of Ukraine the attacks have been aimed mainly at opposition leaders that don't hold a high office (they are at most deputies). However, in the case of Ukraine, long lists of reforms and acts to perform were provided in resolutions and the position of the EU institution (e.g. abovementioned resolution of the European Parliament) and therefore suggestions to solve problems of democracy were more indicative than they were in the case of Slovakia. On the other hand, the EU can venture to be more lenient in the case of Ukraine than in the Slovak case since Ukraine is not going to be a EU member but "merely" an Associated Member and defects of democracy cannot undermine the state of democracy in the EU itself and the functioning of EU institutions themselves.

---

10. to examine promptly and impartially any complaints of torture or other forms of cruel, inhuman or degrading treatment in prisons;

11. to establish an independent and impartial international legal panel to report on possible violations of fundamental rights and freedoms in the cases of Yulia Tymoshenko and other members of her government; notes

12. all judicial proceedings against former and current high-ranking government officials must be conducted in accordance with European standards of fairness, impartiality, transparency and independence; condemns the fact that the Ukrainian authorities are bringing new politically motivated cases against Ms Tymoshenko and others, contrary to the principles of the rule of law;

13. comprehensive reforms, which must be implemented in order to pave the way for Ukraine to converge with European norms and standards.

11.5 Definition of democratic principles in the Slovakia case study

The case of Slovakia can serve as an example of what not to do in order to accomplish a political system that could be considered democratic. From demarches, resolutions of the European Parliament and opinions of the European Commission can be derived a non-exhaustive list of behavioural features of a democratic political regime which conform with the notion of democracy in the Treaty on European Union. Slovakia's case is also more interesting since the EU's objections against the state of democracy and protection of human rights are usually more sabre-rattling than real law enforcement (e.g. the case of Haider's Austria or Orbán's Hungary), but in the case of Slovakia (and similarly in the case of Ukraine) the failure to fulfil political criteria had serious legal consequences in the integration process.

The Copenhagen criteria call for the stability of institutions guaranteeing democracy, the rule of law, human rights and respect for and protection of minorities and the partial explanation of these terms in practice can be the major moral of Slovakia's failure in the accession process. The examples of democratic functioning of institutions could be the following:

1. Parliament shall carry out its duties in conditions which comply with the normal rules for the operation of democracy;
2. Respect for the mandates of members of parliament and the procedures governing the work of parliament shall be guaranteed;
3. Respect for fundamental democratic principles shall include the free exercise of parliamentary mandates;
4. The rights of the opposition shall be respected, particularly with regard to its membership of parliamentary committees;
5. The government or governing majority shall not attempt to deprive democratically elected members of the parliament of their seats;
6. Political and institutional tension shall not infringe on the constitution and shall not run counter to normal democratic practice in the Union;
7. Parliament shall obey the findings of the constitutional court;
8. The government shall fully respect the role and responsibilities of the other institutions and not adopt an attitude which would go beyond the confrontations traditionally accepted in a democracy;
9. The power shall not be concentrated in the hands of the government;

10. Representatives of the opposition shall be involved in government bodies;
11. Adequate control of the work of the secret services by the civil authorities, particularly parliament;
12. Police shall be allowed to complete every inquiry without political interference;
13. All citizens regardless of political affiliation shall have the right to freedom of expression in the media and in public life.

Indeed, it is clear that in a democratic regime it is intolerable to use criminal means in the political struggle or abuse the power over police, prosecutors and courts in order to imprison political opponents for their political acts (e.g. Ukraine).

The case of Slovakia also showed that it is not enough to guarantee the rights of minorities but it is also necessary to not create or contribute to the tension between the majority and minority and the minority shall not feel marginalised.

11.6 The fall of Mečiar's government and a renewal of the dialogue with the EU

Although Mečiar's HZDS won the general election that was held in September 1998 again, it was unable to negotiate a coalition and a new broad governing coalition was formed by former opposition parties: the Slovak Democratic Coalition (itself a right-left coalition of conservatives, liberals, Christian democrats, socialists and also greens) (SDK), post-Communist Party of the Democratic Left (SDL), the Party of Hungarian Coalition (SMK-MKP) and the Party of Civic Understanding[21] (SOP). The new coalition sought to improve relations with Brussels giving a strong priority to satisfying EU political conditions as the most important step towards opening eventual membership negotiations.[22] However, the Regular Report from the Commission on Slovakia's Progress towards Accession in 1998 was already aware of the results of parliamentary

[21] The SOP was without any typical political affiliation and was led by ex-Communist Schuster (who later became President of the Slovak Republic) and ex-HZDS member Hamžík and other well-known public figures.

[22] PRIDHAM, G.: Slovakia's Relations with the European Union 1998 - 2002: Political Conditionality, its Effects and its Limitations. In Slovak Foreign Policy Affairs, Fall 2002, p. 81.

elections but it was published on 4 November 1998[23] so in the time of its preparation Mečiar's government was still incumbent and that is why it found no relevant progress in the fulfilment of political criteria. Although the Commission presented its view that the new situation in Slovakia following the elections allowed for the prospect of opening negotiations on the condition that the regular stable and democratic functioning of its institutions was confirmed, the General Affairs Council did not make any recommendations to the European Council to extend the accession negotiations at the Vienna summit held in December 1998.[24]

Only one year later, in 1999, the second regular report of the European Commission concluded that Slovakia fulfilled the Copenhagen political criteria. The Commission appreciated the following acts and reforms that were aimed at relieving the major failures of democracy pointed out by the EU:

1. Respect to powers of parliament and full participation in its activities;
2. Membership in parliamentary oversight committees was offered to and accepted by the opposition parties, following a proportional representation system, as well as two posts of Deputy Chairmen and the chairs of 6 committees;
3. The adoption of a resolution expressing regret that a member of the former Parliament had been deprived of his mandate;
4. The opposition has also been offered representation on the Supervisory Board of the National Property Fund, which it declined, and in the newly created Councils for TV Broadcasting and Radio Broadcasting, where it was represented;
5. All parliamentary political parties were present in the commission preparing the reform of the constitution;
6. A law on the use of minority languages in official communications entered into force.

[23] Progress Reports from the Commission on Progress towards Accession by each of the candidate countries, 4 November 1998 [online] http://ec.europa.eu/enlargement/archives/key_documents/reports_1998_en.htm

[24] Vienna European Council 11 and 12 December 1998, Presidency Conclusions. [online] http://www.consilium.europa.eu/uedocs/cms_data/docs/pressdata/en/ec/00300-R1.EN8.htm

Thanks to the changes introduced since September 1998 the Commission declared that Slovakia fulfilled the Copenhagen political criteria.[25] The Helsinki European Council in December 1999 endorsed the Commission's assessment that negotiations should be opened[26] and decided to convene bilateral intergovernmental conferences in February 2000 to begin negotiations with Slovakia on the conditions for their entry into the Union.[27]

Afterwards, the third report of 2000 noted that Slovakia continued to meet the political criteria for accession and had further advanced in the consolidation of its democratic system and in the normal functioning of its institutions. Furthermore, the reports for 2001 and 2002 have continued to praise Slovakia for maintaining progress in consolidating and deepening the stability of its democratic institutions while recording deficiencies in particular areas.[28] This democratisation process finally contributed to the successful accession of Slovakia to the European Union.

11.7 Constitutional Reforms in 1999 and 2001 and "Mečiar's heritage"

The Constitution of the Slovak Republic underwent substantial changes by constitutional laws enacted in 1999 and in 2001 that were, inter alia, aimed at stabilising the Slovak constitutional system as well as ensuring effective control mechanisms and independence of judiciary. The major changes regarding the political and the constitutional system were:

1. Direct election of the President of the Republic (1999);
2. A superior territorial unit was introduced as a form of territorial self-administration (2001);
3. The office term of the Chairman and Deputy Chairmen of the Supreme Audit Office were prolonged to 7 years (2001);
4. New and exact rules of parliament deputies were introduced (2001);

---

[25] Regular report from the Commission on Progress towards Accession by each of the candidate countries. COM (99) 500-513, 13 October 1999

[26] SEDELMEIER, U.: EU Enlargement, Identity and the Analysis of European Foreign Policy: Identity Formation Through Policy Practice. Robert Schuman Centre for Advanced Studies. RSC No. 2003/13 European Forum Series. p. 9.

[27] Helsinki European Council 10 and 10 December 1999 Presidency Conclusions. [online] http://www.europarl.europa.eu/summits/hel1_en.htm

[28] PRIDHAM, G.: Slovakia's Relations with the European Union 1998 - 2002: Political Conditionality, its Effects and its Limitations. In Slovak Foreign Policy Affairs, Fall 2002, p. 81.

5. New rules and specification of existing ones regarding the President, Government and Parliament were introduced (2001);
6. New powers of the Constitutional Court including rules on petition of physical and legal persons and remedies (2001);
7. The establishment of the Judicial Council of the Slovak Republic, a body responsible mainly for the selection of judges, that consists of nominees of the Parliament, President, Government and judges (2001);
8. A new system of appointment of judges and Chairmen and Deputy Chairmen of the Supreme Court (2001);
9. The Public Protector of Rights (i.e. ombudsman) was established (2001);
10. New rules of appointment and removal of the Prosecutor General (2001).

From the abovementioned non-exhaustive list of constitutional reforms, it is evident that the change in the political climate was accompanied by extensive constitutional changes that contributed to the stability of political institutions and supported the sustainability of the fulfilment of the Copenhagen criteria.

Dzurinda's government succeeded in eliminating almost all failures of democracy that disqualified Slovakia from the accession process, but the controversial Mečiar amnesties remained in force. Prime Minister Mečiar tried to protect officials of his executive that could be charged with the abduction of President Kováč's son and the obstruction of the referendum by these amnesties. Prime Minister Dzurinda as the acting president tried to abolish these amnesties but the Constitutional Court ruled that the power of the president to grant an amnesty does not include the right of the president to change, in whatever matter, a decision on amnesty that had already been published.[29] Ironically, because of the impossibility of abolishing Mečiar's amnesties the principal suspects, especially the former director of the secret service Ivan Lexa and the former Minister of Interior Gustáv Krajči, cannot be prosecuted and can successfully challenge the Slovak Republic for violation of their rights by the investigation into amnestied crimes. Issues of abolishment still remained open and mainly right-wing parties sought the only way of "constitutional" abolishing of the amnesties in adoption of a constitutional act, i.e. an act with the same legal power as the Constitution. Although several proposals for the

[29] Ruling of the Constitutional Court of the Slovak Republic File Ref. I. ÚS 30/99 of 28 June 1999 published in the Collection of Laws of the Slovak Republic, Part 79, No. 182/1999.

adoption of such a law were raised in Parliament, no attempts to abolish Mečiar's amnesties were successful since "constitutional" majority was never found[30].

11.8 Democratisation Process' Aftermath and Independence of Judiciary

The constitutional reform in 2001 gave judges more independence and self-government especially by establishing the Judicial Council. Although steps to more reliable, independent and effective judiciary were undertaken, the judiciary remains a very distrustful institution. The behaviour of some judges and representatives of the judiciary discredit the whole system of judicial law enforcement. In the first place, it is the personality of Mr. Harabin, current Chairman of the Supreme Court and also the Chairman of the Judiciary Council, who is a former Minister of Justice representing the HZDS in Fico's government in 2006-2009. Mr. Harabin is in permanent conflict with his opponents, critics and also with the Constitutional Court[31]. The judiciary is permanently blamed for nepotism in the selection of judges and higher court officials. Some acts and decisions are also perceived as very controversial, e.g. the Supreme Court itself decided that the financial audit performed by the Ministry of Finance at the Supreme Court is illegal, judges claims for compensation because of discrimination which they see in additional salaries for judges of the Specialised Criminal Court (these cases are normally tried by judges who took similar action and they via facti prepare precedents for their own lawsuits). Since trust in judiciary is one of the pillars of the democratic regime based on the rule of law, it cannot be said that the development of Slovakia to democracy and the rule of law is finished.

11.9 Conclusion

Questions of democracy during the EU integration process of Slovakia in 1994-1999 showed how the EU reacts when political criteria are not met. The EU and its members are, under the Treaty on European Union, legally obliged to obey principles of a democratic regime, protection of

---

[30] Recent attempt led by the Christian Democrats (KDH) failed at the beginning of 2012.

[31] Recently he labelled the Constitutional Court as a political and criminal institute (*SME*, 25.4.2013), [online] http://www.sme.sk/c/6779526/harabin-na-ustavnom-sude-su-druzstevnici.html

human rights, rights of minorities and rule of law, protect those principles and also to promote these principles. This obligation is aimed not only internally (i.e. the Member States shall fulfil criteria themselves) but also externally and shall bind Member States as well as EU institutions in their external relations. Of course, the EU and its Member States seem to be rather lenient on the fulfilment of the Union's principles in international economic Agreements but in the case of "political" Agreements they shall be more rigorous.

In the autumn and winter of 1994 as well as during the following years of Mečiar's government the EU quickly responded to every act that threatened principles of democracy and rule of law and it became evident how failure to comply with democratic criteria can ruin the integration process. On the other hand the integration story of Slovakia shows how a change of political situation and eagerness of the government to introduce a change of political climate from confrontation to cooperation and to carry out constitutional and structural reform could quickly change the attitude of the EU. Therefore Slovakia could serve as an example of how to make progress in integration to those countries whose integration process (Association or Accession to the EU) is inhibited by failure of democratic principles as well as an inspiration for political and constitutional changes.

CHAPTER TWELVE

THE ROLE OF CONSTITUTIONAL COURTS, PARTICULARLY OF THE CONSTITUTIONAL COURT OF THE CZECH REPUBLIC, WHILE INTRODUCING HUMAN RIGHTS

SOŇA MATOCHOVÁ

12.1 European Historical Starting Points

The significance of human rights and its possible role on the constitutional judiciary while both the introduction, protection and enforcement have clearly come forward especially in the period of transformation from the totalitarian regime to the democratic one.[1] Here it is possible to reveal their role very clearly. In the context of the reviewed topic, it is significant to remember that Europe in the 20th century came through the tragic experience of two totalitarian regimes. Both Nazi, fascist and communist ideologies were based on ideas that were in their substance in contradiction with traditionally conceived human rights in the

---

[1] Judgment of the Constitutional Court of the CR Pl. US 14/94: „*The establishment of a totalitarian system always represents a massive assault on mankind and on history itself. ... Its extraordinarily dangerous nature, the fact that it became a social phenomena threatening "the fate of all life on earth" (Preamble to the Charter of Fundamental Rights and Basic Freedoms), also presents reasons as to why the attempt to eradicate all sources of totalitarianism demanded extraordinary legislative measures. In other words, in such situations it is always a matter of eliminating the causes leading to the birth of totalitarianism, of doing away with the sources which could bring on a recurrence of it with all of its horrible features*".

European context[2] and enabled massive, long-term and systematic violation of these rights. The valid legal order did not prevent it.

After World War II, the above situation resulted in a differentiation between legality and legitimacy.[3] It is exactly this situation that is reflected in the so-called Radbruch´s formula,[4] the essence of which is the understanding that law cannot be neutral from the point of value perception. This ex-post rule consists in a quite different approach to law in comparison with pre-war approaches strictly respecting the validity of legal norms.[5] Its author, German legal philosopher Gustav Radbruch (1878 – 1949) became world-famous thanks to his article *Statutory Lawlessness and Supra-Statutory Law* of 1946, published as a reaction to Nazi statute treatment of Jews in 1935. In summary, Radbruch‘s formula argues that where statutory law is incompatible with the requirements of justice "to an intolerable degree", or where statutory law is obviously designed in a way that deliberately negates "the equality that is the core of all justice", statutory law must be disregarded by a judge in favour of the justice principle. Since its first publication in 1946 Germany's Federal Constitutional Court has already accepted this principle in a number of cases.

---

[2] Here, I have in mind the European cultural tradition of human rights as it was continually evolving from the very foundations of European civilization, being formed from Antiquity times through to Christianity and Enlightenment, to current conception of human rights derived from the bitter experience of Nazism and fascism.

[3] Judgment of the Constitutional Court of the CR Pl. US 19/93: „*Whatever the laws of a state are, in a state which is designated as democratic and which proclaims the principle of the sovereignty of the people, no regime other than a democratic regime may be considered as legitimate. Any sort of monopoly on power, in and of itself, rules out the possibility of democratic legitimacy. The starting point of our Constitution is the substantive-rational conception of legitimacy and the law-based state. In the overall structure of a democratic constitutional state and of a functioning democracy, legality mutatis mutandis undoubtedly embodies a part of the legitimacy of the regime, however, these concepts are not quite interchangeable.*

[4] Resolutions of the Constitutional Court of the CR Pl. US 48/05, Pl. US 38/06, Pl. US 14/02 and III. US 671/02 contain in its reasoning reference to Radbruch´s formula.

[5] The normative theory was one of the leading theories of the pre-war period. It is the norm which is the central concept of normative theory. The normative theory considered positive law as the only valid law. In this sense, the positive law is in direct contrast with natural law. The norm is expression of that „what shall to be". As far as the norm content, it can be everything what is possible.

It is important to remember repeatedly that both the current system of international organizations and applicable international treaties created in post-war Europe have been a reaction to the European historical experience during the period of Nazism and fascism. After World War II, a quite new fundamental turnaround towards ethics, morality and law has been initiated. On the basis of horrifying experiences with Nazism and fascism, the individual should have received his rights in a "natural state", i.e. first of all inalienable by any State power. From the same motives the United Nations Universal Human Rights Declaration came out in 1948 stipulating the natural, inherent and inalienable rights of man and citizens.

The post-war arrangement of Europe resulted in a formulation of a human rights concept on a new natural rights basis. Further development was accomplished in 1950 by concluding the Convention on Human Rights and Fundamental Freedoms and creating mechanisms that enabled the enforcement of human rights more effectively (Council of Europe, European Court of Human Rights). Also the European Union itself, although acting primarily as an economic community gradually increasing itself into the sphere of human rights, had the same post-war ethos of its origin. Unfortunately, this post-war human rights development concerned only Western European Countries; it did not include countries behind the iron curtain.

Yet in the period of coping with Nazi and fascist ideology, a new communistic ideology began to govern in Europe.[6] This extremely dangerous ideology simulated the effort to create a socially fair order realised by the division of society into antagonistic classes with different statuses. Some groups of citizens were determined for liquidation or re-education. Whole groups of the population were classed as undesirable: land and factory owners, churches, members of the Western national resistance movement, later on intelligence, believers, or alternative culture movement members. After the period of cruel Stalinist repressions, the regime mitigated forms of its persecution. The citizens were differentiated by unequal access to working positions, property, education and other rights. The ideological concept of State and law, the leading role of the communist party and fear of the State Security´s practices led to a moral devastation of a major part of society.

[6] The Act No. 198/1993 Coll., on the Lawlessness of the Communist Regime, stipulates that any regime based on communist ideology is criminal, illegitimate and abominable.

When “Charter 77”[7] in the then Czechoslovakia was declared on 1 January 1977 containing the requirement to observe both human rights and approved international obligations after the signature of Helsinki Protocols, the regime considered it as its own direct threat. The governing structures were so afraid that the signatories of Charter 77 were persecuted, deprived of personal liberty and followed by State Police at every step. Although human rights were declared in the constitution, they were violated and they were not enforceable. These rights were only nominal. Only the fall of the Berlin Wall started a transformation of post-communist regimes toward democracy.

Only later on did it became clear that the transformation of society would be long term and demanding and that it also requires a change of thinking, new approaches and the acceptance of individual responsibility. The acceptance of moral responsibility for participation in the power mechanism of the communist regime and coping with the communist past to the effect of an analogy with Carl Jasper´s thoughts in his work the Question of Fault,[8, 9] reacting to the situation after World War II in

---

[7] See Judgment of the Constitutional Court of the CR II. US 2268/07 Signatory of Charter 77.

[8] The question of fault in the broader sense urgently emerged after the World War II when it was revealed that legal punishment of Nazi crimes was both very difficult and unsufficient. The German philosopher and psychologist Karl Jaspers in his book „The Question of German Fault“ (*Die Schuldfrage*, 1946) differentiated four levels at which the question of fault could be posed: the criminal, political, moral and metaphysical levelS. According to Jaspers, the moral fault and individual fault in relation to both individuals and groups is with which everybody has to deal with in his/her conscioussness. Similar issues have emerged also after the fall of the communist regime in 1989. In this connection, an American legal theoretician Lon L. Fuller displayd the difficulties which the law must come across in such cases by means of the fictive example of „purple shirts“ regime. L. Fuller: *Morálka práva.* Dodatek. Problém odporného udavače. [Morality of Law. Supplement: The Problem of the Grudge Informers], p. 221 – 228.

[9] The judgment of the Constitutional Court of the CR Pl. US 14/94 explains that rather than being about a presumption of guilt, it is better to speak about a presumption of responsibility. „For it is quite evident that the category of ‘responsibility’ is a much broader concept than that of ‘guilt’, so that in this respect it has a far more extensive value, social, historical, as well as legal, dimension. The determinative factor for defining the category of responsibility is the consciousness of the individual that he himself is answerable for his orientation in life, for his social and value decisions, and that nobody can ever take on this responsibility in his place, neither the society itself nor history. It is mankind's fate that human beings are placed into power relations, and this situation gives rise to

Germany by appeals to moral responsibility, was not either enforced nor perceived as necessary in the post-communist society.[10]

12.2 Place of Constitutional Courts in the Process of Human Rights Protection

The constitutional courts have an indispensable place in the system of advocacy and enforcement of both constitutionality and human rights in Europe. However, certain developments preceded this. The institutional origin of the constitutional judiciary belongs to the period after World War I. It is possible to point out that it had its origin in the constitutions of Czechoslovakia and Austria. The Czech and Austrian models were consistent in essential typological features and so Walter Jellinek (1885–1955) described it as a Czechoslovak-Austrian conception, despite all differences between the above two constitutions.

The continental system of constitutional review had its origin[11] in the thoughts of Hans Kelsen (1881–1973) especially, one of the main representatives of the normative theory of law,[12] about the necessity of constitutional courts as instruments for annulment of unconstitutional acts. While Carl Schmitt (1888-1985) considered the review of constitutionality as a legislative activity, Kelsen considered it as an enforcement of

their responsibility to champion the forces which will make human rights a reality. ..."

[10] The Panel judgment of the Constitutional Court of the CR I. US 517/10 dealt with the question of whether it is possible, in the framework of the right to information, to demand disclosure of information about the membership of current judges in the Communist Party. Although the Constitutional Court granted the complainant and was thus enabled to publish this information, the decision has not been generally accepted by the public.

[11] Georg Jellinek was probably the most significant supporter of concentrated constitutional judiciary. In his work The Constitutional Court for Austria of 1885 he both urgently expressed his opinion against the American model of general review of constitutionality by judges and supported the concentrated review of norms by the Reich Court. In Jana Osterkamp. Ústavní soud v meziválečném Československu 1920-1939: Bezmocní bohové na ústavním nebi. Sborník příspěvků. [The Constitutional Court in Interwar Czechoslovakia in 1920-1939. Powerless gods in constitutional heaven. Collection of Contributions.]

[12] Normative theory was represented both by the so called Vienna Normative School presented by Hans Kelsen and Brno Normative School presented by František Weyr, the Dean of the first Faculty of Law in Brno after the origin of Czechoslovakia. Unlike Hans Kelsen strongly supporting the idea of constitutional court, František Weyr was more sceptical in that respect.

judiciary. He also stated that the result of the above review is the annulment of an act, and thus constitutional judiciary can be described as a negative legislator.[13] According to Kelsen, the constitution which did not introduce constitutional judiciary for the annulment of unconstitutional acts can only mean a non-binding wish:[14] "*The Constitution which does not establish a constitutional court with the power to annul constitutional acts, is a light which does not shine.*"

It is possible to mention generally that we differentiate between an American and European model of review of constitutionality. The continental model of the concentrated judiciary established the constitutional review of acts before the constitutional courts and took it from the ordinary courts disposal, contrary to the American so-called diffuse control of constitutionality according to which every single judge is entitled to check the conformity of law with the constitution. The advantage of a concentrated constitutional judiciary model is its unification. As a result of this review, the constitutional courts can pronounce the unconstitutionality of law with a general effect. The binding force of a judgment is an essential feature of the whole constitutional judiciary concept.[15]

The European constitutional judiciary acquired both a new dimension and impetus for its development after World War II when much more emphasis started to be devoted to the protection of human rights. This was a natural reaction to the brutal harm caused by the value order and democratic principles of Nazi and fascist regimes. For this purpose the institution of the constitutional court was used which originally, in the interwar period, dealt with the formal review of constitutionality in its determined scope.[16] The constitutional courts came to deal with new

[13] *Marcic, René*. Verfassungsgerichtbarkeit und reine Rechtslehre. Wien: 1966, p. 1.

[14] *Kelsen, Hans*. Wesen und Entwicklung der Staatsgerichtsbarkeit. In VVDStR. Berlin: 1929, vol.5, p. 56.

[15] Judgment of the Constitutional Court of the CR III. US 425/97. … „*enforceable judgments of the Constitutional Court are binding on all authorities and persons (Article 89 para. 2 of Constitutional Act No. 1/1993 Coll.)1), such a decision is binding even on the_Constitutional Court itself, in consequence of which, in any further proceedings before it in which the same matter must be decided upon once again (even if in a divergent manner), that decision represents an unavoidable procedural obstacle in the sense of res judicata (§ 35 para. 1 of Act No. 182/1993 Coll., on the Constitutional Court)2), which naturally bars any further review of that matter on the merits whatsoever.*"

[16] Basically we can differentiate among four stages of the European constitutional judiciary development. These are 1. The origin of first Central European interwar constitutional courts, 2. The establishment of constitutional courts after World War

interpretations of the constitution and the value order established by it. They became a specialised institution established for the protection of constitutionality, now broadened to the sphere of human rights protection. As far as value order perception, the German Constitutional Court founded in 1951 assumed an important role in this sense.[17]

Similarly in recent history Central and Eastern European countries came through a unique experience of transformation from a totalitarian regime to a democratic one. In these States, the constitutional courts could arise and fulfil its role only after the fall of communism.[18] It was correctly recognized that in a specific situation characterized on the one hand by legal order formal continuity accompanied by mental and personal continuity with the past regime, and value order discontinuity on the other hand, the constitutional courts could play an important role in the period of transformation towards democratic society and legal State formation.[19]

In this regard the Council of Europe has begun to concentrate its attention on the constitutional judiciary. The Venice Commission of the Council of Europe (European Commission for Democracy through Law)[20] came into existence in May 1990 as an advisory organ of the Council of Europe. It stressed the importance of the constitutional judiciary as a legal guarantee for the development of democracy. It contributes significantly to

---

II, 3. The later stage of the constitional courts establishment in Europe, 4. The establishment of constitutional courts after the fall of communism.

[17] The coming into existence of both the Basic Law of Germany and the German Constitutional Court had been initiated by the political situation after World War II. The example of Germany proves the fundamental role of values in the constitutional courts case law. Exactly the constitutional courts in liberal democracies are the organs which establishes in essential extent the interpretation and application of values creating constitutional order.

[18] Both the mere establishment of the constitutional court in the constitution and its creation has no real sense without the existence of democratic society.

[19] Judgment of the Constitutional Court of the CR Pl. US 19/93: "*Our new Constitution is not founded on neutrality with regard to values, it is not simply a mere demarcation of institutions and processes, rather it incorporates into its text also certain governing ideas, expressing the fundamental, inviolable values of a democratic society. The Czech Constitution accepts and respects the principle of legality as a part of the overall basic outline of a law-based state; positive law does not, however, bind it merely to formal legality, rather the interpretation and application of legal norms are subordinated to their substantive purpose, law is qualified by respect for the basic enacted values of a democratic society and also measures the application of legal norms by these values. This means that even while there is continuity of "old laws" there is a discontinuity in values from the "old regime".*"

[20] See http://www.venice.coe.int.

the acknowledgement of constitutional judiciary issues. The Venice Forum, the place for exchange of information among constitutional courts, has created a database of comparative law in the sphere of constitutional judiciary.

The role of constitutional courts concerns the protection of constitutionality. In order to fulfil this task, some preconditions of various kinds have to be met. The constitutional court has to have its position in the framework of the division of powers. Also the personal composition of the court is extremely important. In the personal profile of individual justices both the highest professional expertise and ethical values should be concentrated. Only a person with such qualities should be appointed as a constitutional court justice. The real acceptance of the court´s role in society, coming from the persuasiveness of its decision-making, is also an element of crucial importance.

Despite the similarity of both legal regulations and cases before constitutional courts, it is possible to say that each of the European constitutional courts is different and specific. For example, if we compare the Constitutional Court of the Czech Republic, the Slovak Republic and Hungary, we would discover differences in connection with the different extent of their powers, constitutional traditions and political development in each given country. It is also obvious that those constitutional courts which were both endowed with greater powers and are characterized by extensive decision-making activities can face more probable conflicts with other organs.[21]

The key role of the constitutional court is determined by its exceptional position that it occupies in the system of the division of powers. On the one hand, it is connected with the judicial system by its possibility to annul judicial decisions, although it is not part of the ordinary court system; on the other hand, it exerts influence over the Parliament through the possibility to annul a provision of law or lower legal regulations as a negative legislator. By means of the constitutionally enshrined power to influence both ordinary courts and legislative or eventually executive

[21] It can be demonstrated by the example of the Hungarian Constitutional Court, once described as a very active constitutional court. Displeasure was probably raised by its broad encroachments. The Fourth Amendment to the Hungarian Constitution passed by the Parliament in March 2013 leads both to restriction of its powers and prevention to cite judgments accepted before the establishment of the new constitution in January last year. As far as the Constitutional Court of the CR, in its second term of office it was often criticized by the President Klaus. The Constitutional Court also clashed with the Parliament in a question of inactivity of the legislator.

power, the constitutional court can perform a concentrated review of constitutionality. In its decision-making, it observes principles of its own self-restraint, minimization of its encroachments and prohibition of arbitrariness.[22] It has to repeatedly find the boundaries of its own constitutionally vested power in its decision-making. Its task is to assess constitutional law questions using constitutional law argumentation. Maybe it is possible to add that the public and media perceive both the questions of constitutional court independence, judicial activism and fair decision-making very sensitively.

If we start with Dworkin´s idea that a constitutional judicial review makes society more fair, and if we overlook the dispute between positive and natural law, it is possible to argue in favour of the above idea by the fact that the existence of the constitutional court means continual and systematic attention addressing issues of constitutionality protection including the protection of human rights, yet with the reservation that the constitutional court, as a negative legislator, cannot select questions for its review. In any case, the judicial review of constitutionality is an important instrument in attracting attention to questions of constitutionality and human rights in any given country.

As the position of constitutional courts is embodied either in a constitution or in constitutional acts, and this means more difficult procedures for approval of amendments, it is absolutely crucial to pass, at the beginning, legal regulations that are faultless in relation both to the constitutional courts´ position and its powers. The key point is that every shortage, incorrectness or inequality in the legal regulations could result later on in serious consequences in relation to the constitutional courts' operation.

Nevertheless, constitutional courts can get into conflict with other State organs, e.g. the president, legislative organ, supreme courts or other concerned entities, which may not agree with its individual decisions or its decision making in general. The constitutional courts decisions also can be, and often actually are, the subject of criticism. In this connection it is necessary to realise that constitutional courts decide about fundamental political, moral and social issues, precisely about those ones which are the most controversial and to which social agreement has not been reached. Thus, the constitutional courts judges that are endowed with guarantees of

[22] See e.g. judgment of the Constitutional Court of the CR Pl. US 11/02 of 11 June, 2003 stating that if the Constitutional Court, a constitutional body, that is, a public authority, is not itself to act arbitrarily, it must feel itself to be bound by its own decisions, and its jurisprudence may depart therefrom only under certain circumstances.

independence have to search with full responsibility for the adequate constitutional answers to the questions raised.

It can be summed up that the role of constitutional courts and the bindingness of their decision-making are both results and a consequence of divisions of power in modern democracies, an instrument of protection of constitutions and a manner of its continual and topical fulfillment. The constitutional courts both clarify a constitution by its interpretative activities and fulfil the content of constitutional rights. They make it both in relation to State organs and citizens. Constitutional courts pronounce themselves through their decisions while the argumentation used in the reasoning of its decisions could impact by its persuasive force.

12.3 The Origin, Position and Powers of the Constitutional Court of the Czech Republic

The first Constitutional Court of the Czech Republic originated in 1993[23] shortly after the independent Czech State came into being, when the President of the Republic appointed 12 of its 15 justices. The remaining justices were appointed in November 1993 and March 1994. However, it was not the first constitutional court in the territory of the Czech Republic. Its predecessor was the Constitutional Court of the Czech and Slovak Federal Republic[24] operating on the basis of the 1991 Constitutional Act. However, this court operated for less than two years in fact. As a result of the dissolution of the federation on 31 December 1992, the federal constitutional court also ceased to exist. Later on, independent constitutional courts in both of the new republics replaced it. Despite the short period of its existence, the federal constitutional court adjudicated on more than a thousand cases,[25] some of them being fundamental from the point of view of the new democratic state foundation.[26] The Constitutional Court of the Czech Republic followed up its activity.

---

[23] The first Constitutional Court of the Czech Republic started its activity on 15 July, 1993.

[24] The federal constitutional court consisted of twelve justices, six of them were the Czechs and six the Slovaks. Its Chairman was Ernest Valko (1950 – 2010).

[25] See The Collection of Resolutions and Judgments of the Constitutional Court of the Czech and Slovak Federal Republic.

[26] Here, it is possible to refer to judgment of the Constitutional Court of the CR Pl. US 5/92 Protection of Democratic Order, Pl. US 1/92 Democratic System, Pl. US 78/92 Retroactivity of Law and I. US 597/92 Rehabilitation.

If we delve yet further into history, we arrive at the earlier mentioned First Republic Constitutional Court[27] which has arisen on the basis of the Constitutional Charter of Czechoslovak Republic from 29 February 1920 published as No. 121/1920 Coll (later on as Constitution of 1920) as the first specialized court in Europe dealing exclusively with constitutional questions. In October 1920, the Constitutional Court of Austria coming from the same common historical guiding sources closely followed it, although coordination or cooperation in the period of their coming into existence has not been proved. We speak here about the Central European model of concentrated constitutional judiciary.

Although the Constitutional Court of Czechoslovakia had operated in the period between 1920-1939, its activity was not continuous. After the end of the first electoral period in 1931, an attempt to elect new judges failed. Therefore judges of the second electoral period were elected as late as 1938. In 1939 this court in fact finished its activity, as it did not operate during World War II. It can be remarked that the court´s decision-making activities were neither extensive nor significant. The constitutional court found difficulties with its position in the system of the division of powers, as it is also reflected in the fact that in some periods it was not elected nor operate. Nevertheless, the mere fact that the constitutional court came into being, as an institution that acquired new significance and proved its purpose after World War II, was of crucial importance.

Although after World War II the First Republics Constitution in Czechoslovakia was only valid till 1948, the constitutional court´s activity was not renewed. In the Constitution of 1948, the constitutional court did not have a place. On the contrary, in 1968, there was an attempt to embody it in the Constitution of the Czechoslovak Socialist Republic, although in fact it had not come into existence. Thus, the existence of the First Republics Constitutional Court did mean, at least for many lawyers during communism, the constant reminder of a missing element in the system of judiciary. The actual renewal of constitutional judiciary occurred only after the Velvet Revolution in 1989.

The current Constitutional Court of the Czech Republic comes from the principles of the European constitutional judiciary; it is outside the ordinary court system and at the same time it represents judicial decision-making about the questions of constitutionality after all remedial measures are exhausted. As is precisely expressed in Art. 83 of the Constitution of the Czech Republic, "*the constitutional court is the judicial organ of*

[27] The Constitutional Court of Czechoslovakia of 1921 consisted of seven judges, three of them were nominated by the President of the Republic, two by the Supreme Court and two by the Supreme Administrative Court.

protection of constitutionality". Under Art. 87 para. 2 of the Constitution of the Czech Republic, *"the decisions of the Constitutional Court are binding for all organs and citizens"*.

The Constitutional Court of the Czech Republic can be characterized as the court endowed by very broad powers, both in the sphere of abstract and specific reviews.[28] Its competences are defined in Art. 87 of the Constitution of the Czech Republic. It encompasses preventive reviews of international treaties, abstract constitutional reviews (reviews of statutes and of other sub-statutory regulations with constitutional order or its individual provisions) and specific reviews of constitutional complaints and various kinds of specialized reviews, for example the review of electoral matters, constitutional charges against the President of the Republic, decisions on the measures necessary to implement a decision of an international tribunal which is binding on the Czech Republic, the dissolution of a political party and competence disputes. The specific constitutional review represents the review of constitutional complaints against final decisions and other encroachments into constitutionally guaranteed fundamental rights and freedoms.

The Constitutional Court decides either in the Plenum composed of all justices or in four three-member panels. In the Plenum, the court usually decides about the annulment of laws or its individual provisions, while panels usually decide about constitutional complaints. According to the Act on the Constitutional Court, a complainant may submit, together with his constitutional complaint, a proposal to annul a statute or some other legal regulations, or individual provision thereof, the application of which resulted in a situation that is the subject of the constitutional complaint. In such a case, a petition to propose the annulment can be submitted by a Panel.[29]

The Constitutional Court is composed of 15 justices appointed for a ten-year period. The President of the Republic with the prior consent of the Senate appoints Justices. Requirements for the function of a constitutional justice are stipulated in Art. 84 para. 3 of the Constitution. Any citizen who has a character beyond reproach is eligible for election to the Senate, has a university legal education, and has been active in the

---

[28] An abstract review is undrestood as the review of laws or its individual provisions, while a specific review is a review in an individual matter of the complainat.

[29] Section 74 and Section 64 para. 1 letter (c) of the Act on the Constitutional Court.

legal profession for a minimum of ten years, may be appointed as a justice of the Constitutional Court.[30]

The performance of the office of justice is incompatible with membership in a political party or political movement. It is also incompatible with the performance of his or her duties for a justice to hold other compensated positions or to engage in some other profit-making activities, with the exception of the management of his own assets and activities of a scholarly, pedagogical, literary or artistic nature, provided that such activities are not to the detriment of the office of justice, its significance and dignity, and do not tend to undermine confidence in the independence and impartiality of the decision-making of the Court.[31]

In the Czech Republic, the constitution does not exclude the repeated appointment of a judge. In making their decisions, the justices of the constitutional court are bound only by the constitutional order (i.e. the constitution, charter, constitutional acts and some international treaties) and the statute under Art. 88 paragraph 1 of the Constitution. A justice of the constitutional court assumes their duties upon taking the oath of office administered by the President of the Republic (Art. 85 para. 1 of the Constitution).[32] The wording of his/her oath refers to the protection of inviolability of natural human rights and the rights of citizens. Thus human rights protection is significantly accentuated.

As far as the requirements for the function of a constitutional court justice, it could be inspiring to cite the opinion of Vladimír Čermák,[33] former justice of the Czech constitutional court, mentioned in his dialogue for the Czech journal Respekt. Here, he stressed that every justice of the constitutional court has to have a perception of law based on moral values. He said that the mere fact that somebody was an expert in criminal law did not mean very much as the constitutional court required other types of perceptions. The expert who is not able to start with a value system of thinking is not a suitable person for the position of a constitutional court

---

[30] Art. 84 para. 3 of the Constitution of the Czech Republic.

[31] Section 4 para. 3 of the Act on the Constitutional Court.

[32] Under Art. 85 para. 2 of the Constitution of the Czech Republic the oath say: "I pledge upon my honor and conscience that I will protect the inviolability of natural human rights and of the rights of citizens, adhere to constitutional acts, and make decisions according to my best convictions, independently and impartially."

[33] Prof. Vladimír Čermák (1930 – 2004), judge of the Constitutional Court of the CR in 1993 – 2003.

justice. The justice of the constitutional court does not decide if anything is legal; an ordinary court does that.[34]

The fact that justices of the constitutional court are appointed for a 10 year period means that the second period of the court´s operation is drawing to an end at the moment.[35,36] The first term of the court´s office can be characterized by the above mentioned strong perception of a law based on moral values closely connected with the personal composition of the court.[37] In the case of the second term of office, the importance of a colourful composition of a court containing judges, attorneys and academics has been underlined. The court also extended the scope of adjudicated questions.

Here, it is useful to remark that the court has solved different issues in relation to the different needs of a relevant term of office, the continuity of the court´s decision-making being preserved at the same time. Whilst the first term of office was more orientated to questions connected with the rule of law in the State and its foundations (the concept of democracy, legality and legitimacy, the rule of law in the State, the substantive core of the constitution, lustration, restitutions, objections of conscience), the second period was orientated more to standard issues of constitutional democracy (the conformity of the Lisbon Treaty with the constitution, the shortening of the electoral period, budget restrictions, health care fees).

---

[34] Vladimír Čermák. Člověk – filozof – soudce. Masarykova univerzita. [Man - Philosopher - Judge]. Brno, 2009. Page 206.

[35] This exchange of justices' occurred in a two-year period as justices had not been appointed at the same time. Currently, four new justices have been appointed. The largest number of judges leave the Court in August 2013.

[36] Chairman Pavel Rychetský, Vice-Chairmen Pavel Holländer and Eliška Wagnerová, justices Stanislav Balík, František Duchoň, Vlasta Formánková, Vojen Güttler, Ivana Janů, Vladimír Kůrka, Dagmar Lastovecká, Jiří Mucha, Jan Musil, Jiří Nykodým, Miloslav Výborný, Michaela Židlická.

[37] For example justices Zdeněk Kessler and Antonín Procházka were prisoners in uranium mines during communism. Vladimír Čermák was deeply interested in questions of democracy during communism and he wrote a four volume work 'Questions of Democracy'. Vladimír Klokočka, Dean of the Faculty of Law in Brno in 1968, fled the country under threat of political persecution after the signature of Charter 77; he was able to obtain a position in the Faculty of the University of Munich. Miloš Holeček was a judge and was disciplinarily punished for a disagreement with the law enabling the punishment of participants of demonstrations „disturbing the socialist legal order". Ivana Janů used her experience from the Constitutional Court of the CR as a judge of the International Criminal Tribunal for Former Yugoslavia. Jiří Malenovský became the judge of the European Court of Justice later on.

Also issues of interpretation and the application of constitutional rights had been elaborated significantly during the second round of the court´s term of office (constitutional law principles, various tests of constitutionality).

As far as the credibility of the constitutional court of the Czech Republic as an institution goes, although it is necessary to consider a public opinion survey with restraint, still it is possible to mention that the Constitutional Court of the Czech Republic belongs to those institutions that are trusted by citizens. According to the latest accessible survey of the STEM agency (Centre of Empirical Surveys) on 27 September 2012, dealing with the confidence of citizens in relation to the highest judicial institutions, 63% of citizens trust the Constitutional Court of the Czech Republic and this confidence is stabilized on the long-term horizon.[38]

As has been already stated, any shortage or systematic fault in the legal regulations can have serious consequences. In the case of the Constitutional Court of the Czech Republic, we can find several shortages. As far as the appointment of constitutional court justices is concerned, such a shortage could be a repeated possibility to appoint a constitutional justice. This is unusual in Europe. The appointment of a majority of justices in one period is rather unpractical from the point of view of decision-making continuity; it would be more suitable if a third of the justices were appointed every three years.[39] As far as the decision making activity of the court goes, adjudication in four Panels does not exclude entirely the potential possibility of different decisions.

To conclude, it is possible to mention that not all constitutional court decisions are accepted without reservations and some of them could be subject to criticism. This is undoubtedly caused by a different opinion both in society and in the framework of political parties and by the complex or controversial character of issues under review. Also the opinions of the constitutional court justices should not be universal. Then they can express their different opinions by means of a dissenting opinion.

12.4 The Constitutional Court of the Czech Republic Case Law

In this year (2013), the Constitutional Court of the Czech Republic will have been functioning for twenty years. From the beginning of its activity,

---

[38] http://www.stem.cz/clanek/1327

[39] In the Czech Republic, there were problems to fill both the „second" and then „third" constitutional court, mainly due to the failure to reach an agreement between the President (Klaus) and the Senate.

there has been an extensive case law of the constitutional court. The court has adjudicated on 50,145 constitutional complaints and issued 3,600 judgments; from this number there were 383 judgments related to the annulment of laws and other legal regulations; furthermore 3,198 judgments related to constitutional complaints and from this number the court (Panels) granted the complainants in 2,809 cases (data to 31 March, 2013, see http://nalus.usoud.cz[40]).[41]

Amongst others, the constitutional court case law reflects moral values as a starting point of a democratic rule of law in the State. The fundamental rights and freedoms in the Czech legal order are at the same time values by which the State is bound in its activities.[42] Although the constitutional court decisions relate to all branches of law, in the context of this contribution dealing with the role of constitutional courts while introducing human rights, it seems appropriate to point out below the value orientated decisions of the Constitutional Court of the Czech Republic which were important for the formation of a democratic State.

Some Selected Important Judgments of the Constitutional Court of the Czech Republic

File No.	*Popular name*	*Date*	*Verdict*
Pl. US 19/93	Lawlessness of Communist Regime	21.12.1993	Rejected
Pl. US 14/94	Legality and Legitimacy	11.4.1994	Rejected, granted
III. US 425/97	Binding Force of a Constitutional Court Judgment	2.4.1998	Granted
Pl. US 9/01	Lustration	5.12.2001	Granted, rejected
I. US 754/01	Interpretation of Restitution Law	23.10.2003	Granted

[40] The Constitutional Court of the CR publishes all its decisions (judgments and resolutions) at web page http://nalus.usoud.cz. It is possible to search here according to various criteria including subject catalogue index and a full text search. Besides that, all Plenum decisions granting the complaint and selected Panel decisions are published in English.

[41] For example, the Constutional Court has dealt with 4914 constitutional complaints in year 2012.

[42] Jan Filip. Ústavní právo [Constitutional Law]. Masarykova Univerzita. Brno, 2008.

File No.	*Popular name*	*Date*	*Verdict*
Pl. US 19/93	Lawlessness of Communist Regime	21.12.1993	Rejected
I. US 38/02	Application of Restitution Law	24.3.2004	Granted, rejected
Pl. US 19/08	Lisbon Treaty I	26.11.2008	Accordance of international treaty with constitution
II. US 2268/07	Signatory of Charter 77	29.2.2008	Granted
Pl. US 29/09	Lisbon Treaty II	3.11.2009	Dismissed as unsubstantiated, accordance of international treaty with constitution
Pl. US 27/09	Shortage of Electoral Period	10.9.2009	Granted
Pl. US 9/07	Church Restitution	1.7.2010	Rejected additive verdict

12.4.A Pl. US 14/94 "Legality and Legitimacy" [43]

In its constitutional complaint, the complainant asked for restitution for confiscated property and at the same time he suggested the annulment of the Beneš decree No. 108/1945 Coll., on the Confiscation of Enemy Property and the Funds of National Renewal. The constitutional court granted the complainant as far as restitution of confiscated property and it rejected the complaint as far as the petition demanded an annulment of a decree. This core judgment is significant especially, both by defining the characteristic features of democratic values and value perception of law as created after World War II. It deals with the differentiation between terms of legality and legitimacy and analyses of democracy as the political system enshrined in the law and explains foundations on which it is based. It describes both the conflict of democracy with totalitarianism and the necessity to defend democracy. Further on, it differentiates between the responsibilities that every citizen has and cannot relieve and fault it in a

[43] Judgment of the Constitutional Court of the CR. Pl. US 14/94 of 8 March, 1995; http://www.usoud.cz/en/.

criminal sense. In general, it serves as a warning to indifference in relation to the establishment of a totalitarian system.

The above judgment, in connection with the adjudication of the petition to annul the Beneš decrees, contains the postulation which can be used generally while evaluating the past in relation to law:

> It is necessary to emphasize, even in a general sense, a basic consideration that is relevant to any sort of evaluation of the past: while it is true in principle that that which emerges from the past must, face to face with the present, pass muster in respect to values; nevertheless, this assessment of the past may not be merely the present passing judgment upon the past. In other words, the present order, which has been enlightened by subsequent events, draws upon those experiences, and looks upon and assesses a great many phenomena with the advantage of hindsight, may not sit in judgment upon the order which prevailed in the past. Pl. US 14/94

14.4.B Pl. US 19/93 "Lawlessness of the Communist Regime" [44]

A group of Deputies of the Parliament of the CR submitted a complaint requesting the annulment of Act No. 198/1993 Coll., regarding the Lawlessness of the Communist Regime and Resistance to it, due to its incompatibility with the constitution and the Charter of Fundamental Rights and Basic Freedoms. The complainants contested provision Section 2 para. 1 of the above act according to which the political regime during the period from 1948–1989 was illegitimate. According to the complainants, "substantive continuity of domestic and international rights is an indication of the legitimacy of the governmental and political regime during the period from 1948–1989". On the contrary, the constitutional court refused the opinion that the political regime in the period from 1948–1989 was legitimate; in this connection, it defined the basic inviolable values of democratic society, the concept of legality and legitimacy and values and principles fundamental from the point of view of political regime legitimacy:

> Our new Constitution is not founded on neutrality with regard to values, it is not simply a mere demarcation of institutions and processes, rather it incorporates into its text also certain governing ideas, expressing the fundamental, inviolable values of a democratic society. The Czech Constitution accepts and respects the principle of legality as a part of the overall basic outline of a law-based state; positive law does not, however,

---

[44] Judgment of the Constitutional Court of the CR Pl. US 19/93 of 21 December, 1993; http://www.usoud.cz/en/.

bind it merely to formal legality, rather the interpretation and application of legal norms are subordinated to their substantive purpose, law is qualified by respect for the basic enacted values of a democratic society and also measures the application of legal norms by these values. This means that even while there is continuity of "old laws" there is a discontinuity in values from the "old regime”.

This conception of the constitutional state rejects the formal-rational legitimacy of a regime and the formal law-based state. Whatever the laws of a state are, in a state which is designated as democratic and which proclaims the principle of the sovereignty of the people, no regime other than a democratic regime may be considered as legitimate. Any sort of monopoly on power, in and of itself, rules out the possibility of democratic legitimacy. The starting point of our Constitution is the substantive-rational conception of legitimacy and the law-based state. In the overall structure of a democratic constitutional state and of a functioning democracy, legality mutatis mutandis undoubtedly embodies a part of the legitimacy of the regime, however, these concepts are not quite interchangeable. In a regime, in which hardly anybody was unaware that the elections were not elections, that the parties were not parties, that democracy was not democracy and that the law was not law [at least not in the sense of a law-based state, since the application of the law was politically schizophrenic and everywhere discarded when the interests of those governing entered into the picture], in such a regime it is even less possible to reduce the concept of legitimacy to that of the formal legality of normative legal regulation.

A political regime is legitimate if, on the whole, the majority of citizens accepts it. Political regimes which lack democratic substance avoid empirical verifications of legitimacy in favour of ideological arguments, primarily from the perspective of formal-rational legality. In this they are facilitated by the fact that consolidated governmental power is not just a fact of political power, but at the same time of legally organized power. However, it is precisely in such a regime that politics most differs from law and legality from legitimacy. For this reason, not even the continuity of law signifies recognition of the legitimacy of the communist regime. It cannot be asserted that every act or all conduct, so long as it does not cross over the line given by law, is legitimate, because, in this way, legality becomes a convenient substitute for an absent legitimacy.

The legitimacy of a political regime cannot rest solely upon the formal legal component because the values and principles upon which a regime is built are not just of a legal, but first of all of a political nature. Those principles of the Czech Constitution, such as the sovereignty of the people, representative democracy, and a law-based state, are principles of the political organization of society, which are not entirely normatively definable. Positive law proceeds from them, however normative regulation does not make up the full contents of these principles - something apart from it remains. Pl. US 19/93

12.4.C Pl. US 9/01 "Lustration" [45]

The so-called large Lustration Law was passed in the Czech Republic after the Velvet Revolution. By its approval, the legislator wanted to protect newly established institutions from the influence of the former communist State Security (StB) and people connected with it.[46] This above act stipulated pre-conditions for holding certain offices in governmental bodies and organizations of the Czech Republic. In this connection the constitutional court stated that the large and small lustration laws still protect an existing public interest, or, in other words, they pursued a legitimate aim, which is the active protection of a democratic state from the dangers which could be brought to it by insufficiently loyal and little trustworthy public services:

> Determination of the degree of development of democracy in a particular state is a social and political question, not a constitutional law question. Thus, the Constitutional Court is not able to review the claim of "culmination" or, on the contrary "non-culmination" of the democratic process by the means which it has at its disposal.
>
> A democratic state, and not only in a transitional period after the fall of totalitarianism, can tie an individual's entry into state administration and public services, and continuing in them, to meeting certain prerequisites, in particular meeting the requirement of (political) loyalty. The Constitutional Court begins with the premise that the concept of "loyalty" must be interpreted – like other key concepts, e.g. impartiality and independence of courts – by two complementary methods. The concept of loyalty covers the level of loyalty of each individual active in public services, and the level of loyalty of the public services as a whole. Here it is not only relevant whether the public services are actually loyal, but also whether they appear loyal to the public. For that it is necessary that doubts about their loyalty not arise. Such doubts undermine the public's trust in the public services and also in the democratic state which these services represent. Untrustworthy public services and state administration as a result endanger democracy, and a democratic state is entitled to defend itself against such danger by ensuring that the public services cannot appear untrustworthy to the public by eliminating reasons for doubts.
>
> The Constitutional Court of the CR, in agreement with its Czechoslovak predecessor, considers the closer connection of persons with the totalitarian regime and its repressive components to still be a relevant

---

[45] Judgment of the Constitutional Court of the CR Pl. US 9/01 of 5 December, 2001; http://www.usoud.cz/en/.

[46] In March 2003 the Ministry of Interior of the CR published an official list of 75 thousand registered collaborators.

circumstance which can cast doubt on political loyalty and damage the trustworthiness of the public services of a democratic state and also threaten such a state and its establishment. At the present time other newly democratic European states view this aspect of the past of their public representatives and bureaucrats analogously.

The Constitutional Court is aware that an individual's attitudes to the democratic establishment are determined primarily by his actual actions. The longer the period which has passed from the collapse of the totalitarian regime, the more and the more thoroughly will an individual's attitude to the democratic state be verified by his daily interaction with it and with the democratic society. In other words, with the passing of time the relative significance of attitudes and the position of persons in the totalitarian state certainly does not disappear, but certainly does decrease. There is evidently consensus in Europe in this regard. Pl. US 9/01

12.4.D II. US 2268/07 "Signatory of Charter 77" [47]

The complainant was a member of New Orientation, a group of clergies and laymen in the framework of the Protestant Church criticizing the political situation during the communist regime; he was also a signatory of Charter 77. In 1978, the complainant assaulted a member of the National Security Force after he had provoked him. He was found guilty for the criminal act of attempted assault on a public official and subversion of the state and convicted to an unconditional sentence of imprisonment for eight months. The complainant believed that the case was actually a political one. In 2007, the Minister of Justice filed a complaint of a violation of law against the criminal judgment related to the complainant. The Supreme Court denied the complaint; it stated that the complainant's actions corresponded to all the elements of the criminal act of an assault on a public official. According to the complainant, the Supreme Court must have known that the petitioner had been subject to persecution for a considerable period under the Communist regime. In its judgment, the Constitutional Court stated that the Supreme Court failed if it did not adjudicate the case in the broader context of the communist regime persecution. It considered the alleged criminal offence as a massive attack on the human dignity of the complainant. It also stressed that the trust of the public in the judiciary is the most precious value the judiciary has:

---

[47] Judgment of the Constitutional Court of the CR II. US 2268/07 of 29 February, 2008; http://www.usoud.cz/en/.

The Supreme Court was in error when, whilst evaluating the complaints on the violation of the law with respect to the contested resolution, it was satisfied merely with the criminal file and the statement of the public prosecutor and the petitioner. From the reasons specified above, it should have been clear that the case must be clarified within an even broader context, which for understandable reasons cannot be delineated merely from the original criminal files. This broader context is constituted by data which the Constitutional Court procured from public sources (see Section III, clauses 29-35). Findings from these sources complement the criminal file in terms of clarifying such gaps in knowledge which were not (and could not have been) closed with evidence in the original criminal proceedings, as the intentions of the State Police were not even in compliance with the valid legal regulations then. This broader context indicates that in fact any reason was sought out to constrain the personal freedom of the petitioner, so as to preclude his activities within the Evangelical Church of Czech Brethren (ECCB)....

The Evangelical Church of Czech Brethren (ECCB) was the largest Protestant church in the territory of the then Czech Socialist Republic. Elaboration of the ECCB as an internal enemy of the state commenced after February 1948 and ended with the fall of the Communist regime at the close of 1989. The State Police ranked the ECCB as one of the most "reactionary" and most dangerous churches: "Until the present time, the Evangelical Church of Czech Brethren has not ceased to apply its traditional orthodoxy, at some points exalted to extreme anti-socialist forms. It has been a bastion of resistance against the socialist order in the Czechoslovak Socialist Republic, has relations to right-wing and anti-socialist subjects in order to jointly instigate and support negative campaigns related to internal policy and aimed against the Communist Party. Out of all the movements existing within the Evangelical Church of Czech Brethren, 'New Orientation'–a formation of clergy and laymen–is a proponent, bearer and promoter of hostile attitudes against the state." (p. 20 of the document).... The State Police formally undertook operative elaboration of the Evangelical Church of Czech Brethren on the basis of the following political criminal acts: subversion of the state (§ 98), sedition (§ 100), misuse of religious office (§ 101), damnification of interests of the state abroad (§ 112), and obstruction of supervision over church and religious institutions (§ 178) (p. 21 of the document)....

An essential condition for the existence of an independent judiciary is the trust of the public in the judges seeking just decisions adopted on the basis of law. Without public trust in the judge's procedure being fair and in compliance with high moral standards, the judiciary cannot function properly. The trust of the public in the judiciary is the most precious value the judiciary has; such a trust is also one of the most valuable virtues for each citizen of a state. H. de Balzac said: "Lack of trust in a judicial system is the beginning of the end for society." However, the trust of the public is not given freely, it must be earned. Maintaining it is more difficult than losing it. Years of hard work and endeavour may be thrown away due to one lapse in judgment. Each and every judge must bear this in mind when taking a decision in a case; a judge, unlike the legislature, does not enforce their own will, but should always enforce the law through a constitutionally conformable interpretation.

In the words of Justice Douglas: "The more transparent and outright the manner of argument, the closer one is to democracy. This is reflected in Cardozo's 'openness'. The principle of complete openness has the same substantiation in state institutions' agenda as in economy. A judiciary discovering reasons for their choosing a course of action earns understanding. Trust based on understanding is more permanent and resolute than that based on fear and forced respect." (Douglas, W.: Stare Decisis, 49 Colum. L. Rev. 735, 754 [1949]).

Human dignity as a value is intrinsic to the foundations of the entire scheme of fundamental rights as contained within the constitutional order. The entitlement of every individual to enjoy respect and recognition as a human being is related to human dignity, implying a prohibition of rendering a man a mere object of a state's will, or prohibition of exposing a person to such actions which cast doubts on such a person's quality as a subject. II. US 2268/07

12.4.E I. US 754/01 and I. US 38/02 "Restitution of property" [48, 49]

In the Czech Republic, after the fall of the communist regime in 1989, the partial restitution of property was realized on the basis of acts on mitigation of consequences of certain property and other injustices. It is stated that restitutions in the Czech Republic were the most extensive of the post communist countries. The restitution related to property taken away illegally during the "decisive period", that is, the period from 25 February 1948 until 1 January 1990. Restitution laws have also been repeatedly subject to review before the constitutional court, both in the framework of abstract and specific reviews. The court significantly contributed to both the interpretation and application of restitution laws, as we can see from the reasoning below:

The Constitutional Court would emphasize that with the restitution laws the democratic law-based state is endeavoring at least partially to alleviate

[48] Judgment I. US 754/01 of the Constitutional Court of the CR of 23 October, 2003; http://www.usoud.cz/en/.

[49] Judgment I. US 38/02 of the Constitutional Court of the CR of 24 March, 2004; http://www.usoud.cz/en/.

the consequences of past property injustices, and state bodies are obliged to conduct themselves in accordance with the applicable restitution law in harmony with the statutory interests of persons who should be at least partially compensated for injuries inflicted upon them by the totalitarian communist regime. This partial compensation cannot be seen, for example, in an outcome where, although the restitution claim is determined to be well-founded, the entitled persons merely receives free of charge another parcel of land owned by the state or is awarded financial compensation. The guiding principle must always be the above-stated intent of the restitution law, in the interpretation of which preference must in principle be given to turning over the original plot, or plots, of land, should the restituent pursue that outcome and should the law not rule it out." (I. US 754/01)

"In applying the restitution acts, a too restrictive, or formalistic, approach must not be taken, on the contrary, they must be applied in a very sensitive manner, always with the circumstances of the particular case in mind, and above all the cited purpose and significance of the act. As far as concerns the above-stated central question relating to the necessity of the precise individualization or specification of the items demanded, under the sanction that the claim would otherwise be extinguished, it would perhaps be possible to agree with the ordinary courts' conclusions if this matter had not concerned an enormous extent of moveable property, but about several items where it would be entirely and without any doubt evident that it was within the restituent's power to specify in detail the property in question within the time period allowed by the statute.

If there exists several possible interpretations of a particular legal enactment or of certain of its provisions, consideration must be given to the intent of the legal rule. In the case of Act No. 87/1991 Coll. that intent is doubtless the effort to mitigate the consequences of certain property injustices committed by the totalitarian state in the decisive period. If two equally valid interpretations are possible, one of which is broad and the other narrow, between them the court must select that which corresponds to further interpretive methods, in particular teleological reasoning. The ratio legis of the restitution acts is to redress, at least to a certain degree, the consequences of the infringement of the fundamental rights of natural and legal persons in the totalitarian era. Thus, a constitutionally conforming interpretation is generally a broad one: a statute and its individual provisions must be interpreted in such a way that, by applying them, it is possible to attain the aim pursued by the legislature.

When interpreting the relevant provisions of the restitution acts, it also cannot be overlooked that it was a totalitarian state which illegally stripped its citizens of their property and that subsequently state bodies dealt with that property in an arbitrary fashion for a period of nearly 40 years, in the course of which movable property was appropriated and in fact relocated to various places; therefore, the Constitutional Court is convinced that the consequences of these or similar transactions cannot now be interpreted, in principle, solely to the detriment of the entitled persons. It is necessary always to proceed on the basis of the circumstances of the particular, concrete case. I. US 38/02.

12.4.F Pl. US 9/07 "Church Restitution" [50]

A group of senators of the Parliament of the Czech Republic filed a complaint in which they requested the annulment of Section 29 of the Act on Land, a so-called blocking provision or provision of "a blocking nature" according to which such property as was originally owned by churches, religious orders and congregations cannot be transferred to the ownership of third parties prior to the adoption of an act regarding such property. Although a special legal regulation satisfying the entitlement of churches should have been passed, the legislator did not carry out any steps and the intended legal regulation was not passed in a period of 19 years. The length of this transitionary period of restriction of ownership rights was not limited by the act. As a result of this, part of the owners, especially municipalities, could not run a business as the property relations had not been satisfied. After adjudication of the case, the constitutional court has found no reasons for granting the petition for annulment of Section 29 of the Act on Land, since said provisions are not unconstitutional. The constitutional court has found that the purpose, as well as the means contained in the contested provisions stand up, when tested against the constitutional principles:

> It follows from the meaning of the contested provision and the hitherto interpretation of the same by the Constitutional Court (continuation to the above-recapitulated case law) that their purpose is not only the actual "blockage" of a certain part of state property (partly also property registered as owned by third parties, particularly municipalities); that is, for example, attempts to preserve a certain status quo in terms of property. The nature of the contested provisions must be seen in particular in the commitment (pledge) of the legislature, at a deferred time, to adopt a legal arrangement settling the historic property of churches and religious communities, which would take into account objective particulars of the matter under discussion and actually consummates the provisions of § 29 of the Act on Land.
>
> The above-specified purpose of § 29 of the Act on Land must be observed in the context of the value foundation for restitution and rehabilitation law and the case law of the Constitutional Court. The

[50] Judgment Pl. US 9/07 of the Constitutional Court of the CR of 1 July, 2010; http://www.usoud.cz/en/.

legislature embodied the primary value points in the preambles and introductory provisions of restitution acts and rehabilitation acts and Act No. 198/1993 Coll. on Lawlessness of the Communist Regime and on Resistance to the Same. The Constitutional Court explicitly declared the non-legitimacy of the regime and its acts from 1948 to 1989 in its key Judgment file No. Pl. US 19/93, dated 21 December 1993. In addition, it is necessary to emphasise that the issue of the restitution under consideration is not seen by the Constitutional Court, even through the distance of two decades, as one of historic injustice that would stretch beyond the instruments of a rule of law state.

Long-term inactivity on the part of the Parliament of the Czech Republic consisting in non-adoption of a special legal regulation governing disposal of property, the original owners of which were churches, religious orders and congregations, violates Article 1 paragraph 1 of the Constitution of the Czech Republic, Article 4 paragraph 1, Article 11 paragraph 1, paragraph 4 of the Charter of Fundamental Rights and Basic Freedoms, and Article 1 paragraph 1 of Protocol No. 1 to the Convention for the Protection of Human Rights and Fundamental Freedoms. Pl. US 9/07.

12.4.G Pl. US 19/08 "Lisbon Treaty" Pl. US 19/08 [51]

A group of senators claimed to review the conformity of the Lisbon Treaty with the Constitution, both as a whole and individual provision thereof. Here, the constitutional court has dealt for the first time with a preventive review of an international treaty. In this judgment, the constitutional court has interpreted such concepts as sovereignty, transfer of certain powers of the Czech Republic to international bodies, the substantive core of the constitution and conditional conferral of powers:

> 105. The global scene can no longer be seen only as a world of isolated states. It is generally accepted that the state and its sovereignty are undergoing change, and that no state is such a unitary, separate organization as classical theories assumed in the past. An international political system is being created in the global scale that lacks institutionalized rules of its own self-government, such as the international system created by sovereign states had until now. It is an existential interest of the integrating European civilization to appear in global competition as an important and respected force. These processes quite clearly demonstrate that the sovereign legitimate state power must necessarily observe the ongoing developmental trends and attempt to approach them, understand them, and gradually subject this spontaneous

[51] Judgment Pl. US 19/08 of the Constitutional Court of the CR of 26 November, 2008; http://www.usoud.cz/en/.

globalization process, lacking hierarchical organization, to the order of democratic legitimacy…

The European Union has advanced by far the furthest in the concept of pooled sovereignty, and today is creating an entity sui generis, which is difficult to classify in classical political science categories. It is more a linguistic question whether to describe the integration process as a "loss" of part of sovereignty, or competences, or, somewhat more fittingly, as, e.g., "lending, ceding" of part of the competence of a sovereign. It may seem paradoxical that they key expression of state sovereignty is the ability to dispose of one's sovereignty (or part of it), or to temporarily or even permanently cede certain competences.

93. As the Constitutional Court has already stated above, within the applied point of reference, the constitutional order of the Czech Republic, it is the essential requirements of a democratic, law-based state – whose amendment is impermissible under Art. 9 par. 2 of the Constitution – that represent the central criterion. A more detailed description of the content of these essential requirements of a democratic, law-based state, which usually have the character of general principles, is the result, in specific cases, of interpretation by bodies that apply the Constitution. The Constitutional Court of the Czech Republic, in its historically first judgment, stated that our Constitution is not based on a neutrality of values, it is not a mere definition of institutions and processes (judgment file no. Pl. US 19/93, judgment file no. Pl. US 14/1994 Coll.).

120. In view of the foregoing, the Constitutional Court states (and repeats) that the Constitutional Court generally recognizes the functionality of the EU institutional framework for ensuring review of the scope of the exercise of conferred competences; however, its position may change in the future if it appears that this framework is demonstrably non-functional. In terms of the constitutional order of the Czech Republic – and within it especially in view of the material core of the Constitution – what is important is not only the actual text and content of the Treaty of Lisbon, but also its future concrete application. Pl. US 19/08.

12.4.H Pl. US 29/09 „Lisbon II“ [52]

In the judgment Lisbon II, dealing again with objections to the Lisbon Treaty filed by a group of senators, it answered some other procedural questions in the proceedings on the preventive review of international treaties with constitutional orders (e.g. interpretations of *rei iudicatae*, time limits for submitting a petition to open proceedings on the conformity of an international treaty with the constitutional order). The constitutional court also pointed out that, in a modern democratic State governed by the

[52] Judgment of the Constitutional Court of the CR Pl. US 29/09 of 3 November, 2009; http://www.usoud.cz/en/.

rule of law, the sovereignty of the State is not an aim in and of itself, that is, in isolation, but is a means for fulfilling the fundamental values on which the construction of a democratic State governed by the rule of law stands:

> The Court points out that, in a modern democratic state governed by the rule of law, the sovereignty of the state is not an aim in and of itself, that is, in isolation, but is a means for fulfilling the fundamental values on which the construction of a democratic state governed by the rule of law stands. It then concluded that the transfer of certain state competences, that arises from the free will of the sovereign, and will continue to be exercised with the sovereign's participation in a manner that is agreed upon in advance and is subject to review, is not a conceptual weakening of sovereignty, but, on the contrary, can lead to strengthening it within the joint actions of an integrated whole. … A key manifestation of a state's sovereignty is the ability to continue to manage its sovereignty (or part of it), or to cede certain powers temporarily or permanently. Pl. US 29/09.

14.4.I Pl. US 27/09 "Shortening the Term of Office of the Chamber of Deputies" [53]

In his constitutional complaint, a Deputy of the Chamber of Deputies of the Parliament sought the annulment of the Decision of the President of the Republic no. 207/2009 Coll., on Calling Elections to the Chamber of Deputies of the Czech Republic. At the same time he was filing a petition seeking the annulment of constitutional Act no. 195/2009 Coll., on Shortening the Fifth Term of Office of the Chamber of Deputies. He objected that the cited decision of the President and Act violated his right to uninterrupted exercise of a public office. As far as the contested act, he believed that it changed the essential requirements for a democratic State governed by the rule of law which are impermissible under Art. 9 para. 2 of the Constitution:

> In its case law, the Constitutional Court emphatically made clear the need to protect the material focus of the constitutional order, and, partly abstractly and partly casuistically, indicated its structure, as well as the fact that its consequences apply not only to the democratic legislature, but to the Constitutional Court itself.
>
> Insofar as the Constitutional Court articulates the need to include the category of constitutional acts within the term "statute" in Art. 87 par. 1

[53] Judgment of the Constitutional Court of the CR Pl. US 27/09 of 10 September, 2009; http://www.usoud.cz/en/.

let. a) of the Constitution, in terms of reviewing them for consistency with Art. 9 par. 2 of the Constitution, with direct derogative consequences, it does so in connection to its case law, beginning with the key judgment file no. Pl. US 19/93, and does so in accordance with the values and principles that guide constitutional systems in democratic countries. Protection of the material core of the Constitution, i.e. the imperative that the essential requirements for a democratic state governed by the rule of law, under Art. 9 par. 2 of the Constitution, are non-changeable, is not a mere slogan or proclamation, but a constitutional provision with normative consequences. In No. 78 of The Federalist Papers, Alexander Hamilton wrote that "the courts were designed to be an intermediate body between the people and the legislature, in order, among other things, to keep the latter within the limits assigned to their authority." Without the projection of Art. 9 par. 2 of the Constitution into interpretation of Art. 87 par. 1 let. a) of the Constitution, the non-changeability of the essential requirements for a democratic state governed by the rule of law would lose its normative nature and remain merely a political, or moral challenge.

An ad hoc constitutional act (for an individual instance) is not a supplement or amendment to the Constitution. In content, a constitutional act for an individual instance can take two forms – either it involves time-limited suspension of the Constitution, or a substantive, or personal, exception from the general validity of the constitutional framework.

A supplement to the constitution can be characterized by the fact that the supplemented constitutional provision does not change, and the supplemented and supplementing provisions are not inconsistent. An amendment to the constitution means that a particular constitutional provision is annulled or partly annulled and perhaps (not necessarily) a new provision is established. In a breach, the constitution is not annulled, but the breached (in this case, suspended) provision and the breaching (in this case, suspending) provision are inconsistent.

Constitutional Act no. 195/2009 Coll. is a constitutional act only in form, but not in substance. In substance it is an individual legal act affecting not a generally defined circle of addressees and situations, but a specifically designated subject (the Chamber of Deputies of the Parliament of the Czech Republic elected in 2006) and a specific situation (ending its term of office on the day of elections, which are to be held by 15 October 2009, and shortening deadlines under the Act on Elections to the Parliament of the Czech Republic and under the Administrative Procedure Code, only for this instance). This fact is expressly stated not only in Art. 1 of this constitutional Act, but also in Art. 2 (which is a direct amendment to statutes implemented by the constitutional act!), which contains the express formulation concerning the shortening of deadlines, "for this instance."

The original constitutional framers, in Art. 9 par. 2 of the Constitution, placed the democratic principle and the principle of a law-based state on the same level among the principles that fundamentally identify the constitutional system of the Czech Republic. As the Constitutional Court's case law indicates, violating the principle of generality of laws falls within the realm of impermissible interference with a law-based state. Possible exceptions are either cases of accepting application of law in the form of a statute (e.g. an act on the state budget), or cases of express authorization to issue an ad hoc statute (e.g. constitutional acts issued under Art. 11 and Art. 100 par. 3 of the Constitution) or ad hoc statutes whose issuance is supported by exceptional reasons that meet the condition of the proportionality test (e.g. restitution acts containing lists).

In the absence of a constitutional authorization to issue constitutional acts ad hoc, the constitutional conformity of a constitutional act adopted inconsistently with the constitutionally defined scope of the competence of Parliament could be established only by protection of the material core under Art. 9 par. 2 of the Constitution. In other words, protection of the democratic state governed by the rule of law by adopting an ad hoc constitutional act could be accepted in absolutely exceptional circumstances (such as a state of war or natural catastrophe that are not addressed by either the Constitution or by constitutional Act no. 110/1998 Coll., on the Security of the Czech Republic, as amended by constitutional Act no. 300/2000 Coll.), but that procedure would have to meet the requirements that follow from the principle of proportionality. Pl. US 27/09

12.5 Conclusion

Constitutional courts as specialised institutions of concentrated constitutional reviews emerged for the first time in the inter-war period, namely in constitutions of Czechoslovakia and Austria in 1920; we speak about the origin of European constitutional judiciary. Nevertheless, they became much more important after the fall of Nazism and fascism and later on communism, i.e. in connection with the need to stress the perception of law based on ethical values. The constitutional judiciary is an important phenomenon of the rule of law in the State. Its role consists of the protection of constitutionality containing protection of human or fundamental rights. Constitutional courts have a unique position in the framework of the division of powers in relation towards both ordinary courts (power to annul their decisions) and to parliament (power to annul laws or its provisions). They pronounce themselves as a negative legislator to the most complex political, social and moral issues from the point of view of constitutionality. In doing that, they find the limits of constitutional review; their task is not to review legality. The essential qualification to be a justice of the constitutional court consists not only in an expert qualification, but also in the perception of values embodied in fundamental rights. In their decision-making adjudication, constitutional courts should use persuasive reasoning. The existence of the constitutional court means continual and systematic attention devoted to issues of constitutionality and interpretation of fundamental rights content. The role of constitutional courts is not done in advance; it is searched and fulfilled repeatedly in connection with adjudication of different issues related to the development of society.

CHAPTER THIRTEEN

THE HISTORICAL AND THEORETICAL ASPECT OF APPROXIMATION OF LAW IN CENTRAL EUROPE

VLASTA KUNOVÁ

13.1 Introduction

The unification of law or legal convergence consists in purposeful activities jointly undertaken by unifying entities with a view to adopting uniform texts of legal standards and subsequently transposing them as valid law into the legal systems of the countries concerned in line with their international commitments. These activities result in the creation of a set of unified standards.[1]

The process of the unification of law can be perceived in two ways. Firstly, it represents unification of law at the level of the creation of law, i.e. unification of legislation. Secondly, it means unification of the application of law, i.e. uniform interpretation and application of law by courts.[2]

In private international law, classical unification of law was carried out by incorporating a uniform wording of a legal standard (legal institution) into the text of an international treaty. The same outcome can be achieved by an international organisation through its statute. It creates an obligation for State parties to transpose agreed standards into their legal systems and to refrain from their unilateral change. The States may take over uniform legal provisions also on a voluntary basis: in this case we speak about

[1] See Kučera, Zdeněk. *Mezinárodní právo soukromé.* Brno: 1994. p. 56.
[2] See also Štefanovič, Milan. *Svetové právne systémy.* Bratislava: BVSP, 2007. p. 36.

practical implementation of the objectives and functions of unified international standards.[3]

A distinction should be made between unification of law and approximation or harmonisation of law. The latter concept denotes an activity that does not result in the adoption of identical legal provisions, but leads only to a greater or lesser degree of their similarity or correspondence.[4]

On the one hand, unification and also approximation (harmonisation) can have the form of intra-state unification when the legal environment comprises of at least two legal systems. The efforts at unifying the law at the intra-state level existed also during the so-called First Czechoslovak Republic (1918–1938). The type of unification that is the most frequently applied in Europe is a so-called inter-state unification–of the kind that took place between the Scandinavian countries (Denmark, Norway, Sweden, Finland and Iceland). In both cases, difficulties were encountered at the concluding stage of unification (or approximation).[5]

A completely new form of unification of law and legal convergence is currently taking place at the level of the EU. It emanates from the supranational concept of the EU and the loyalty principle.[6] On this basis, part of the competences of the Member States have been conferred upon the European Union; as a result, the EU may adopt legal acts that take precedence over the law of its Member States and that are directly applicable in these States.[7] According to the loyalty principle, Member States are required to ensure the fulfilment of the obligations arising out of the treaties or resulting from the acts of the EU.[8] According to Art. 114 of the TFEU, approximation of laws is one of the key instruments for the functioning of the internal market of the EU.

Unification of law and legal alignment are among the key unifying factors in the European Union framework.

---

[3] See Kunová,Vlasta. Od pridruženia k členstvu Slovenskej republiky v Európskej únii. In Čorba, Juraj at all. Európske právo na Slovensku. Bratislava: Nadácia Kalligram, 2003. p.110.

[4] Compare Kunová,Vlasta. Od pridruženia k členstvu Slovenskej republiky v Európskej únii. In Juraj Čorba, et al. Európske právo na Slovensku. Bratislava: Nadácia Kalligram, 2003. 109.; See Šišková, Naděžda. *Základni otázky sbližování českého práva s právem ES. Codex Bohemia,* 1998. p. 18.

[5] See Bogdan, Michael. Nordická legislatívna spolupráca - príklad harmonizácie právnych poriadkov. In *Právny obzor*, 1993.1. p. 58.

[6] Tichý, Luboš. et al. Evropské právo. Prague: C.H.BECK, 2011. 4 revised. p. 68.

[7] set out for the first time by the Court of Justice in Case 6/64 Costa v. ENEL.

[8] See Art. 4; par 3 of the TEU.

13.2 Historical background

Unification and approximation of law within the EU are globalisation phenomena in law, their roots dating back to the Middle Ages[9].

Addressing the issue of legal convergence is a challenging task. Where should I begin? In the first place, I must emphasise that my primary focus will be on the research into unification phenomena in the region of Central Europe, with an excursion into a more distant past. The most highly developed law in the times of Antiquity was the law of ancient Romans. In addition to the positive influences of ancient Romans in other fields, Roman law represented a grandiose achievement of the spirit of Roman civilisation.[10] In this regard, the fusion of *ius civile* with *ius gentium* may be perceived as a first successful step towards unification. Another historic form of legal assimilation is the reception of law.[11] The reception of law means not only that one country takes over the law of another country; it also includes the shaping of a country's legal system following the model of another country.[12] The concept of the reception of law is used most often in connection with the process of the imitation of Roman law in continental European countries. That process was taking place roughly between the 12th and the 16th centuries and it left an indelible mark on the countries of the European continent of that time, from the eastern shores of the Atlantic to the western borders of Russia. Roman law is also associated with the law of universities, where it was developed and cultivated by prominent legal scholars. It was not only a propaedeutic subject, but also a living example suitable for practical applications. Finally, *ius commune* represents historic foundations for *ius commune europeo*.[13] As a matter of interest, I would like to stress that Roman law is still being taught at all law faculties in Central Europe today. It represents a return to the old traditions of continental Europe and constitutes a unifying link with Western legal culture. The idea of "natural law", i.e. the law that belongs to all animals and/or living creatures, also originated in ancient Rome.[14] Naturally, Central Europe was influenced also by canonical law–another unifying element in the evolution of legal thinking. In the Middle Ages,

---

[9] See Fischer, Peter et al. *Europa Recht*. Vienna: Linde Verlag, 2002. p. 17.

[10] See Urfus ,Valentin. *Historické základy novodobého práva soukromého.*Prague: C. H. BECK, 1994. p. 1.

[11] See also Knapp, Viktor. *Velké právní systémy.* Prague: C. H. BECK, 1996. p. 213.

[12] Ibid.

[13] See Bartošek, Milan. *Dejiny římskeho práva.* Prague: Academia, 1988.

[14] Ulpianus (D.1,1,1,3)

German mining and municipal rights were introduced and exercised in the territory of Slovakia. They took root in Slovakia along with the technical know-how on gold and silver mining. The import of German law to Slovakia at that time represented a clearly positive moment in our legal development.[15]

A new era of European legal history was ushered in with the emergence of natural law in the 17th century. It introduced a supranational element into the legal history of Europe. As already stated, it may be traced back to old Greek philosophy, and also to Roman law. However, the Modern Age gave it a new, rational content. In German philosophy, this law is referred to as "Vernunfrecht".[16] Its representative is Dutch lawyer Hugo Grotius and his work "*De iure belli ac pacis*." The idea that there is only one law that exists independently on the positive law is as old as mankind itself. However, Grotius's teachings gave it a rational core. The rational perception of natural law heralded the advent of a new civil society. Natural law theories are closely linked with the Enlightenment and they undoubtedly represent the philosophical backdrop to the present-day globalisation tendencies in European law as a whole. On the one hand, major European codifications of civil law reflected the national ambitions of their drafters. They are often considered as supremely national achievements of the human mind. On the other hand, almost all civil codes have their roots in Roman law, which was their unifying element. In the case of Slovakia, the text of the Czechoslovak Civil Code was drawn up in the 1950s under the influence of "Allgemeines Buergerliches Gesetzbuch (1811)." Thus, in the early stages of the socialist period in Czechoslovakia, it was still possible to derive inspiration from a Western model. However, the only models that were allowed in our legal system in the subsequent periods were those of other Communist countries and, in particular, of the Soviet Union. European civil codes served as models for many countries not only in Europe, but also in other continents. The adoption of a code always brings greater clarity to the law in force, its systemisation, and represents a global element in the development of law.[17]

---

[15] Štefanovič, Milan. *Svetové právne systémy.* Bratislava: BVSP, 2007. p. 23.

[16] Bartošek, Milan. *Dejiny římskeho práva.* Prague: Academia, 1988.

[17] See von Münch, I.v. Export a import práva. In *Právní rozhledy.* 1995. 3. p. 107-109.

13.3 The Concept of Droit Commun de l'Humanité

The process of legal convergence represented a major milestone in the early 20th century. A World Congress of Comparative Law was held in 1900 in Paris. The Congress focused, inter alia, on the development of common law. That was the time when the notion of the so-called common legislative law started to be used. Moreover, H. Levy-Ullmann and his reflections about the creation of global law of the 20th century influenced the legal science of that period. Italian lawyer del Vecchio saw the future in a comparative legal science that can effectively contribute as a great source of inspiration for the coming together of various legal systems across the world.[18] The concept of the so-called *droit commun de l'humanité* proposed by Raymond Saleilles may sound like a fantasy, but it represents the basis for the reflections about the so-called *ius unum*. The Czech legal theoretician Viktor Knapp does not believe that legal systems of individual countries are separated by insurmountable and insuperable barriers.[19] While it is true that individual laws are tied to a certain territory, the law as such is not. An interesting fact is that law is not protected by a copyright. It may therefore be used at will as a model for legislative proposals, copied and exported from or imported to other countries practically without any restriction. There are scores of examples of such "robberies of law", as certain German authors call this phenomenon.[20]

13.4 The Process of Approximation of Slovak Law with EC/EU Law

In the post-1989 period, Slovakia started to transform its legal system. I know from my own experience that these processes were often unstructured and non-systemic. Slovak lawmakers were drawing on foreign models depending on their subjective experience. The prevailing criteria included the knowledge of a language, personal contacts, availability of a legal model and sometimes even the party of the affiliation of the drafters of legal texts.[21] Thus, Slovak criminal law drew on certain American models, which it is very difficult to transpose into our

---

[18] See Knapp, Viktor. *Velké právní systémy.* Prague: C. H. BECK, 1996. p. 213, p.10-11.

[19] Ibid. 209.

[20] See von Münch, I.v. Export a import práva. In *Právní rozhledy.* 1995. 3. p.108.

[21] Kunová, Vlasta. *Globalization and Law.* In *After Fifty Years the Coming Challenges*. Coimbra: Almedia, 2007. p. 62.

legal reality. Apart from that the alignment of Slovak law with EU law represented a positive moment in our legal reform.[22]

The Europe Agreement Establishing an Association between the European Communities and Their Member States, of the One Part, and the Slovak Republic, of the Other Part, was adopted on 4 October 1993 in Luxembourg by signing the Final Act. In conformity with its Article 123, this international treaty entered into force on 1 February 1995. In the Slovak Republic, the Europe Agreement was published in the Collection of Laws under No. 157/1998. In the European Union, it was published in the Official Journal of the European Communities as L 359 of 31 December 1994. The European Agreement is an important instrument and basic document for aligning Slovak law with the law of the European Communities.

The articles related to the harmonisation of national legislation with EC/EU law are found in all Association agreements concluded with the countries of Central and Eastern Europe. The commitment to legal alignment is fulfilled by means of general harmonisation measures and provisions governing certain specific areas.

As has been mentioned above, the key legal instrument was the European Agreement on Association of 1993, namely its articles 69 and 70.[23]

Under the Agreement, Slovakia gave an undertaking to align its entire existing and future legal system with the law of the EU. Legal alignment was governed by clear rules, centrally coordinated by the European Commission, and financed from EU PHARE funds. Right from the outset, it was clear that the process will transcend the limits and barriers represented by national interests. This was a dynamic process driven by the concern that the failure to fulfil the obligation of implementing the *acquis communautaire* could mean an end to integration ambitions of a candidate country. New members of the EU were mutually harmonising their legal systems at a relatively fast pace, bringing them closer also to the so-called comparandum, i.e. EU law. Legal comparative science attaches a

---

[22] Compare Kunová, Vlasta. Od pridruženia k členstvu Slovenskej republiky v Európskej únii. In Juraj Čorba, et al. Európske právo na Slovensku. Bratislava: Nadácia Kalligram, 2003. p.109.

[23] Maresceau, Marc. Europe Agreements: A New Form of Cooperation between the European Community and Central and Eastern Europe. In *East and Central European States and the European Communities: Legal Adaptation to the Market Economy*. Baden-Baden: Nomos Verlaggesellschaft, 1995. p. 209-233.
Kunova, Vlasta. Ibid p.109.

high value to the following positive attributes of the process of approximation (I will use Slovakia as an example):

- democratisation of the national legal system
- stabilisation of the national legal systems
- modernisation of the legislation[24]
- systematic character of the legal reforms[25]

---

[24] Compatibility clause and concordance tables are very modern instruments of comparative methods for evaluation of approximation of laws. The key purpose of the clause was to ascertain the degree of compatibility between the Slovak legal regulation and the relevant Community legislation. In the compatibility clause, the bodies submitting Government bills must state the degree of compliance of a draft legal regulation with the law of the European Union. The degree of compliance may be: full; partial; none; the draft legal regulation is incompatible. The compatibility clause also specified whether the subject covered by the draft legal regulation:
a) Was provided for in the law of the European Union; b) was not provided for in the law of the European Union;
The compatibility clause should have a constitutive rather than a declaratory character.
Annex 1a) to the Legislative Rules of the Government of the Slovak Republic includes the description of the table of concordance between a legal regulation and the law of the European Communities and the law of the European Union. Concordance tables serve as auxiliary instruments providing broader information about the compatibility of a Slovak legal norm with EU law. Concordance tables contain also information about the method of transposition of EU law, i. e. standard transposition, transposition with options, or transposition at full discretion of the Member State. The control of compatibility was performed at the governmental level by the relevant section of the Institute for Approximation of Law of the Slovak Government's Office. No concordance tables were prepared for private bills of MPs which must contain only the compatibility clause.
[25] Systematic character was manifested in the Association Agreement: Under the Agreement we distinguish general harmonisation measures (art. 69 and 70), special harmonisation measures (Article 57 paragraph 5, Article 62 paragraph 1, Article 64 paragraphs 2 and 5, Article 66, Article 67 paragraph 1, Article 75 paragraph 1, Article 78 paragraph 1, Article 81 paragraph 3, Article 82 paragraph 3, Article 84 paragraph 1, Article 86 paragraph 2, Article 92 paragraph 1 and Article 93 paragraph 1) and technical harmonisation measures (Art. 75). See also the White Paper adopted by the European Council, the document under the title the "White Paper" in June 1995. Preparation of the Associated Countries of Central and Eastern Europe for Integration into the Internal Market of the Union. The White Paper applied to six Central and Eastern European countries that signed Europe Agreements with the EU (Poland, Hungary, the Czech Republic, the Slovak Republic, Bulgaria, Rumania) and the countries expected to conclude Association

- dynamic quality and flexibility of the whole process
- central coordination by the institutions of the EU
- high professionalism of the EU experts
- the exchange of EU and local experts
- enrichment of the legal terminology
- uniform know-how on the transposition of EU law in new Member States or candidate countries
- organisation of seminars and training activities for local experts
- technical assistance to the candidate country in the process of harmonisation (Art. 71 of the Europe Agreement)

Legal approximation consisted of two elements. Firstly, convergence of the legal systems of candidate countries with EU law, i.e. the process of ensuring a certain degree of uniformity of these legal systems; secondly, legal unification. A parallel process of a gradual elimination of differences between the legal systems of the Member States–referred to in legal theory as harmonisation of law–was also taking place.[26] The process of legal convergence within the EU continues and, at the same time, constitutes one of the most important instruments for external relations of the EU. I will mention, by way of example, several projects that involved Slovak legal experts: The preparation of the Ukrainian Parliament for legal approximation,[27] EU seat for Serbia, transfer of experience to Belarus,[28]

Agreements in the near future (Estonia, Latvia, Lithuania, Slovenia). The number of addressees of the White Paper is not final and may increase. The White Paper has the character of a systematic manual containing basic information about the state of legislation and other relevant data in selected areas of the EU internal market, and recommendations concerning optimum procedures to be used by the associated countries in their harmonisation efforts.

26 Libanský. Václav. Harmonizace čs. práva s právem ES. In *Právo a zákonnost*. 1992. 4. p. 197.

[27] The need and necessity of harmonization of the Ukrainian law with the European law was declared at the beginning of the reconstruction of the Ukrainian state. Ukraine signed the Partnership and Cooperation Agreement (PCA) with the EU in the Summer of 1994. This document proclaimed a strategic goal of European integration for Ukraine, Ukraine has committed to approximate its legislation in 16 key sectors; currently the Association Treaty is foreseen to be signed. See in detail Petrov, Roman. Transpozicija „acquis“ Evropejskogo Sojuza v pravovije sistemi tretich stran. Kijev: Istina, 2011. p.294-364.

[28] See in details In Kunova,Vlasta et al. European Union – Support via experience, assistence and training. Bratislava: Comenius University, Faculty of Law, 2005. p.75. In Kunova, Vlasta and Vrabko, Marian et al. Experience of the Slovak

approximation projects in Moldavia etc.[29] The EU provides important assistance also to non-member states of the EU in the Mediterranean area. Also the countries of Asia, especially China and Japan, are interested in approximating their laws with the European Union. Several top American universities offer EU law courses.[30] As regards to the companies in Slovakia, especially those with US investors, they pay attention mainly to the EU competition law. We are clearly faced with the so-called migration of law, as a result of which law is becoming an object of imitation and intellectual admiration. Law is being taken over at an almost informal level. The process of legal approximation and harmonisation in the framework of the EU has transcended narrow regional legal concepts. This was the first time in the history of law that targeted activities in the legislative area have proven to be so effective. It is worth noting that this process relies on voluntary engagement, since the States introduced the elements of European law into their legal systems for pragmatic reasons. The EU does not exert pressure on the candidate countries to make them fulfil their commitments in the area of legal transposition (except for the observance of the general principle *pacta sunt servanda*). The situation is different in those Member States where the enforcement in this area relies on sanctions and on non-contractual liability of the State for the incorrect transposition of Community law. The Alignment of individual state laws with EU law undoubtedly represents one of the most successful projects of the EU. It represents a distinct move towards the concept of "*ius unum,*" which certain legal sceptics are reluctant to recognise. The EU law constitutes a mixture of continental and Anglo-Saxon legal systems. This has been the first time in the legal history of Central European countries that they are experiencing such a massive influx of elements of common law. In the early 1990s I met a well-known English philosopher, Professor Roger Scruton, in Bratislava. He suggested that English judges should replace Slovak judges. He argued that because of the notorious problem of corruption in the courts of several new members of the EU, such a substitution could help address the critical situation. Naturally, this unrealistic proposal was turned down as slightly eccentric. After all, Great Britain was not even able to exert a more substantial influence on the law of India whose legal system represents a mixture of several influences.

Republic from the Membership in the European Union. Bratislava: Comenius University, Faculty of Law, 2008 .p. 299.

[29] Petrov, R.A.: Transpozicia "acquis" Europejskogo Sojuza v pravovyje sistemy tretijich stran, Publishing Istina, Kiev, 2011,.p 159;193; 198.

[30] Free Trade Zone negotiations between EU and US started on 8 July 2013 in Washington

This means that where the imposition of influence as a kind of legal expansion proved to be ineffective, the same purpose may be now achieved through the process of approximation of national legal systems with EU law. Continental lawyers are increasingly getting used to referring to the decisions of the European Court of Justice, which often fills the gaps in the EU legal system. Even more, they are obliged to apply them in the right way, as stated in the well-known Kobler case C-224/01. Permit me please another personal reminiscence. During my study stay at the ECJ in Luxembourg in the 1990s, I had the privilege of consulting Advocate General Francis Jacobs on certain outstanding legal issues. He gave a very a good answer to my question "Do the decisions of the Court constitute a source of law in the EU?" He replied, "We should not theoreticise too much about these questions." This, I believe, is the cornerstone for the success of the convergence method. It is flexible, and it meets the practical needs of the new global era. It has not become an academic issue; quite the contrary; the first who must come to terms with it are the lawmakers followed by the judges, later on comes the turn of the academic institution with its comments. I could draw an analogy between this process and the reception of Roman law, where the practical needs of the period made it necessary to apply the perfect legal institutions of the ancient Romans. The EC/EU law represents an even greater challenge since, in several respects, it represents an absolutely original production of the human mind. Similarly to Roman law, EU law is becoming a new means of communication, at least among European lawyers. Graduates of even a short legal course are familiar with the cases of Van Gend en Loos or Cassis de Dijon. Legal terminology of the EU has enriched the linguistic culture of all the countries that have adopted it and tends to constantly develop. Multilingualism, which–especially for lawyers–is a necessity, cultivates the legal language, increasing its clarity. Obviously, there are still those who oppose and criticise this trend but, on the whole, its effect on the development of the legal language and of the speech in general is positive. These reflections logically lead to the conclusion that, to be successful, legal processes involving the unification and/or approximation of law must result from practical needs. If they emerge only as romantic ideas of a group of enthusiastic visionaries, they are bound to fail. By the same token, it would not be appropriate to impose the law of another country as a model in those situations where it has no practical applicability. The history of law offers the example of countries subjected to the dominance of the Soviet Union that were forced, without much success, to deviate from their legal traditions. Legal discontinuity imposed on these countries negatively marked their legal development for many years. We could mention, for instance, the forced interference with civil law in the former East Germany (DDR), but also the Civil Code adopted in Czechoslovakia in 1964, whose revised provisions continue to be in force up to the present (in Slovakia). Such interferences with legal continuity create a very strong legal uncertainty. Another negative phenomenon consists in excessively frequent changes of the legislation. A critical observation could be made in this regard also in connection with frequent amendments to the primary law of the EU. It should, however, be recognised that the drafters of the revisions to the founding treaties of the EU are often driven by the aim of increasing the transparency of the EU's legislation and improving the effectiveness of its decision-making, and by an effort at incorporating the decisions of the Court of Justice. But, on the whole, the process of the transposition of EU law into national legal systems has been very positive, and will most probably result in a significant move of the law towards the maximum achievable convergence of legal cultures. Approximation as a new comparative method has made it possible also for the former Soviet bloc countries to accelerate the reforms of their legal systems in the direction of their democratisation and modernisation. An "*acquis associatif*" started to emerge already in the pre-accession period–a mix of legal systems of candidate countries with the *acquis communautaire*".[31] This mix is homogeneous and displays similarities with EU law. Because of the complexity of the issues related to approximation it appeared to be necessary to make full use of intellectual capacities, without any outside pressure; as a result, lawyers could be distinguished as those who responded to the changes in a flexible manner or those who were unable to move away from their thinking stereotypes. It is also true, however, that even among western European lawyers there was a number of those failed to surmount the regional boundaries of legal thinking, representing today the conservative wing of the legal community. I believe that the importance of the penetration of EU law through the protective shield of national law will also continue in the future,[32] in spite of a certain hindrance to the application of the principle of precedence and the direct effect of EU law due to the fact that it has not been declared *expressis verbis* in the Lisbon Treaty. The

[31] I used the term *acquis associatif* for the first time at the Conference - The Role of the Judiciary in Implementation and Enforcement of EC Law-From Association to Accession held in Vienna 2003; since that time, it has been used as a "terminus technicus" in professional terminology. See also Kunová, Vlasta. Od pridruženia k členstvu Slovenskej republiky v Európskej únii. In Čorba, Juraj et al. Európske právo na Slovensku. Bratislava: Nadácia Kalligram, 2003. p,109.
[32] Fischer. Peter. *European Law*. Bratislava: BVSP, 2006.p.61.

introduction of the concept of damage compensation and State liability for incorrect transposition are also the factors that encourage the States to fulfil their membership obligations, as evident from their increasingly uniform legal provisions.[33] This contention may be supported also by the fact that, with only a few exceptions, Member States respect the legal principle of the uniform interpretation of EU law.[34] For the countries of the former Soviet bloc, accession to the EU and the subsequent adoption of its legal system represented the achievement of their pre-accession ambitions. This was not a one-off process, because the preparations stretched over a period of almost 10 years. This targeted and purposeful process was part of the transformation of the entire legal system of these countries and consolidated the legal environment, making it more systematic, and contributed to its modernisation. Its ultimate outcome is the fact that these countries have become participants in the process that heralds new civilisation challenges. However, approximation may also give rise to particular risks that we cannot disregard in our research. After our experiences they include mainly:

- the absence of an assessment of the social and economic impact on State's legislation
- underdeveloped inter-institutional framework for approximation (HR capacity)
- the problem of the incompatibility of EU law with national legal traditions
- lobbyism and its influence on the legislation of the Member States
- ineffective national coordination of EU matters at the level of the executive and legislative powers
- the problem with the application of EU law by Member State courts (lack of training in the EU matters and the weak experiences of judges, problems with corruption in new MS)
- shortages of national/local experts in the area of EU law at the beginning of the approximation process
- the lack of comparative literature in the area of law approximation theory

[33] See Cases C - 6 and 9/90 Frankovich and C - 46 a 48/93 Brasserie du Pecheur/Factortame III.

[34] The application of EU law by national courts was addressed, inter alia, in Cases 106/77 Simenthal II and Case 314/85 Foto-Frost.

Notwithstanding these risk phenomena, the approximation of law can be evaluated as a positive factor in the transformation of law in the Slovak Republic.

13.5 The approximation of Law and Human Rights Protection in Europe

The stability of institutions guaranteeing democracy, the rule of law, human rights and the respect of and protection of minorities represents another important criterion for effective cooperation with the EU.[35] For that reason another important element for legal alignment in Europe is respecting the fundamental rights as stipulated in the European standards of the Human Rights protection. A new legislative basis of the protection of the fundamental rights introduced in the Lisbon Treaty represents a more transparent obligation to be fulfilled by the candidate states.[36]

The implementation of the European Convention for the Protection of Human Rights and Fundamental Freedoms, signed in 1950 in Rome represents a positive moment for the legal alignment in the European area. The international monitoring of the decisions of national courts contributes to the stabilisation and democratisation of the judiciary, in particular in the countries that have difficulties with negative phenomena in their judiciary (corruption, lack of impartiality, lack of professional competence). Moreover, the ECHR has contributed to promoting a universalist perception of the protection of human rights and fundamental freedoms and has reached a wider audience through its intelligible and transparent decisions.[37]

The common protection of the fundamental rights has not been the subject of my research. Nevertheless, the respect of them creates an integral part of the approximation process (e.g. the situation in Belarus and Ukraine).

---

[35] Compare Kunová, Vlasta. Od pridruženia k členstvu Slovenskej republiky v Európskej únii. In Čorba, Juraj. et al. Európske právo na Slovensku. Bratislava: Nadácia Kalligram, 2003. p109.

[36] Art 6 of the TEU; Art 21, par. 1, 2, of the TEU

[37] Strážnická, Viera. Efektívnosť kontrolného systému Európskeho dohovoru o ochrane ľudských práv. In Ľudské práva v súčasnom globalizovanom svete. [Human rights in the current globalised world]. Bratislava: Comenius University FSEV, 2012.p.10 – 18.

13.6 A Concluding Reflection

My chapter has mentioned some historical and theoretical aspects of the approximation of law. Because of the extensity of my research aim, it has not been possible to examine the issue in more depth. However, my conclusions demonstrate that the factors mentioned above have exerted an important and, what is more, positive influence on the legal reality of the new EU Member States from the post-socialist bloc. In spite of their initial legal divergences,[38] the legal systems of these States are currently showing signs of convergence. This is a good sign, especially for the advocates of globalisation and for those visionaries who promote the idea of a uniform world law (Lex multiplex ius unum).

This has been the first time in the history of legal comparative science that a targeted and methodically well-designed reform of the transformation of law has recorded positive results both at the legislative level and at the level of the application of law. In the future, it will be very interesting to examine the evolution of the relationships between EU law and international law. It will also be of considerable interest to observe the attitude of aother world entities operating in the EU region to a certain predominance of EU law. At any rate, advances towards unification of EU law will lead to a general unification of Europe and to the enhancement of European identity in a number of areas.

Our analysis indicates that while the processes of legal convergence in the past were more or less spontaneous, the European Union applies today a well-designed method based on highly sophisticated comparative know-how. Our examples from the past demonstrate that, to achieve a successful unification, the system developed to transform the law in the direction of legal convergence must contain the elements of a perfect system, sophisticated procedures and must aim at unifying not only the legislation but also the application of law. It appears that a well-designed method of legal convergence calls for central regulation. Legal alignment leads to expanding the idea of European integration and, as such, it undoubtedly represents a phenomenon having a certain political influence, not only in Europe but also in other parts of the word. For the new Member States of the EU, it represents the road towards modernisation of their legal systems, and their democratisation. The Lisbon Treaty as a key constitutional document that entered into effect on 1 December 2009; it provides also for the possibility of certain new derogations from the

---

[38] E.g. the split of the Czech and Slovak Federal Republic and of its legal system in 1989.

harmonisation and unification of law. In my view, the most important one is the derogation from the so-called direct effect of the provisions of the Charter of Fundamental Rights granted to the UK and Poland.[39] Fundamental rights of the citizens of these countries will be considerably restricted, in sharp contrast to the theory of natural law. I hope, however, that this will apply only for a short period of time. From the legal point of view, the procedure of granting derogations represents a relatively complicated part of the decision-making processes of the EU. There is an evident effort by the Union to limit the granting of derogations only where they are considered to be absolutely necessary and in cases where political, economic or social conditions in the member States call for a special approach. Our research has confirmed that the process of approximation of law can be a useful instrument for effective cooperation with the Eastern Partnership countries.

[39] Protocol 30 of the Lisbon Treaty.

CHAPTER FOURTEEN

APPROXIMATION OF COMPETITION LAWS: LESSONS LEARNED IN CENTRAL EUROPE

MICHAL PETR

14.1 Introduction

Under the current Partnership and Cooperation Agreement, Ukraine is obliged to work to remedy or remove through the application of its competition laws or otherwise restrictions on competition by enterprises or caused by State intervention in so far as they may affect trade between the EU and Ukraine. The precise competition rules, comparable to those included in the Treaty on the Functioning of the EU, will however only be set by the Association Agreement. Even more important is that the aim of the Agreement is not only to harmonize the EU and Ukrainian competition law but to liberalise its entire economy and create a Deep and Comprehensive Free Trade Area.

The countries of Central Europe have undergone similar developments. After the series of revolutions in 1989, they had to completely liberalise their state-controlled economies; they adopted competition regimes and over the next decade, harmonised these regulations with the EU. Such an approximation brought profound changes to their economic and competition policy. A similar experience may be expected to happen in Ukraine as well.

This article will discuss the challenges facing Ukrainian competition regime, taking into account the recent experience of Central European countries. It will briefly discuss the basic principles of EU competition law and describe the development of competition law of Ukraine, taking into account further developments foreseen by the Association Agreement. Parallels between Ukraine and the countries of Central Europe will then be discussed; so as to identify the future challenges the Ukrainian competition regime might be faced with.

14.2 Overview: the EU Competition Law

It is not the aim of this article to discuss the EU competition law; we will therefore only briefly outline its basic characteristic in order to be able to make a comparison with the Ukrainian regime.

By the term *competition law* we understand the regulation of undertakings possessing–either individually or jointly–such market power that would enable them to distort competition in the market, most apparently by increasing prices above market levels. Competition law thus prohibits certain forms of coordinated conduct of the undertakings, the so-called *anti-competitive agreements*, and of their unilateral conduct, i.e. the *abuse of dominant position*. The EU competition law is also concerned with *concentrations*, i.e. with ascertaining the future effects of structural changes in the markets due to mergers and acquisitions; mergers leading to substantial lessening of competition will be prohibited.

The legal basis for competition law constitutes the Treaty on the Functioning of the European Union (hereinafter referred to as the "Treaty"). The concept of agreements is defined in Article 101 and the dominant position in Article 102 of the Treaty. Merger control is not based on the Treaty itself, but on a Council regulation (hereinafter referred to as the "Merger Regulation").[1]

The Treaty identifies the concepts of agreements and dominance only in general terms, refined further by jurisprudence of the Court of Justice (hereinafter referred to as "ECJ"). The agreements are described as any direct or indirect contacts between undertakings, *the object or effect whereof is either to influence the conduct on the market of an actual or potential competitor or to disclose to such a competitor the course of conduct which they themselves have decided to adopt or contemplate adopting on the market.*[2] Since coordination among independent undertakings is necessary to achieve market power enabling them to distort competition, anticompetitive agreements are generally referred to as *collusive conduct.*

Not every collusion between undertakings is prohibited, only those agreements, which have *as their object or effect the prevention, restriction or distortion of competition within the internal market*, e.g. agreements which directly or indirectly fix purchase or selling prices, share markets or sources of supply, apply dissimilar conditions to equivalent transactions with other trading parties, thereby placing them at a competitive

[1] Council Regulation (EC) No 139/2004 on the control of concentrations between undertakings (the EC Merger Regulation), OJ L 24, 29. 1. 2004, p. 1.
[2] ECJ judgement *40/73 Suiker Unie*, [1975] ECR 1663, 174.

disadvantage, etc.[3] European competition authorities regard horizontal agreements which have the distortion of competition as their object, the so called *cartels*, to be the most harmful, and consider them their priority.

An exemption may be granted for an anticompetitive agreement, allowing its parties to carry it out. Under the conditions of Article 101 (3) of the Treaty, every agreement fulfilling the conditions specified therein is *ex lege* and *ab initio* valid, without any notification being necessary.[4] To simplify the position of smaller undertakings, the *de minimis* rule is in place, exempting most of the agreements among undertakings with low market shares.[5] Exemptions are also granted by the European Commission to specific agreements in specific areas; these are known as *block exemptions*. For example, in the Block Exemptions on Vertical Agreements the Commission specifies which obligations the producers may set to their distributors.[6]

The dominant position is described in the case-law as *a position of economic strength enjoyed by an undertaking which enables it to prevent effective competition being maintained on the relevant market by giving it the power to behave to an appreciable extent independently of its competitors, customers and ultimately of its customers*.[7] Since the dominant undertaking itself holds sufficient market power to distort competition and no collusion with other undertakings is thus needed, its behaviour is generally referred to as *unilateral conduct*.

The competition law prohibits not the dominant position as such, but its abuse; according to the ECJ, *the concept of abuse is an objective concept relating to the behaviour of an undertaking in a dominant position which is such as to influence the structure of a market where, as a result of the very presence of the undertaking in question, the degree of competition is weakened and which, through recourse to methods different from those which condition normal competition in products or services on the basis of*

[3] Art. 101 (1) of the Treaty.

[4] This *ex lege* system replaced the previous regime of *individual exemptions*, under which the agreements had to be notified to the European Commission, that could decide that they are compatible with Article 101 of the Treaty, i. e. grant an individual exemption. Nowadays, the undertakings have to perform the assessment themselves.

[5] Commission Notice on agreements of minor importance which do not appreciably restrict competition under Article 81(1) of the Treaty establishing the European Community (de minimis). OJ C 368, 22. 12. 2001, p. 13.

[6] Commission Regulation 330/2010 of 20 April 2010 on the application of Article 101(3) of the Treaty on the Functioning of the European Union to categories of vertical agreements and concerted practices. OJ L 102, 23. 4. 2010, p. 1.

[7] ECJ judgement *27/76 United Brands*, [1978] ECR 207.

the transactions of commercial operators, has the effect of hindering the maintenance of the degree of competition still existing in the market or the growth of that competition.[8] The conduct perceived as abusive includes imposing unfair purchase or selling prices, limiting production, markets or technical development to the prejudice of consumers, making the conclusion of contracts subject to acceptance by the other parties of supplementary obligations which, by their nature or according to commercial usage, have no connection with the subject of such contracts, etc.[9] It is possible to distinguish between exploitative abusive practices, which the dominant undertakings employ in order to extract unfair advantages out of their market strength (e.g. excessive pricing), and exclusionary practices, aimed at pushing rivals of the dominant undertaking out of the market. Exploitative practices are regarded to be the priority of European competition authorities.[10]

As far as merger control is concerned, a concentration is deemed to arise where a change of control on a lasting basis results from the merger of two or more previously independent undertakings, or from the acquisition of control over the other undertaking.[11] A concentration of undertakings, the annual turnover of which exceeds certain limits (known as *notification thresholds*), needs to be notified to the European Commission.[12] The Commission will ascertain whether the concentration does not *significantly impede effective competition in the common market, in particular as a result of the creation or strengthening of a dominant position*;[13] this assessment is known as the *SIEC test*. Only if the Commission decides that the competition will not be impeded may the concentration be implemented.

14.3 Ukrainian Competition Law

In Ukraine, the competition law stems directly from the Constitution,[14] which not only generally proclaims the *right to entrepreneurial activity*, but states specifically that the State *shall ensure the protection of*

---

[8] ECJ judgement *85/76 Hoffmann – La Roche*, [1979] ECR 461.
[9] Art. 102 of the Treaty.
[10] Guidance on its enforcement priorities in applying Article 82 of the EC Treaty to abusive exclusionary conduct by dominant undertakings, OJ C 45, 24.2.2009, p. 7.
[11] Merger Regulation, Art. 3.
[12] Merger Regulation, Art. 1.
[13] Merger Regulation, Art. 2.
[14] Art. 42 of the Constitution of Ukraine, the Official Journal of the Verkhovna Rada (hereinafter referred to as „OJVR") 1996, No. 30, p. 141.

competition in pursuit of entrepreneurial activities and that, in particular, *abuse of a monopolistic position* and other forms of *unlawful restriction of competition* shall be prohibited.

Competition law thus has a very strong position in Ukrainian legal order. In fact, even though most of the constitutions of the EU countries include concepts close to the "right to entrepreneurial activity" and some of them even mention competition law as a means to safeguard this right, specific instruments of competition law are almost never mentioned. It is therefore noteworthy that the Constitution puts emphasis specifically on "abuse of monopolistic position", i.e. abuse of dominance in the EU terminology. It will be discussed below that unilateral conduct indeed constitutes the core of Ukrainian enforcement activity.

14.3.A Introduction of Antitrust Regulation

The first law on the protection of competition was adopted even before the Constitution, in 1992 (hereinafter referred to as the "Antimonopoly Act 1992").[15]

It is important to keep in mind the specific legal and economic context under which this law was adopted. The starting point was a completely state-controlled economy, with many undertakings enjoying a monopolistic position. There was no competition in the sense as it is understood in liberal economies–the entire production was state-planned, all the prices were regulated.

At the same time, Ukraine seceded from the USSR and many trade and economic links had to be re-established. As a result, Ukraine's GDP was significantly decreasing through most of the 1990s and the inflation, especially in the early years of independence, was staggering, exceeding 10,000% in 1993.[16] This experience alone might help explain why the activities of the Antimonopoly Committee of Ukraine (hereinafter referred to as the "AMCU") are even today so much focused on the price-related abuses of dominance, in particular excessive pricing (see below).

The Antimonopoly Act 1992 reflected this reality and enabled a very simple determination of a dominant position–any undertaking with a market share exceeding 35% was deemed to hold a monopoly position;[17] in case of an abuse, the AMCU was allowed to order a compulsory split-

[15] The act on the limitation of monopolism and the prevention of unfair competition in entrepreneurial activities, OJVR 1992, No 12, p. 64.
[16] For statistical data, see Ukraine. Country Report No. 05/21. IMF, 2005.
[17] Antimonopoly Act 1992, Art. 1.

up of the dominant.[18] On the other hand, the agreements were defined very vaguely (*anticompetitive concerted actions*)[19] and not much attention was devoted to them by the AMCU. The Antimonopoly Act 1992 also contained some form of merger control. It however covered virtually any form of business (and even public authority) restructuring,[20] not the *concentrations* as understood by EU competition law, and even though these transactions were subject to the consent of the AMCU, no relevant criteria were given as to which transactions would be cleared and which prohibited.

It also ought to be mentioned that the Antimonopoly Act 1992 contained specific provisions protecting the undertakings against discriminatory interventions by public authorities.[21]

The Antimonopoly Act 1992 thus introduced some rudimentary forms of competition regulations, including prohibition of anticompetitive agreements, abuse of dominance and merger control; it was however significantly different from the EU competition regime. Nonetheless, such regulation might have been well suited to the period when the entire economy needed to be privatised and liberalised and when the nascent competition might have been distorted by public authorities, used to intervene heavily in the economy, and by the monopolies and ex-monopolies, ready to exploit their market power.[22]

Even the then structure and functioning of the AMCU reflected this specific transitory period. The 1993 law on the Antimonopoly Committee of Ukraine (hereinafter referred to as the "AMCU Act")[23] foresaw a competition authority subordinate to the government (Cabinet of Ministers), the chairman of AMCU himself being a Minister. Such an arrangement was undoubtedly efficient, as the Chairman of the Competition Authority was directly involved in the government's discussions concerning economic reforms and privatisation, it was however hardly a structure guaranteeing independence of competition policy. This system was changed in 1996, and the President of Ukraine currently appoints the Chairman of AMCU.

---

[18] Antimonopoly Act 1992, Art. 16.
[19] Antimonopoly Act 1992, Art. 5.
[20] Antimonopoly Act 1992, Art. 14.
[21] Antimonopoly Act 1992, Art. 6.
[22] For the sake of completeness, AMCU was also responsible for the protection against unfair competition on the basis of the Law on the protection from unfair competition, OJVR 1996, No. 36, p. 164.
[23] The law on the Antimonopoly Committee of Ukraine, OJVR 1993, No. 50, p. 472.

The AMCU has been fully operational since 1995, when its regional branches were established. Since then, a stunning number of decisions have been adopted. As is clear from Graph 1, the vast majority of cases concerned different forms of abuse of dominance, in particular price related, and a significant number of decisions were addressed to public authorities; on the other hand, the number of decisions on anticompetitive agreements was rather low.[24] The AMCU itself blames the low number of decisions on agreements on an inappropriate regulation and lack of investigatory powers.[25]

Graph 1: AMCU decisions 1995 – 2002

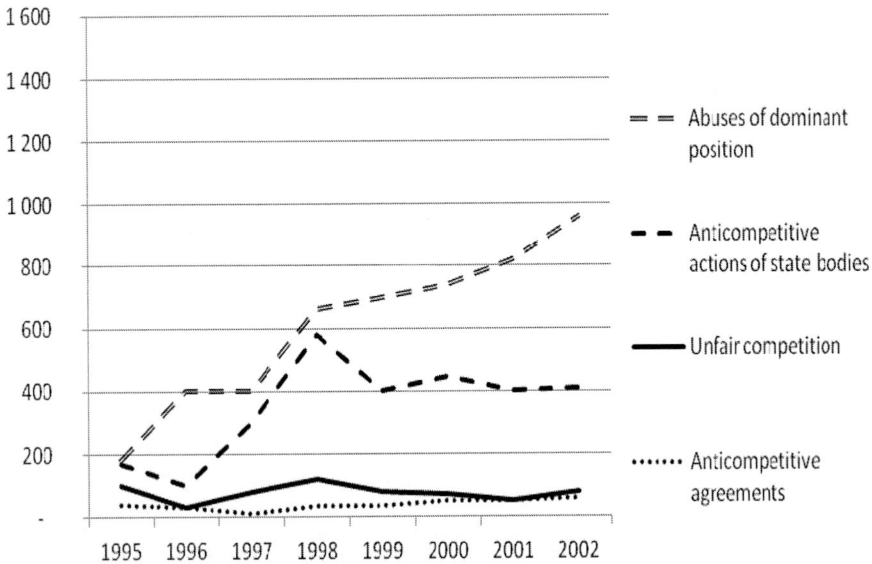

[24] The numbers in the graph were compiled out of AMCU Annual Reports by *Jakubiak, M.* Analysis of factors contributing to the adoption of competition law in Ukraine. Implications for other developing countries. Published by the Institue for Economic Research, Halle, 2005. The article is available at: http://www.iwh-halle.de/projects/competition_policy/Ukraine_Country_Study.pdf [31. 3. 2013].

[25] Contribution of Ukraine for the OECD Global Forum on Competition, 26 September 2001, CNM/GF/COMP/WD (2001)7.

Also the trend in the number of decisions is telling: only in the area of unilateral conduct are the number of decisions growing, whereas in other areas, it stays more or less at the same level.

The strong emphasis on unilateral conduct is even more obvious from Graph 2, covering the years 1998–2001 and showing the relative ratio of decisions concerning different practices,[26] with unilateral conduct constituting almost half of AMCUs enforcement, on the one hand, and anticompetitive agreements representing barely 2% thereof, on the other.

Graph 2: AMCU decisions 1998 - 2001

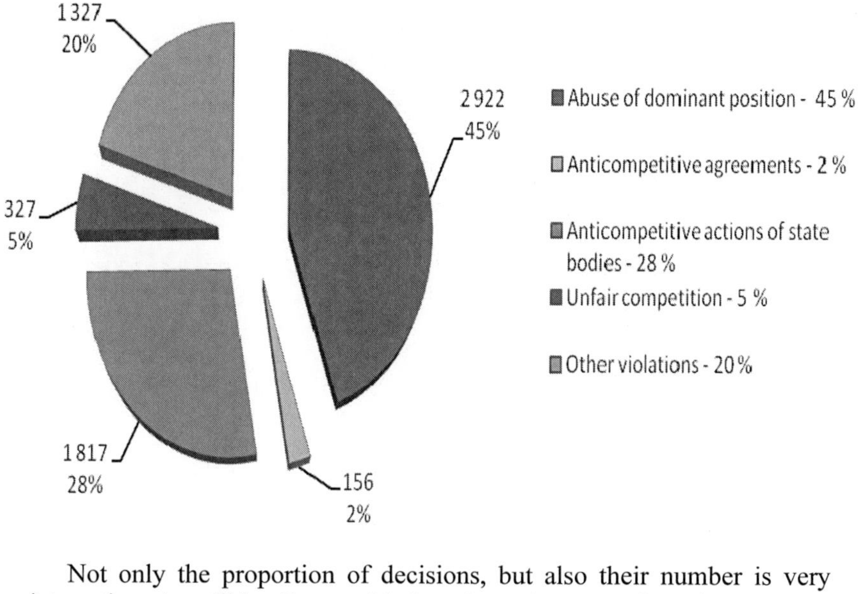

Not only the proportion of decisions, but also their number is very interesting. As will be discussed below, it vastly outnumbers the output of competition authorities from comparable EU countries.

14.3.B The Partnership and Cooperation Agreement

In March 1998, the Partnership and Cooperation Agreement between the EU and Ukraine (hereinafter referred to as the "Partnership Agreement")

---

[26] The numbers in the graph were compiled from Ukraine's contribution to the OECD Global Forum on Competition, 17 January 2003, CCNM/GF/COMP/WD (2003)10.

entered into force.[27] It contains several provisions concerning competition, which are however very broadly formulated–the parties to the Cooperation Agreement are obliged to *ensure that they have and enforce laws addressing restrictions on competition by enterprises.*[28] It does not provide any further clarification as to what should be the content of such laws. Ukraine however commits itself to endeavour to ensure that its legislation will be gradually made compatible with the EU one, mentioning–among others–specifically the rules on competition.[29]

As far as the competition law is concerned, the Partnership Agreement itself does not bring any significant change. It however oriented Ukrainian competition law towards the EU one, and thus started the gradual process of harmonization, as is obvious from the new Competition Act, adopted in 2001. It needs not to be emphasised that the Partnership and Cooperation Agreement had the same effects on other economic policies of Ukraine as well.

14.3.C The Competition Act 2001

In 2001, a new Competition Act (hereinafter referred to as the "Competition Act 2001") was adopted.[30] The new law moves Ukrainian competition regulation significantly towards the EU model; noteworthy national specifics however remain in force.

The new competition act introduces a standard definition of anticompetitive agreements.[31] Even a leniency programme was announced,[32] reflecting in principle the type I. leniency (immunity) in the EU.[33] There is a general exemption enabling small and medium enterprises[34] to conclude

---

[27] Partnership and cooperation agreement between the European Communities and their member states, of the one part, and the Ukraine, of the other part, OJ L 49, 19. 2. 1998, p. 3.

[28] Partnership Agreement, Art. 49.

[29] Partnership Agreement, Art. 51.

[30] The law on economic competition protection, OJVR 2001, No. 12, p. 64.

[31] Competition Act 2001, Art. 5.

[32] Competition Act 2001, Art. 6.

[33] Commission notice on immunity from fines and reduction of fines in cartel cases.
OJ C 298, 8. 12. 2006, p. 17.

[34] According to Art. 1 of the Competition Act 2001, an SME *is an undertaking, whose income (revenue) resulting from the sale of products for the latest financial year or value of assets does not exceed an amount equivalent to 500 000 EUR, if in markets, in which it operates, competitors having a significantly bigger market share are present.*

agreements on joint procurement of goods.[35] A block exemption for vertical sales is also available.[36] The system of individual exemptions is still in place in Ukraine, requiring the undertakings to seek clearance of certain agreements.[37] The list of conditions under which the AMCU may grant an individual exemption is considerably longer than the EU one;[38] for example, agreements optimizing export or import of goods or rationalization of production are covered. The most important distinction from the EU system is, however, the power of the government to exempt even the agreements not cleared by AMCU, if *the positive effect for public interests prevails over adverse consequences of competition restriction.*[39]

As far as unilateral practices are concerned, the dominant position is no longer tied with a specific market share. Undertakings whose market share exceeds 35% are however still presumed to be dominant, unless they can demonstrate they are subject to considerable competition restraints from their competitors.[40] The definition of a dominant position is thus still not fully in line with the effects-based approach favoured by the European Commission.[41] The list of abusive practices covers the standard examples.[42]

The definition of concentrations has also been harmonised with the EU concept, covering mergers and acquisitions;[43] Ukrainian law does not however distinguish between sole and joint control and it is not clear whether a change in the quality of control would constitute a

[35] Competition Act 2001, Art. 7.
[36] Competition Act 2001, Art. 8.
[37] Competition Act 2001, Art. 10.
[38] According to Art. 101 (3) of the Treaty on the Functioning of the European Union, only *agreements which contribute to improving the production or distribution of goods or to promoting technical or economic progress, while allowing consumers a fair share of the resulting benefit*, and *which do not impose on the undertakings concerned restrictions which are not indispensable to the attainment of these objectives* and do not *afford such undertakings the possibility of eliminating competition in respect of a substantial part of the products in question* are exempted.
[39] Competition Act 2001, Art. 10.
[40] Competition Act 2001, Art. 12.
[41] See the Commission's *Guidance on its enforcement priorities in applying Article 82 of the EC Treaty to abusive exclusionary conduct by dominant undertakings*, supra 7.
[42] Competition Act 2001, Art. 13.
[43] Competition Act 2001, Art. 22.

concentration.[44] The notification thresholds are based alternatively on (relatively low) turnovers[45] and market shares;[46] the turnover of the acquired undertaking does not cover only the part over which the control will be established after the concentration, but also the part that will thereafter lose control. The AMCU assesses whether the concentration would result in a monopolization or significant restriction of competition in the market,[47] which corresponds in principle to the SIEC test. Similarly to the regulation of anticompetitive agreements, the government may clear even the mergers not authorised by AMCU.[48]

Even under the new Competition Law, AMCU has retained supervision over public authorities, which *shall be bound to assist the development of competition*[49] and are prohibited from performing anticompetitive actions, including legislation and decision making.[50] AMCU is also still responsible for the protection against unfair competition.[51]

As well as before, AMCU has kept its focus on unilateral conduct. As is apparent from Graph 3,[52] the ratio of decisions taken in different areas of AMCUs competence remains basically the same,[53] but the absolute numbers of decisions taken grew to surprising heights, totally incomparable to the EU practice.

---

[44] *Vovk, T., Voznyuk, O.* Ukraine: Overview. In: *The European Antitrust Review 2013*, Global Competition Review.

[45] According to Art. 24 of the Competition Act 2001, concentrations of undertakings with turnovers exceeding 12 mil. EUR worldwide and 1 mil. EUR in the Ukraine are in principle subject to notification.

[46] According to Art. 24 of the Competition Act 2001, concentrations of undertakings whose combined market share exceed 35% are in principle subject to notification.

[47] Competition Act 2001, Art. 25.

[48] Competition Act 2001, Art. 25.

[49] Competition Act 2001, Art. 4.

[50] Competition Act 2001, Art. 15.

[51] The Unfair Competition Act.

[52] The numbers in the graph were compiled from Ukraine's annual report to the OECD, 29 October 2012, DAF/COMP/AR (2012) 49.

[53] It ought to be mentioned that the amount of agreements has slightly grown to almost 10%.

Graph 3: AMCU decisions 2011

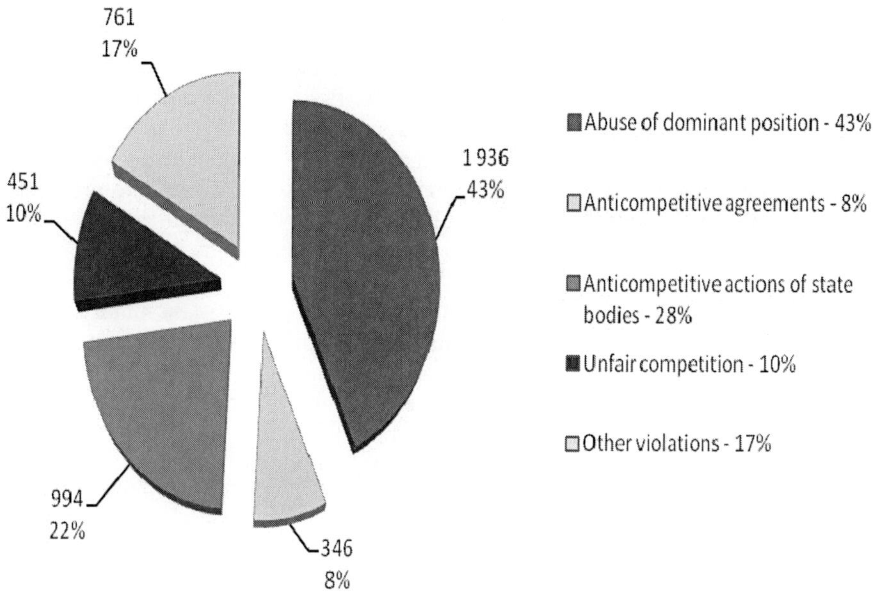

14.4 Parallels with Central Europe

The experience of Ukraine is unique, and making any comparisons with other countries is therefore tricky. Nonetheless, the countries of Central Europe have likewise moved from a completely state-controlled economy to a free market, and the Association with the EU contributed significantly to their transformation. These countries have also first taken inspiration in some aspects of the EU law and only later advanced to full harmonisation.

Some parallels are indeed striking. In the Czech Republic, for example, the head of the competition authority was also a member of the government, so that he could participate in the discussions concerning economic reforms and in particular privatization; a fully independent competition authority was established only in 1996. Also similarly to Ukraine, the existence of a dominant position was until 2001 irrebuttably presumed for undertakings whose market share exceeded 30% in the Czech Republic.[54]

It therefore seems plausible that if a competition regime is being introduced in a country with no (immediate) history of a free market, it will probably go through similar stages. At first, the competition policy will be closely linked with the overall economic policy of the government and only later will it become apparent that independence of the competition authority needs to be guaranteed. Also the Competition law will probably be initially based on simplified concepts (e.g. irrebuttable presumptions of dominance) and only later redefined in line with the more economic approach (see below).

One aspect is however significantly different, and it is the number of decisions taken by AMCU every year. It is difficult to relate Ukraine with Central European countries, only Poland may have a comparable number of inhabitants.[55] From this point of view, the enforcement ratio between agreements and unilateral conduct is broadly comparable: even Poland investigates considerably more cases of unilateral conduct than of agreements; the majority of cases dealt with by the Polish competition authority are however those concerning collective consumer interests (see Graph 4), which to a certain extent corresponds to unfair competition.[56]

What is outstanding is the absolute number of decisions: the AMCU currently issues more than ten times as many decisions as the Polish competition authority, and more than 20 times as many in the area of unilateral conduct (see Graph 5).[57] Although higher enforcement activity generally indicates efficiency of a competition authority, it is improbable that the AMCU would be ten times more efficient than the Polish competition authority. The only explanation then is that the AMCU is not yet dealing with the most complex cases and that the complexity of economic analysis is not as robust as is now the case within the EU, especially with respect to abuse of dominance.

---

[54] This led in at least one case to an absurd conclusion that there were two dominant undertakings in the same market (individually, not as a collective dominance).

[55] Also the structure of Polish competition authority is to a certain extent comparable: it also deals not only with antitrust, but also with unfair competition (specifically with collective consumer interests), and it is divided into central headquarters and regional offices.

[56] The numbers in the graph were compiled from the Poland's annual reports, published at: http://www.uokik.gov.pl/reports_on_activities.php [31. 3. 2013].

[57] The numbers in the graph were compiled from graphs 3 and 4.

Graph 4: decisions of Polish competition authority 2011

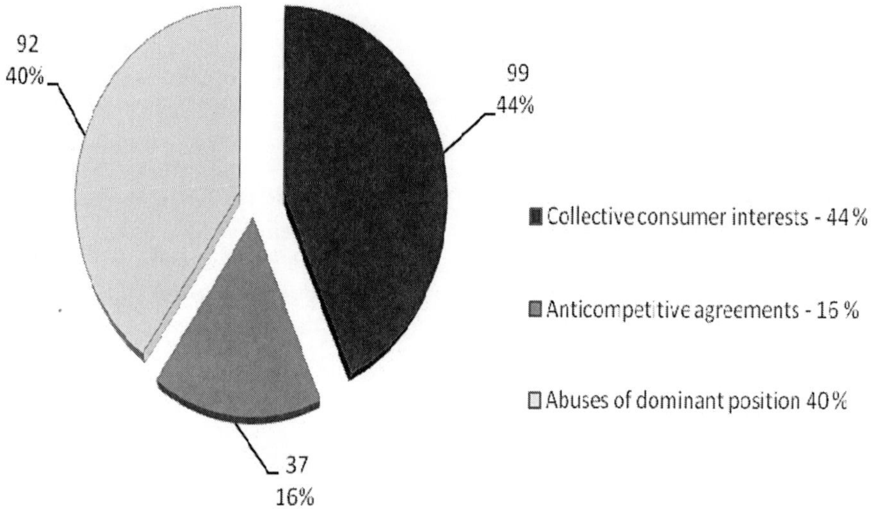

Graph 5: decisions of Polish and Ukrainian competition authorities 2011

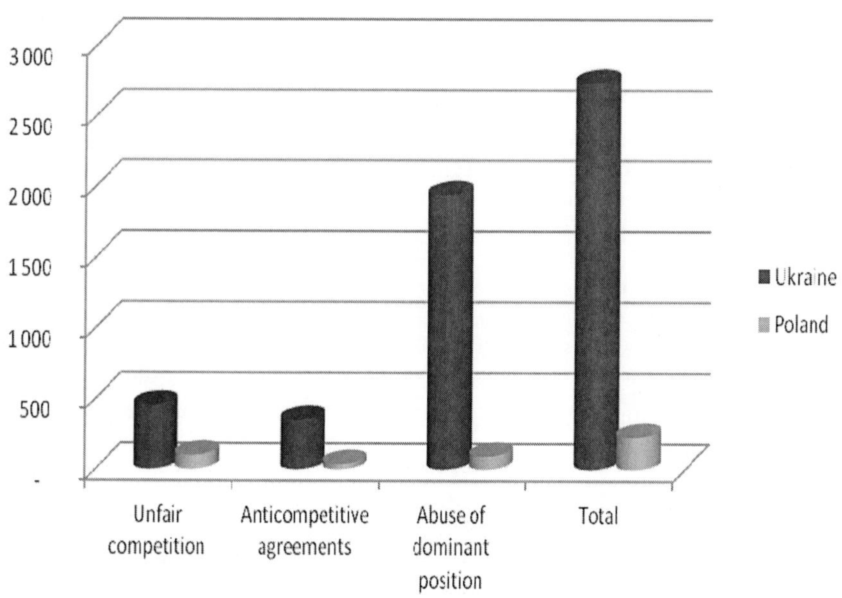

It is obvious from the above that Ukraine currently exhibits a competition law broadly in line with the EU one and the AMCU issues an overwhelming number of decisions every year. Even a cursory look at the state of the Ukrainian economy however suggests that deep structural reforms are still needed in order to establish an efficient market economy; similarly, the colossal number of AMCUs decisions itself suggest that the economic analysis underlying them cannot be compared with the EU standard.

Far reaching changes, concerning both the AMCUs enforcement and the overall economic regulation of Ukraine thus seem to be necessary. The Association Agreement, which shall approximate Ukrainian law and practice to the EU one, could be a stimulus not only for the regulation itself, but especially for the enforcement practice.

14.5 The Association Agreement

Negotiations on the Association Agreement commenced in 2007 and by the end of 2011, completion of negotiations were announced at the Ukraine–EU Summit held in Kiev. The text of the agreement has not yet been officially published;[58] numerous publications however discuss its content.

The aim of the Agreement is to promote gradual rapprochement between the EU and Ukraine, based on common values and close and privileged links. The Agreement covers most of the areas of EU *acquis*; for the purposes of this article, however, the establishment of the Deep and Comprehensive Free Trade Area (hereinafter referred to as "DCFTA") is of crucial importance. The Agreement shall support Ukrainian efforts to complete the transition into a functioning market economy through the progressive approximation of its legislation to that of the EU and thus establish conditions for enhanced economic and trade relations leading towards Ukraine's gradual integration in the EU Internal Market.[59]

Competition law had a significant role to play while establishing the EU's Internal Market, and it will be similarly important for DCFTA. The Association Agreement therefore clearly proclaims that agreements distorting competition, abuse of a dominant position and concentrations which result in monopolization or substantial restrictions of competition

---

[58] It is however accessible at certain web sites, e.g. http://glavcom.ua/pub/2012_11_19_EU_Ukraine_Association_Agreement_English.pdf [31. 3. 2013].

[59] Association Agreement, Art. 1.

are inconsistent with it;[60] Ukraine thus undertakes to approximate its Competition law and practices to the correspondent EU *acquis* within three years of the entry into force of the agreement.[61] Ukraine shall also ensure that public enterprises and enterprises entrusted with special or exclusive rights are subject to competition laws.[62]

The Association Agreement covers not only questions of substantial law. An authority responsible for effective enforcement of competition law shall be maintained and appropriately equipped, and the parties to the proceedings shall enjoy the right to be heard; decisions of the competition authority shall be subject to court review.[63]

The Association Agreement thus has potential to fully harmonise not only the competition law of Ukraine and the EU, but especially the enforcement practices of competition authorities. In order to achieve this, the AMCU will undoubtedly be faced with several challenges. Here the experiences of Central European countries might be especially valuable, since they had to follow the same path in the past.

14.6 Future Challenges

Ukraine decided to implement the competition policy 20 years ago and the text of its competition law is, to a great extent, in line with modern competition laws throughout the world. It is however not yet possible to claim that Ukraine has a fully functioning market economy and anti-trust regime. It is obvious that even the best competition law cannot change the broader economic reality, which is still in need of deep structural reforms.

The AMCU is very well aware of that and it has prepared an ambitious Competition Development Programme in Ukraine for 2013–2023, approved in 2012 by the President of Ukraine.[64] The programme aims at structural changes in all areas of the economy, including industrial, investment, agriculture, foreign trade and pricing policy. At the same time, the United Nations Conference on Trade and Development (UNCTAD) has commenced a peer-review of Ukraine that will result in suggestions for amendments of not only the competition law, but other regulations as well.

---

[60] Association Agreement, Art. 254.
[61] Association Agreement, Art. 256.
[62] Association Agreement, Art. 257.
[63] Association Agreement, Art. 255.
[64] Ukraine's annual report to the OECD, *supra* 52.

The crucial role will however be played by the Association Agreement. As Ukraine will be obliged to harmonise its economic legislation with the EU *acquis* and liberalise its markets with a view of implementing the DCFTA, a broad structural reform will have to be performed, allowing for the competition policy to be efficiently implemented.

Even though it is obvious that Ukraine has still a long way to go, it is safe to presume that two fundamental changes concerning both material and procedural law will have to take place.

14.6.A A more economic approach

In the area of material law, several changes will probably be necessary. Concerning agreements, it might be advisable to switch from individual exemptions to the *ex lege* system, as the EU law has done, or to introduce a standard *de minimis* rule. As far as dominance is concerned, the presumption of a 35% market share (even though rebuttable) will probably have to be abandoned. And in the area of concentrations, the notification criteria should be revisited, strengthening the *local nexus* of the transaction under review to the Ukrainian markets. These changes, however extensive, are nonetheless not a change of the basic paradigm and their realization should not pose insurmountable obstacles. Much more difficult (and at the same time critical) will be the introduction of a more thorough assessment of the effects of anticompetitive practices.

The assessment of undertakings' conduct and appraisal of whether it is capable of distorting competition should not be based on the form of the conduct in question, but solely on a rigorous economic analysis. This is the central theme of the so called "more economic approach" to competition law, prevailing at well-established competition authorities throughout the world. The analysis should be "more economic" i.e. based more on econometrics and economic analysis, and "less legal" i.e. not based on presumptions. Even though such an approach is intuitively correct, it is vastly more complicated than the "traditional" one.[65]

Implementing the more economic approach requires dedicated support not only from the competition authority itself, but also from the stakeholders. As the Central European experience shows, it is necessary to establish a specialised department (usually called the "Chief Economist Department") equipped not only with sophisticated software, but also with top economists; even this might be demanding for a staff-constrained

[65] See e.g. *Fisher, F. M.* Economic Analysis and „Bright-Line Tests". Journal of Competition Law and Economics (2008) 4 (1): 129-153.

agency. Long-term training is necessary, which consumes both time and resources, and there is always a risk that once state employees reach a certain level of knowledge, they will leave the authority and enter private practice; the high employee turnover in chief economist departments throughout Europe underlines this point.

When an effective chief economic department is indeed established (which requires years rather than months), the way the authority works and affects the undertakings will change. In order to perform the econometric tests, vast amounts of data are required not only from the undertakings concerned but from other market players as well. Consumer tests are often needed. That results in a situation where the competition authority delivers significantly less decisions, but at the same time requires much more cooperation from the market players.

We have already noted that the number of cases decided by AMCU every year is more than ten times higher than in comparable countries in Central Europe. We therefore predict that with the more economic approach, the number of cases will drop dramatically. It might however be difficult for a competition authority, especially in a country where a competition policy has not yet been fully established, to explain that a ten-fold decrease in output (and thus also in fines collected) is a step forward. Ukraine however does not have any other choice if it wants to establish the DCFTA and implement a modern competition policy.

14.6.B Fair trial

Whereas the relevance of the "legal approach" decreases in the material assessment of conduct under review, it will be more and more relevant with respect to the procedural part of the assessment. The question of due process is currently as important as the question of whether certain conduct is in fact legal or not. It is even more so in countries with limited experience with competition law. Experience shows that in all Central European countries judges often tend to scrutinize more thoroughly the requirements of procedural law, in which they are experts, and try to avoid the complex questions of competition economics, which are novel to them. Establishing long term cooperation with the judges and if possible, conducting joint seminars allowing judges to appreciate the economic analysis, is in itself a very challenging task.

The AMCU can expect the parties of the proceedings to flood it with dozens of objections, many of which might not have been solved before by national case law: were the parties granted sufficient access to file? Were they allowed to be heard as required by the European Convention on

Human Rights? Was the right not to incriminate oneself respected? To what extent may the rights, granted by the European Convention on Human Rights to natural persons, be applied to companies and other legal persons?

An effective competition authority requires adequate investigatory powers. Experience has shown that the most important tool of investigation is the unannounced on-site inspections, poetically named "dawn raids", granting the competition agencies power to search any documentation in any form available in the premises, including computer data. Many objections will arise in connection with dawn raids, among others: can the authority search computers, which may contain not only business, but also private data? How to handle documents which the undertaking labels as a legal profession privilege? May the police be involved during inspections?

Here again, the Association Agreement may play a crucial role. As the Ukraine undertakes to implement the entire *acquis*, case law of the ECJ will have to be taken into consideration. The AMCU will thus have the advantage of relying on the ECJ jurisprudence, where most of these questions have already been settled, and even more importantly, Ukrainian courts will have to interpret Ukrainian law in line with them.

14.7 Conclusions

Ukraine has managed to adopt a competition law which is already based on the EU one, and its full harmonization will therefore not be extremely difficult. Nevertheless, even though the AMCU adopts thousands of decisions every year, it is still not possible to claim that Ukraine has developed into a fully functioning market economy with a sufficiently embedded competition regime.

Broader regulatory changes of the entire economy are therefore necessary, liberalizing it and enabling the competition to flourish. At the same time, the AMCU needs to embrace the more economic approach and prepare itself for numerous legal quarrels concerning fair trial.

In both these aspects, the Association Agreement may play a critical role as it envisages far reaching adjustments of regulations with a view of implementing the DCFTA and enables the Ukrainian authorities to rely on the EU *acquis*.

CHAPTER FIFTEEN

THE EUROPEANIZATION OF LAW CURRICULA IN EASTERN PARTNERSHIP COUNTRIES: BEST PRACTICES OF EU MEMBER STATES

TANEL KERIKMÄE
AND KATRIN NYMAN-METCALF

15.1 Europeanization

The ambitious title of this paper necessitates a closer look at terminology in order to guarantee that "Europeanization" in the legal context can be understood uniformly. Most likely, the Europeanization of a legal or judicial system is not equivalent with the Europeanization of a law curriculum. This is especially true as there are still different doctrinal approaches to teaching law, but also as Europe is changing rapidly and the expectations and relations to the European Union (EU) of third countries may vary considerably. Among definitions of "Europeanization" we find that of Bulmer and Olsen indicating that the most important elements of the process of Europeanization are related to legal society, namely "central penetration of national systems of governance" but also "exporting forms of political organization".[1] The term itself is deployed where the EU seeks to export its values.[2] Transferring "Europe" means, above all, transferring European(ized) beliefs and values but also European rules and norms (and their interpretative concepts reflected in general legal culture). It goes without saying that today Europe has to work hard on determining its own future–this also influences the relations with Eastern Partnership countries.

---

[1] Bulmer. S., 2008. Theorizing Europeanization, in: New Research Agendas. Ed by Paolo Graziano and Maarten P. Vink. New York: Palgrave Macmillan.
[2] Ibid, p.47

In order to transmit values to others, it is essential to be clear what those value are and what it represents to incorporate them.

In this context of a re-evaluation of concepts and beliefs, it could still be hoped for that the Europeanization of law curricula could be a valuable process and a basis for introducing (new) principles in legal societies in transformational countries. That is why such a process should not be directly influenced by political events (such as after-crisis rescue plans) in Europe but rather focus on main ideas and the formation of legal arguments in the EU legal space. Here, it is possible to make a comparison with the United States legal system (although there are several discrepancies) to agree that the legal policy should not interfere with the legal theory. As Bermann puts it "…while federalization (or de-federalization) of American law is unquestionably an important and indeed controversial subject, it has little to do with the law becoming more or becoming less 'Americanized.'"[3] So, despite the recent debate on (neo) Federalism, the Europeanization of law curricula should avoid being dogmatic or influenced by political ideas before they are implemented by legal norms. This would guarantee that the principle of the rule of law is the basis of the curricula.

A very important issue is that when talking about European law it is necessary to make a distinction between European law in a broader context and EU law. The first dimension is wider and includes also European intergovernmental treaties and importantly the European Convention of Human Rights (ECHR). The success of the ECHR and the European Court on Human Rights (ECtHR) has led many commentators to see enforceable human rights law as a predominantly European concept.[4] In any event, a strong role for human rights is definitely an important part of Europeanization legal training.

We will return to the question of differences between European countries, including between EU Member States later, but even here we want to emphasize that it is possible to talk about Europeanization and European values while recognizing that such differences exist, provided–

---

[3] George A. Bermann *Americanization and Europeanization of Law: Are there Cultural Aspects?*, Columbia University School of Law (New York), See: http://www.learningace.com/doc/2475419/e9423681b2e7795d4dc7d39702070085/cornellconferencebermann

[4] Stéphanie Hennette-Vauchez "Human Rights Law as an Academic Discipline" in Antoine Vauchez and Bruno de Witte (eds.) *Lawyering Europe. European Law as a Transnational Social Field,* Hart Publishing, Oxford/Portland 2013, pp. 117-133 at p. 120. She mentions the ECHR as the emblem (the model?) of international human rights law.

as we do it–the values and the principles are seen at a higher level of abstraction, at which individual solutions in practice do not disturb the idea of common values.

15.2 Best practises of EU member states

It would be rather impossible to discuss and analyse in detail all the various initiatives and practical attempts of the EU or its Member States to Europeanize Eastern Partnership countries′ law curricula. Instead, this paper reflects on the main theoretical ideas on Europeanization deriving from scholars of EU Member States that may or should influence composing a "EU friendly" law curricula in different countries.

As mentioned, Europeanization of the legal system as such and of legal education should be seen separately. However, these processes are closely interrelated and most authors discuss primarily the general law issues, keeping in mind that the curricula changes should be a prerequisite for future changes. Ziller states: "Europeanization of law may be understood as a phenomenon of broadening of the scope of European law, as well as the emergence of new legal disciplines in Europe, linked to European integration"[5] From this quote, two important aspects may be distilled. "Broadening the scope means that the legal scholars are innovative and, with the help of the basic values seek solutions *de lege ferenda*."

Europeanization outside of just the curricula includes notions such as the strengthening of democracy and the protection of human rights, making this something more than just a national concern. Bieber brings the European Convention and Court of Human Rights and rights deriving from EU law as examples.[6] He states: "Establishing a constitutional setting which combines the exercise of power at a national with a supranational level may increase the inclusiveness of the exercise of power, the respect for minority rights and its efficiency, because it may be a more genuine reflection of the interest of the peoples."[7]

Williams on the other hand stresses the failure of the EU to establish strong democratic structures as something that serves to diminish conceptions of liberty in the EU. Early on in the history of the EU, the ECJ did not pay much attention to enforcing democracy. Williams feels this left

---

[5] Jacques Ziller "Europeanisation of Law: From the Enlargement of the Areas of European Law to a Transformation of the Law of the Member States" *EUI Working Paper LAW* No. 2006/19

[6] R. Bieber "The Lissabon-Urteil: An Association of Sovereign States", European Constitutional Law Review 5 (2009) pp at p 400.

[7] *Ibid.*, p 400.

the EU a bit outside of the idea of supporting an ideological notion of democracy. In his view, the latter attempts to inscribe democracy as a value that the EU supports in provisions on citizenship or transparency for example are "vaguely desperate". He also sees ambivalence regarding the rule of law.[8] Williams puts these weaknesses down to an absence of a philosophy of law for the EU. His ideas are linked to the debate on whether there is a European demos, a people through which the demands for democracy can be raised. The German Constitutional Court in 2009 pronounced that there are no such demos.[9] The development of the EU does show how a practical and functional cooperation can lead to more ideological cooperation and to notions of shared values. Williams is one of many authors who see the process of values and practical tasks to enforce these values as a bit backward, with cooperation on a wide range of issues first and then when such cooperation shows it is essential to have and protect common values, such values are found or created. In Williams' view the paramount consideration when it comes to EU protection of values is still to protect the integrity of the EU legal system. [10] The much noted Kadi case[11] where the ECJ stated that public international law (in the form of UN resolutions) cannot be applied if it conflicts with EU fundamental principles thus is also mainly an attempt to save the system, not so much to certain specific rights.

Such debates in their detail are more relevant for EU Member States, but the existence of these discussions and the critical thinking around the EU based on values rather than just on institutional issues should have a place in any Europeanization of studies.

It is clear that the content of legal curricula will have an influence on the legal community. If only university curricula are altered to take into consideration "new" topics or different values, the effect will be rather slow, as the students will only come out into active service after some years. However, as there should be and in most countries normally is, a close connection between teaching and research, modern notions are spread also in other ways and become part of the legal discourse of the country. Academics who play an active role in introducing new topics or new ways of thinking can thus have an important effect on legal

---

[8] A. Williams "Philosophy of EU law", pp Oxford Journal of Legal Studies Vol. 29 Autumn 2009 at p 568.

[9] Bundesverfassungsgericht (Germany) 30 June 2009, available (also in English) at http://www.bundesverfassungsgericht.de/entscheidungen/es20090630_2bve000208 en.html

[10] Williams (2009) especially pp 570-571 and pp 575-576.

[11] Case Kadi C-402/05P (2008)

developments, whether or not they are directly involved in the legislative process (as experts or similar). Hennette-Vauchez mentions academics that played a great role in introducing human rights as essential parts of the European legal curricula, especially in the 1960s.[12]

Among the best practices of EU Member States, the emphasis on skills and not just knowledge as a component of legal education should certainly be mentioned. Practicing European law requires specific skills,[13] but this has also led to a more general understanding that not just factual knowledge is important but also the ability to use this and put it into best effect.

15.3 The EU influence on legal studies in the EU

Legal curricula in EU Member States have gradually been influenced in different ways by a process of Europeanization. Just like the process for Eastern Partnership countries being different from country to country, both in scope and in timing, the process within the EU has been anything but unified, even if looking simultaneously only at countries that joined at the same time. For the whole of the EU the picture is obviously even more varied, as the actual Europeanization process as such only developed rather slowly from the creation of the EU (or rather its predecessor the European Community, EC).

In the early days of European unification, legal education was not changed much or influenced by the emergence of the new organisations. What happened was that some specialised programmes were introduced (for example the College of Europe in Bruges) and many of the early European officials trained in such institutions.[14] Evidently, with the growth of the areas of competence of the EC and later EU as well as enlargements of the EU, European studies could not stay exclusive in this

---

[12] Hennette-Vauchez (2013) p. 132.

[13] Antoine Vauchez "Introduction. Euro-lawyering, Transnational Social Fields and European Policy Building" in Antoine Vauchez and Bruno de Witte (eds.) *Lawyering Europe. European Law as a Transnational Social Field,* Hart Publishing, Oxford/Portland 2013 pp. 1-17 at p. 5.

[14] Bruno de Witte "European Union Law: A Unified Academic Discipline?" in Antoine Vauchez and Bruno de Witte (eds.) *Lawyering Europe. European Law as a Transnational Social Field,* Hart Publishing, Oxford/Portland 2013 pp. 101-116 at p 103. The Jean Monnet Action Programme, a funding scheme to promote university teaching on questions of European integration was started in 1989. *Ibid.* p. 115.

way but a process of Europeanization of many legal topics as taught in most European universities began.

De Witte[15] points out that legal scholars normally do not write about their scholarship as such, in the same way as, for example, political to social scholars. This means that there is not much written about the nature of European legal scholarship and the possible differences between countries. Legal scholars tend to go directly to the topic of their research with only limited theoretical discussions around the research. It is thus easier to see differences in, for example, how courts or administrative bodies use a doctrine (where there are substantial differences between EU Member States) than in how this doctrine is born.[16] De Witte points to a fragmentation because of the different way EU law is taught in different countries and presented in literature of different countries.[17] Although we do not challenge this view, we maintain that at a higher level of abstraction, common principles can still be found.

The legal systems and also the legal training in EU Member States have been influenced by the EU not just in the direct and obvious manner that EU law is now part of the legal system of the Member States and has to be taught at university as well as implemented by courts and administrative organs or incorporated by legislators. Commentators also recognize other influences on the legal style or style of governance in EU Member States, wider than that which is necessary because of EU Membership. Kelemen talks about "Eurolegalism" as a change to the regulatory style of Europe brought on by the more complex regulatory environment in the integrated Europe where freer markets and deregulation lead to a need for more formal, transparent and juridical regulatory rule-making as well as of the specific legal style introduced in relation to corporate and competition law.[18] With a deepening of the supranational legal framework, the EU in some ways moves closer to the US model of a regulatory state, where law is very important to structure regulation, rather than more flexible schemes that were possible in Europe earlier when the areas and matters to be regulated were much less

[15] *Ibid.* p. 101-102.
[16] *Ibid.*
[17] *Ibid.* p. 108.
[18] R. Daniel Kelemen "Eurolegalism and the European Legal Field" in Antoine Vauchez and Bruno de Witte (eds.) *Lawyering Europe. European Law as a Transnational Social Field,* Hart Publishing, Oxford/Portland 2013, pp. 243-257 at pp. 244-245 and p. 248.

extensive.[19] Also such changes have influenced the demands put on legal education and have entailed Europeanization in EU Member States. Activities such as lobbying and other public affairs related tasks have led to a special course on EU issues including law for non-lawyers[20]–also that is an element of Europeanization that affects legal curricula as some tasks related to law take on a different aspect and are no longer primarily within the domain of the (traditional) legal professional.

It is more difficult to determine if the cultural and traditional differences between legal education and its role in society in EU Member States has changed because of the EU or any other processes of Europeanization. In the Eastern and Central European EU Member States, as society changed so cardinally after the fall of Communism, there are fewer special historical and traditional factors linked to studying law. The clearest example of such factors is to be found in the United Kingdom where for example the need to work for free in order to qualify has meant that the social diversification among law students is minimal. However, also in Scandinavia and Germany law faculties retain at least some characteristics of institutions for the elite.[21] Law students are influenced by the atmosphere in which they study and with an increasing number of students studying in foreign countries and reading literature in other languages, legal thinking is shaped in different ways that are not based necessarily on nationality.[22]

The EU is often seen as a construction for which law and legal knowledge is of the utmost importance, which has led to a big influence of legally trained persons for the development of the Union. With the increased complexity of the EU as it covers more and more areas, one would perhaps expect an even greater role for lawyers, but in fact the proportion of persons with a legal background in important positions in the main intergovernmental body, the Commission, has decreased in recent

---

[19] Bronwen Morgan and Karen Yeung *An Introduction to Law and Regulation,* Cambridge University Press, Cambridge 2007, p. 312.

[20] Christian Lahusen "Lawyers and Consultants at the EU" in Antoine Vauchez and Bruno de Witte (eds.) *Lawyering Europe. European Law as a Transnational Social Field,* Hart Publishing, Oxford/Portland 2013, pp. 177-194 at p. 187 and p. 189.

[21] This is discussed from a slightly different angle by Yves Dezalay "Opportunities and Limits of a Weak Field" in Antoine Vauchez and Bruno de Witte (eds.) *Lawyering Europe. European Law as a Transnational Social Field,* Hart Publishing, Oxford/Portland 2013, pp. 259-282 at pp. 262-263.

[22] De Witte (2013) p. 107.

years as shown by the analysis of Georgakakis and de Lassalle.[23] This does not necessarily mean a decrease in the importance of law and legal training, but it can be seen as recognition of the mentioned extension of the EU competence to many new areas, which necessitates specialist competence in various matters.

15.4 Eurocurricula for Eastern Partnership countries

The authors are familiar with several law curricula of universities in Eastern Partnership countries and based on this knowledge would rather claim that beside the titles of the courses included in these academic programmes, there are other more essential aspects that should be kept in mind but are often neglected when evaluating the "Europeaness" of the curricula. For example, one of the current authors recently provided suggestions to Moldavian universities on the Europeanization of their curricula. Despite many good initiatives and positive developments, the conclusions were rather critical, emphasising the underlying sources of the problems with insufficient Europeanization, which are more critical than the surface work with changing titles or introducing new topics. This is not to be overly critical of any one country, but rather to point to what is needed in order to achieve the best results–also from the point of view of such European scholars who have as their mission to Europeanize law curricula in certain countries.

Our main analysis is related to the teaching methods and "European spirit" of the teaching process that is not often visible. In many instances, teaching methods are not specified, although interactive tools and e-environments are inseparable parts of any contemporary law school and the use of such methods is an element of Europeanization. Grading and assessment methods are also often not specified. In Europe, there is a trend to use cumulative assessment rather than one decisive final exam. Another issue is that literature is usually provided only in the domestic language (or Russian). When certain international elements and the EU legal system are included in the curricula, a comprehensive understanding of some foreign (European) literature seems to be unavoidable. It would be advisable to let the students themselves find sources for their independent creative work

---

[23] Didier Georgakakis and Marine de Lassalle "Where Have all the Lawyers Gone?" in Antoine Vauchez and Bruno de Witte (eds.) *Lawyering Europe. European Law as a Transnational Social Field,* Hart Publishing, Oxford/Portland 2013, pp. 137-151 at pp. 148-149.

and research. Also this is an element of the Europeanization of the teaching process.

Learning outcomes, which are central for testing the quality of the curricula in Europe, are in many Eastern Partnership countries not always visible and should be presented more systematically and concretely. Often the question arises: is it possible for a student to make choices and combine his/her own study path? To introduce the spirit of Europeanization it should be possible to have law curricula based on individuals′ rights and freedoms, combining the roles of State, society, and citizens. This shift in the mind-set of professors is a crucial question if we would like to avoid the formalistic approach and be result-oriented.

When teaching European topics, practice should have a central role. General theory of law is often presented in an old-fashioned way. For example, constitutional law seems often to be just a course on the judicial system and administrative law. Contemporary courses related to the subject matter should include the methods of interpretation, constitutional doctrines, principles and case-law. Furthermore, for the legal protection of human rights it is very useful to use case-law (and then the selection of the cases would be a part of compulsory literature). In courses on EU law, the Charter of Fundamental Rights is not often mentioned. The Lisbon Treaty and the Charter should be presented as recent and quite innovative milestones of development of the whole European legal system. The courses often lack general concepts and problems (universality, "new human rights", derogations, exceptions, direct applicability, criteria for identifying human rights violations and victims, etc.). It seems that too much attention is focused on institutional frameworks rather than on concrete human rights.

In the study of EU law it is essential to include contemporary issues like crisis regulation mechanisms such as the European Stability Mechanism (ESM). Why this is important is because it includes essential conceptual issues like the collision between supranational and national law (with Karlsruhe–German Constitutional Court-cases for example). Also, a separate section should be dedicated to enlargement law (accession treaties) and pre-accession legal strategies. It is also important to know how to read EU law. Courses include too much institutional framework issues without sufficient focus on concepts and legal principles.

Another example is criminal procedure law. Here the suggestion is to use the jurisprudence under Article 6 of the European Convention of Human Rights (right to fair trial). As for courses related to the legal profession ethical issues should be added, including professional codes of ethics and other such matters that form an important basis for the work of the profession in democratic states. The study of cases and problems related to Eastern countries′ legal professionals would benefit from comparative analysis with EU countries.

In addition to Moldova, examples from Ukraine can be mentioned. Lvov University named after Ivan Frank, has several centres related to EU Member State legal systems (German, Austrian, Polish) that may give students and scholars some support in their achievements. However, EU law is not included in the curricula. You may find several courses on American law, such as "Introduction to the American Criminal Justice System" (example from Taras Schevchenko National University of Kyiv) or elements of German law at Ukrainian universities. Sometimes it seems that there is a struggle of whether to prefer US or EU legal approaches that may cause confusion among students. Some of the Eastern Partnership universities contain a special compulsory course on European law (Belarussian State University).

The other important issue of Europeanization is related to academic research that is a basis for good quality teaching. This would require the Eastern Partnership countries to understand the need for peer-reviewed journals, projects with solid consortia.

The formation of a knowledge-based society is one of the main goals of the EU. If the EU wishes to become a "citizens Europe", there must be a common understanding of the legal framework among the Member States, EU institutions and citizens to avoid non-equality of EU Members. This understanding has to be grounded on the rule of law and supported with continuous dialogue in which the constitutional norms play a central role.[24] This ideal should also be applied to the relationship with the Eastern Partnership countries, reflected in the law curricula in local universities. Besides developments in EU law as such, conceptual approaches should be taught with emphasis on learning outcomes.

15.5 What does the East need?

The crucial question is: what should the theoretical difference of the Europeanization of law curricula of EU Member States and the curricula of the Eastern Partnership countries be?

---

[24] See: Tanel Kerikmäe "Estonia as a EU member state in the context of deliberative supranationalism: Lack of pro-active constitutional dialogue" in *Post-Enlargement Constitutionalization in Central and Eastern Europe* Ed. By Alexander Morawa, Ashgate Publishing Ltd, Farnham, 2010

It seems that in both cases, the main purpose is the same. As stated by Ziller[25] "Europeanization has three main consequences:

- a fundamental change in the systems of sources of law;
- unifying legal culture;
- changes in terms of methodology of legal sciences.

All these three strategic objectives can be constantly reviewed in EU universities but can also be a basis for curricula reform in Eastern Partnership law schools.

Additionally, we would propose the use of selected categories of Europeanization, proposed by Harmsen and Wilson,[26] in light of law curricula. There are interesting moments beside traditional propositions that can fill certain gaps in Europeanization, especially of Eastern Partnership countries′ curricula. One of these aspects, "Europeanization as policy isomorphism", would mean that not only EU legislative acts should be taken into account but also "intensive transnational cooperation fostered by European integration".[27] It means that the curricula should, beside EU legal developments see also the legal cooperation schemes between Member States (such as consultative actions when composing a consortium in case of infringement procedure, following each others′ requests for preliminary rulings, judgements of higher courts, intergovernmental agreements etc.).

Europeanization means that law adapts to a post-national environment and even if this only applies to members of the EU as such and to some extent to members of the ECHR, the idea of an increasingly integrated world "where neither the cultural and normative values, nor the available pool of social knowledge upon which law rests, can ultimately be taken for granted"[28] also has a wider application.

Another useful aspect would be to include critical approaches as we often see isolated courses rather than telling a story of one, unified and perfect EU legal system. "Europeanization as a problem and opportunity for domestic policy management"–as Harmsen and Wilson state: "Governments must find the means to reconcile potentially contradictory

---

[25] Jacques Ziller, ibid.

[26] Robert Harmsen and Thomas M. Wilson "Approaches to Europeanization" *Yearbook of European Studies* 14 (2000), pp. 13-26.

[27] *Ibid.* p 15

[28] Mark Dawson "Soft Law and the Rule of Law in the EU" in Antoine Vauchez and Bruno de Witte (eds.) *Lawyering Europe. European Law as a Transnational Social Field,* Hart Publishing, Oxford/Portland 2013, pp. 221-241 at p. 223.

European and domestic choices".[29] Although we claimed in the first part of the current paper that policy making and law should not be mixed to avoid the prevalence of the thoughts of specific schools or political interest-groups over the legal principles-especially legal certainty and rule of law-the models, techniques and hard-cases on collisions in the multi-level legal space that reflect tensions as well as pragmatic solution-seeking should be reflected. It would give the right impression that the EU legal system is not dogmatic but rather a developing legal system where the constitutional values are (especially after the crisis) derived from dialogue and a certain level of reciprocity, rather than a dictate.[30] It is not so much about policy choices but rather testing the EU legal norms through the basic legal values common to the Member States and the EU.

De Witte points out that initially a large extent were in favour of deeper integration (or at least having been perceived thus), EU legal scholarship in the Member States has become much more multi-facetted and also critical.[31] This is a normal and positive development, as it allows scholarship to play a real role in the debate and development of society.

Beside "Europeanization as modernization and joining Europe", that are core elements and the main reasons for third countries to include European courses in their law curricula. We would emphasise the relevance of the aspect of "Europeanization as the reconstruction of identities".[32] The Europeanization of the law curricula should not purely introduce new disciplines and procedures, but provide a deep insight into European legal culture to prepare a shift in the mind-set of the lawyers and frame a new identity for the legal system that needs to be Europeanized. Here, we would get inspiration from Maduro who states that "it will not be sufficient, however, to increase the importance attached to EU law in the curricula of European law schools. A first step will be to 'Europeanise' the teaching of the other legal subjects".[33] The Europeanization of the law

---

[29] Hamsen & Wilson (2000) p. 15

[30] See Tanel Kerikmäe "Estonia as a EU member state in the context of deliberative supranationalism: Lack of pro-active constitutional dialogue" in *Post-Enlargement Constitutionalization in Central and Eastern Europe* Ed. By Alexander Morawa, Ashgate Publishing Ltd, Farnham, 2010; and Tanel Kerikmäe and Katrin Nyman-Metcalf "Karlsruhe vs. Lissabon: an Overture to a Constitutional Dialogue?" *European Journal of Law Reform* 2011:12 pp. 373 - 387

[31] De Witte (2013) p. 105.

[32] Harmsen & Wilson (2000), pp. 16-17

[33] Miguel Poiares Maduro "Legal Education and the Europeanization and Globalization of Law" Policy Paper 10/01, February 2010, *Contraditório*, www.contraditorio.pt, (also published as an Editorial Note in the Croatian Yearbook of European Law & Policy 2010, p. 5)

curricula of the Eastern Partnership countries should probably not do it to such an extent as the Member States. However, the biggest problem is that in many curricula the few courses of EU institutional law or common market law are isolated from other legal subjects taught. It also means that the knowledge received from these courses remains isolated and somewhat useless, as the graduate cannot find the relationship between EU law and different legal areas such as constitutional law, family law, private law and so on.

One of the aspects that Maduro emphasises[34] is that the practice of law is increasingly international, therefore, the claim that Eastern Partnership lawyers do not need a substantial knowledge in European law that reflects changes in different regulatory fields, is not justified. Although not candidate States, Eastern Partners have strategies to increase business relations with Europe–for that, there is a need for qualified lawyers who know the legal cultures of both sides. Also, the judiciary should be Europeanized–especially with the purpose of encouraging judges "to apply international and EU law in their decisions".[35]

15.6 Is the succesful tranposition of values possible?

This paper will not discuss the general question of whether it is possible and to what extent to make "legal transplants". There is abundant literature on the matter and although a basic understanding of this matter is needed to understand the discussion on Europeanization of legal curricula–especially the more fundamental and philosophical aspects of this question–we presume that the reader has a basic knowledge of this debate and we thus concentrate for reasons of space on the curricula as such. However, even in this limited context it is necessary to reflect as a conclusion on preconditions for a successful introduction of "European" norms and principles in the legal education of the Eastern Partnership States.

Where there are examples of a rather rapid acceptance of a common set of ideas and the possibility to move in accord toward a common goal, this is often coupled with a limited size of the community in question and shared traditions, cultural norms and so on. This said, what constitutes such commonality can be more varied than just pointing to States with a

---

[34] Maduro (2010) p. 6

[35] Roman Petrov and Paul Kalinichenko "The Europeanization of third country judiciaries through the application of the EU *Aquis*: The cases of Russia and Ukraine." *International & Comparative Law Quarterly,* vol. 60, issue 2, 2011, p. 8

very similar history or geographical proximity. Indeed, a shared understanding of the goal to be achieved and a shared notion of what this goal is, most likely matters more than external circumstances.[36] The EU as the most important regional integration organisation influences the view on regional integration, as a model and an example of what is possible. The EU experience can be a strong precedent for other parts of the world and its experiences are also of interest for this reason: as analogies for other regions. It may be discussed whether the EU can be a model in its specifics or if it is rather an example of what is possible as an idea.[37] In any event, the ability to discuss and consider such ideas should be transmitted through studies also.

The question of legal transplants is increasingly relevant in many areas of the law, as the process of globalisation as well as the transition of many States to a market economy and democracy in a relatively short time period, mean that there are numerous situations in which countries use the laws of other countries as models for their own new laws. Legal transplants are not unproblematic as any law is an element in an organic system and must be able to interact with the other elements of this system. An alien transplant may not be able to fulfil this role. The fact that the situations of using many legal transplants often come at a time of upheaval generally does not make the exercise any easier in the country. At the same time, there is nothing to gain from constantly re-inventing the wheel and legal transplants can support faster reform and closer integration into value systems. Having the ability to critically analyse "best practices" and international norms is an essential component of legal studies and Europeanization of curricula also means: to be able to be critical of the EU!

---

[36] Hennette-Vauchez discusses the common notion of a mission by the founders of the European Convention and Court of Human Rights. Hennette-Vauchez (2013), p. 123.

[37] C. Hall "Constitutionalism as Liberal-Juridical Consciousness: Echoes from international law's past" in *Leiden Journal of International Law* 22 (2009) pp 251-287 at pp 276-277.

CONCLUSIONS

SUMMARIZATION AND FORMULATION PROPOSALS *DE LEGE FERENDA*

The Eastern Partnership clearly occupies a privileged position in the Union's external relations and constitutes an important 'Eastern axis' of the European Neighbourhood Policy, along with its Southern/Mediterranean dimension. The Treaty of Lisbon confirmed the importance of cooperation with Neighbouring countries in Art. 8 TEU, which is a framework provision and a 'declaration of intent' to foster relations with the Union's neighbours.

The establishment of the ENP was inspired mainly by the EU's fifth enlargement which necessitated the elaboration of a new comprehensive framework for the EU's relations with its new neighbours, bringing together the previous EU policies towards its neighbours. However, from its very inception the ENP covered two distinctly different groups of states, which impeded the EU's efforts to create a cohesive approach fully applicable to all of the neighbouring countries. The lack of consensus among the EU Member States for the finality of the ENP and the unwillingness of a certain neighbouring country to become a "permanent neighbour" provoked the geographical split of the ENP, resulting in the establishment of the UfM and the EaP. Whereas the UfM is an international organisation with its own institutional framework, the EaP is perceived as a specific form of cooperation between the EU and its Eastern neighbours, implemented within the ENP framework.

Thus provisions in Article 8 TEU of the Lisbon Treaty allow for the adoption of two not entirely coherent approaches. The first option is to conclude a specific external agreement on as precise a legal basis as possible; the other–and in our view more likely–option is to use flexibly the vague definitions of Association, EFTC and ENP to account for the political will of the other party. Differences between these concepts of external relations, and even more so their overlapping, indeed give the EU quite a lot of leeway allowing it to reflect the political wishes of the non-EU contractual parties and, at the same time, to respect the EU principle of delegated powers which is a requirement for any EU action to have a sufficient legal basis in the Treaties.

In this context, Article 8 TEU (ENP) can be evaluated as an *alternative* to Article 217 TFEU (Association). Some countries do not wish to be "Associated" because of their political ego (Russia, in the past also Switzerland); other countries require Association status (because of the vision of future membership) even if the EU is not that enthusiastic about it.

The examination of the new formulations of the provisions in the field of External Relations law of the Union brought by the Lisbon Treaty enable us to conclude, that whilst article 212 TFEU on EFTC introduces a clear link to the development policy, article 8 TEU on ENP talks about privileged relations and bears thus more resemblance to Association pursuant to Article 217 TFEU.

The preparation of the EU-Ukraine Association Agreement indicates the future orientation and the prospects for Eastern Partnership countries, which can be a transition to more privileged links with the Union in the form of a future Association relationship. In this sense the Eastern partnership could be evaluated to a certain intermediate level (grade) to the Association.

This conclusion is also proved by the fact that the drafts of the new Association Agreements with some other States of the Eastern partnership (Moldova and Georgia) were already prepared on the basis of this "model" Association treaty of the new generation.

The analytical view of the previous Association Agreements with the states of Central and Eastern Europe and their comparison thereof with the new EU-Ukraine Agreement proves that as concerns the European Agreements, the issues of approximation of law have been left open to a broader discretion and consideration of the candidate states themselves, including the provision of legally non-binding instruments (for example the White Paper).

Unlike the European Agreements, the EU-Ukraine Association Agreement brings specified procedures, methods and detailed instructions in the form of legal obligations as concerns the adoption of the Union legislation, including the institutional questions, determination of the time sequence for ensuring that compatibility has been reached in the particular norms and monitoring the fulfilment of these obligations (in the framework of so-called regulatory approximation).

Even though the above outlined new concept may seem to be a little bit "paternalistic" at first sight in comparison with the previous Europe Association Agreements, nevertheless it must be taken into consideration that to the more extensive obligations in approximation of law correspond the substantially extended pattern of "assistance counter-obligations" on the Union side.

In other words, it can be concluded, that the generally declared principle "more for more" will be fully applicable in the field of the legal approximation as well. Besides the précised specification of the ratione materiae and materiae temporis enables the effective monitoring of the contractual obligations, including the respect to rule of law and human rights.

The Ukraine has managed to adopt a competition law that is already based on the EU one, and its full harmonization will therefore not be extremely difficult. Nevertheless, even though the AMCU adopts thousands of decisions every year, it is still not possible to claim that Ukraine has developed into a fully functioning market economy with a sufficiently embedded competition regime.

Broader regulatory changes of the entire economy are therefore necessary, liberalizing it and enabling the competition to flourish. At the same time, the AMCU needs to embrace the more economic approach and prepare itself for numerous legal quarrels concerning fair trial.

In both these aspects, the Association Agreement may play a crucial role as it envisages far reaching adjustments of regulations with a view to implementing the DCFTA and enables the Ukrainian authorities to rely on the EU *acquis*.

Subsequently, we argue that the future EU–Ukraine AA should be regarded as a sophisticated tool of EU external policy. Recognising the established role of the EU as a "rule generator", we acknowledge that the objectives and scope of the EU–Ukraine AA serves as an appropriate "wrapping" for the export of EU-generated rules (EU acquis) abroad. Similar to a missionary, the EU–Ukraine AA pursues an objective of the gradual establishment of a friendly legal environment beyond EU borders through the export of its values, principles, and legal heritage abroad underpinned by the existence of binding harmonisation/approximation commitments.

The Association Agreement with Ukraine confirmed also the greater accentuation of the importance of the guarantees in the field of human rights and democratic principles (the deepening of the general trend which was started by the conclusion of the Europe Agreements of the second generation).

The rule of law is an essential cornerstone of the legal acquies of the European Union. It includes three general dimensions: the trans-national dimension between the Member States (I), the internal dimension of the

European Union (II) and the domestic dimension of every Member State (III).

The Rule of Law as a constitutive value of the European Union in the inner legal structure of the European Union is placed right at the beginning of the Treaty on the European Union in two of its lead provisions. The first one says, "the Union´s aim is to promote peace, its values and the well-being of its people." The other one answers the question how the values are substantially composed. It reads "the Union is founded on the values of respect of human dignity, freedom, democracy, equality, the rule of law and respect for human rights." Here we encounter the explicit expression "rule of law" (in German "Rechtsstaatlichkeit" which corresponds to the fundamental principle embodied in Articles 20 and 23 of the Basic Law – "Grundgesetz" of Germany).

The EU and its members are legally obliged under the Treaty on European Union to obey the principles of a democratic regime, the protection of human rights, rights of minorities and the rule of law, protect those principles and also to promote those principles. This obligation is aimed not only internally (i.e. the Member States shall fulfil criteria themselves) but also externally and shall bind Member States as well as EU institutions in their external relations.

As a consequence for the external relations of the Union the provision on the Union´s neighbourhood policy includes this requirement when prescribing that "the Union shall develop a special relationship with neighbouring countries, aiming to establish an area of prosperity and good neighbourliness, founded on the values of the Union."

The rule of law also encloses the requirement of authority and effective enforcement of judicial decisions. Such a situation is functionally closely linked to a general social acceptance and appreciation of judicial decisions. In the tradition of Immanuel Kant the latter can be considered to mirror an essential element of an enlightened society and polity. The experience in Central and Eastern European States after 1989 shows that this social foundation of the rule of law is specifically a great challenge in polities which transform from dictatorships into free societies.

From a formal point of view, all three sources of fundamental rights mentioned in Article 6 TEU (Charter, ECHR and general principles of law) are independent, parallel and have a similar binding force. However, having regard to the structure of this provision, the explicitly recognised legal value of the Charter and its detailed catalogue of rights, the authors of the Treaties have made it clear that the Charter shall become the main and preferred source of fundamental rights in the Union legal order. The Court of Justice has respected this will and it has been, in particular, gradually ceasing to refer to general principles of law. Thus, when possible, the Court of Justice started replacing the analysis based on general principles of law by the one based on the Charter and the latter is thus replacing, step-by-step, the general principles in its case-law. Furthermore, the Court of Justice prefers to refer to the Charter instead of the ECHR, even in cases in which referring courts or applicants base their arguments on provisions of the ECHR. In some cases, the Court of Justice preferred however to complete the provisions of the Charter by references to the provisions of the ECHR.[1] The Court of justice clearly demonstrated this attitude in Volker und Markus Schecke.

This new conception of the protection of fundamental rights, based on the coexistence of several formal sources of law, has given rise to three main consequences. First of all, the Charter has become a central instrument for the protection of fundamental rights in the Union legal order (I). At the same time, the Court of Justice has lost a part of its discretionary power in this field (II). Finally, the level of protection of fundamental rights has been increased (III).

The understanding of Article 2 TEU as an obligation of the Member States is supported by the Treaty´s provision of accession. Article 49 TEU provides that any European State "which respects the values referred to in Article 2 and is committed to promoting them may apply to become a member of the Union". It is noteworthy that the text provides that this requirement has to already be fulfilled at the time at which the application for membership is lodged. It certainly would be paradoxical if this requirement for a State would vanish at the moment when this State becomes a member of the Union.

Questions of democracy during the EU integration process of Slovakia in 1994–1999 confirmed the essential significance of their requirements and showed how the EU reacts when political criteria are not met.

In the autumn and winter of 1994 as well as during the following years of Mečiar's government the EU quickly responded to every act that threatened the principles of democracy and the rule of law and it became evident how failure to comply with the democratic criteria can ruin the integration process. On the other hand, the integration story of Slovakia shows how a change of political situation and eagerness of the government to introduce a change of political climate from confrontation to cooperation and to carry out constitutional and structural reforms could

[1] See Cases C-163/10 *Patriciello* [2011] ECR I-7565, paragraph 31; C-391/09 *Runevič-Vardyn and Wardyn* [2011] ECR I-3787, paragraph 66; C-208/09 *Sayn-Wittgenstein* [2010] ECR I-13693, paragraph 52 and C-145/09 *Tsakouridis* [2010] ECR I- 11979, paragraph 52.

quickly change the attitude of the EU. Therefore Slovakia could serve as an example of how to make progress in integration of those countries whose integration process (Association or Accession to the EU) is inhibited by the failure of democratic principles as well as an inspiration for political and constitutional changes.

The relevant material also demanded the examination and the research of the role of the Constitutional courts and in the issues of constitutionality and the interpretation of fundamental rights content.

Constitutional courts as specialised institutions of concentrated constitutional review became much more important after the fall of Nazism and fascism and later on communism, i.e. in connection with the need to stress the perception of a law based on ethical values. The constitutional judiciary is an important phenomenon of the rule of law in the state. Its role consists of the protection of constitutionality containing the protection of human or fundamental rights. Constitutional courts have a unique position in the framework of the division of powers in relation towards both ordinary courts (power to annul their decisions) and to parliament (power to annul laws or its provisions). They pronounce themselves as a negative legislator to the most complex political, social and moral issues from the point of view of constitutionality. In doing that, they find the limits of constitutional review; their task is not to review legality. The essential qualification to be a Justice of the Constitutional court consists not only in an expert qualification, but also in the perception of the values embodied in the fundamental rights.

The research was also focused on a detailed characteristic of the European Neighbourhood Policy towards the South Caucasus States, namely Armenia, Azerbaijan and Georgia, and finding out what might be the reasons for the EU engaging in such close cooperation with these countries.

The research shows that the prevention of possible problems coming from the region, or caused by instability there, is definitely a motivating factor for the EU to have a special, closer relationship with the region, having a special policy towards it and putting in an effort to reform and modernize the countries there. These possible problems (such as drug trafficking, illegal immigration, human trafficking, terrorism), might have a direct effect on the EU itself and therefore become a threat to its safety. That is why the EU is very much interested in being more active in this region, being able to monitor the situation very closely, having the possibility to influence the countries more on their way to modernization and democratization, carrying on necessary reforms, in order to build more successful states, with strong democratic institutions, a stable market economy, with the values that are common to Europe and in general, a safe and stable, developing country. As stability in the region would mean stability and safety on the EU borders in general.

Estonia and Georgia provide examples of two quite different roads taken by post-Soviet states, but roads that in some ways have converged on similar goals. Still, the timing of steps taken to reform the countries and the consistency of such reforms have meant that now Estonia is in a position to assist its partner and such assistance has in many ways proven to be more consistent and effective than that of European and Euro-Atlantic organisations in general.

Nowadays Estonia, which is interested in closing the gap between the West and other post-Soviet States [Galbreath, Lamoreaux 2006:98], and thus acquire more allies in the enlarged Europe, continues its cooperation with Georgia.

We believe that the concept of post-Soviet countries does not make sense anymore. Some successful examples, such as Estonia, have proven that being a post-Soviet country does not prevent the economy from blooming; Estonia has fulfilled the EU criteria of membership, is involved in the Euro zone, belongs to NATO and is perfectly capable of taking care of its own economic affairs. The same refers to Slovakia and the Czech Republic; the ways of legal and political transformation were the subjects of examination in this study. Nevertheless, international opinion including at the highest level among the states of "Old Europe" and other groups of countries together based only on a shared history. Due to this, the post-Soviets are striving for closer cooperation with each other in order to lose the negative connotations of being Eastern European countries that are too fragile in the economic sense to be in collaboration with. Two decades have passed since the collapse of the Soviet Union and the decline of World War II dividing lines: it should now be high time to accept that those countries that have gained independence and have proven thriving economies are worthy of being regarded as full members of the European family and indeed instrumental in assisting those yet not quite as far on the road to "Westernization".

Last, but not least, the research focused on the Europeanization of legal curricula – especially the more fundamental and philosophical aspects of this question and discussed the general question of whether it is possible and to what extent to make "legal transplants".

However even in this limited context it is necessary to reflect as a conclusion on the preconditions for a successful introduction of "European" norms and principles in legal education of the Eastern Partnership States.

Hence scholars, legislators, administrators and judges are foremost responsible for creating and supporting this respect – in the common interest of the desired high standards of societal civilisation in Europe.

Since its establishment at the Prague Summit in 2009, the Eastern Partnership, as is shown, has flourished and a complex framework of legal and political instruments have been created, along with the necessary financial resources to implement the defined objectives (in this respect apprehensions were not justified, that it will be unnecessary tool). However, the overall success of this project will be put to the test in the near future, and some tangible results (the signing and the initiating of AAs/DCFTAs) would be much needed and appreciated.

Current political unrests and demonstrations in Ukraine in connection with the delay of the signature of the EU-Ukraine Association Agreement showed also that the mentioned contract instrument is considered to be a key indicator in geopolitical terms, as a concrete expression and powerful symbol of future orientation and inclination of this former Soviet Republic either towards the European Union, or to Russia. At the moment of writing of these lines the dramatic events in Ukraine are taking place and the definite fate of the Agreement is still not known. Although we believe that the analysis of this document, which was done in the monograph, will help to explain (even partly) the substance, reason, and core of this development. In this respect the envisaged signature and the implementation of the EU-Ukraine Association Agreement and the realisation of this "pilot project" will influence significantly not only the destiny of Ukraine itself, but some other countries of the former Soviet empire as well.

The future dynamics and progress of the Eastern Partnership depend on it to a great extent, as much as the stability and security of the Union depends on the developments in its neighbourhood.

LIST OF ABBREVIATIONS AND ACRONYMS

AA	Association Agreement
AMCU Act	Law on the Antimonopoly Committee of Ukraine, OJVR 1993, No. 50, p. 472
Antimonopoly Act 1992	Act on the limitation of monopolism and the prevention of unfair competition in entrepreneurial activities, OJVR 1992, No 12, p. 64
AP	Action Plan
CEE	Central and Eastern Europe
CFSP	Common Foreign and Security Policy
CIB	Comprehensive Institution-Building
CIS	Commonwealth of Independent States
CJEU	Court of Justice of the European Union
Coll.	Collection of Law of the Slovak Republic/Czechoslovak Socialist/ Czech and Slovak Federal Republic
Competition Act 2001	Law on economic competition protection, OJVR 2001, No. 12, p. 64
COREPER	Committee of Permanent
Representatives	
CS	Common Strategy
CSCE	Commission on Security and
Cooperation in Europe	
DCFTA	Deep and Comprehensive Free Trade Area
DU	Democratic Union
EA	Europe Agreement
EAEC	European Atomic Energy Community
EaP	Eastern Partnership
EC	European Community
ECEAP	Estonian Centre of Eastern Partnership
ECJ	European Court of Justice
ECR	European Court Reports
ECtHR	European Court on Human Rights
EEC	European Economic Community

EFTA	European Free Trade Association
EFTC	Economic, Financial and Technical Cooperation
ECHR	European Convention of Human Rights
ENP	European Neighbourhood Policy
ENP	European Neighbourhood Policy
ESM	European Stability Mechanism
EU	European Union
EUMM	European Union monitoring mission
EURATOM	Treaty establishing the European Atomic Energy Community
HZDS	Movement for Democratic Slovakia
ICC	International Criminal Court
ICT	Information and Communications Technology
IIFFMC	Independent International Fact-Finding Mission on the Conflict in Georgia
JHA	Justice and Home Affairs
KDH	Christian-Democratic Movement
LGDJ	Librairie générale de droit et de jurisprudence
Merger Regulation	Council Regulation (EC) No 139/2004 on the control of concentrations between undertakings (the EC Merger Regulation), OJ L 24, 29. 1. 2004, p. 1
NATO	North Atlantic Treaty Organisation
NATO	North Atlantic Treaty Organization
NIS	Newly Independent States
O.J.	Official Journal of the European Union
OCT	Overseas Countries and Territories
OECD	Organisation for Economic Cooperation and Development
OJ	Official Journal of the European Union
OVJR	Official Journal of the Verkhovna Rada
Partnership Agreement	Partnership and cooperation agreement between the European Communities and their member states, of the one part, and the Ukraine, of the other part, OJ L 49, 19. 2. 1998, p. 3

PCA	Partnership and Cooperation Agreement
SAA	Stabilisation and Association Agreement
SAPC	Stabilisation and Association Parliamentary Committee
SDK	Slovak Democratic Coalition
SDL	Party of the Democratic Left
SMK-MKP	Party of Hungarian Coalition
SNS	Slovak National Party
SOP	Party of Civic Understanding
TEAEC	Treaty on the European Atomic Energy Community
TEC	Treaty on the European Community CFSP Common Foreign and Security Policy
TEU	Treaty on European Union
TFEU	Treaty on the Functioning of the European Union
UEPLAC	Ukrainian-European Legal Advice Center
UN	United Nations
UNDP	United Nations Development Programme
UNSC	United Nations Security Council
US	United States
WMD	Weapons of Mass Destruction
WTO	World Trade Organisation

BIBLIOGRAPHY

Adams, M., ed.: Judging Europe´s Judges, The Legitimacy of the Case Law of the European Court of Justice, Hart Publishing, Oxford and Portland, Oregon 2013.; Agreement on the European Economic Area, OJ No L1, 3.1.1994, p. 3

Bartošek, M.: *Dejiny římskeho práva.* Prague: Academia, 1988.

Bechev D., Nicolaidis K. (2010) >From Policy to Polity: Can the EU's Special Relations with its Neighbourhood be Decentred? Journal of Common Market Studies, Vol. 43, No. 3: 475-500

Bogdan, M.: "Nordická legislatívna spolupráca - príklad harmonizácie právnych poriadkov". ("Nordic Legislative Cooperation – an Example of Harmonisation of Legal Systems"). *Právny obzor* 1 ,1993.

Cesta do Evropské unie. No. 9, Ministerstvo pro místní rozvoj ČR, Praha, 1997, p. 12

Coppieters, B.; Legvold, R. (2005): *Statehood and Security: Georgia after the Rose Revolution.* Cambridge, Mass: MIT Press.

Cornell, S. E.; Tsereteli, M.; Socor, V. (2005): "Geostrategic Implications of the Baku-Tbilisi-Ceyhan Pipeline".

Cremona, M.: Citizens of Third Countries: Movement and Employment of Migrant workers within the European Union in: Legal Issues of European Integration, ELR 1995, vol. 2, p. 94.

Cremona, M.: The European Neighbourhood Policy–More than a Partnership?. In: Cremona M. (ed.), Developments in EU External Relations Law, Oxford University Press, 2008, p. 282.

Corrias, L.: Tha passivity of Law. Competence and Constitution in the European Court of Justice. Dordrecht: Springer, 2011, p. 171.

David,R.: and Grassmann, G.: *Die Einfurung in die grossen Rechtsysteme der Gegenwart.* München: C. H. BECK, 1988.

Dobrovoljec, D.; Nyman-Metcalf, K. (2001): "Enlargement of the European Union a – Regatta with moving goal posts?" *European Journal of Law Reform* 3(2): 131-147.

Dragneva R., Wolczuk K. (2012) EU Law Export to the Eastern Neighbourhood. In: Paul James Cardwell (ed.) EU External Relations Law and Policy in the Post-Lisbon Era. T.M.C. ASSER Press, the Hague, pp. 217-240

Eeckhout, P.: EU External Relations Law, 2. Edition, Oxford University Press, Oxford - New York, 2012, p. 127.

Eeckhout, P.: The External Relations Law of the European Union, Oxford University Press, Oxford - New York, 2004, p. 190-191.

Elsuwege, P. V.: Variable Geometry in the European Neighbourhood Policy. The principle of Differentiation and its Consequences, in: Lannon, E. (ed.): The European Neighbourhood Policy's Challenges, P. I. E. Peter Lang, Brussels 2012, p. 59

Experience of the Slovak Republic From Membership In The European Union (Opyt Slovakii po Členstvu v ES).: Scientific Editors-Kunova,V and Vrabko, M, Comenius University Bratislava Faculty of Law, 2008, pages 299

Fierro E. (2003) The EU's Approach to Human Rights Conditionality in Practice. Martinus Nijhoff Publishers, the Hague

Fischer, P.: and others, eds. *Europa Recht*. Vienna: Linde Verlag, 2002.

Fischer, P.: *European Law*. Bratislava: BVSP, 2006.

Galbreath, J.; Lamoreaux, W. (2006): "What Democratizing Countries May (Hope to) Get from Abroad?" Kasekamp, A.; Pääbo, H. (eds.): *Promoting Democratic Values in the Enlarging Europe: The Changing Role of the Baltic States from Importers to Exporters*. Tartu: Tartu University Press.

Ghazaryan N. (2012) Pre and Post-Lisbon Institutional Trends in the EU's Neighbourhood. In: P.J. Cardwell (ed.) EU External Relations Law and Policy in the Post-Lisbon Era. T.M.C. Asser Press, the Hague, pp. 199-216

Hanf D. (2011) The ENP in the Light of the New "Neighbourhood Clause". Research Paper in Law, No. 2/2011, College of Europe, Bruges

Hartley T.C.: The Foundations of European Union law, 7th Edition, Oxford University Press, Oxford- New York, 2010, p. 72.

Hartley T.C.: The foundations of the European Union, 7th edition Oxford University Press, Oxford and New York, 2010, p. 193 – 197;

Havránek, J. et al.: Právní teorie. "Juridica Brunencia", Brno 1995, p. 138, 139

Henderson, K.: Slovakia and the democratic criteria of EU accession. In Henderson, K. (ed.): Back to Europe: Central and Eastern Europe and the European Union. London : UCL Press, 1999, p. 210-229.

Hillion C. (2008) The EU's Neighbourhood Policy towards Eastern Europe. In: A. Dashwood and M. Maresceau (eds) Law and Practice of EU External Relations: Salient Features of a Changing Landscapes. Cambridge University Press, Cambridge, pp. 309-333

Hillion C., Mayhew A. (2009) The Eastern Partnership–something new or window-dressing, SEI Working Paper No. 109

Honcová, R.: Procesy sbližování práva – některé aspekty, Právník 1998/8 p. 686.

http://eeas.europe.eu/top_stories/140912_ukraine_en.htm

Inglis, K.: EU Enlargement: Membership Conditions Applies to Future and Potential Member States, in Blockmans, S., Lazowski, A., ed.: The European Union and its Neighbours, A Legal Appraisal of the EU's policies of stabilisation, partnership and integration. T. M. C. Asser Press, The Hague, 2006, p. 63 - 67.

Kalenský, P.: Právo Evropských společenství a čs. právní řád se zřetelem k přístupu Československa. Právník, 1991/6, p. 542

Kerikmäe, T.; Nyman-Metcalf, K.; Põder, M. L. (2010): "The August 2008 Russian-Georgian War: Issues of International Law". *Baltic Yearbook of International Law* 10: 1-27.

Knapp, V.: *Velké právní systémy.* Prague: C. H. BECK, 1996.

Kučera, Z.: Mezinárodní právo soukromé. Brno: 1994.

Kunová, V.: Globalization and Law in After Fifty Years the Coming Challenges. Coimbra: Almedia, 2007.

Kunová, V.: *Od pridruženia k členstvu Slovenskej republiky v Európskej únii.* (From Association to Membership of the Slovak Republic in the European Union). *Európske právo na Slovensku.* Bratislava: Nadácia Kalligram, 2003.

Lannon E., van Elsuwege P. (2004) The EU's Northern Dimension and the EMP-ENP: Institutional Frameworks and Decision Making Process Compared. In: P. Xuereb (ed.) The European Union and Mediterranean–The Mediterranean's European Challenge. European Documentation and Research Center, Malta, pp. 3-71

Lannon, E. (2008) Union for the Mediterranean: Building on the Barcelona Acquis. European Union Institute for Security Studies Reports, Paris, pp.1-32

LEŠKO, M: Mečiar a mečiarizmus: politik bez škrupúľ, politika bez zábran. Bratislava : VMV 1996, 239 p.

Lesser, I. (2007) "Global Trends, Regional Consequences: Wider Strategic Influences on the Black Sea", Xenophon Paper, No 4. International Centre for Black Sea Studies publications.

Libanský, V.: "Harmonizace čs. práva s právem ES". *Právo a zákonnost*, 4, 1992.

Libanský, V.: Harmonizace čs. Práva s právem ES, Právo a zákonnost, 1992, vol. 4, p. 197

Linz, J. J. - Stephan, A.: Problems of Democratic Transition and Consolidation: Southern Europe, South America, and Post-Communist Europe. Baltimore: JHU Press, 2011, 504 p.

Lucas, E. (2008): *New Cold War*. London: Bloomsbury.

Malová, D. - Rybář, M.: European Union's Policies towards Slovakia. Carrots and Sticks of Political Conditionality. In RUPNIK, J-ZIELONKA, J (eds.): The Road to the European Union. Volume 1. Manchester University Press, 2003, p. 98-112

Maresceau, M.: 'Europe Agreements': A New Form of Cooperation between the European Community and Central and Eastern Europe", in *East and Central European States and the European Communities: Legal Adaptation to the Market Economy.* Baden-Baden: Nomos Verlaggesellschaft, 1995.

Maresceau, M.: On Association partnership, pre-accession and accession, in: Maresceau, (ed.): Enlarging the European Union, Longman, London- New York, 1997, p. 3-12.

Maresceau, M.: On Association, Partnership, Pre-accession and Accession, in Marescean, M (ed.): Enlarging the European Union, Relation between the EU and Central and Eastern Europe, Longman, London and New York, 1997, p. 7.

Mayhew, A. (2007): *A certain idea of Europe: Can European integration survive eastern enlargement?* London: The University of Sussex Lecture.

McGoldric, D.: Internal Relations Law if the European Union, Longman, London and New York, 1997, p. 79-83

Münch, I.: "Export a import práva". *Právní rozhledy* 3, 1995.

Nodia, G. (2006): "What Democratizing Countries May (Hope to) Get from Abroad?" Kasekamp, A.; Pääbo, H. (eds.): *Promoting Democratic Values in the Enlarging Europe: The Changing Role of the Baltic States from Importers to Exporters*. Tartu: Tartu University Press.

Nodia, G. (ed.): *The Caucasus Institute for Peace, Democracy and Development*. Tbilisi: CIPDO.

Nyman-Metcalf, K. (2006): "Common values as a basis for integration: Is there an end to Europe?" Kasekamp, A.; Pääbo, H. (eds.): *Promoting Democratic Values in the Enlarging Europe: The Changing Role of the Baltic States from Importers to Exporters*. Tartu: Tartu University Press.

Palivec, J.: Aktuální problémy aproximace práve ČR s právem ES. Přehled předpisů Evropských společenství, 1997, vol. 1, p. 4.

Panke, D.: The effectiveness of the European Court of Justice. Why reluctant states comply. Manchester: Manchester University Press, 2010, p. 329.

Pauknerová, M.: Asociační dohoda – některé teoretické a praktické otázky, Právník, 1995, vol. 9, p. 841

Pauknerová, M.: Asociační dohoda – některé teoretické a praktické otázky, Právník, 1995/2, p. 849.

Petrov, R.A.: Transpozicia "acquis" Europejskogo Sojuza v pravovyje sistemy tretijich stran, Publishing Istina, Kiev, 2011, p. 19-36.

Pitrová, L, Pomahač, R.: Průvodce judikaturou Evropského soudního dvora, Linde, Praha, 2001, p.265.

Pridham, G.: Slovakia's Relations with the European Union 1998 - 2002: Political Conditionality, its Effects and its Limitations. In Slovak Foreign Policy Affairs, Fall 2002, p. 75-89.

Prodi R. A wider Europe: A Proximity Policy as the Key to Stability. Brussels, 5-6 December 2002, SPEECH/02/619.

Prodi R. (2002) "A Wider Europe - A Proximity Policy as the Key to Stability", Sixth ECSA-World Conference, "Peace, Security and Stability International Dialogue and the Role of the EU"

Racius, E. (2006): "Baltic Democracy Exporters to Central Asia? A Lithuanian Perspective". Kasekamp, A.; Pääbo, H. (eds.): *Promoting Democratic Values in the Enlarging Europe: The Changing Role of the Baltic States from Importers to Exporters*. Tartu: Tartu University Press.

Sedelmeier, U.: EU Enlargement, Identity and the Analysis of European Foreign Policy: Identity Formation Through Policy Practice. Robert Schuman Centre for Advanced Studies. RSC No. 2003/13 European Forum Series. 29 p.

Senden L. (2005) Soft Law in European Community Law. Hart Publishing, Oxford

Šišková, N.: Bílá kniha jako nástroj sbližování práva přidruženého státu s acquis communautaire vnitřního trhu, Právní rozhledy, 1999/ No5, p. 288

Šišková, N.: Obecné otázky sbližování českého práva s právem ES, Právník 1998/8, p. 704

Šišková, N.: Základní otázky sbližování českého práva s právem ES, Codex Bohemia, Prague, 1998.

Smith K.E. (2005) Enlargement and Conditionality: Incompatible or Mutually Reinforcing? In: R. Youngs (ed.) New Terms of Engagement: Global Europe Report 02. Foreign Policy Centre, London, pp. 23-29

Stainer, J., Woods, L.: EU law, 10th edition, Oxford University Press, Oxford – New York, 2609, p. 360-384.
Starr, S. F; Corell, S. E. (eds.): *The Baku-Tbilisi-Ceyhan Pipeline: Oil Window to the West*. Uppsala: Central Asia – Caucasus Institute & Silk Road Studies Program.
Štefanovič, M.:. *Svetové právne systémy*. Bratislava: BVSP, 2007.
Svák, J.: *Advokát pred európskymi súdmi*. Bratislava: Poradca podnikateľa, 2004.
Svoboda, P.: K právní povaze tzv. asociačních dohod a sekundárního asociačního práva, Právník, 1996, vol.3, p. 201-206
Svoboda, P.: v teorii a praxi Evropská unie, Právník, 1994, vol. 2, p. 164
Svoboda, P.: Právo vnějších vztahů EU, C. H. Beck third edition, Praha, 2010, p. 209
Technická harmonizace. Cesta do Evropské unie, vol. No. 4. Ministerstvo hospodářství ČR, Praha 1996, p. 32
Tichý,,L. and others.: Evropské právo, (4 Revised) 2011, C. H. Beck, p. 953
Urfus, V.: Historické základy novodobého práva soukromého. Prague: C. H. Beck, 1994.
Vachudova, M. A.: Europe Undivided: Democracy, Leverage, and Integration After Communism. Oxford: Oxford University Press, 2005, 341 p.
Van Vooren B. (2011) EU External Relations Law and the Neighbourhood Policy: A Paradigm for Coherence. Routledge, London
Zemánek, J..: The Czech pre-European Union accession experience from legal approximation and its relevance for the Eastern partnership, in: The Eastern Partnership and the Europe 2020 strategy: Visions of leading policy makers and academics, Directorate-General for Education and culture, Publications Office of the European Union, Luxembourg, 2012, p.89
Zweigert, K.: and Kötz, H.: Introduction To Comparative Law. (3 Revised). Oxford, 1998.

Internet Sources

Civil Georgia (2010): *Tagliavini's Report Heard at PACE Debates*. http://www.civil.ge/eng/article.php?id=22235 (January 2013).
Civil Georgia EU Offers Close Partnership to its Six Neighbors. Available at: http://www.civil.ge/eng/article.php?id=20070
Civil Georgia European Neighborhood Policy for the region. Available at: http://www.civil.ge/geo/article.php?id=15653

Conclusions of the European Council, Kopenhagen 21-22.6.1993,7/A/iii, JN 180/93, p.13.Dinana, D. (2000) Encyclopedia of the European Union. Macmillan press

Estonia (2008): *Joint Declaration of Estonian, Latvian, Lithuanian and Polish Presidents on the situation in Georgia.* http://www.president.ee/en/media/press-releases/1721-joint-declaration-of-estonian-latvian-lithuanian-and-polish-presidents-on-the-situation-in-georgia/ (January 2013).

Estonia (2008): *President Ilves to Javier Solana: The European Union should be the spokesperson for the cessation of Russia's attacks on Georgia.* http://www.president.ee/en/media/press-releases/1723-president-ilves-to-javier-solana-the-european-union-should-be-the-spokesperson-for-the-cessation-of-russiaas-attacks-on-georgia/ (January 2013).

Estonia (2011): *Georgia. Bilateral development co-operation.* http://www.vm.ee/?q=en/node/4081 (January 2013).

Estonia (2011): *Strategy for Estonian Development Cooperation and Humanitarian Aid 2011–2015.* http://www.vm.ee/sites/default/files/Arengukava2011-2015_ENG.pdf (January 2013).

Estonia (2012): *A dynamic Economy.* http://estonia.eu/about-estonia/economy-a-it/a-dynamic-economy.html (December 2012).

Estonia (2012): *Estonia and Georgia. Bilateral Relations.* http://www.vm.ee/?q=en/node/79 (January 2013).

Estonia (2012): *Välisminister Urmas Paet: Eesti toetab Gruusia lähenemist Euroopa Liidule ja NATOle (Estonian minister of foreign affars Urmas Paet: Estonia suppoerts Georgia's moving closer to the EU and NATO).* http://www.vm.ee/?q=node/15351&ref=avaflash (January 2013).

Estonian Center of Eastern Partnership (2012): *Seminar on effective management of the EU Assistance to EaP countries in Tbilisi, Georgia.* http://www.eceap.eu/events.asp?id=68&wa_site_id=4 (January 2013).

EU- Ukraine Association Agreement. "Guide to the Association Agreement." http://eeas.europa.eu /images/top-stories/140912-C; http://www.sonsilium.europa.eu/uedocs/ems_Dat

Europa – Eastern Eastern Partnership Summit to strengthen EU links with Eastern Europe and South Caucasus. Available at: http://europa.eu/rapid/pressReleasesAction.do?reference=IP/09/700&format=HTML&aged=0language=DE&guiLanguage=en

Europa – EU Delegations. Delegation of the EU to Georgia. Available at:

http://eeas.europa.eu/delegations/georgia/eu_georgia/political_relations/index_en.htm

Europa – summaries of EU legislation. European Neighbourhood Policy: recommendations for Armenia, Azerbaijan and Georgia and for Egypt and Lebanon. Available at: http://europa.eu/legislation_summaries/external_relations/relations_with_third_countries/eastern_europe_and_central_asia/r14103_en.htm

European Commission (2009) Progress Report Armenia. Available at: http://ec.europa.eu/world/enp/pdf/progress2009/sec09_511_en.pdf

European Commission (2009) Progress Report Azerbaijan. Available at: http://ec.europa.eu/world/enp/pdf/progress2009/sec09_512_en.pdf

European Commission (2009) Progress Report Georgia. Available at: http://ec.europa.eu/world/enp/pdf/progress2009/sec09_513_en.pdf

European Commission uropean Neighborhood Policy. Available at: http://ec.europa.eu/world/enp/index_en.htm

European Council. European Council in Copenhagen (1993): *Conclusions of the presidency*. http://ue.eu.int/ueDocs/cms_Data/docs/pressdata/en/ec/72921.pdf (January 2013).

European Parliament. The South Caucasus (Armenia, Azerbaijan, Georgia) Available at: http://circa.europa.eu/irc/opoce/fact_sheets/info/data/relations/relations/article_7242_en.htm

European Union (2012): *Joint statement by High Representative/Vice-President Catherine Ashton and Commissioner Štefan Füle, on EU-Georgia relations and the upcoming elections*. http://www.consilium.europa.eu/uedocs/cms_Data/docs/pressdata/EN/foraff/132250.pdf (January 2013).

European Union External Action. European Neighborhood Policy – Overview. Available at: http://eeas.europa.eu/enp/index_en.htm

European Union External Caucasus Research Centre (2011): *Knowledge and Attitudes toward the EU in Georgia*. http://crrccenters.org/activities/research/?id=38 (January 2013).

European Union Monitoring Mission in Georgia. Delegation of the European Union to Georgia. http://eumm.eu/en/eu_in_georgia/delegation_of_the_eu_commission (January 2013).

European Union, Delegation to Georgia. *Eastern Partnership*. http://eeas.europa.eu/delegations/georgia/eu_georgia/political_relations/political_framework/eastern_partnership/index_en.htm (January 2013).

European Union, Delegation to Georgia. *Political and economic relations*.

http://eeas.europa.eu/delegations/georgia/eu_georgia/political_relations /index_en.htm (January 2013).

European Union, Delegation to Georgia. *The role of the EU delegation*. http://eeas.europa.eu/delegations/georgia/about_us/delegation_role/ind ex_en.htm (January 2013).

European Union. EUR-Lex, Access to European Union Law. http://eur-lex.europa.eu/LexUriServ/LexUriServ.do?uri=CELEX:21999A0804(0 1):EN:NOT (January 2013).

EU-Ukraine Association Agreement – Guide to the Association Agreement, p. 5, available at: http://eeas.europa.eu/top_stories/2012/140912_ukraine_en.htm

EU Ukraine Association Agreement, http://eeas.europa.eu/top_stories/2012/140912_ukraine_en.htm, references from 21.9.2012

Fűle, Š.: Ukraine and the world: Addressing Tomorrow´s challenges Together, 9th Yalta Meeting, Ukraine 13 September 2012, Press Releases, available at http://europa.eu/pressReleasesAction.do?reference=SPEECH/12/603af ormat=H, 21.9.2012, p. 3.

Fűle, Š.: Ambitions of EU and East Partners for the Vilnius summit, 28.5.2013 available at http//europa.eu/rapid/press-release_SPEECH-13-477_en.htm, p. 2, navšíveno 4.6.2013

Fűle, Š.: Ukraine and the world: Addressing Tomorrow´s challenges Together, 9th Yalta Meeting, Ukraine, 13 September 2012, Press Releases, available at http://europa.eu/pressReleasesAction.do?reference=SPEECH/12/603af ormat=H, 21.9.2012, p. 3

Georgia (2007): *Presidents of Georgia and Estonia conduct joint press conference*. http://www.president.gov.ge/ge/PressOffice/News?2416 (January 2013).

Georgia (2012): *Georgian Prime-Minister meets President of Estonian Parliament*. http://www.government.gov.ge/index.php?lang_id=geo&sec_id=251& info_id=33266 (January 2013).

http://glavcom.ua/pub/2012_11_19_EU_Ukraine_Association: Agreement_English.pdf [31.3.2013]

Independent International Fact-Finding Mission on the Conflict in Georgia (2009): *Report*, volume II. http://www.ceiig.ch/pdf/IIFFMCG_Volume_II.pdf (January 2013).

Meister, S. (2010): *Tangled Up in Blue and Gold*. https://ip-journal.dgap. org/en/ip-journal/regions/tangled-blue-and-gold (January 2013).

News. Az Energy not EU's only interest in South Caucasus. Available at: http://www.news.az/articles/politics/3268

Nodia, G. (2007): "Political Forum: 10 Questions on Georgia's Political Development".

Nodia, G. (2008): *The war for Georgia: Russia, the west, the future.* http://www.opendemocracy.net/article/georgia-under-fire-the-power-of-russian-resentment (January 2013).

Nuriev, Elkhan (2007) The EU policy in south Caucasus: The Case of post-soviet Azerbaijan New opportunities and future prospects. Available at: http://swp-berlin.org/fileadmin/contents/products/arbeits papiere/SWP_RP_Nuriyev_ks.pdf

Poviliunas, Audrius (2006) South Caucasus in The Context of European Neighbourhood Policy, Lithuanian foreign policy review. Available at: http://www.lfpr.lt/uploads/File/2006/Poviliunas.pdf

Puppo, L. (2007) The South Caucasus countries and the ENP: Three different paths to Europe? Available at: http://www.un-az.org/undp/bulnews45/caucasus.php

Tangiashvili, N., Kobaladze, M. (2006) EU- Georgian Neigborhood Relations. Central European University

The International Institute for Education Policy, Planning and Management (2007): *Education on Shadow Market: Monitoring of Private Tutoring.* http://www.apkhazava.gol.ge/EPPM/Private%20Tutoring%20in%20G eorgia.pdf (January 2013).

United Press International (2012): *Russia not ready to talk with Georgia. Dmitry Medvedev about relationship with Georgia.* http://www.upi.com/Top_News/World-News/2012/01/25/Russia-not-ready-to-talk-with-Georgia/UPI-47981327505851/ (January 2013).

World Bank (2009): *Georgia – Education System Realignment and Strengthening Program Project.* http://documents.worldbank.org/curated/en/1999/07/440949/georgia-education-system-realignment-strengthening-program-project (January 2013).

World Bank (2009): *Georgia: Implementation Completion and Results Report: Poverty Reduction Support Operations I–IV. Document of the World Bank, Report No: ICR00001018.* http://www-wds.worldbank .org/external/default/WDSContentServer/WDSP/IB/2010/01/13/00033 4955_20100113015515/Rendered/PDF/ICR10180Multip1C0disclosed 011111101.pdf (January 2013).

World Trade Organization. Members and Observers. Available at: http://www.wto.org/english/thewto_e/whatis_e/tif_e/org6_e.htm